MONOGRAPHS
SOCIETY FOR RESEA
CHILD DEVELO

SERIAL NO. 209, VOL. 50, NOS. 1-2

GROWING POINTS OF ATTACHMENT
THEORY AND RESEARCH

EDITED BY

INGE BRETHERTON
COLORADO STATE UNIVERSITY

EVERETT WATERS
STATE UNIVERSITY OF NEW YORK AT STONY BROOK

MONOGRAPHS OF THE SOCIETY FOR RESEARCH IN CHILD
DEVELOPMENT, SERIAL NO. 209, VOL. 50, NOS. 1–2

CONTENTS

ABSTRACT

BRETHERTON, INGE, and WATERS, EVERETT (Eds.). Growing Points of Attachment Theory and Research. *Monographs of the Society for Research in Child
Development*, 1985, **50**(1–2, Serial No. 209).

Research guided by attachment theory as formulated by Bowlby and
Ainsworth is branching out in exciting new directions. The 12 chapters
collected together in this *Monograph* present theoretical and methodological
tools that will facilitate further research on attachment across the life span,
across generations, and across cultures.

The *Monograph* is divided into 4 parts. Part 1 provides the theoretical
framework, emphasizing the ethological and the psychoanalytic roots of
attachment theory. Two central ideas in attachment theory are highlighted:
attachment as grounded in a behavioral-motivational control system whose
set-goal is felt security, and the notion that individuals construct internal
working models of self and attachment figures that guide the interpretation
and production of behavior. These themes are repeatedly taken up in other
chapters of the *Monograph*.

Part 2 is concerned with translating theory into measurement. In Chapter II, Waters and Deane present a Q-sort suitable for assessing attachment
security in 12–36-month-olds. This instrument is based on Bowlby's control
systems model of attachment. In Chapter III, Main, Kaplan, and Cassidy
offer a variety of highly original measures for assessing security in children
and adults that have been validated against attachment classifications in
infancy. These measures open new avenues for research by moving the
study of attachment to the level of representation.

Part 3 (Chaps. IV–IX) is organized around issues in adaptation,
maladaptation, and intergenerational transmission. Vaughn, Deane, and

Waters (Chap. IV) examine short-term and long-term adaptations to non-maternal care. Findings on short-term adaptation to high-quality day care seemed benign; those on long-term adaptation illustrate that outcome is jointly dependent on attachment security and on whether or when the mother returns to work. In Chapter V, Dontas, Maratos, Fafoutis, and Karangelis present a field study, conducted in a model infant home in Greece, describing 8–12-month-olds' 2-week adaptations to a new principal caregiver (the adoptive mother) in a supportive setting. The theme of Chapters VI and VII is continuity of adaptation from infancy to early childhood in a poverty and in a middle-class sample. Significant relationships between early insecure attachment classification and later preschool behavior problems are reported for the poverty sample (Erickson, Sroufe, & Egeland, Chap. VI) but not for the middle-class sample (Bates, Maslin, & Frankel, Chap. VII), despite the fact that mother-infant interaction at 6, 13, and 24 months was related to attachment classifications in predictable ways. In Chapter VIII, Schneider-Rosen, Braunwald, Carlson, and Cicchetti discuss infants' adaption to maltreatment. They report a preponderance of insecure attachment classifications at 12, 18, and 24 months, with avoidant classifications becoming dominant at the later ages. Secure attachment in abused children is explained in terms of multifactorial compensatory and potentiating influences. In the concluding chapter of this section, Ricks reviews intergenerational effects related to attachment. Two domains are considered: effects of early separation and familial disruption on parental behavior in the next generation, and continuity in quality of attachment.

Part 4 (Chaps. X–XII) is devoted to cross-national research on attachment in infancy. Grossmann, Grossmann, Spangler, Suess, and Unzner (Chap. X) present findings for North German mother-infant pairs, observed at home and in the Strange Situation. This first attempt at replicating the classic Baltimore study corroborated associations between Strange Situation classifications and maternal sensitivity to infant signals reported by Ainsworth and her colleagues. However, the overrepresentation of group A (avoidant) classifications in this sample is ascribed to a culturally valued emphasis on early independence rather than to maternal rejection. In Chapter XI, Sagi, Lamb, Lewkowicz, Shoham, Dvir, and Estes report a high proportion of insecure-resistant (C) classifications in 12-month-old Israeli kibbutz infants, who were observed with mother, father, and metapelet. This finding is explained in terms of heightened stranger anxiety rather than insecurity. A comparison group of Israeli city infants in day care resembled U.S. samples in terms of Strange Situation groups. The insecure-resistant group (C) was also overrepresented in Japan (Miyake, Chen, & Campos, Chap. XII), where C classification was correlated with neonatal temperament but also with maternal interactive behavior. In view of the infants' lack of experience with nonfamilial care, the C classification in Japan is not interpreted as an index of insecure-resistant attachment.

Two additional themes running through the *Monograph* deserve special mention. These are (*a*) a concern with epigenetic explanations, charting different developmental pathways for secure and insecure infants, and (*b*) consideration of exceptional cases that do not, at first sight, fit predictions derived from the epigenetic perspective.

PREFACE

The 12 chapters in this *Monograph* document the achievements and growing points of a theory still in the making. Attachment theory, closely associated with the names of Bowlby and Ainsworth, has generated a considerable amount of research in the past 10 years and is about to enter a new phase. However, before reflecting on the new directions in which the theory is now taking us, it may be useful to trace briefly its roots in the past.

Bowlby's interest in loss of parent figures began in 1927 when he worked in a home for emotionally disturbed boys. This experience led to his decision to become a child psychiatrist and psychoanalyst. Ainsworth's interest in security was inspired by the work of William Blatz at Toronto, under whom she wrote a dissertation in 1939 entitled "An Evaluation of Adjustment, Based upon the Concept of Security." Bowlby's and Ainsworth's paths crossed after World War II when Bowlby established a special research unit at the Tavistock Clinic in London, designed to examine young children's responses to separation from the mother. Among those who worked there over the years were Anthony Ambrose, Christoph Heinecke, Colin Murray Parkes (who is now studying adult attachments), James Robertson, and Rudolph Schaffer. Mary Ainsworth was associated with this research unit from 1950 to 1954.

During this period John Bowlby, through discussions with Robert Hinde and Julian Huxley, became interested in how ethological principles might contribute to our understanding of the infant's tie to the mother. Although at first unconvinced by Bowlby's new approach, Mary Ainsworth applied some of his ideas to her subsequent study of infancy in Uganda in 1955, long before the first formulation of attachment theory appeared in print in 1958.

Throughout the 1960s Bowlby repeatedly convened the Tavistock

Mother-Infant Interaction seminars, whose participants included Mary Ainsworth and many other well-known names in the field: Jacob Gewirtz, David Hamburg, Harry Harlow, Robert Hinde, Hanus Papoušek, Heinz Prechtl, Harriet Rheingold, Henry Ricciuti, Jay Rosenblatt, Len Rosenblum, Louis Sander, Rudolph Schaffer, and Peter Wolff, a group quite diverse in background and theoretical orientation. The further development of attachment theory benefited from the spirited discussions at these seminars and from the empirical research they engendered. This included Ainsworth's Baltimore study, begun in 1963. The first Strange Situation was conducted 20 years ago, in 1964. In 1969 John Bowlby published the first volume of the attachment and loss trilogy, *Attachment,* which was followed by *Separation* in 1973 and *Loss* in 1980. Many of the insights gained from Mary Ainsworth's Baltimore study, especially those pertaining to individual differences in the security of infant-mother attachment, were incorporated in these volumes.

In the early 1970s, research in mother-infant attachment began to accelerate. At Johns Hopkins University and later at Virginia, Mary Ainsworth and her associates worked with a large group of graduate and undergraduate students. Some of them (Inge Bretherton, Jude Cassidy, Michael Lamb, Mary Main, and Everett Waters) are contributors to this volume. Another contributor, Klaus Grossmann, was a repeated visitor at Baltimore. In 1973, Everett Waters's move from undergraduate study at Johns Hopkins University to graduate study at Minnesota led to the formation of the Minnesota attachment group. In addition to Alan Sroufe and Everett Waters, several other members of that group are represented in this volume (Dante Cicchetti, Byron Egeland, Martha Erickson, Margaret Ricks, and Brian Vaughn). After publication of the volume *Patterns of Attachment* (Ainsworth, Blehar, Waters, & Wall, 1978), a substantial number of investigators not directly connected with Mary Ainsworth, Alan Sroufe, and their associates and students began to test some of the claims of attachment theory (represented in this volume by Jack Bates, Cleo Dontas, Kazuo Miyake, and their colleagues).

This *Monograph* was inspired by presentations at the International Conference on Infant Studies at Austin, Texas, in 1982. Attachment beyond early infancy, attachment across generations, and attachment across cultures were new themes that called for publication in a special volume in which the growing points of the theory could be clearly documented. The resulting *Monograph* is divided into four parts. Each part, with the exception of Part 1, is preceded by a short introduction. The content will therefore be only briefly summarized here. Chapter I is intended to provide an overall framework, emphasizing the psychoanalytic as well as the ethological heritage of attachment theory and suggesting future directions for research. In Part 2, Chapters II and III, for the first time since the creation of the

Strange Situation, offer new theoretically based assessments of attachment. The chapters in Part 3 consider attachment and the concept of adaptation versus maladaptation in the context of transitions to new caregivers (Chaps. IV, V), the prediction of later behavior problems (Chaps. VI, VII), maltreatment (Chap. VIII), and the intergenerational transmission of attachment patterns (Chap. IX). Part 4 is devoted to cross-national studies of attachment in infancy, raising the question of adaptation in the context of cultural differences (in North Germany, Israeli kibbutzim, and Japan).

We would like to thank the contributors to this *Monograph* for their cooperation, responsiveness, and patience in bringing this collaborative effort to fruition. We are also grateful to Eleanor Maccoby and Joy Osofsky for their careful, detailed, and helpful critiques. Looking toward the future, we hope that the *Monograph* will inspire continued refinement and elaboration of attachment theory. A recurrent theme in many chapters of this volume is the representational aspect of attachment relationships. This, we believe, will become the unifying framework for further studies of attachment across the life span, across generations, and across cultures. Beyond this, we also hope that the *Monograph* will lead toward a synthesis with converging findings from other theoretical approaches. Relationships among measures of parental acceptance and warmth, and a child's self-esteem, empathy, social competence, and effective coping, have been reported in literature from other perspectives, including psychoanalysis, cognitive personality theory, and social learning theory. The field may not be quite ready for the grand synthesis we envision, but we believe that we can dimly perceive its outlines.

I. B.
E. W.

I. ATTACHMENT THEORY: RETROSPECT AND PROSPECT

INGE BRETHERTON

Colorado State University

This chapter has several major aims. The first is to provide an overview of attachment theory as presented by John Bowlby in the three volumes of *Attachment and Loss* (1969/1982b, 1973, 1980), giving special emphasis to two major ideas: (1) attachment as grounded in a motivational-behavioral control system that is preferentially responsive to a small number of familiar caregiving figures and (2) the construction of complementary internal working models of attachment figures and of the self through which the history of specific attachment relationships is integrated into the personality structure. These two concepts, but especially the notion of internal working models, will be used in the second section of the chapter to interpret refinements and elaborations of the theory that have been primarily the result of the work and influence of Mary Ainsworth. Topics discussed are maternal and infant contributions to the quality of attachment relationships, stability and change in the quality of attachment relationships, carryover effects from earlier to later relationships, and intergenerational transmission of attachment patterns as an intracultural and cross-cultural phenomenon. An attempt is made to clarify a variety of theoretical points and to discuss others that remain to be clarified. Finally, I consider how recent insights into the development of socioemotional understanding and the development of event representation can be integrated into attachment theory to shed new light on the origins of individual differences in personality development. In doing so, I have also attempted to provide a framework for the studies presented in this volume.

During the writing of this chapter, I received support from the John D. and Catherine T. MacArthur Foundation Network on the Transition from Infancy to Early Childhood, which is gratefully acknowledged. I would also like to thank Mary Ainsworth, Jay Belsky, John Bowlby, and Mary Main for critical and encouraging comments on earlier versions of this manuscript. Mary Main's critique was especially helpful. Finally, although this chapter is offered as an introductory framework to this volume, I do not presume to represent the views of other contributors.

THE ONTOGENESIS OF ATTACHMENT THEORY

Attachment in the Narrow Sense

The impetus that moved Bowlby (1958, 1969/1982b, 1973, 1980) to formulate attachment theory came from findings demonstrating pervasive ill effects of institutional and hospital care on infants and young children (e.g., Bender & Yarnell, 1941; Goldfarb, 1943; Skodak & Skeels, 1949; Spitz, 1946), findings that could not be explained in terms of the then prevailing secondary drive theories (see Maccoby & Masters, 1970, for a summary of the social learning and psychoanalytic versions of this point of view). The theoretical underpinnings of the new theory came from ethology, control systems theory, and cognitive science, but the influence of psychoanalytic principles is pervasive, especially in the later volumes of the attachment trilogy (Bowlby, 1969/1982b, 1973, 1980).

Historically, attachment theory was developed as an alternative to psychoanalytic theories of object relations (Bowlby, 1982a) in order to explain (1) why mere separation should cause anxiety; (2) the similarities between adult and childhood mourning; and (3) defensive processes (selective exclusion of signals from within and without that would normally be implicated in the activation of attachment behavior).

"Attachment," as conceptualized by Bowlby, was not meant to be taken as a simple synonym for the term "social bond," nor was it meant to apply to all aspects of child-parent relationships. It is often overlooked that Bowlby believed that the roles of attachment figure and playmate were conceptually distinct (Bowlby, 1969/1982b, p. 307). A child is said to seek the attachment figure when under stress but to seek a playmate when in good spirits. Because the two roles are not incompatible, it is possible for one person (e.g., the caregiver) to fill both.

With respect to the formulation of attachment theory, this position has a number of implications. First, it is now clear that the term "attachment" used in this narrower, technical sense does not cover the playful interactions studied by Brazelton (e.g., Brazelton, Koslowski, & Main, 1974) and Stern (e.g., Stern, 1977), even though these play an important role in mother-infant relationships. This point is treated at much greater length in Bretherton (1980). Second, it becomes evident that one useful way of describing relationships is in terms of the variety of the partners' shared interaction plans or programs. For example, a person may be a child's principal attachment figure but not the child's most important or preferred playmate. Conversely, it is quite conceivable for a preferred playmate to have only a very minimal role as an attachment figure. Such an approach to the study of relationships has been proposed by several authors (Bretherton, 1980;

Hinde, 1976, 1982a; Parkes, 1982) and is espoused by Bowlby in the revised edition of *Attachment* (1969/1982b).

In his influential article "On Describing Relationships," Hinde (1976) suggested that relationships can be characterized along the following dimensions: (1) content of component interactions; (2) diversity of component interactions; (3) reciprocity versus complementarity of interactions; (4) qualities of the component interactions (meshing, mutual goal alignment); (5) relative frequency and patterning of component interactions; (6) multidimensional qualities such as "affectionateness" that cannot be described in terms of any one dimension such as warmth or possessiveness; (7) each partner's level of moral and cognitive functioning; and (8) penetration or degree of mutual disclosure, openness, and intimacy.

Hinde's first three points have to do with the content of relationships, points 4, 6, 7, and 8 with qualitative aspects of relationships. Point 5 relates to both. In applying this framework to attachment, the following may be claimed. The content of attachment relationships (point 1) is concerned with security regulation where the attached person seeks and the attachment figure provides security (and protection, soothing, comfort, and help). The attachment partnership is thus an asymmetrical or complementary one (point 3) except in circumstances in which both partners play the role of attachment figure vis-à-vis one another. Additional plans shared by attachment partners may involve the reciprocal roles of playmate and the complementary roles of teacher-pupil, to mention just two examples (point 2). The parent-child relationship is therefore neither exclusively reciprocal nor exclusively complementary (point 3). It would be reasonable to assume that the attachment component and the play component of a relationship would show qualitative consistency (see Ainsworth, Blehar, Waters, & Wall, 1978; Bates, Maslin, & Frankel, in this vol., for supportive evidence). To throw more light on this question, it might be fruitful to describe how frequently, warmly, and deeply attachment partners interact with one another across the full range of their shared plans (points 4, 6, 7, 8). It will be especially important to do this for both parents. Although neither father nor mother tends to play an exclusive role as attachment figure or playmate, the relative predominance of the attachment and play components may vary (point 5). Several authors have documented that in Western cultures mother tends to become the preferred attachment figure whereas father tends to become the preferred playmate (e.g., Lamb, 1976, 1977, 1978; Lytton, 1980). There is also evidence that in some cultures reciprocal play does *not* play an important role in the early mother-infant relationship. For example, in a study of Mayan Indians in Mexico, Brazelton (1977) observed few maternal attempts at eliciting social responses from infants by talking or face-to-face interaction, although mothers were quite solicitous in response to infant distress.

The Attachment System

Having discussed the place of attachment within the more general framework of relationships, we can now consider Bowlby's conceptualization of attachment as a goal-corrected control system (see Waters & Deane, 1982, for an excellent summary of the properties of systems). The term "attachment behavioral system" (I prefer "attachment system") refers to a psychological organization hypothesized to exist within a person. This system is so constituted that feelings of security and actual conditions of safety are highly correlated, although the correlation is by no means perfect. Seen from an outside observer's viewpoint the system's set-goal is to regulate behaviors designed to maintain or obtain proximity to and contact with a discriminated person or persons referred to as the attachment figure(s). From the psychological vantage point of the attached person, however, the system's set-goal is felt security (Bischof, 1975). Both the external and the internal perspectives are useful and necessary, but the distinction should be kept clearly in mind. Attachment behavior tends to be most obvious when the attached person is frightened, fatigued, or sick and is assuaged when the attachment figure provides protection, help, and soothing. The mere knowledge that an attachment figure is available and responsive provides a strong and pervasive feeling of security and so encourages the person to value and continue the relationship (Bowlby, 1982a, p. 668). Finally, although attachment behavior is most noticeable in early childhood, it can be observed throughout the life cycle, especially in stressful situations.

Because attachment behaviors closely resemble behaviors that had been described as dependent in the context of social learning theory, the new attachment construct was initially assimilated to the well-established concept of dependency (see Sroufe, Fox, & Pancake, 1983, for an extensive discussion). However, despite superficial similarities, there are substantial differences between the two theoretical approaches. Dependency had been conceptualized as a personality trait. Attachment, by contrast, refers to a relationship with a discriminated person or persons. No biological function had been attributed to dependent behaviors. Attachment behaviors, on the other hand, are believed to have the biological function of protecting the attached individual from physical and psychological harm. Indeed, Bowlby (1982a) proposed that attachment behavior rivals mating and feeding behavior in biological importance and that the attachment system has its own distinct internal motivation. It is in claiming that the attachment system is a distinct motivational system that Bowlby most profoundly diverges from traditional psychoanalytic theory.

In an even more general sense, attachment to persons and places and fear of the novel and strange may—in Bowlby's view—be interpreted as part of a group of behavioral systems whose function it is to maintain a relatively steady state between an individual and his or her environment (Bowlby, 1973). Such homeostatic systems may be regarded as an "outer ring" of life-maintaining systems complementary to the "inner ring" of systems that maintain physiological homeostasis. As long as the outer ring (the behavioral-motivational) systems successfully maintain an individual within a familiar environment, the load placed on the systems maintaining physiological homeostasis is lessened (see Bowlby, 1973, pp. 149–150).

This notion has received strong support from recent studies of nonhuman primates by Reite and his colleagues (Reite, Short, Seiler, & Pauley, 1981). These investigators showed that pigtail macaque infants whose mother was removed from the social group underwent profound physiological changes suggestive of a general impairment of autonomic homeostatic functioning (decreases in heart rate and body temperature, sleep disturbances, and changes in EEG power spectra).

In Bowlby's view the essentially "conservative" homeostatic systems are antithetical to systems mediating exploratory and other forms of information- and stimulation-seeking behaviors. A child's behavior may then be seen as the outcome of the interplay of such systems (Bischof, 1975; Bretherton & Ainsworth, 1974). Although the propensity for exploration may take the child away from the attachment figure, the experience of fear and stress takes the child toward the attachment figure. The joint operation of these antithetical propensities facilitates exploration under reasonably safe conditions. When no apparent danger threatens, the child can (but need not necessarily) explore at a fair distance from the caregiver, but when stress-arousing stimuli are present, the attachment system pulls the child closer to available protection. A cautionary note may be in order here. Although the function of attachment in an evolutionary sense may be homeostasis with regard to the environment, it is experienced by the attached person as a psychological bond to the attachment figure who plays the part of secure base and haven.

The attachment system envisaged by Bowlby (1969/1982b, 1973) does not become organized until sometime during the second half of the first year, although it builds on component systems that are operative earlier. Even at birth human infants show behaviors that appear to have the function of bringing them into closer proximity and interaction with a caregiver. In the course of the first few months these behaviors come to be preferentially directed toward discriminated persons (e.g., crying when mother but not a visitor leaves the room or lifting the arms toward the mother but not a visitor in greeting; see Stayton, Ainsworth, & Main, 1973). However, it is only during the second 6 months that these proximity and interaction promoting behaviors are integrated into a coherent system, organized around a particular figure or figures. It is to the focusing (preferential activation) of this system with respect to a small hierarchy of familiar figures and its resistance to "reprogramming" that the term "attachment," as formulated by Bowlby (1969/1982b) and Ainsworth (1973), is properly applied.

Support for the hypothesis that earlier signaling behaviors come, around 9 months of age, to be incorporated into a goal-corrected system of proximity/security regulation, which now also includes locomotion, is largely indirect. One such indirect piece of information is Yarrow's (1967) finding that a child moved from a foster home to a permanent adoptive home before the age of 6 months tends to show only transitory distress. By contrast, a change in primary caregivers between the ages of 7 and 12 months invariably entailed much more pervasive disturbance (increased crying and clinginess, apathy, and eating and sleeping disturbance). The fact that this change is roughly associated with the onset of locomotion makes evolutionary sense (Freedman, 1974; Stayton, Hogan, & Ainsworth, 1971). Independent locomotion enables the child to leave the mother. A system that ensures that a child's explorations do not take it too far from a protective figure can thus plausibly be viewed as having survival value.

In some precocial birds such a system is ready to become organized around a discriminated object shortly after hatching by a process known as imprinting. Bowlby compared attachment to, but did not equate it with, imprinting in precocial avian species as described by Lorenz (1935/1957) in an influential paper entitled "Companionship in Bird Life." Although much attention has been paid to imprinting in precocial birds such as geese and ducks, Lorenz's article also contains a description of delayed filial attachment that resembles the human situation somewhat more closely. Jackdaws are altricial. Immediately on hatching, they are capable of neither independent locomotion nor independent feeding. During this period, young jackdaws shy away from a human intruder who takes them from the nest but soon come to beg for food from their new foster parent. However, after about 20 days, when jackdaws begin to follow their parents in flight, filial behavior can no longer be redirected to a human caregiver (Lorenz, 1935/1957, pp. 106–107 [in the 1957 ed.]).

Although the description of filial imprinting in jackdaws offers a better analogy to human attachment than filial imprinting in precocial birds does, it is of course unlikely that attachment processes in birds and humans are based on homologous brain structures and processes, despite the fact that behavioral indicators are strikingly similar in avian and mammalian species (following, distress on separation). Nevertheless, insights gained from the study of one species can be instrumental in formulating new questions about the development of similar behavior in another. At the very least the comparison shows that filial attachments can exist in the absence of all the complexities of primate cognition. Whereas there is more justification for a direct comparison of filial attachment across primate species, species-specific affective-cognitive differences between human and nonhuman primates are likely to have a pervasive effect on how attachment operates and comes to be experienced. I will return to this point after a more detailed discussion of the functioning of the attachment system as conceptualized by Bowlby (1969/1982b, 1973, 1980).

In order to clarify the complexity of the system Bowlby envisaged, I have constructed a diagram (see Fig. 1, adapted from Bretherton, 1980). This diagram attempts to spell out the interrelationships among the subsystems constituting and serving the attachment system. It may look unnecessarily intricate, but it is in fact a gross oversimplification of what a complete specification of the system would have to look like. My primary objective is to show interrelations (informational flow between subsystems) rather than to elaborate on the functioning of the separate subsystems.

Several important features of the hypothesized system should be noted. First, although an attachment relationship exists dyadically between two individuals, the system described by Bowlby concerns the organization of a system within the attached person (see also Hinde, 1982a; Sroufe & Fleeson, in press). This system, like filial attachment in birds, is preferentially organized around discriminated partners. In some species such a focused system exists in only one of the partners (the parent of the infant). In human and nonhuman primates the attachment relationship is best conceptualized as based on the joint functioning of a filial and a parental attachment system. So far it is largely the human filial system that has been studied, for reasons that will be considered later. Nevertheless, as we shall see shortly, the system within the individual represents the dyadic relationship.

The attachment system requires, uses, and seeks several types of information that are taken in through the sensory systems: clues to danger (physical and psychological) and the availability of an attachment figure (physical and psychological). Bowlby (1969/1982b) originally suggested that the system functioned episodically or was activated by perceived danger and deactivated (terminated) by perceived safety. I strongly believe (Bretherton, 1980) that much is to be gained by thinking of the system as continuously active. To do so clarifies and simplifies the relationship between two phenomena that had previously been regarded as distinct: the so-called secure base phenomenon (a concept contributed to attachment theory by Ainsworth) and security seeking (seeking proximity, contact, and protection/comfort). When the child feels secure (the system has assessed the environment as nonthreatening), the "pull" of the attachment figure becomes weaker, but there are limits on how far away from the attachment figure the child will explore (see, e.g., Anderson, 1972). In this case the child is using the attachment figure as a secure base. However, when the child perceives the environment as mildly alarming, the system's proximity set-goal will change, pulling the child closer to the attachment figure. Anticipated nonresponsiveness on the part of the attachment figure will have a similar, but

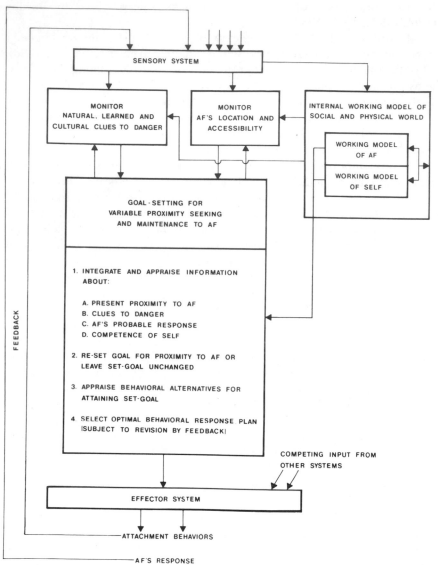

FIG. 1.—The attachment system: a simplified model of a control system for the regulation of proximity to and contact with an attachment figure.

more permanent, effect on the proximity set-goal as the perception of danger. In the first case, attachment behavior seems prudent, in the second anxious (the child has to take more than optimal responsibility for maintaining proximity). Conflicted behavior emerges when the exploratory system evaluates a stimulus as highly attractive while the fear system evaluates the same stimulus as threatening. Under such circumstances, the child may exhibit oscillating intention movements toward the stimulus and the attachment figure (Bretherton & Ainsworth, 1974). Finally, if the environment is appraised as highly threatening or stressful, mere proximity no longer suffices. Contact seeking is instituted, with a number of important consequences. If the attachment figure does not perceive the situation as dangerous, he or she can comfort the child but also attempt to teach coping behaviors. If the attachment figure perceives danger, the couple can leave the situation together. The latter situation is not usually tested in laboratory studies of attachment. In situations where the child is uncertain about how to appraise a stimulus, he or she may seek information about its meaning by referencing the mother's face. This behavior, known as social referencing (Campos & Stenberg, 1981; Emde, 1983; Klinnert, Campos, Sorce, Emde, & Svejda, 1983), can, in my view, be understood as a special form of attachment behavior.

Internal Working Models of Attachment Figures and the Self

The relative safety or danger of a situation and an attachment figure's availability and responsiveness are, according to Bowlby (1969/1982b), not appraised completely afresh every time. Through continual transactions with the world of persons and objects, the child constructs increasingly complex internal working models of that world and of the significant persons in it, including the self (Bowlby, 1969/1982b, 1973, 1980). These models are useful in appraising and guiding behavior in new situations. For example, if the child's experience had led him or her to construct a model of the attachment figure as a person likely to provide support when needed, close monitoring of the figure's whereabouts may be less necessary than when such responsiveness cannot be counted on.

Although Bowlby's notion of internal working models is compatible with Piaget's (1954) theory of representation, it was not inspired by Piaget's work but derives from an influential book by Craik, who states: "If the organism carries a small-scale model of external reality and of its own possible actions within its head, it is able to try out various alternatives, conclude which is the best of them, react to future situations before they arise, utilize the knowledge of past events in dealing with the present and future, and in every way to react in a much fuller, safer and more competent manner to the emergencies which face it" (1943, p. 61).

As a conceptual metaphor, the term "internal working model" has several advantages. First, the adjective "working" draws attention to the dynamic aspects of representation. By operating on mental models, an individual can generate interpretations of the present and evaluate alternative courses of future action. Second, the word "model" implies construction, and hence development, with later, more complex working models coming to replace earlier and simpler versions.

Internal working models of attachment figures and self, once organized, tend to operate outside conscious awareness. For this reason, and because new information is assimilated to existing models, the models tend to be resistant to dramatic change (Bowlby, 1980). However, to remain serviceable, internal working models of attachment figures *must* be revised, especially in childhood, when development is rapid. As the child's affective-cognitive understanding grows, internal models of self, social partners, and the physical world increase in sophistication. Hence, behaviors regulated by the attachment system may change substantially over age, even though the basic interrelationships among the component subsystems remain unaltered. As children become better able to assess the intentions and motives of attachment figures, as they acquire improved coping skills and learn to make better appraisals of what is dangerous, attachment behavior becomes more subtle. In older children the power of the attachment system is therefore highly visible only in stressful situations. The waning of attachment behavior does not, however, imply the waning of the attachment system. Loss of a principal attachment figure and attachment to new principal figures is perhaps more difficult in the later preschool years than in infancy even though attachment behavior is much more conspicuous at the earlier ages.

Because the internal working models of self and attachment figures are constructed out of dyadic experiences, they may at first be closely intertwined. Indeed, in early development it may be preferable to speak of an internal working model of the relationship (Main, Kaplan, & Cassidy, in this vol.). However, even when the models of self and other have become distinct, they represent obverse aspects of the same relationship and cannot be understood without reference to each other. For example, if an attachment figure frequently rejects or ridicules the child's bids for comfort in stressful situations, the child may come to develop not only an internal working model of the parent as rejecting but also one of himself or herself as not worthy of help and comfort. Conversely, if the attachment figure gives help and comfort when needed, the child will tend to develop a working model of the parent as loving and of himself or herself as a person worthy of such support (Bowlby, 1973). Similar ideas, but clothed in somewhat different terminology, have been proposed by a number of other investigators. For example, Sroufe and Fleeson (in press) have recently postulated that, in the course of continuous interaction, individuals learn or internalize both sides of a relationship. Thus, a child who trusts the parents to give needed emotional support will also learn the complementary parental role and be able to enact it later when he or she becomes a parent. Epstein (1980) also sees the construction of the self system as based on dyadic processes (see Ricks, in this vol., for a review). Indeed, the general idea that concepts of self and other are developed interdependently is not new (e.g., Baldwin, 1911; Cooley, 1902; Mead, 1934; Sullivan, 1953). What is new are the constructivist-developmental and interpersonal connotations inherent in the metaphor of internal working models. I believe that this approach will also throw new light on the psychoanalytic concepts of introjection, projection, identification, and superego formation to which the notion of internal working models of self and attachment figures is closely related (see Barkow, 1977, for a discussion of internal models and superego).

The picture I have just drawn is still too simple, however. Bowlby (1973) notes that some clinical data can best be explained by supposing that individuals sometimes operate with two or more working models of the same attachment figure and two or more models of self:

> When multiple models of a single figure are operative they are likely to differ in regard to their origin, their dominance and the exent to which the subject is aware of them. In a person suffering from emotional disturbance it is common to find that the model that has greatest influence on his perceptions and forecasts, and therefore on his feelings and behavior, is one that developed during his early years and is constructed along fairly primitive lines, but that the person may be relatively unaware of; while simultaneously there is operating within him a second, and perhaps radically incompatible, model, that developed later, that is much more sophisticated, and that the person is more clearly aware of and that he may mistakenly assume to be dominant. [Bowlby, 1973, p. 205]

This position is related to a theory of defensive processes (developed more fully in Bowlby, 1980) wherein incompatible models of attachment figures are understood as the product of incompatible interpretations of experience that may become defensively dissociated. Such dissociations are especially likely when the child cannot cope with viewing rejecting parents in an unfavorable light or when parents attempt to persuade the child to interpret their rejecting behavior as loving. Representational homeostasis, based on defensive exclusion of representations that cause painful feelings, may provide emotional relief. However, it also forces a person to work with an inadequate model of reality, leading to inappropriate, perhaps even pathological, behavior. Yet because the material is defensively excluded from awareness, it cannot be restructured or updated as a serviceable model should be (Bowlby, 1973, 1980).

In summary, Bowlby's most significant conceptual contributions to attachment theory are (1) that the attachment system may be regarded as a behavioral—and, I would add, ideational—control system with its own distinct motivation (distinct from systems regulating sexual and feeding behavior) and (2) that individual differences in the functioning of that system appear to be closely tied to an individual's working model of self, others, and the world. The manner in which early patterns of interaction with attachment figures come to be organized into more traitlike interactional styles is not yet completely clear. That attachment patterns established in infancy play a significant role in the patterning of the personality was proposed not only by Bowlby (1973) but also by Ainsworth (1967), Hinde (1982a), Main et al. (in this vol.), Ricks (in this vol.), and Sroufe and Fleeson (in press). Recent advances in attachment research will now be reviewed with this point of view in mind.

INDIVIDUAL DIFFERENCES IN ATTACHMENT AND PERSONALITY DEVELOPMENT

In his later years Freud described the child's relationship to the mother in very powerful terms, calling it "unique, without parallel, established unalterably for a whole lifetime as the first and strongest love-object and as the prototype of all later love relations—for both sexes" (Freud, 1940, p. 188).

This statement is silent about the respective contributions of infant and mother to the developing relationship. It claims merely that a pattern, established during the early years, will remain stable and be perpetuated in other relationships. What is the evidence for maternal and infant contributions to the organization of attachment patterns and for the stability of such patterns once established?

Direction of Effects

Effects of maternal behavior.—Perhaps because attachment theory is rooted in findings on maternal deprivation, investigators initially focused on maternal influences. A second major reason for this emphasis was the belief that what the mother brings to an interaction with her neonate is far more complex than what the infant brings. The mother's contribution to the new relationship "derives not only from her biological make-up, but from a long history of interpersonal relations with her family of origin and from absorbing the values and practices of her culture" (Bowlby, 1969/1982b, p. 342). Attachment research provides fairly solid support for this position.

Ainsworth's Baltimore study, based on prolonged monthly observations of mothers and infants in the home, revealed that maternal sensitivity to the infant's signals during feeding, face-to-face play, physical contact, and distress episodes in the course of the first 3 months was predictive of the quality of the relationship during the fourth quarter of the first year. Maternal responsiveness to infant crying during the first quarter bore no relationship to concurrent infant crying. However, by the fourth quarter, infants whose mothers had responded promptly and appropriately to their crying early on now cried less. Maternal sensitivity to infants' signals during feeding, play, and episodes of close bodily contact in the course of the first 3 months also turned out to be correlated with the infant's behavior at 12 months in a naturalistic laboratory procedure known as the Strange Situation (See Ainsworth et al., 1978, for an overview; see also Ainsworth & Bell, 1969; Blehar, Lieberman, & Ainsworth, 1977; Stayton & Ainsworth, 1973; Tracy & Ainsworth, 1981).

The Strange Situation consists of a standard series of eight episodes. Infants are observed in an unfamiliar playroom, where they are given an opportunity to explore toys as well as to interact with an unfamiliar adult in the presence and in the absence of the mother. Although Ainsworth originally devised this situation to assess the effect of maternal absence on infant exploration (see Ainsworth & Wittig, 1969), the infants' behavior during reunion with the mother turned out to be of unexpected interest. Some infants behaved as anticipated. They approached the mother and sought physical contact with her if they had been overtly distressed by the separation, or if they had not become distressed, they greeted her and sought interaction (group B). Other infants, however, snubbed or avoided the mother on her return (group A), and yet others (group C) showed angry, resistant behavior interspersed with attachment behavior (see Ainsworth, Bell, & Stayton, 1971, 1972).

Ainsworth was alerted to the avoidant (group A) and resistant (group C) reunion patterns in the Strange Situation because they resembled reunion behaviors typically observed in children after longer, more traumatic separations (e.g., Robertson, 1953; see also Main et al., in this vol., for a detailed discussion). The Strange Situation derives its validity as an assessment of attachment quality not from this direct resemblance, however, but rather from the systematic and extensive correlations of infant behavior in this situation with maternal and infant behavior in the home throughout the first year of life.

Avoidance of the mother during the two reunion episodes of the Strange Situation was predictable not only from maternal insensitivity to infant signals in a variety of contexts during the first 3 months of life but also from the mother's verbally and behaviorally stated dislike of physical contact with the infant during the first quarter (Ainsworth et al., 1978), an attitude that remained stable over the first year (Main & Weston, 1982). Main and Weston also report that infants from the Baltimore study who avoided their mothers on reunion during the Strange Situation showed unpredictable episodes of aggression toward her at home. These results were corroborated in laboratory studies at Berkeley by Main, Tomasini, and Tolan (1979) and by Main and Stadtman (1981). These authors also report that mothers of infants classified as avoidant in the Strange Situation were generally low in emotional expressiveness, even in response to the sometimes highly aggressive behavior of their infants. In a more recent analysis of the Berkeley data, Main (in press) further showed that observed parental dislike of physical contact with the infant could be predicted from ratings of parental reports regarding rejection in childhood. The resistant reunion pattern (group C) in the Strange Situation involves a combination of contact-seeking and tantrumy behavior toward the mother. In the Baltimore data, this pattern was related not to maternal rejection of the infant's bids for physical contact but to maternal inconsistency in responding throughout the first year (Ainsworth et al., 1978).

Because of their correlations with infant and maternal behaviors in the home, avoidant or resistant reunion patterns in the Strange Situation are interpreted by Ainsworth et al. (1978) as distortions of the optimal functioning of the attachment system. Nonoptimal functioning of a system is, of course, preferable to complete malfunction. Hence many biological systems are evolutionarily adapted to permit ontogenetic adaptation to a range of environmental circumstances, even though the likelihood of survival may not be equally good throughout that range (Lorenz, 1965; see Main, 1981, for an extensive theoretical discussion of this point with respect to avoidance). Avoidant behavior in attachment relationships may represent the infant's adaptation to specific caregiver styles. Yet such patterns are not regarded as one of a variety of equally desirable patterns by attachment theorists (Ainsworth, 1984). This can perhaps be clarified by taking a more extreme example. Abused children may engage in a number of behavioral adaptations that lessen the likelihood of further abuse, but to have to make such an adaptation may foreclose optimal adaptation in other social relationships (see Ainsworth, 1984; Schneider-Rosen, Braunwald, Carlson, & Cicchetti, in this vol.).

The original finding that particular infant patterns of proximity, contact, and interaction regulation in the Strange Situation tend to be associated with the quality of maternal caregiving earlier in the first year came from Ainsworth's sample of 23 Baltimore infants (see Ainsworth et al., 1978). More recently, additional corroborating evidence has become available. Grossmann, Grossmann, Spangler, Suess, and Unzner (in this vol.) found that maternal sensitivity to infant signals at 2 and 6 months was related to later secure attachment classifications in a sample of 49 North German infants, although the differences failed to reach significance at 10 months. For a U.S. sample, Maslin (1983) reported that composite scores of maternal warmth and affectionate behavior during two 3-hour home observations at 6 months predicted secure attachment classifications in the Strange Situation at 12 months. In addition, Belsky, Rovine, and Taylor (1984) found that a measure that they interpret as an index of maternal sensitivity (obtained during mother-infant interaction in the home) was predictive of secure attachment assessed in the Strange Situation. Although these findings certainly do not rule out the possibility that the mother herself was influenced by the infant, they strongly suggest a consistent and therefore measurable influence by the mother on the organization of the emerging attachment relationship.

Infant effects.—Efforts to investigate infant effects on the quality of later infant-mother attachment were, in part, precipitated by the results reported in the section on maternal effects. Findings are mixed, with some studies showing effects and others not. In fact, Ainsworth (1983) speculates that an infant's influence on the mother may be masked by maternal responsiveness to signals because such behavior is individually attuned to particular infants.

In a poverty sample studied in Minnesota no relationships were found among early Apgar scores, the Neonatal Behavioral Assessment Scale (NBAS; see Brazelton, 1973), nurses' ratings of the neonate at the hospital, and secure (group B) versus avoidant (group A) patterns as assessed in the Ainsworth Strange Situation (Egeland & Farber, 1984; Waters, Vaughn, & Egeland, 1980), although Waters et al. did uncover links between neonatal behavior (Apgar scores, motor maturity, and state regulation) and resistant patterns (group C). Miyake, Chen, and Campos (in this vol.), using observational measures, found that Japanese infants who later showed resistant reunion patterns in the Strange Situation with their mothers had been more prone to cry as neonates.

Belsky et al. (1984) found no correlations between secure attachment to the mother at 12 months and maternal ratings of infant temperament at 3 and 9 months. Egeland and Farber (1984) also failed to find associations between assessments of attachment security at 12 months and temperament measures derived from behavioral observations at 3 months and Carey temperament scores at 6 months. Miyake et al. (in this vol.) were able to predict resistant reunion patterns in the Strange Situation at 1 year of age from measures of irritability (fussing and crying) in home observations at 3 months. These authors are the only investigators so far to have noted consistent irritability from the neonatal period to 3 months. Other reports of significant correlations between temperament beyond the neonatal period and attachment assessments at 12 months cannot unambiguously be interpreted in terms of infant constitution. For example, Bates et al. (in this vol.) report correlations between a small number of their many temperament ratings at 6 and 13 months and Strange Situation classifications at 12 months. As these authors point out, however, temperament ratings at later ages may already be the product of mutually negotiated patterns of interaction. For the same reason a study by Bretherton, O'Connell, and Tracy (1980) that found relationships between Strange Situation classifications and the mother's rating of her own and her infant's temperament cannot be interpreted in terms of infant constitution alone. In that study infants classified in subgroups B_1 and B_2 during the Strange Situation were judged by their mothers to be significantly more sociable with strangers (the mothers in turn rated themselves as more extraverted).

Most interesting to me are studies documenting interactive effects of neonatal temperament assessments and maternal behavior. Such an approach is most closely in accord with Bowlby's epigenetic view of developing attachment patterns: "Thus at conception development turns on interaction between the newly formed genome and the intrauterine environment; at birth it turns on interaction between the physiological constitution, including germinal mental structure, of the neonate and the family, or non-family, into which he is born; and at each age successively it turns on the personality structure then present and the family and, later, the wider social environments then current" (1973, chap. 22, p. 364).

Thus, Crockenberg (1981) was able to predict insecure attachment patterns at 12 months from neonatal irritability as assessed during the NBAS (Brazelton, 1973), but only for infants whose mothers were relatively unresponsive to their infant's crying at 3 months and who had little social support available to them. Grossmann et al. (in this vol.) found that a high score for neonatal orienting and/or a high maternal sensitivity rating at 6 months accounted for 94% of children classified as group B with their mothers at 12 months. This suggests that there may be two pathways to a secure attachment, a mistaken conclusion. About half the infants classified as insecurely attached (groups A and C) would be misidentified by this procedure. Hence other variables must also contribute substantially to quality of attachment as assessed by the Strange Situation. In the Miyake et al. (in this vol.) study, early irritability identified almost all the infants later classified as resistant (group C). However, a substantial number (33%) of infants judged securely attached (group B) at 1 year had also been irritable earlier. Irritability did not ipso facto lead to insecure attachments. Finally, Minde (personal communication, March 1984) reports that infants rated as having an easy temperament at 6 months but a difficult temperament at 12 months had mothers who were rated as highly insensitive at 6 months. In contrast, infants rated as difficult at 6 months, but easy at 12 months, had mothers who were rated as highly sensitive at 6 months.

The findings obtained so far suggest that it might be fruitful to conduct longitudinal studies specifically designed to go beyond the search for general maternal or infant effects and to chart in more detail the epigenetic pathways that produce the patterning of attachment relationships. There is at present no justification for supposing that the quality of future attachment relationships is fully determined by an infant's temperamental disposition at birth.

The next question to be addressed is the extent to which the relationship once patterned remains, as Freud predicted, unalterable and prototypical of other relationships.

Stability in the Quality of Attachment Patterns

In studies of middle-class families there is indeed evidence for stability of attachment patterns, at least from 12 to 18 months. Children who exhibit a particular nonoptimal (A or C) pattern of reunion behavior in the Strange Situation at 12 months tend to show a similar nonoptimal pattern at 18 months. The same is true for the optimal (B) pattern, which also tends to be consistent at both ages (Connell, 1976; Main & Weston, 1981; Waters, 1978). Moreover, Main et al. (in this vol.) were able to document considerable stability from 12 months to 6 years of age when infants in their original sample were seen again in a Strange Situation–like setting (an additional disorganized/disoriented classification of Strange Situation behavior was used in that study; see Main & Solomon, in press).

On the other hand, we have no evidence that the quality of a relationship once formed is necessarily unalterable. Changing life circumstances can make a substantial difference. One study (Vaughn, Egeland, Sroufe, & Waters, 1979) discovered an association between stressful events in the child's family during the 12–18-months period and changes to a nonoptimal attachment pattern in the Strange Situation; another (Thompson, Lamb, & Estes, 1982) reported findings suggesting that life stresses may lead to beneficial *or* detrimental reorganizations of an attachment relationship. In maltreating families the quality of the mother-infant relationship tends to deteriorate from 12 to 18 months (Egeland & Sroufe, 1981a, 1981b; Schneider-Rosen et al., in this vol.). This is particularly true where the mother is depressed and psychologically unavailable. Egeland and Sroufe compared the effects of (1) physical abuse and hostility, (2) psychological unavailability or depression, and (3) neglect or failure to provide proper care. In comparison with a control group, children in all three maltreatment groups were more likely to be classified as insecurely attached at 18 months. The strongest effect, however, was obtained for psychological unavailability. At 12 months 43%, but at 18 months 86%, of children with psychologically unavailable mothers were classified as avoidant (group A) in the Strange Situation; the remainder were placed in the resistant category (group C). Paradoxically, psychological unavailability alone appeared to be more damaging than psychological unavailability paired with physical abuse. Egeland and Sroufe speculate that any form of contact (and I would say response) may be better than no contact or response. It is especially noteworthy that children of psychologically unavailable mothers were lively babies at 3 months but that their functioning had begun to decline markedly even by 6 months.

Not all changes in the patterning of attachment relations are necessarily permanent. In addition to more long-term changes in the quality of relationships, there seem to be temporary perturbations, such as increased clinginess after separations (see Robertson & Robertson, 1971). However, the distinction between temporary fluctuations and more enduring changes in the quality of a relationship is difficult to make without longitudinal data and needs further study. Moreover, even if apparently permanent changes from insecure to secure attachment relationships are found, this does not necessarily imply that earlier experiences are erased (see Erickson, Sroufe, & Egeland, in this vol.). Studies of increased vulnerability, despite apparent changes for the better, are required.

Predictive Validity of Early Attachment Patterns

If the Strange Situation assesses (as is claimed) the child's trust in the physical and emotional availability of an attachment figure, one ought to find that attachment classifications are related to the child's functioning in other areas. A considerable body of research has largely supported the claim that mastery motivation is associated with secure attachment. Some studies also report correlations of attachment security with cognitive development, though—surprisingly—hardly ever with language acquisition (for reviews, see Ainsworth et al., 1978; Bates, Bretherton, Beeghly-Smith, & McNew, 1983; Bretherton, Bates, Benigni, Camaioni, & Volterra, 1979). Particularly interesting in this regard are studies by Main (1973) and Matas, Arend, and Sroufe (1978). Main found that toddlers earlier classified as securely attached had longer attention spans and displayed more positive affect during free play. Matas et al. found that children judged securely attached at 12 and/or 18 months confidently attempted solutions to easy tool-using tasks. When challenged with more difficult tool-using tasks, the same children enlisted their mothers' support in order to achieve a solution. This was not the case for insecure 2-year-olds, who were frustrated, whiney, and negativistic, whether trying to solve the easy or the difficult problems. Those classified as avoidant in the Strange Situation sought little help from their mothers, even when unable to achieve a solution on their own. Mothers of avoidant children, conversely, showed little affective investment in their children's activities, offering only minimal support even with hard tasks (see also Arend, Gove, & Sroufe, 1979; Bates et al., in this vol.). Confidence in the mother's physical and psychological availability appears to lay the groundwork for autonomous exploration and problem solving, coupled with the expectation that help will be forthcoming when needed. Thus attention span and persistence, which have often been regarded as traitlike, perhaps constitutionally based, qualities, may be at least in part a product of particular relationship patterns.

Fairly strong evidence for carryover effects from early attachments to later social relationships has also been obtained. Bowlby's epigenetic perspective offers several reasons why this might be the case. Because family environments tend to be relatively stable, the pressures that lead a child to adopt a particular developmental pathway are likely to persist. Internal models of self and significant figures, once constructed, tend to have an additional stabilizing influence because they influence construal of present experience. Finally, environmental and intrapersonal processes do not work independently. Structures residing in the personality tend to determine the relationships and situations that an individual actively seeks or actively avoids. Thus the environment should be viewed not as a purely external influence but as partially created by the individual (Bowlby, 1973, pp. 368–369).

Several studies published by Sroufe, Egeland, and their colleagues have found classifications in the Strange Situation to predict social functioning in the preschool with teachers and peers. Children classified as securely attached to their mothers at 12 and/or 18 months were rated higher on positive affect and lower on negative affect by their preschool teachers (Sroufe, Schork, Motti, Lawroski, & LaFreniere, 1984). They were also judged more empathic and compliant (LaFreniere & Sroufe, in press; Waters, Wippman, & Sroufe, 1979; see also Londerville & Main, 1981; and Main & Weston, 1981, for independent corroboration).

More recently, findings concerning play between peers who exhibited optimal or nonoptimal attachment patterns at 12 and 18 months have been reported by the Minnesota group (Sroufe, 1983). Children classified as resistant on the basis of their reunion behavior in the Strange Situation showed ineptness in their transactions with peers, whereas the children classified as avoidant tended to be hostile or distant. Moreover, children classified as avoidant at 12 and/or 18 months frequently did not seek teachers when injured, disappointed, or otherwise stressed. The resistant group showed more chronic low-level dependency, being constantly near or oriented to the teachers. Erickson et al. (in this vol.) report that children classified as resistant or avoidant in the Strange Situation at 12 and 18 months are more likely to present behavior problems in the preschool later. Bates et al. (in this vol.) report correlations of attachment classifications at 12 months with mother-infant interaction and the Matas et al. (1978) problem-solving tasks at 24 months but could not predict preschool-age behavior problems (perceived by the mother and a secondary caregiver). One explanation for these discrepant results is the fact that the mothers in the Erickson et al. study came from a poverty sample, where life stresses were more frequent and familial support less available than was presumably the case in the middle-class two-parent sample studied by Bates et al. In addition, the children in the Erickson et al. study were a special subsample who had been assigned the same attachment classification at 12 and 18 months, a factor that leads one to expect more continuity.

George and Main (1979) also present evidence suggesting carryover effects from early attachments to later relationships. From research showing correlations between physical rejection by the mother and nonoptimal attachment patterns in the Strange Situation, they predicted that physically abused children should show avoidant behavior to secondary caregivers and peers, a prediction for which they found partial confirmation. Abused toddlers observed with peers and caregivers in a day-care center avoided friendly overtures significantly more often than a contrast group of nonabused children. The abused children were also more likely to threaten and assault their companions and to show unpredictable aggressive behavior toward them.

I interpret the above findings as generally supporting Bowlby's notion that internal working models of attachment figures come to govern behavior in new relationships. His corollary, that the internal working models of self and of attachment figures are interdependent, is also in accord with present findings. Children who were judged to have secure attachments to their mothers in the second year tended to show more ego resilience and to be rated as more socially competent in the preschool (Arend et al., 1979; Waters et al., 1979). The same children also obtained significantly higher scores on a self-esteem Q-sort devised by Waters.

Social Transmission

In view of the fact that children seem to repeat early relationship patterns in their later relationships, the question naturally arises whether parents are reenacting patterns they themselves experienced as children. This question can be asked about individuals within cultures (intergenerational effects) and societies (cross-cultural effects). I will consider the transmission of individual patterns first.

Intergenerational effects.—Several studies (reviewed in detail by Ricks, in this vol.) have shown that a parent's internal model of childhood attachments in turn governs how the parent behaves as attachment figure vis-à-vis his or her own child. This could, I propose, be explained in two ways. The individual may be using the internal model of the parent to guide his or her own parenting behavior (identification). This identificatory explanation is also implicit in Sroufe and Fleeson's (in press) notion that a child internalizes both sides of a relationship. Alternatively, a person's parental behavior may be guided by the current self model, which has its roots in the earlier relationship with parents. I am not sure that present findings permit a choice between these two explanations. Indeed, both may be operating.

In studies investigating intergenerational transmission of attachment patterns, parents whose children are directly observed with them in the Strange Situation and other settings are interviewed about their own childhood experiences. Morris (1980) collected maternal interview histories (coded by blind judges) and compared these to the children's Strange Situation classifications. Reported lack of stable family relationships and the mother's perception of her own mother as low in nurturance and competence predicted anxious patterns. Ricks (1982, 1983) found that mothers of infants judged securely attached in relation to them had more positive recollections of childhood relationships with their mothers, fathers, and peers than did mothers of infants seen as anxious. The results concerning mother acceptance were particularly strong, with few cases of overlap between mothers of children showing the B (secure) pattern as opposed to the A (avoidant) and C (resistant) patterns in the Strange Situation. Main et al. (in this vol.) found significant correlations between a child's attachment classification with mother and with father at 12 or 18 months and the respective parent's conceptualization of his or her own early attachments. Ratings were made from detailed interviews, to reflect the parents' current thinking about the meaning of their early attachment relationships in general, that is, without considering separately the interviewed parent's reported relationship to father and to mother, a point to which I will return later. In a second, more detailed study of mothers only, Main and Goldwyn (in press) report that mothers who idealize their parents when speaking about them in very general terms, but who report quite rejecting behavior when talking about specific memories, tend to have children who avoid them during the reunion episodes of the Strange Situation. This was, however, not the case for a subsample of mothers who were able to express anger about having been rejected or who expressed forgiveness.

These findings suggest to me that it is not a person's internal working models of attachment figures per se but how the person construes these internal models in adulthood that appears to be involved in intergenerational transmission. True to Bowlby's hypothesis, the social transmission of adverse patterns appears to be more likely when the parent is using two incompatible models of his or her own attachment figures, with explicit awareness only of the idealized model. When early rejection is understood as an attribute of the parent, not as a reflection of the self, the repetition of patterns experienced in childhood is apparently less likely. Something like counteridentification may be possible, a term I use here in analogy to the concept of counterimitation in social learning theory (Bandura, 1971). By counteridentification I mean a process whereby the person has acquired and stored an internal working model of the parental figure but is actively and deliberately resisting identification with it (see also Fraiberg, Adelson, & Shapiro's classic 1975 article on "ghosts in the nursery").

Cross-cultural data.—In studying cultural transmission we examine how groups of individuals are patterned by cultural practices and how that pattern is passed on to the next generation. Note that we are now talking about individual differences between societies, not persons.

Despite the fact that Mary Ainsworth's first insights regarding the origin of individual differences in the attachment relationship were developed in the course of her study of infancy in Uganda (1967), cross-cultural studies of attachment based on the Bowlby-Ainsworth formulations have since been rare. Grossmann et al.'s (in this vol.) recent study of North German families has begun to remedy this situation. Like Ainsworth, Grossmann et al. examined relationships between quality of mother-infant interaction during lengthy home visits and later reunion behavior in the Strange Situation. In Japan, Miyake et al. (in this vol.) have also studied infant behavior in the Strange Situation in relation to neonatal temperament and mother-infant interaction at several ages. In Israel, Sagi et al. (in this vol.) observed kibbutz-reared infants in the Strange Situation with mother, father, and substitute caregiver.

Two obvious conclusions emerge from these findings. First, the majority of infants in North Germany, Japan, and Israel could be classified into the patterns observed by Ainsworth et al. (1978) in the Strange Situation with a U.S. sample, although a sizable proportion of Israeli infants did not complete two full separations because of inordinate distress. Second, the proportion of infants classified into each group was at variance with distributions reported for the United States. In North Germany, the avoidant group (A) predominated over the secure group (B), which is most common in the United States. By contrast, in Japanese and Israeli kibbutz infants, resistant (C) infants were significantly more numerous than was expected on the basis of U.S. findings. A recent dissertation by Li-Repac (1982) on Chinese-American families is especially interesting in this regard. An unexpectedly high proportion of group C patterns was identified, but the inflated proportion of C classifications tended to be associated with nonacculturated families. In more acculturated families fewer children were classified as group C and more as group A.

Hinde (1982a), in discussing patterns of attachment, emphasized that we should think of attachment behavior as adapted not to an ideal partner but to a variety of possible partners. Animals, he claims, are evolutionarily adapted to adapt ontogenetically, that is, to have conditional strategies that permit a range of styles and a capacity to select those that best fit specific environmental circumstances. Cultural variations engender different experiences, leading to different relationship patterns. Even within a culture the behavior of males and females is patterned differentially. For this reason, Hinde proposed, what is best must be considered against the whole background of family, social groups, and cultural beliefs. A mother-child relation that produces successful adults in one situation will not necessarily do so in another.

The findings reported in this volume support Hinde's claim, in the sense that cultural reasons may be advanced to account for differential proportions of infants classified as secure, avoidant, and resistant in the Strange Situation. Grossmann et al. (in this vol.) ascribe the high proportion of group A infants in North Germany to cultural pressures on mothers to engage in independence training. Miyake et al. (in this vol.) believe that the preponderance of group C classifications in their sample is due to the extreme stressfulness of the Strange Situation for babies who have almost no experience with nonfamilial caregivers. Sagi et al. (in this vol.) also claim that the Strange Situation is much more stressful for kibbutz infants because of extremely high levels of stranger anxiety.

Support for Hinde's thesis is not unequivocal, however. It is not the case that cross-cultural studies have uncovered completely different correlational patterns among variables. To the contrary, the relationships of maternal behavior with Strange Situation classifications are remarkably similar to those obtained for the Baltimore sample (Ainsworth et al., 1978). It has already been noted that Grossmann et al. (in this vol.) found an association between early maternal sensitivity and secure attachment classifications at 12 months. Grossmann et al. were also able to replicate several other findings. For example, they, like Bell and Ainsworth (1972), discovered that maternal responsiveness to crying was associated with less infant distress during the fourth quarter of the first year. Along the same lines, Li Repac (1982) notes that American-Chinese parents whose infants were classified as resistant were less responsive to their infants' vocalizations, caressed and kissed them less during the home visit, and were less willing to respond to the infants' requests for support. By contrast, American-Chinese parents who fostered autonomy in a supportive context had children who had low resistance scores in the Strange Situation.

A cross-cultural survey of the effects of parental acceptance or rejection (Rohner, 1975) corroborates the correlational patterns obtained in attachment research. Studies of 101 different communities from the Human Relations Area Files were included in the survey, representing a stratified sample of the world's known and adequately described social systems. Ratings of acceptance or rejection were based on parental behavior to children between

2 and 6 years of age because insufficient material was available for infancy. Results were as follows. In societies that are highly accepting of children, the children tended to be more self-reliant and achievement motivated, although the correlation with achievement motivation does not carry through to adulthood. In societies where children are rejected, children and adults tended to be emotionally unresponsive, more dependent, less emotionally stable, and less able to become involved in affectionate relationships and to show more aggressive behavior and hostility. In such societies, adults are less likely to give sympathy to people in need and more likely to have low self-esteem (for a replication of the latter finding, see Allen, 1967).

The survey also uncovered a worldwide correlation between child acceptance and households in which fathers are significantly involved in child care and/or in which grandparents are available as substitute caregivers. These findings are consistent with an earlier cross-cultural study by Minturn and Lambert (1964) and with at least two U.S. studies. For example, Crockenberg (1981) reports that the availability of social support was significantly correlated with maternal responsiveness to the infant and with secure attachment classification at 12 months. Also in line with the cross-cultural data, Easterbrooks and Goldberg (1984) found paternal involvement to be related to patterns of secure attachment to the mother in the Strange Situation. It appears that principal attachment figures can function more supportively when they themselves receive the support of others.

Finally, Rohner's (1975) survey demonstrated a strong tendency to view the supernatural world as hostile and malevolent in societies with high ratings for parental rejection (for similar cross-cultural findings, see Lambert, Triandis, & Wolf, 1959; Spiro & D'Andrade, 1958; Whiting, 1959).

It is easy to find fault with cross-cultural surveys based on the Human Relations Area Files. It must be emphasized, however, that Rohner only chose to include ethnographies that fulfilled certain requirements (the information given was firsthand, and the ethnographer spoke the native language and stayed with the society for a prolonged period). After careful reading of his survey—including the extensive appendixes—I feel that Rohner's general conclusions regarding the deleterious effects of parental rejection on the development of intimate human relationships deserve to be taken seriously. I am particularly impressed with the fact that correlates of acceptance or rejection among societies read uncannily like the sequelae of secure and insecure attachment reported by Sroufe (1983) for a sample of preschoolers in Minnesota.

Not many ethnographies contain the detailed information needed to go beyond global questions regarding correlates of parental acceptance or rejection. The few that do suggest that cross-cultural studies more directly guided by attachment theory might be extremely productive. To illustrate what I have in mind, I will present brief descriptions from two contrasting societies, the Tikopia (Firth, 1936) and a Balinese village community (Bateson & Mead, 1942).

Tikopia, a small coral island in the Solomon archipelago (Micronesia), was studied in the late 1920s. The Tikopia are remarkable for their very articulate beliefs about infants' relations to parents and strangers. Firth quotes a verbatim account by one of the chiefs:

> The child knows its own mother and its own father also by tokens—it looks constantly on them. The infant recognizes its parents while it yet cannot speak. Faces only are recognized; therefore when it looks then on faces which are different, the infant cries. The babe which has not yet made speech [i.e., begun to speak properly], if its father be absent, be he gone to the woods or hither for a stroll, it seeks then for its father, cries, cries, cries, calling "Pa! Pa E! Pa E! Pa, pa, pa, pa!" That is, it knows the relatives, but it weeps for its father. When they listen to it, crying "pa, pa, pa, pa" thereupon someone goes out to look for him. When the father is found he asks "What?" "Come to the child who has cried and cried for you; cried Pa awfully!" Thereupon its father goes over, lifts it up on his arms, and so looking at its father it stops and does not cry. And the infant scolds its father, "You went-went-went-went!"
> [1936, p. 157]

Firth, who visited the Tikopia long before the formulation of attachment theory, was at first skeptical of such accounts. However, subsequent observations convinced him that young children indeed followed their parents about, cried when they were absent, were soothed when they returned, and ran to them when danger threatened. Although the Tikopia recognized the primacy of the child's attachment to parents, they were also concerned that this attachment not be too exclusive. In accord with the theory that interaction, not kinship, breeds attachment, important relatives would establish relations with the infant by engaging in a special kind of talk, called "fakasanisani." This consisted of bending over the infant, murmuring: "You remember me. I am your father. When I go away, you come and seek for me. . . ." These same relatives later supported the child by offering physical contact in times of stress, a practice that continued into adulthood.

The Balinese village community described by Bateson and Mead (1942) made very different uses of the attachment system. Mothers employed simulated fear to control their infants' movement, crying out, "Aroh! wildcat!" or "Aroh! Caterpillar" even when no danger threatened. Infants who did not yet understand the content of these warnings seemed to respond to the mother's fearful tone of voice. This practice represents, I suggest, a manipulation of the attachment system for ulterior purposes.

Mothers also teased the infants in play interactions. When an infant responded to the mother's playful stimulation by becoming engaged, she reciprocated with a blank ("away") look. Although infants reacted cheerfully to this treatment in the early months, it did eventually lead to temper tantrums and sulkiness. By 2–3 years of age, children ceased to pay overt attention to it. One has the strong impression that the children were being trained not to respond to provocation, to disengage emotional expression from emotional experience, a valued ability among the Balinese.

The attitudes toward attachment held by the Tikopia and the Balinese villagers were strikingly different. The Tikopia respected attachments to primary and secondary caregivers. Supportive relationships, often involving physical contact, were highly valued throughout life, and no one was expected to sacrifice strong feelings to appearances (Firth, 1936). In the Balinese community the aesthetic form of outward behavior was regarded as more important than the person's actual feelings. Thus the functioning of the attachment system is molded by different cultural ideals and beliefs. With the proviso that the respective ethnographies give a reasonably representative account of societal practices, cultural relativism would lead one to call both patterns ontogenetically adaptive. A member of one of these two societies would probably feel ill at ease in the other. From a universalist position, and taking the quality of intimate relationships as a focus of comparison, the Tikopia pattern might be termed a more optimal ontogenetic adaptation. We are once more faced with the dilemma I considered in my earlier discussion of secure versus insecure mother-infant attachments within cultures. Avoidance of the mother may be adaptive for a child whose mother dislikes physical contact, but only in the sense of "best fit under the circumstances." Implicit in Bowlby's and Ainsworth's work is the notion that optimal ontogenetic adaptation of the attachment system occurs under circumstances in which major caregivers accept the child's needs. Although flexibly adaptive to a range of caregiver behaviors, the attachment system is postulated to have a central bias that represents an evolutionary or phylogenetic adaptation (Ainsworth, 1984).

How can we resolve the conflict between relativism and universalism? Although I feel that such conflict is unavoidable, I also believe that both approaches to the study of attachment have their place, depending on whether the research questions have to do with an individual's adaptation to a specific society or with a worldwide comparison of societal practices. Perhaps the wisest statement regarding this problem was made by Erik Erikson in *Childhood and Society* (1963): that certain basic things must happen in the parent-child relationship and that beyond these there is leeway for what may happen.

FUTURE DIRECTIONS: THE STUDY OF INTERNAL WORKING MODELS

Bowlby's (1973) original claim, that a person develops complementary working models of self and of caregivers in the context of first attachments, models that come to determine how future relations are established and maintained, receives fairly solid support from the intracultural studies conducted within the United States as well as from the cross-cultural and intergenerational studies I have just reviewed. There is, however, a serious problem with the view that early models of attachment figures become the basis of generalized working models for potential partners. This derives from findings that the quality of a child's relationship to the mother can be quite different from the quality of relationships to other attachment figures or—to phrase it in Freudian terms—that the attachment relationship with the mother is not the prototype for all others.

The Problem of Nonconcordant Relationships to Different Attachment Figures

If the infant's relationship with the mother is prototypical, then the quality of infant-mother attachment should be congruent with the quality of infant-father attachment. I can recall a time when such a belief was informally held by some investigators. However, it has now been amply documented that the quality of an infant's relationship to mother and to father, at least as assessed in the Strange Situation, can be quite divergent. The first such study was conducted by Lamb (1977). The second was undertaken by Main and Weston (1981), who assessed infants with father and mother at 12 and 18 months. Main and Weston observed considerable longitudinal stability in the relationship with each parent. However, as in Lamb's study, there was no concordance of secure, resistant, and avoidant patterns with respect to mother and to father. Similar findings were obtained by Grossmann and Grossmann (1981a) in Germany, by Sagi et al. (in this vol.) in Israel, where the infant was assessed with father, mother, and metapelet, and by Krentz (1983) in the United States, where infants were seen with the day-care giver and with the mother.

How can we reconcile repeated reports that a child's history of attachment to the mother matters for later relationships with findings that quality of attachment to mother and to father is not generally concordant? To put it differently, what happens to the internal model of the self when a child feels secure in the relationship with one parent and not with the other? Which of these relationships is the one carried forward into other relationships, or are both carried forward in different types of relationships? Or are these the wrong questions to ask?

Encouraging evidence regarding the importance of relationship histories (Sroufe's term; see Sroufe & Fleeson, in press) or of internal models constructed within specific present or past relationships comes from many quarters, not only from studies of attachment. For example, psychoanalysts have long claimed that a person's relationship with the analyst (transference) is assimilated to the parent-child relationship, that is, perceived in accordance with the model the patient has constructed of the parent (Bowlby, 1973; Osofsky, 1982). Clinical material offered in the course of psychotherapy also suggests continuity in relationship patterns. Cottrell (1969; cited in Sroufe & Fleeson, in press) offers a case history describing a patient's harsh treatment of his young son, apparently carried forward from the patient's relationship with his father. This contrasted with the patient's tender treatment of his wife, carried forward from the mother-son relationship. Depending on the partner, the patient seemed to have two distinct selves.

Main et al. (in this vol.) offer some relevant insights, although these do not address the problem posed by Cottrell's case study. They found that an assessment of the child's representation of attachment at 6 years of age (in response to a family picture and to a projective test about separation) were highly predictable from attachment classification with the mother, but not with the father, 5 years earlier. These results, which were completely unexpected, suggest to me that, in the construction of the working model of the self, one parent, probably the principal attachment figure, may be much more influential than the other. Rick's intergenerational data (1983) point in the same direction. A mother's reported acceptance by her own mother was particularly strongly related to her infant's attachment security as evaluated in the Strange Situation at 12 months.

Questions Raised by Nonconcordant Attachments
and Tools to Answer Them

A myriad of questions pose themselves on the basis of the findings and ambiguities reviewed here. Some of these are:

1. Is an integrated internal working model of the self built from participation in a number of nonconcordant relationships? If so, how and when? Or are self models, developed in different relationships, only partially integrated or sometimes not at all? (See Fairbairn, 1940, pp. 7–8, for similar ideas.)

2. When and how are normative working models of "father," "mother," and "person" constructed, presumably out of representations derived from a variety of experienced and observed interactions?

3. When are specific as opposed to normative models used to guide behavior in new relationships?

4. Under what circumstances can processes I have called counteridentification prevent an internal model of a major attachment figure from providing the model for the attached person's future relationships, especially with his or her own children? At what periods in the life span is such restructuring most likely?

5. Does it make sense to rate the overall quality of a relationship, or might it be more useful to assess different aspects (e.g., attachment and play) separately?

To answer such questions we need tools for studying the development of internal working models. Here, I suggest, it may be fruitful to make a concerted effort to integrate into attachment theory recent advances regarding the development of social-emotional understanding, communication, and general representational processes, a task begun by Marvin (1977; Marvin, Greenberg, & Mosler, 1976) and continued by Main et al. (in this vol.) and Cassidy (1985).

Some insights into when to start looking can, I propose, be gained from studies of social understanding spanning the transition from the first to the second year. These concern the emergence of intentional communication (Bates, Camaioni, & Volterra, 1975; Bretherton & Bates, 1979; Bruner, 1975; Greenfield & Smith, 1976), of affective referencing (Campos & Stenberg, 1981; Emde, 1983; Feinman & Lewis, 1983; Klinnert et al., 1983), of shared reference (Butterworth, 1979; Scaife & Bruner, 1975), of shared interest in mutual plans (Trevarthen & Hubley, 1979), and of the ability to entertain short-term hypotheses about the probable actions of others (Littenberg, Tulkin, & Kagan, 1971). These studies offer what I consider persuasive evidence for an emerging ability to attribute subjectivity (internal states) to others and even for a budding realization that information about subjective states can be interpersonally communicated (Bretherton, McNew, & Beeghly-Smith, 1981).

It is self-evident that the massive new findings in the area of social cognition (see Shantz, 1983, for a wide-ranging review) must be taken into account in studying the development of internal working models. It may be less obvious that insights gained from studies of memory and cognition are also highly relevant. Bowlby (1980) pointed out that the distinction between episodic and semantic memory made by Tulving (1972) may be especially helpful here. Episodic memory refers to instances where a specific, autobiographical event can be recalled. Tulving contrasted episodic with semantic memory, which is a generalized representation of world knowledge (semantic networks encode such information as, "Down" is the opposite of "up").

Although it is plausible to suppose that autobiographical memories of specific episodes play a role in the construction of internal models, I find even more suggestive the recent work on event schemas (Mandler, 1979, 1983), on active structural networks (Norman & Rumelhart, 1975), and on scripts (Schank & Abelson, 1977). Event schemas or scripts are dynamic frameworks containing skeletal information on the who, what, when, where, why, and how of events. It is suggested that such schemas are constructed through the repeated experience of similar events. Once constructed, they can be used to predict future events, to guide decision making, and to infer unstated components of verbal narrative. The script or generalized event schema, in the words of Nelson and Gruendel (1981), is a cognitive model of experienced events, though I would prefer to speak of a mental instead of a cognitive model. Experienced events also include affective components. Hence, when a script is instantiated or called up in order to think about, predict, or guide action, affective components are represented along with perceptual/cognitive ones. It is indeed puzzling that in using the term "representation" most developmental psychologists (though not clinicians) tend, implicitly or explicitly, to restrict its meaning to cognitive processes. Much could, I propose, be gained by explicitly including the representation of affective appraisals in the study of event schemas.

Research on the development of scripts or event schemas in young children between 3 and 5 years of age (Nelson, 1981; Nelson & Gruendel, 1981) has demonstrated that they have considerable knowledge of the structure of routine events. Even the youngest children reported action sequences in the correct order, although their reports were less detailed than those of the older preschoolers. Events in which action sequences were causally connected to each other appeared to be especially salient even to 3-year-olds, and—interestingly, from the perspective of internal models—the youngest children seemed to store only extraordinary events as episodic (autobiographical) memories. The youngest children produced scripts when asked to recall a specific instance of a routine event such as eating dinner last night (Nelson & Ross, 1982). At even earlier ages than those studied by Nelson and her colleagues observation of symbolic play provides some insight into children's developing event schemas (Bretherton, 1984).

On the basis of findings described here, Nelson and Gruendel (1981) propose that event schemas or generalized event representations are the basic modules of mental representation from which higher order understandings are derived by application of additional abstracting processes (see also Mandler, 1979). Higher-order structures mentioned by Nelson and Gruendel included such disparate things as classification hierarchies and role concepts. I submit that event schemas developed in interaction with specific persons are also the raw material from which young children construct internal (affective/cognitive) working models of the self and of significant others, including attachment figures. Therefore, students of attachment might find techniques developed in the context of event representation helpful in attempting to investigate the development of internal working models.

In addition, it may be useful to think of the internal working model of the self and of attachment figures as a multilayered hierarchical network of representations. This idea is derived from Epstein's work regarding the self theory (1980; see Ricks [in this vol.], for a more detailed discussion). Epstein proposed that an individual's self theory consists of a hierarchy of major and minor postulates, a notion that can also be conceptualized in terms of event schemas. At the bottom of the hierarchy are basic-level event schemas, derived from significant repeated experiences with specific attachment figures. From these basic-level representations ("My mother comforts me when I get hurt"), multiple levels of ever more general schemas regarding the attachment figure and the self are abstracted ("My mother cares for me when I need her"). As long as the broader, top-level generalizations correspond fairly closely to the basic level representations, the individual will have serviceable and coherent models of self and attachment figures. In this case, updating of the working models will be a relatively straightforward task.

However, should the basic level schemas become disconnected from the high-level general schemas, difficulties are likely to ensue. Schemas of rejecting parents are likely to be associated with feelings of pain and anger. At the same time, it is threatening for a young child to experience anger toward the persons from whom he or she expects protection. One way out of this dilemma is to disconnect the affect from the painful event schema (masterfully described by Fraiberg et al., 1975). In such cases, the person can recall rejecting parental behavior but without the negative feelings that had formerly been associated with it. A second way out is to banish anxiety-provoking event schemas from awareness altogether (see Main et al., in this vol.; Ricks, in this vol.). Not only the feeling but also the event itself is now inaccessible to conscious recall. Both types of representational homeostasis appear to be counterproductive because both result in the construction of inconsistent representations. When the high-level postulates that are accessible to awareness are no longer in accord with the defensively excluded lower level postulates (event schemas of everyday rejection by parents), reorganization of the internal model of self and attachment figure becomes problematic.

Up to this point, my discussion has been almost exclusively focused on the internal working models constructed by the attached person, not the attachment figure. This is not because I regard the internal working models constructed by attachment figures as unimportant. To the contrary. I consider it unfortunate that studies of attachment relations as experienced and represented by the attachment figure are almost nonexistent. Even when adults' internal working models of attachment relationships have been examined, investigators were interested in them only in terms of the adult's childhood experiences with parents. The failure to study the parental attachment system, including parents' internal working models of attachment relationships, is a serious shortcoming of attachment research. The exclusive study of attachment from the perspective of the attached person has, I believe, led us to focus on the caregiver's physical and psychological availability, responsiveness, and sensitivity to signals. Yet it is probably wrong to conceive of the attachment figure in a purely responsive role. We can assume that the parent or caregiver adult already has constructed a generalized or normative model of infants, perhaps even a vague model of the specific infant before that infant is born (see Stern, 1977, for an example where this appeared to make a difference). We can also assume that such working models guide, from the outset, not only an attachment figure's behavior in individual circumstances but also long-term goals and planning for their attainment (Bretherton, 1980).

Some might say that we ought to study the caregiver-child relationship as one system. It is, of course, true that an attachment relationship—or any relationship, for that matter—is the joint work of two persons (achieved within the framework of a particular family and a particular culture). In this sense it is appropriate to consider the caregiver-infant relationship as a system (Sander, 1977). However, a representational view of relationships such as the one proposed here underscores that the two partners have, in another sense, two relationships: the relationships as mentally represented by the attached person and by the attachment figure.

The relevant questions therefore become still more complex. Not only must we ask whether a person constructs a separate self model within every important relationship and how these models become integrated, and not only must we discover under what circumstances individuals tend to exclude defensively from awareness affective and/or cognitive aspects of their internal working models (leading to multiple and incompatible models of the same attachment figure). We must also ask questions about the congruency of a relationship as represented by the attached person and by the attachment figure. Indeed, in caregiver-infant attachment relationships the representations cannot be congruent because the infant's symbolic capacities are much more primitive than those of the adult. What are the implications of such incongruencies, whether in terms of conceptual level alone or in terms of affective alignment as well? Although the answers to these questions will not be easy to obtain, I believe that, with the aid of new tools now available to us, we will be able to make considerable progress.

CONCLUDING REMARKS

In this chapter, I have made much of the significance of internal models of self and attachment figures. However, in conclusion, I would like to reemphasize that the development of relationships and their mental representation rests on more than symbolic capacities. In terms of attachment theory, internal working models of self and attachment figures are constructed in the context of a motivational-behavioral control system. This system steers behavior along particular channels and leads a person to expect, within certian limits, certain types of behavioral input from the partner. The system may be adapted to function within certain ranges of input, but as one moves toward the limits of that range (too much rejection, neglect or abuse of the child by the attachment figure, or, on the other hand, overprotection and restriction of the child's exploration due to anxiety about the child's safety or a desire to retain the child as attachment figure), its functioning may become not merely suboptimal but distorted. The positive or negative affective/cognitive appraisal of a partner's behavior, according to this view, is, to a significant part, governed by built-in motivational and evaluative processes. Acceptance and emotional support by a parent are inherently evaluated as positive, rejection and nonsupport as negative. I therefore believe that a theory of human attachment relationships, indeed of human relationships in general, cannot be based on very general affective/cognitive and communicative capacities alone. Such a theory must also take into account the set-goals of relevant motivational-behavioral systems.

THEORY AND ASSESSMENT:
INTRODUCTION TO PART 2

The development of a theory is dependent on its successful translation into measurement. Until very recently the only theory-based method for assessing patterns of attachment has been the Ainsworth Strange Situation. In spite of a host of studies exploring a variety of antecedents, concomitants, and sequelae of the Strange Situation attachment classifications, there have been few serious efforts to create alternatives to the Strange Situation or to devise procedures for evaluating attachment patterns in older children and adults. Fortunately, this situation is beginning to change. In Part 2, Waters and Deane (Chap. II) and Main, Kaplan, and Cassidy (Chap. III) describe a variety of new methods for assessing individual differences in security of attachment in toddlers, children, and adults.

Waters and Deane have created a Q-sort for assessing secure attachment in toddlers. Their measure is closely tied to Bowlby's control systems model of attachment. It is evaluated in terms of criteria for valid theory-based assessments that have applicability beyond this particular measure. The principal criterion (borrowed from Loevinger, 1957) is structural fidelity or the extent to which a measure reflects important aspects of the construct it is designed to assess. Additional criteria are that the measure must make reference to observable behavior in context, evaluate affective-cognitive relationships, allow for qualitative developmental change, detect coherence in development over time despite behavioral change, and discriminate the construct from similar constructs associated with other theoretical perspectives.

The attachment Q-set consists of 100 statements that permit an observer to describe individual differences in the functioning of the attachment system or, to phrase it in representational terms, to describe the child's internal working model of the attachment relationship as inferred from behavior. The measure has been tested for children between 12 and 36 months. Parents and independent observers have achieved high levels of agreement. Waters and Deane have also used this instrument for the purpose of scientific clarification. By asking other investigators to perform criterion sorts describing the prototypical secure, dependent, and sociable child, they tested the extent to which researchers of different theoretical persuasions could agree on the meaning of attachment and related constructs such as dependency and sociability.

The Q-sort developed by Waters and Deane follows the psychometric tradition of measurement by creating profiles from a composite of items. The assessments presented by Main et al., by contrast, examine the structure and pattern of a person's behavior across a whole event or interview. The structural fidelity of their measures derives both from the theoretical relevance of the eliciting stimuli and situations and from the systems of interpretation (ratings and classifications) applied to the resulting responses. The authors suggest that individual differences in attachment relationships in children and adults can best be pursued by moving to the level of representation. For the children, representational measures included responses to a family photograph in the parents' absence and the child's responses to a series of pictures of parent-child separations (devised by Klagsbrun & Bowlby, 1976). A dyadic measure was based on the fluidity of parent-child dialogue after a 1-hour separation, assessed from verbatim transcripts. The parents' internal working model of early attachment relationships was assessed via the Berkeley Adult Attachment Interview designed by Main, Goldwyn, and Kaplan (see Main, 1985). It probes for descriptions and evaluations of attachment relationships in childhood, paying particular attention to statements regarding an inability to recall childhood, coherent versus incoherent discussion of childhood attachments, and presence versus absence of idealization of attachment figures. Ratings were made from the interview transcripts in their entirety, after careful study of themes and theme developments. All the new child and adult measures were validated against the children's Strange Situation classifications at 12 months with mother and at 18 months with father. Strong continuity in security of attachment from infancy to childhood and from parental interview evaluations of childhood to their own infants' security at 12 and 18 months was documented.

The new measures presented in this part not only make significant theoretical contributions in and of themselves but will also permit us to pursue the study of attachment beyond infancy and across infancy with vigor and effectiveness.

I. B.

II. DEFINING AND ASSESSING INDIVIDUAL DIFFERENCES IN ATTACHMENT RELATIONSHIPS: Q-METHODOLOGY AND THE ORGANIZATION OF BEHAVIOR IN INFANCY AND EARLY CHILDHOOD

EVERETT WATERS AND KATHLEEN E. DEANE

State University of New York at Stony Brook

At times, it seems as if attachment research could fall victim to its own success. In the span of barely 15 years, we have come to accept Freud's view that attachment in infancy constitutes a genuine love relationship. We have recognized that this relationship is closely tracked by patterns of behavior toward caregivers and that this behavior is complexly organized, goal-corrected, and sensitive to environmental input. We have also adapted observational techniques employed by behavioral biologists and learned to examine infant behavior in detail and in context. As a result we have learned a great deal about attachment and exploratory behavior and about the organization and motivation of proximity seeking, contact maintaining, avoidance, and resistant behavior during separation and reunion.

As a direct result of these accomplishments, we have been able to standardize and validate useful techniques for assessing individual differences in attachment behavior and in the infant's ability to use an adult as a secure base from which to explore. These tools have enabled us to outline the antecedents of individual differences in attachment behavior and to establish that attachment relationships can be markedly stable over significant periods of time. At the same time, we have been able to rule out both intelligence and temperament as alternative explanations of individual dif-

This research was funded in part by a grant from the Foundation for Child Development (Program for Young Scholars in Social and Affective Development). The authors wish to thank the many colleagues who contributed their expertise to this project by performing the criterion Q-sorts for security, dependency, sociability, and social desirability.

ferences in secure versus anxious attachment and to demonstrate that patterns of attachment can change in response to significant changes in patterns of care. Evidence that infants who are secure with one parent are not necessarily secure with the other is particularly decisive on the distinction between attachment and temperament and confirms that our assessments reflect characteristics of specific relationships rather than traits of particular infants.

In the midst of these and other advances that are well documented in this *Monograph*, it is easy to lose sight of the fact that there have been very few nonlaboratory observations of attachment behavior during the last 10 years. Reports on attachment behavior outside the 12–18 month age range have also been few and far between. Questions about what is learned during the formation of attachment relationships, about the course of attachment after infancy, and about individual differences beyond security and anxiety have received surprisingly little attention. Unfortunately, the longer these questions are left unanswered, the more difficult it becomes to design incisive research or to assimilate new data. In fact, most of the recent data on the correlates of secure versus anxious attachment are simply being assimilated to the general hypothesis that "all good things go together." This provides little guidance for further research and almost insures that each new study will be less and less incisive. It also introduces the risk that the attachment construct will lose its definition and once again fall in among the feckless personality trait variables from which it was only recently rescued.

ATTACHMENT AND THE SECURE BASE PHENOMENON

The cornerstone of Bowlby's attachment theory was replacement of psychoanalytic drive reduction theory with a control systems analysis. In Bowlby's view, the apparently purposive behavior of infants toward caregivers can be explained in terms of a behavioral control system, which functions to maintain a balance between attachment and exploratory behavior across a wide range of contexts. In familiar contexts, and in the absence of what Bowlby called "natural cues to danger," the balance favors exploration punctuated by periodic checks on the adult's location. In other contexts, which may have entailed risk of injury or predation in the environment to which humans are adapted or which may have been associated with negative consequences in a particular infant's experience, the balance favors physical contact over exploration. When the control system operates as designed, it enables the infant to play an active role in its own behavior and development and facilitates both social and cognitive development. The operation of an attachment control system over time is referred to as the secure base phenomenon.

When Bowlby (1969/1982b) introduced behavioral control systems into attachment theory, he was addressing a very specific problem related to the motivational model underlying attachment theory. Aside from this, his interest was primarily in attachment as an emotional bond. Since the publication of the first volume of *Attachment and Loss,* many elaborations and alternatives to the emotional bond concept have been proposed. The infant-adult bond has been variously conceptualized as a traitlike variable (e.g., Coates, Anderson, & Hartup, 1972), a response class (e.g., Masters & Wellman, 1974), a relationship (e.g., Hinde, 1976, 1979), one facet of a broader social network (Weinraub, Brooks, & Lewis, 1977), and an organizational construct (Sroufe & Waters, 1977).

Each of these proposals conveys something important and well worth incorporating into assessment and empirical research. But unfortunately, insights and alternatives have rarely been presented in terms that are easily translated into assessment procedures. This poses several problems. First, theories that are not readily translated into assessment procedures are not easily tested. Second, a test or task cannot be made relevant to attachment theory by fiat. Unless a procedure is carefully tailored to assess attachment as it is defined in theory, it can only generate irrelevant and unassimilable data. This is hard to achieve when attachment is defined in psychodynamic, organismic, or contextual terms. But when attachment is closely tied to the performance of a behavioral control system, a clear relationship to patterns of secure base behavior in the home is easily defended as the criterion against which the construct validity of any attachment measure has to be assessed.

While Ainsworth clearly shares Bowlby's view that attachment is an emotional bond, she has come closer than anyone else to equating attachment per se with the control system that organizes attachment behavior. In her early cross-cultural work (Ainsworth, 1967) and in her Baltimore longitudinal study (Ainsworth et al., 1971), she detailed the infant's use of an adult as a secure base from which to explore. In addition she proposed that secure base behavior across time and across situations, rather than separation protest per se, is the most decisive evidence of attachment in infancy (Ainsworth, 1973). Finally, she has conceptualized secure versus anxious attachment in terms of differences in the infant's ability to use an adult as a secure base in naturalistic settings (Ainsworth et al., 1971).

When attachment is identified with a behavioral control system, specific behavioral referents are built into the definition of the construct. As a result, assessment problems become more tractable, and it is easier to say exactly what the development of attachment is supposed to be the development of. In addition, emphasis on a behavioral control system is entirely consistent with the notion that attachment is learned (Waters & Deane, 1982). Once we are past this perennial stumbling block, we can move directly to more significant issues: what is learned in the acquisition of a first attachment, what role (if any) do species-specific biases in learning ability play in the acquisition of attachment, and what is learned in forming a first attachment that facilitates acquisition of attachment to additional caregivers?

A second advantage of identifying attachment with an underlying control system is that the performance of a control system is easier to assess than a relationship, an organizational construct, or a social network. In addition, reference to a control system and to patterns of secure base behavior suggests criteria against which various approaches to assessment can be evaluated. This is most important because, as we have indicated in several recent papers (e.g., Waters & Deane, 1982), incongruous weddings of theory and assessment have led to fruitless controversy and wasted effort. In addition, they have been extremely difficult to unravel (Waters & Deane, 1982).

The primary disadvantages seem to be that the control system/secure base perspective is not as relevant to describing or explaining responses to loss of attachment figures as we might like and that there is the risk that we may reify the behavioral system, only to discover later that it is more useful as a metaphor than as an explanation for attachment behavior. At the same time, our inability to assess attachment beyond a limited age range is becoming a more acute problem, and the trend away from research on attachment per se toward the study of attachment correlates continues. Hence, for the moment, the advantages in tying the attachment construct closely to an underlying behavioral system and to the secure base phenomenon seem to outweigh the disadvantages.

CRITERIA AGAINST WHICH ASSESSMENT PROCEDURES CAN BE EVALUATED

When attachment is conceptualized in terms of a behavioral control system and closely tied to the secure base phenomenon, we can define seven criteria against which any measure can be evaluated. Where measures are not available or where conventional measures fall short, the same criteria can serve as guidelines in the development of new measures.

Structural Fidelity

In her classic monograph on the relationship between psychological assessment and psychological theory, Loevinger (1957) outlined a number of important conditions for valid assessment. Among these she included the notion that a measure should provide data congruent with the type of construct it is designed to assess. Quantitative traits call for continuous variables;

taxonomic entities call for classification rather than measurement; multiple components call for multidimensional assessment. When theory and measurement are congruent in this respect, the measure affords structural fidelity.

The defining characteristic of the attachment system is reference to a set-goal. That is, the measure of a control system should be in terms not of gross behavioral output but of success or failure at some regulatory function (i.e., adaptiveness). This involves assessment across time and across the range of stimuli to which the system is responsive. As long as the distinction between (quantitative) output and (qualitative) performance is maintained, adaptiveness can certainly be measured in terms of a continuous variable.

Reference to Behavior

The control systems described by Ainsworth et al. (1971), Bischof (1975), Bowlby (1969/1982b), Bretherton (1980), and Waters and Deane (1982) all incorporate, inter alia, sensitivity to stimuli in the social environment. In addition, each of these control systems generates observable behavioral output. Thus measures of individual differences in attachment should make specific reference to behavior. This might involve defining behavioral variables as narrow as "clinging to mother's leg" or as broad as "contact maintaining" (which might include reaching, clinging, resisting being put down, etc.).

Once these primary data have been collected via time sampling, rating, or some other method, it may be economical to describe the performance of the attachment behavioral system in terms of trait descriptive adjectives. For example, it is more economical to describe a child as "secure" than it is to say that the child explores and approaches novelty more readily when the adult is present, monitors adult location and behavior spontaneously and effectively, is more tolerant of self-initiated separation than of adult moving away, retreats to adult when distressed, is not angry after brief separation, finds physical contact a potent stimulus for terminating distress, prefers to be comforted by this adult, et cetera. The essential point is that an attachment measure should provide primary data that have clear behavioral referents. Trait language should be used only to summarize behavior—never as a substitute; never as an explanation.

Take the Context of Behavior into Account

The control systems described by Ainsworth et al. (1971), Bischof (1975), Bowlby (1969/1982b), Bretherton (1980), and Waters and Deane (1982) all make specific reference to the context in which attachment behavior occurs. This involves both the context provided by objects and events in the environment and the context provided by the infant's or child's ongoing behavior. For example, approaches to the mother may be phenotypically similar; but, within a control systems perspective, some are "exploratory approaches" (i.e., not attachment behavior), and some are "proximity seeking" or even a "retreat" from a stranger (i.e., cornerstones of the secure base phenomenon). Similarly, an incomplete approach in a nonseparation context has to be distinguished from an incomplete approach when the caregiver returns after a separation. Such distinctions have to be made because phenotypically similar behaviors often have dramatically different external correlates when the context in which behavior occurs is taken into account (e.g., Hay, 1980; Sroufe & Waters, 1977; Tracy, Lamb, & Ainsworth, 1976; Waters, Matas, & Sroufe, 1975).

The emphasis that control systems theory places on the context in which behavior occurs has two important implications for assessment. First, an attachment measure should explicitly recognize that a given behavior can be congruent with the system's set-goal in one context and incongruent, even irrelevant to the attachment construct, in other contexts. Second, a measure should preserve or incorporate information that allows us to score different behaviors as equivalent when their outcome vis à vis the control system's set-goal is equivalent.

Evaluate Relationships among Affect, Cognition, and Behavior

Each of the control system models mentioned above includes sensitivity to affective, cognitive, and behavioral cues. The primary effect of affective inputs seems to be on the set-goal of the attachment behavioral system. Infants are more tolerant of separation and explore farther away when they are alert and not distressed. They are less tolerant of separation and generally demand more physical contact when they are ill, hungry, concerned by recent experiences, et cetera.

The primary role of cognitive and behavioral input to the control system is regulatory. Cognition plays a critical role in monitoring adult behavior and accessibility, in recognizing and evaluating events in the environment, and in exploratory interactions with toys and people. Finally, behavior is the attachment control system's effector mechanism. It is used to correct deviations from the set-goal by changing the proximity of the infant to the caregiver or by stimulating changes in the caregiver's behavior.

All these are monitored and integrated in order to keep the balance between contact and exploration within the limits defined by the control system's set-goal. None of them has any decisive meaning to the control system, except in the context of the others. Accordingly, any attachment assessment should include data from all three domains.

Allow for Nonquantitative Developmental Change

There are many ways in which the operation and output of a control system can change during development. Some of the more important among these include changes in the system's set-goal, in the inputs to which the system is sensitive, in the integration of system components, in the behaviors through which adaptive response is effected, and in the relationship between the system in question and other behavioral systems. Each of these involves the structure and configuration of the control system and may or may not alter the rate of any particular behavior. Accordingly, an attachment measure should anticipate the problem of detecting and describing change in how the behavioral system operates. Emphasis on age changes in the frequency of particular behaviors will not suffice.

Detect Coherence over Time Even in the Context of Behavioral Change

As described above, an attachment measure that offers structural fidelity will employ a criterion of "adaptiveness" (i.e., how well is the system tracking its set-goal?) rather than assess the quantity of behavioral output per se. While both criteria involve assessment over time, they refer primarily to cross-sectional assessment. A related criterion is that a measure should be able to detect consistency (if any) in adaptive functioning across age, even when there are developmental changes in the behavior through which adaptive response is effected.

An Additional Criterion: Discriminant Validation

The behaviors initiated, modulated, or terminated by an attachment control system are not properly part of the system. They belong to the infant's or child's repertoire of action skills. Thus the phenotypically similar behaviors can be performed in the service of attachment in one context and be unrelated to the attachment control system's activity in another. This raises two problems that psychometricians have discussed in terms of discriminant validity. First, data collected to assess attachment may be subject to alternative interpretations, especially in terms of temperament, intelligence, and other trait constructs. The most decisive approach to this is to incorporate assessment of these variables into the procedure for assessing attachment. This enables us to evaluate and rule out plausible alternative interpretations. A second problem arises from the fact that evaluative biases can easily intrude into observational data (e.g., the tendency to attribute socially desirable secure base behavior to preferred subjects).

One response to this is to anticipate it and to employ assessment strategies and observational designs that minimize or attenuate observer biases. An additional strategy is to include specific assessment of social desirability bias in the measure. Discriminant assessment is an important component of any individual differences assessment, regardless of how attachment is conceptualized.

EVALUATION OF CONVENTIONAL ASSESSMENT METHODS

When trait ratings, time sampling, and the widely used Strange Situation procedure are evaluated in terms of these criteria, each shows a unique pattern of assets and liabilities. A brief review of these conventional assessment methods can be quite useful since even methods that fail to meet one or more of the criteria mentioned above are likely to have particular strengths that should be incorporated into some other method to provide better assessment.

Trait Ratings

The primary advantages of rating methods are flexibility and economy. In terms of the criteria outlined above, rating methods excel in their ability to take the context in which behavior occurs into account and in their sensitivity to coherence over time, in the context of underlying behavioral change. These advantages arise from the ability of (some) human judges to apply complex cognitions in the task of summarizing and of scaling diverse behavioral inputs in terms of a theoretically defined criterion such as security. (See Meehl, 1973, for detailed consideration of the conditions under which clinical judgment is both useful and economical.) In principle, rating methods are quite amenable to discriminant validation, though it is rarely undertaken with the care it deserves.

The primary disadvantages of rating methods are that they offer little in the way of structural fidelity since attachment is not a trait, that when primary data are collected in terms of ratings it is impossible to recover the behavioral details on which the ratings were based, and that ratings are exceptionally susceptible to intrusion of biases, response sets, and global rating styles. As a result, ratings are coercive; they force us to see the phenomenon in terms of constructs built into the rating scale and limit our ability to construct and evaluate alternatives without new data. Rating methods also tend to be conservative. The set adopted in rating a particular construct works against the adoption of new perspectives during observation.

Rating methods are not well suited to analyses of nonquantitative developmental change, even though they can enable us to see beyond age changes in specific behaviors in order to detect continuity of adaptation. In particular, rating data do not provide the behavioral detail necessary to analyze developmental changes in a behavioral system's set-goal, the inputs to which a system is sensitive, or relationships among system components.

Finally, ratings generally incorporate information about affect, cognition, and behavior. Thus they can be quite useful if the alternative is a method that tends to overlook any of these domains. At the same time, it is inherently difficult to separate affect, cognition, and behavioral variance in rating data. Moreover, in most contexts, a process level analysis of affect-cognition-behavior interplay is much more valuable than approaches that emphasize correlations and components of summary score variance without respect to the sequencing of events in real time.

Observational Data: Frequency Counts and Time Sampling

The primary advantage of frequency counts and time sampling procedures is that they retain much of the behavioral detail that is sacrificed in rating methods. At the same time, they are extremely expensive to employ. In terms of the criteria outlined above, observational data can afford considerable structural fidelity if the categories of observation are tailored to the design of the behavioral system and take the context in which behavior occurs into account. In practice, most observational scoring schemes are extremely insensitive. They tend to aggregate broad ranges of phenotypically similar behavior, even where the same behavior has markedly different implications for control system functioning in different situational or behavioral contexts (e.g., Coates, Anderson, & Hartup, 1972).

Individual differences in observational data across time have traditionally been analyzed in terms of stability within particular behavior categories (e.g., Masters & Wellman, 1974). Unfortunately, the stability of specific behaviors clearly underestimates the coherence and consistency of adaptive functioning across periods of significant behavioral change (Waters & Sroufe, 1983). In principle, we can define behavior categories that have clear implications for adaptive functioning at various ages and intercorrelate scores on age appropriate measures across time intervals. Alternatively, we can employ observational protocols that are sufficiently detailed to support secondary data reduction, in which frequency counts or time sampling data are reduced to ratings.

Unfortunately, very little of the potential inherent in observational data has been realized in developmental research. Several problems have contributed to this. First among these is the lack of conceptual analysis and the relative unfamiliarity with the target behaviors reflected in most lists of observation categories. Aside from this, time sampling and frequency counting tax the skill, patience, and endurance of even the most dedicated researcher. In addition, the number of behavior categories that can be assessed at once (or in one viewing of a video record) is quite small while at the same time the number of behavior categories increases dramatically when distinctions among superficially similar behaviors are made and when the context in which behavior occurs is taken into account. Finally, many behaviors that are of interest in developmental research occur at low and/or uneven frequencies. This poses serious problems for the collection of psychometrically reliable data unless very substantial periods of observation are devoted to each subject (Waters, 1978).

The Ainsworth Strange Situation Procedure

The Ainsworth Strange Situation procedure involves both a standardized observation context and a set of scoring protocols. Both the observation context and the scoring system were developed with explicit reference to an attachment behavioral control system. The separation-reunion episodes of the Strange Situation were designed to reproduce mild to moderately stressful challenges to the attachment behavioral system that occur in everyday situations. The system for scoring interactive behavior in the Strange Situation is explicitly designed to evaluate the adaptive functioning of the attachment control system. That is, it parses behavior in terms of inputs and contexts that are theoretically relevant to the control system's task of maintaining an optimal balance between proximity and exploration. Accordingly, the assessment affords exceptional structural fidelity.

In research on individual differences, the Strange Situation procedure is more a psychometric instrument than an observational measure because the behavior observed in the laboratory is not, in and of itself, the behavior of interest. That is, crying in the Strange Situation is not assessed as a sample of crying rate in the home, nor are rates of proximity seeking, avoidant behavior, or resistant behavior in the laboratory expected to correlate with rates of similar behavior at home. These behaviors are assessed in the Strange Situation as signs or predictors of the control system's ability to operate over a wide range of contexts and to organize behavior toward the adult over significant periods of time.

The validity of Strange Situation assessment depends on its ability to substitute for extensive assessment of the secure base phenomenon in naturalistic contexts. The primary evidence in support of the procedure's external validity is detailed in Ainsworth et al. (1978). If the relationship between Strange Situation classifications and the secure base phenomenon at home was not evident in empirical data, the procedure might still provide valuable data on the quality of attachment relationships. But we would be unable to explain why or how.

The principal limitations of the Strange Situation procedure are that it is only applicable within a narrow age range (perhaps as narrow as 12–18 months), that repeated assessments have to be spaced to prevent strong carryover effects, and that the situation and scoring procedures do not lend themselves to research on developmental changes in the attachment control system. The procedure is also expensive to administer and score, and scoring is difficult to learn without direct instruction.

One additional aspect of the Strange Situation procedure seems problematic. The scoring system that is best validated for research on individual differences involves taxonomic classification rather than quantitative assessment. Moreover, the distribution of subjects across the avoidant, secure, and resistant categories is markedly unbalanced. As a result, the data gleaned from the procedure offer less information and fewer options for data analysis and require larger samples than either rating or time sampling methods. It can be argued, however, that taxonomic assessment is part and parcel of the procedure's structural fidelity, which may explain why the classification system has had markedly greater external validity than any other scheme for scoring Strange Situation data.

Summary

Each of the conventional methods for assessing attachment behavior has a distinct pattern of strengths and weaknesses. Ratings are economical and flexible, but they do not provide behavioral detail or structural fidelity. They are coercive and conservative. Observational methods preserve behavioral detail, but they tend to become unmanageable when we try to take the behavioral context into account. In addition, observational methods are rarely informed by theory or pilot observation and thus often fail to deliver on much of their potential.

The Strange Situation procedure affords well-validated assessment, but it is applicable only to a very limited age range. It is not well suited to research on important issues in attachment theory that call for multiple assessments or for assessment of developmental change. The procedure is also difficult to score and yields taxonomic rather than quantitative data.

In brief, none of the conventional methods for assessing attachment meet all the criteria outlined above. Thus there is a compelling case for developing alternative measurement strategies.

THE Q-SORT METHOD: AN ALTERNATIVE APPROACH TO ATTACHMENT ASSESSMENT

The Q-sort method was introduced by Stephenson (1953) and has been used extensively in personality assessment and developmental research (e.g.,

Baumrind, 1968; Bem & Funder, 1978; Block, 1961/1978; Block & Block, 1980; Roberts, Block, & Block, 1984; Waters, Garber, Gornal, & Vaughn, 1983). Q-sort methodology consists of three components: procedures for developing sets of descriptive items to which scores are to be assigned; procedures assigning scores to items by sorting them into a rank order, from most characteristic to most uncharacteristic within each subject; and a wide variety of procedures for data reduction and analysis.

During the last 2 years we have developed and pilot tested a 100-item Q-set that allows us to meet each of the criteria for attachment assessment outlined above and at the same time affords the psychometric and data-analytic advantages that are unique to the Q-sort method. As is not the case with conventional trait assessment Q-sets, each item in this Q-set makes specific reference to behavior. Many of the items qualify their behavioral referents by specifying a specific context. The Attachment Q-set covers a broad range of secure base and exploratory behavior, affective response, social referencing, and other aspects of social cognition. Accordingly, the Q-set can be construed as an overview of the entire domain of attachment relevant behavior, as currently understood within an ethological/control systems perspective.

The Q-set: A Vocabulary for Describing Attachment Behavior

Each item in the attachment behavior Q-set consists of an item title and more specific descriptive statements printed individually on cards. These items constitute a standard vocabulary for describing individual differences within a particular domain of personality, attitudes, or behavior. Q-set items can easily be written to refer to specific behaviors or to behavior in specific contexts. In addition to describing individuals, Q-sets can also be used to operationalize constructs in terms of an array of scores on a specific set of relevant items.

Use of a standard multiple-item vocabulary for assessment has many advantages. The development of the Q-set itself demands close examination of theory and reference to extensive clinical or observational data. What is the range of behavior relevant to a particular construct or set of constructs that might be assessed with the Q-set? What contexts are salient in evaluating construct relevant behavior? Construction of a Q-set forces us to consider process-oriented models of behavior and behavioral organization in detail. We are also forced to clarify distinctions and ambiguities that are more easily glossed over in designing rating scales. A well-designed Q-set is thus a powerful tool for transferring theoretical and behavior sophistication to new observers.

Use of a standard Q-set insures that diverse observers evaluate the same content in describing each subject. The use of a broad-band item set is also economical. After individuals have been described in terms of a particular Q-set, a wide range of variables can be scored from this description, including variables that attracted attention only after data collection was completed (see Data Reduction and Analytic Strategies below).

Q-Sorting Procedure

When judges or observers use a Q-set to describe a subject, they sort the items (on cards) into piles whose designations range from most characteristic to least characteristic of a particular subject. This is usually accomplished in several steps, by sorting the items into three piles and then subdividing these into a total of nine. Then, working from the outer piles toward the center, each pile is adjusted so that the final sort conforms to a symmetrical, unimodal distribution with specified numbers of items in each of the nine piles (i.e., 5, 8, 12, 16, 18, 16, 12, 8, and 5).

Each item is scored in terms of its placement (piles 1–9) in the distribution (e.g., each of the five items in pile 9 receives a score of 9, each of the five items in pile 1 receives a score of 1, and so forth). When several sorters describe the same subject, a composite description can be constructed by averaging the scores assigned by each sorter to each item.

The primary advantages of the Q-sort method are that observers can be kept unaware of the constructs that will be scored from the data they provide; that observers are not required to have detailed knowledge of norms for each item, as they are for conventional rating methods; that response biases are reduced by sorting items into a fixed distribution; that the significance of a behavior is clearly distinguished from the frequency with which it occurs; that each item is explicitly scored in the context of a well-defined set of other items; and that data from different samples can be compared directly because sample norms do not enter into the scoring. In addition, description of subjects in terms of an array of scores on items with highly specific content affords a wide range of analytic possibilities that are not available when rating procedures are employed to summarize a wide range of information in a single score.

Data Reduction and Analytic Strategies

As mentioned above, the Q-sort method involves describing a subject in terms of an array of scores on a standard set of items. One of the greatest advantages of this approach is the wide range of data reduction and analytic strategies that can be employed in such data.

Reliability assessment.—Agreement between independent observers provides evidence that they are performing their tasks similarly (i.e., that they are in some sense interchangeable). This is important when one observer is very experienced or can otherwise be considered the criterion against which correct scoring should be assessed and when the observations of different subjects are undertaken by different observers.

Unfortunately, agreement per se does not decisively establish that observations are accurate. It merely suggests that observers have performed similarly. More important, agreement does not imply that the observations on which observers agree are typical or representative of the subjects' mean rates or relative performances. This is especially problematic when data are based on very brief encounters with a subject, as in many field studies and most laboratory procedures.

The psychometric reliability of a measure reflects the extent to which the scores assigned to individual subjects are representative of their typical or "true" scores over the entire set of comparable occasions that might have been assessed. When data are unreliable, correlations among scores are attenuated and the statistical power of group comparisons is diminished. In most developmental research, observational data tend to be extremely accurate but may be unrepresentative (when this distinction is not made, reliability in the sense of representativeness is generally not evaluated).

In Q-sort data, agreement can be assessed in terms of the reliability of individual items or of an entire sort. Item agreement is assessed by intercorrelating the scores assigned by two sorters across a sample of subjects. Agreement on a complete sort can be assessed within each subject by intercorrelating the arrays of scores assigned to a particular subject by two sorters, and mean agreement can be assessed by computing the average agreement across all the subjects in a sample.

In general, it is extremely useful to have several sorters describe each subject in a study because the reliability of a Q-sort description increases when several sorts are averaged to obtain a composite Q-sort description. This is simply an instance of the well-known relationship between test length (each Q-sort description being considered a single item) and reliability (Ghiselli, Campbell, & Zedeck, 1981) and of the notion that the more points of view and the more observational occasions included in a description, the more representative the description will be (Rushton, Brainerd, & Pressley, 1983).

When several Q-sorts are obtained to describe a single subject or a single hypothetical construct, the reliability of a composite of these sorts can be assessed by computing the mean intercorrelation among the scores that several expert raters assign on a particular item across all the subjects in a sample and then applying the Spearman-Brown formula (Ghiselli et al., 1981). In additon, since each subject is described in terms of an array of scores for the complete Q-set, the reliability of the full Q-sort description of any individual subject can be obtained by intercorrelating the arrays of scores assigned to the subject by several observers and applying the same Spearman-Brown formula.

The significance of these reliability coefficients is that they indicate the proportion of variance in a set of data that is reliable (as opposed to indicating error), that they can be used to determine the degree to which correlations and the power of statistical tests will be attenuated as a consequence of error variance in the data, and that they can be used to determine how much observation time would be necessary to obtain reliable Q-sort descriptions. Psychometric reliability estimates can also be computed for rating data and observations (e.g., Waters, 1978), though they are rarely reported in developmental research. A special advantage of Q-sort data is that reliability coefficients can be computed for individual subjects as well as for a sample at large. By indicating when additional data should be collected on a particular subject, this provides a useful approach to quality control in Q-sort data.

Analysis of individual items.—The most obvious approach to Q-sort data is simply to treat the scores assigned to subjects on the Q-set items as separate scores on so many different variables. These scores can be correlated with other data, or groups can be compared in terms of item-by-item significance tests (e.g., Vaughn, Deane, & Waters, in this vol.; Waters et al., 1983; Waters et al., 1979). Since this typically involves a large number of statistical tests, it is important to deal with the fact that a certain number of significant results will occur by chance. One approach is simply to employ conservative significance criteria. An alternative is to undertake a cluster analysis of the variables on which significant results are obtained and to emphasize domains of significant effects rather than specific items in interpretations and discussion.

Subsets of items as scales.—A wide variety of procedures can be used to compose scales from selected Q-set items after a complete Q-set has been sorted. These range from using rational criteria to select items on the basis of specific content to using cluster analysis or factor analysis for empirical item analysis. The full range of item-weighting procedures can also be employed. When the scores assigned to a selected subset of items are summed or weighted and summed, the total score can be used as an index of a single construct. The reliability of such a score can be determined from the mean intercorrelations among the items included in the scale (Ghiselli, Campbell, & Zedeck, 1981).

Criterion sorting.—Judges can use a Q-set to operationalize important attachment constructs by sorting the items to describe a hypothetically most secure, dependent, or sociable subject. Item-by-item comparisons between the placement of items by sorters defining one construct and sorters using the same items to define a different construct can be used to evaluate similarities and differences among related constructs (e.g., Deane & Waters, 1984; Waters, Noyes, Vaughn, & Ricks, in press).

When constructs have been defined in this way, subjects can be scored on each construct by computing the correlaton between the composite description of the "hypothetically most *x* subject" and the Q-sort description of a particular subject (i.e., the correlation between two arrays of scores within each subject). The correlation coefficient between the construct definition and the description of the subject is used as the subject's score on that construct. The more similar the subject is to the hypothetically most extreme subject, the higher the subject's score on the construct.

This procedure has several important advantages. First, it enables us to place some distance between the observers who collect the primary data in a study and the constructs that will be scored from their data. Biases and halo effects are much less likely to intrude when observers use a Q-set to "describe a subject's behavior" without reference to any specific constructs than when observers are asked to assign ratings on the constructs themselves. Second, it allows us to employ experts' definitions of a construct to score subjects without having to enlist the experts as observers.

The criterion-sort procedure also insures that the full range of relevant behavior is considered in assigning scores on a construct. Most constructs have implications for a wide range of behaviors. And in principle a high score should be reserved for subjects who have a broad profile of construct-relevant behavior. In practice, raters who have a particular construct in mind respond strongly to positive evidence (e.g., to a few clear signs of insecurity in a particular interaction). As a result, moderate to high scores are often assigned to subjects whose behavior is unexceptional in much of the domain relevant to the construct. In contrast, a Q-sorter's task is to describe the subject's behavior with equal attention to every Q-set item. After the subject has been described in detail, a high correlation between this description and a criterion sort implies exceptional behavior across a significant range of construct-relevant behavior. Isolated events are much less likely to result in high scores in Q-sort data than they would be with conventional rating methods.

Finally, this procedure enables us to develop criterion sorts and assign scores on new variables long after data collection has been completed. This is a great advantage in longitudinal research. Interpreting unexpected results or alternative hypotheses is often facilitated by the ability to score subjects on a variable for which no specific measure was included in the study.

Cluster analysis of subjects.—In many research contexts, it is useful to identify homogeneous subsets of subjects within a sample. In some cases, taxonomic analysis of the sample is significant in itself. In other cases, this is merely a step toward analysis of a hypothesis that may fit a subset of the sample better than the sample as a whole. Q-sort data lend themselves to this kind of analysis quite readily because intercorrelations among subjects (sometimes called Q-correlations) can be computed across selected items or across an entire Q-set. These correlations reflect the similarities and differences among subjects and can easily be employed in cluster analyses of subjects.

Once homogeneous subsets of a sample are identified, they can be characterized in terms of mean profiles on individual Q-set items. Comparisons among the subsets can also be made in terms of mean scores on Q-set items or group differences on data from other sources via discriminant analysis. Once subsets of a sample have been adequately characterized, etiological hypotheses, differential predictive hypotheses, et cetera can be made with reference to specific groups. Block (1971) and Block (1969a) have demonstrated the power of this type of data analysis in several longitudinal studies of personality development.

An Attachment Behavior Q-Set for Infancy and Early Childhood

The Attachment Q-set was developed and revised in four stages. In the first stage we reviewed the literature on attachment theory and attachment behavior in American and other samples. In the course of this review, we compiled a list of behaviors and contexts that were mentioned in theoretical articles or empirical research. In addition, we developed a list of constructs that one might want to score from a well-designed Attachment Q-set. These included security, dependency, detachment, self-efficacy, several aspects of object orientation, communication skills, predominant mood, response to physical comforting, fearfulness, anger, and trust. In a series of home visits, we rated infants and toddlers on each of these variables and subsequently specified the particular behaviors that had led to or seemed congruent with these ratings. These, plus the behaviors mentioned in the literature, constituted a preliminary item set. We then listed each of our preliminary items on cards and defined behavioral responses that would be considered the opposite of each item.

In a second series of home visits, we used the preliminary item set to describe the behavior of infants and toddlers. Behaviors that never occurred, could not be sorted with good agreement, or had very little variance across subjects were revised or eliminated. In addition, a number of items were qualified, and in several instances a single item was replaced with two or more items in order to distinguish among theoretically significant contexts.

In the third stage of development, we categorized the entire set of items and opposites and then eliminated either the item or its opposite in order to balance social desirability within each category. At this point the item set consisted of 100 items. The content categories and the number of items per category are presented in Table 1.

TABLE 1

ATTACHMENT Q-SET: CONTENT CLUSTERS

Cluster Description	Items (N)
Attachment behavioral system:	
Attachment/exploration balance	12
Differential responsiveness to parents	9
Affectivity	19
Social interaction	18
Object manipulation	14
Independence/dependency	14
Social perceptiveness	8
Endurance/resiliency	6
Total	100

In the final stage of development, we asked parents to familiarize themselves with the items and use them to describe their own infant's or toddler's
behavior. Two observers visited each of the subjects for 3–4 hours at home
on two occasions and used the items to describe the subjects' behavior. Items
on which it was difficult to obtain agreement between observers were
clarified. A number of items were restated to eliminate technical terms that
the mothers asked to have defined (further effort is still needed in this
direction). Finally, items for which the opposite behavior (i.e., the meaning
of low placement in the sort) was unclear were revised. The opposite of the
behavior described in these items was added in italics at the bottom of the
card on which the item is printed.

In the present item set, each item consists of a title and a definition that
refers to specific behaviors and relevant contexts, and opposites are defined
in italics as needed. The item titles for the Attachment Q-set are listed by
item number in the Appendix.[1]

The Attachment Q-Set in Naturalistic Contexts

In a recent study, we visited 50 3-year-olds in their homes and collected
Q-sort descriptions of each child's behavior from observers as well as from
the child's mother (Deane & Waters, 1984). Three visits were scheduled at
the family's convenience. On the first occasion, Observer 1 visited for 3–4
hours, accompanying the parent and child throughout the home, around
the yard and neighborhood, and on any excursions away from home. The
observer was responsive to bids for interaction. On the second occasion,

---

[1] The complete items and sorting instructions are available from the authors, Department of Psychology, State University of New York, Stony Brook, NY 11794.

both Observer 1 and Observer 2 visited the family for 3–4 hours. The purpose of a joint visit was to allow the now familiar observer to introduce the second observer to the family. The third visit was made by Observer 2 alone. Both graduate students and undergraduates served as observers.

After completing two visits, the observers sorted the items as described above. Correlations between the two Q-sort descriptions of each child ranged from .75 to .95. Thus 6–8 hours over two occasions provides sufficient information for sorters to provide highly reliable data.

When the series of visits with a family was completed, the procedure for providing a complete Q-sort was explained to the mother, and she was asked to familiarize herself with the Q-set by sorting the cards into three piles (characteristic, neither characteristic nor uncharacteristic, and uncharacteristic). She was encouraged to ask about both the items and the sorting procedure.

During the following week, the mother observed her child with the intent of providing a Q-sort description at the end of the week. During the next week, she observed again and completed a second sort. These two sorts were averaged together to yield a composite description of the child. The correlation between the composite mother's sort and a similar composite of the observers' descriptions of her child ranged from .59 to .93. The mean correlation was .80. Examination of differences between mothers' and observers' sorts indicated that, in many instances, the differences were clearly examples of the mother having better access to the behavior than the observers did.

These results provide clear evidence that mothers can provide exceptional data on their children's attachment behavior when they are informed in advance of what they should observe and how it is to be reported and when the procedure for reporting involves nonevaluatively stated items and a forced choice procedure such as a Q-sort.

We are currently in the midst of a similar study of 1-year-olds. While the Q-set items seem equally relevant at this age, it appears that three visits may be more appropriate than two. The items do not seem appropriate for infants under 10 months.

Criterion Sorts: Security, Dependency, Sociability,
and Social Desirability

In addition to our observational studies, we have used the Attachment Q-set in a study of security and related concepts as they apply to children aged 12 months and 3 years (Deane & Waters, 1984). Forty-three Ph.D. psychologists familiar with developmental theories of security, dependency, or sociability provided Q-sort definitions of these constructs. Eight independent sorts were collected for each construct as it applies at each age.[2] In addition, eight Ph.D. students in developmental psychology sorted the items in the Attachment Q-set into nine piles ranging from most socially desirable to least socially desirable for each age. The sorters represented a wide range of theoretical perspectives in contemporary developmental psychology, from behaviorally oriented child clinicians to eclectic cognitive social learning theorists to psychodynamically trained personality researchers.

The mean item placements of each item in the security, dependency, sociability, and social desirability sorts for 12 and 36 months are listed in the Appendix. There was exceptionally good agreement as to the Q-sort definitions of each construct at each age. The mean correlations among criterion sorts ranged from .70 to .80. There were no obvious patterns of agreement or disagreement related to the sorter's theoretical orientation. The sorts for each construct were averaged to provide a composite definition of each construct at each age. The reliabilities of these composites were > .95 for each construct at each age. Thus the Attachment Q-set enables us to develop extremely reliable consensual definitions of these constructs from a relatively small number of sorters.

As indicated above, these criterion sorts can be used to assign scores to individual subjects by computing the correlation between the criterion sort and the array of scores assigned as a description of the subject in question. The Q-sort method clearly provides an economical means of informing and standardizing assessment of these abstract constructs across laboratories.

Conceptual similarity.—Correlations across criterion sorts indicate the degree of conceptual similarity among different constructs. In the present data, security and dependency, which have often been used interchangeably and occasionally as opposites, are conceptually orthogonal at 12 months ($r = -.09$) and somewhat negatively correlated when they are defined with ref-

---

[2] Criterion sorts were provided by Everett Waters, Alan Sroufe, Mary Ainsworth, Mary Blehar, Mary Main, Donelda Stayton, Donna Weston, and Joan Stevenson-Hinde (security: 12 months); Everett Waters, Mary Blehar, Alan Sroufe, Brian Vaughn, Inge Bretherton, Robert Marvin, Leah Matas, and Alicia Lieberman (security: 36 months); Willard Hartup, Joseph Campos, Eleanor Maccoby, Carl Corter, Susan Goldberg, Margaret Ricks, Brian Vaughn, and Donna Bradshaw (dependency: 12 months); John Masters, Tiffany Field, Jay Belsky, Mavis Hetherington, Ken Rubin, Kathleen Deane, Barbara Caparulo, and Mary Main (dependency: 36 months); Ross Parke, Allison Clarke-Stewart, George Morgan, Carol Eckerman, Mary Rothbart, Hill Goldsmith, Marguerite Stevenson, and Marilyn Svejda (sociability: 12 months); Wanda Bronson, Marian Radke-Yarrow, Thomas Berndt, Sandra Scarr, Wyndol Furman, Dante Cicchetti, Karen Rosen, and Sarah Sternglanz (sociability: 36 months); JoEllen Hoffman, Carol Friedman, Terri Lomenick, Pat Murray, Miriam Kramer, Stacy Vedder, Joyce Prigot, and an anonymous student, State University of New York (social desirability: 12 months); and Virginia Tinsley, Donna Cox, Lucille Anderson, Charlotte Jungblat, Carol Andreason, Marlene Zelek, Jan Pederson, and Paul Dores (social desirability: 36 months).

erence to 36-month-olds ($r = -.36$). This kind of data can inform developmental theory and also provide both justification and procedures for developing age appropriate assessment of important constructs.

Our criterion sorts also indicate that security and sociability are conceptualized similarly for both 12- and 36-month-olds ($r = .82, .88$). That is, psychologists are somewhat more sensitive to (or more aware of) normative trends in attachment behavior than in sociability.

Deane & Waters (1984) present analyses of item differences among these conceptual sorts as well as correlations among security, dependency, and sociability scores assigned to individual subjects. They also describe procedures for evaluating the effects of social desirability variance on conceptual sorts and for assigning scores to one criterion sort while holding variance in the other sorts constant.

In brief, detailed analysis of criterion sorts can sensitize us to our own theoretical expectations and provide a foundation for empirical research that leads to improved conceptual definitions and better measurement.

Evaluation

Even at this early stage in our research it is evident that the Q-sort method holds considerable promise for assessing attachment relationships in a wide range of ages and, insofar as parents continue to provide good data, in quite large samples. The method shows every indication of meeting each of the criteria outlined above for assessing attachment from an ethological/control systems perspective. The level of behavioral detail and context specification achieved in the Attachment Q-set items affords considerable structural fidelity vis à vis a control system view of the secure base phenomenon.

The Attachment Q-set and the data analytic procedures available for use with Q-sort data seem well suited to the task of examining relationships among affect, cognition, and behavior in the attachment domain. The Q-sort method also lends itself to analyses of both quantitative and qualitative developmental change. Finally, the Q-sort method is ideally suited to assessment of discriminant validity and to statistical control of sources of variance in scores computed from criterion sorts.

While data obtained via the Attachment Q-set are not merely trait ratings, they are not quite behavioral observations either. They are behavior relevant, however; and they are economical to obtain. As a result, they can play an important role in research designed to find out what the answers to important questions are going to be like. It is only when we know what the answers to our important questions are like and where they are to be found that we can design strategic observational and experimental studies that can ultimately provide decisive answers.

APPENDIX

TABLE A1

CRITERION SORTS FOR ATTACHMENT CONSTRUCTS

Item Titles[a]	Security		Dependency		Sociability		Social Desirability	
	12	36	12	36	12	36	12	36
1. Remains fearful of moving toys or animals	4.00	3.38	5.87	6.12	3.37	3.37	3.12	3.25
2. Eager to demonstrate songs, games, or other behavior	5.37	6.62	3.75	4.37	7.75	7.50	6.37	6.50
3. Predominant mood is happy	8.25	7.87	3.62	3.25	7.25	7.00	8.12	8.62
4. Easily comforted by adult	8.25	8.12	3.37	3.75	6.87	7.12	8.50	7.00
5. Approaches adult to interact	4.50	4.12	7.25	7.00	6.62	5.87	5.87	5.00
6. Prefers tasks and activities that are not difficult	4.50	4.37	5.75	6.62	4.87	4.37	4.37	4.00
7. Is often unaware of changes in adult's location or activities	3.50	4.75	1.37	2.25	3.62	4.25	4.37	6.00
8. Laughs easily with observer	6.25	5.87	3.00	3.37	8.00	7.62	7.00	7.62
9. Does not babble or talk when playing alone	4.00	4.50	5.12	5.12	3.12	3.75	4.12	4.25
10. Avoids or rejects new people	3.62	3.37	6.50	7.62	1.37	1.37	2.87	2.75
11. Does not recognize distress in adult	3.75	3.37	4.00	4.62	3.25	3.00	3.25	3.62
12. Bouts of exploration and play away from the adult are brief	2.62	1.75	7.87	7.50	5.00	3.50	3.37	3.87
13. Becomes bored quickly	4.12	4.25	5.50	5.62	4.00	4.00	3.12	2.62
14. Does not accept adult's affectionate behaviors to others	3.87	3.87	6.25	7.25	3.87	3.12	2.37	2.87
15. Prefers female adults	5.12	5.12	6.00	5.37	4.75	5.00	5.00	4.75
16. Is upset by negative evaluations or disapproval from adult	6.37	5.50	7.75	7.25	5.75	6.37	6.12	5.25
17. Does not share willingly	4.12	3.25	5.50	5.62	2.25	2.63	2.87	2.62
18. Actively solicits comforting from adult when distressed	8.37	8.00	6.50	7.75	7.37	7.37	7.37	6.25
19. Explores objects thoroughly	7.00	6.25	4.25	3.75	4.75	5.50	6.25	6.62
20. Distressed by separation at home	2.62	1.37	7.75	7.62	4.12	3.00	3.87	3.50
21. Is indifferent to observer's invitations to play	3.75	3.12	4.75	6.25	1.37	1.75	3.37	3.50
22. Easily distracted from distress	6.25	6.50	3.37	3.00	6.37	5.62	7.25	7.12
23. Has good endurance, is not easily tired	5.75	5.75	4.00	4.37	5.37	5.87	6.25	6.50

CONSTRUCT

Item								
24. Proximity/exploration/proximity cycles are evident in ½–1-hour observations	8.00	5.62	5.62	4.25	6.50	6.12	6.00	5.25
25. Is affectively responsive and expressive	7.87	7.87	4.87	3.87	8.25	7.87	8.25	7.87
26. Does not cry hard from minor injuries	6.12	5.25	2.25	2.25	5.12	5.25	6.75	7.00
27. Is careful with toys	6.00	5.25	4.62	4.87	4.87	5.37	6.12	6.50
28. Is not adaptable when moved from one activity to another	3.25	4.13	6.37	6.62	3.87	3.75	2.37	2.75
29. Cries to prevent separation	4.00	3.25	8.25	7.75	4.25	4.12	4.25	3.62
30. Is responsive to distress in adult	6.25	6.87	4.62	4.12	7.25	7.62	6.75	7.12
31. Does not look to adult for reassurance when wary	1.75	2.37	1.75	2.62	2.62	3.50	3.00	3.75
32. Initiates interaction with familiarized adults	6.87	7.12	3.25	3.12	8.12	8.75	7.50	7.12
33. Maximum good mood requires adult's presence	5.00	4.00	7.25	7.37	5.75	4.37	3.37	3.12
34. Does not attempt to approach or follow when adult moves away	3.87	4.12	2.37	1.75	3.12	3.87	4.75	5.25
35. Prefers to be comforted by adult	7.75	6.62	7.62	7.00	4.62	5.00	4.37	4.62
36. Greets adult spontaneously	8.75	8.37	4.87	4.00	8.75	8.12	7.63	7.25
37. Is demanding and impatient	3.00	2.75	7.87	7.62	4.25	3.75	2.50	1.87
38. Aware of social environment	6.87	7.37	6.00	5.87	8.12	8.00	7.87	7.50
39. Hesitates or does not repeat previously prohibited behavior	6.50	6.75	5.50	5.25	5.62	5.75	6.87	6.25
40. Acts to maintain social interaction	7.25	6.75	4.37	3.75	8.62	8.75	8.25	8.00
41. Is flexible in trying to communicate clearly with adults	7.12	7.62	3.12	4.12	7.00	7.50	7.12	7.00
42. Is independent with most adults	5.75	6.87	2.00	1.12	5.87	6.87	6.75	7.37
43. Returns from exploration and play often spontaneous at home	7.75	6.87	7.00	6.12	7.25	6.50	6.37	5.62
44. Does not solicit or enjoy physical contact with nonfamily adults	4.62	4.25	5.00	5.87	2.50	2.50	3.62	3.37
45. Actively solicits assistance or comfort after minor injury	7.37	6.37	7.12	7.75	6.62	6.87	6.50	5.25
46. Gross motor control is not smooth and coordinated	4.50	4.87	5.25	5.25	4.87	5.00	4.00	4.00
47. Interacts directly with adults	7.25	7.75	5.50	5.37	8.50	8.62	6.12	6.87
48. Lacks self-confidence	3.50	2.12	7.50	7.62	4.00	4.12	3.50	2.37
49. Prefers realistic play	5.00	4.37	4.62	5.00	4.37	4.50	4.75	4.25
50. Behaves in a nurturant or parental way toward toys during play	6.12	7.00	4.37	6.37	6.37	6.62	6.50	6.37
51. Does not accept adult's assurances when wary in familiar contexts	2.25	2.62	6.25	5.87	2.25	2.62	2.62	4.12

TABLE A1 (Continued)

	CONSTRUCT							
	Security		Dependency		Sociability		Social Desirability	
ITEM TITLES[a]	12	36	12	36	12	36	12	36
52. Transition from exploration to proximity and contact is not executed smoothly	2.00	2.12	5.62	5.12	3.00	3.12	3.37	3.00
53. Does not solicit or enjoy affectionate physical contact with adult	1.50	2.12	2.50	3.25	1.62	1.62	1.37	1.75
54. Expects adult will be unresponsive	1.37	1.25	5.62	5.37	2.62	1.75	2.25	2.00
55. Cries in response to separation	5.62	3.87	8.37	7.87	4.87	4.37	4.37	3.75
56. Does not display tension movements	6.25	5.25	3.62	3.12	5.50	5.62	5.50	5.87
57. Average activity level is high	5.12	5.12	4.37	4.12	4.75	5.75	4.87	5.75
58. Is not compliant with adult control	2.75	2.75	4.37	4.37	2.75	3.62	3.25	2.62
59. Is attracted to novelty rather than familiarity	6.62	6.37	3.37	2.62	6.12	6.25	6.87	7.50
60. Sleeps on a regular schedule	5.75	5.25	4.75	4.50	4.75	4.87	6.37	6.12
61. Is not bolder or more confident to play when adult is nearby	3.12	3.75	2.37	3.50	4.00	4.37	4.37	4.50
62. Becomes distressed when social interaction is blocked or becomes difficult	3.87	3.87	7.00	7.50	5.62	4.12	3.87	3.37
63. Becomes distressed when adult moves away	3.87	3.25	8.25	8.00	4.75	3.75	3.62	3.62
64. Does not solicit or enjoy playful physical contact with adult	2.25	1.87	3.12	4.12	1.75	1.62	1.50	2.25
65. Object oriented in play preferences	3.12	3.87	3.62	4.00	2.00	2.00	3.37	3.37
66. Does not persist when nonsocial goals are blocked	3.50	3.62	5.87	6.50	4.62	4.25	3.75	3.37
67. Sleeps lightly (even if regularly)	4.75	4.75	5.25	5.13	4.87	4.87	3.87	4.50
68. Transition from proximity and contact to exploration is not executed smoothly	2.00	2.25	7.00	6.75	3.25	3.62	3.37	3.62
69. Is independent with adult	5.12	7.12	1.12	1.12	5.87	7.12	6.62	7.75
70. Is indirect or hesitant in making observations or requests	3.75	3.37	5.12	5.00	3.25	3.00	4.25	3.50
71. Prefers animate toys	5.25	5.50	4.62	4.75	6.00	5.62	5.25	5.25
72. Does not stay closer to adult in unfamiliar settings	2.50	4.37	1.75	1.25	4.12	4.25	4.62	5.37
73. Accepts assistance	7.37	7.00	6.12	6.37	6.87	7.00	7.50	7.75

64

No.	Item								
74.	Is demanding when initiating activities with adult	3.37	3.12	8.50	7.50	3.75	3.75	3.25	3.12
75.	Cries often (regardless of intensity or duration)	2.50	2.87	7.12	7.62	3.50	3.50	2.37	3.12
76.	Expresses enjoyment of accomplishing or achieving	7.00	7.12	4.00	3.87	6.87	6.62	8.00	7.87
77.	Affective sharing occurs during play	8.25	8.12	4.37	4.62	8.62	8.37	7.87	7.37
78.	Does not restart crying readily after crying and calming down	7.75	7.00	2.50	3.00	5.50	6.25	6.50	6.75
79.	Imitates observer's behavior	5.87	5.62	3.75	3.75	7.50	7.00	5.75	5.75
80.	Is more tolerant of self-initiated separation than of adult-initiated separation	5.75	6.25	6.62	6.25	5.37	5.50	6.12	5.37
81.	Is creative with objects or social roles in play	5.62	6.25	3.87	4.12	5.00	5.37	6.25	7.87
82.	Easily becomes angry with adult	2.00	3.37	5.62	6.87	3.25	3.37	2.25	2.00
83.	Recovers from minor injuries slowly	4.75	4.50	6.00	6.12	4.62	4.62	3.62	3.62
84.	Does not adapt active play to avoid hurting adult	3.75	2.87	5.12	4.75	3.87	2.87	2.75	2.00
85.	Requires encouragement to keep constructively occupied	3.25	3.75	7.37	7.12	4.87	4.12	3.37	3.00
86.	Does not accept adult's assurances when wary in unfamiliar places	2.00	2.75	6.50	6.75	2.00	2.62	2.50	3.25
87.	Does not laugh easily with adult	3.00	3.50	5.37	5.37	1.62	2.37	2.37	3.12
88.	Imitates adult's behavior	5.87	6.62	5.50	4.25	7.62	7.00	6.87	6.25
89.	Proximity/exploration/proximity cycles are evident in 3–5-hour observations	6.87	8.25	4.87	4.62	6.12	5.50	5.62	6.12
90.	Shows signs of self-control	6.37	7.87	3.50	4.25	5.62	5.75	6.87	7.12
91.	Rarely asks for help	3.87	4.37	1.37	1.75	3.12	3.37	4.25	5.00
92.	Does not become angry with toys	6.62	6.12	4.25	3.87	5.00	6.00	6.12	6.75
93.	Accepts adult's attention to others	6.75	6.75	3.50	2.25	6.37	6.75	7.50	6.87
94.	Returns from exploration and play are often spontaneous in unfamiliar environments	7.75	7.00	6.50	6.50	6.75	7.12	6.00	5.75
95.	Child's observations and requests are often difficult to understand	3.87	4.12	4.87	5.25	3.87	4.37	3.62	3.50
96.	Is obedient when adults give instructions	7.37	7.00	5.50	5.12	5.87	6.00	7.25	6.00
97.	Is not wary of new objects	5.37	5.75	2.75	2.25	6.12	6.00	6.12	6.00
98.	Does not prefer physical contact with adult	2.00	3.00	2.50	3.50	3.37	4.12	4.87	4.37
99.	Fine motor manipulation is not skillful	4.87	4.87	5.25	5.12	4.87	4.87	4.75	4.87
100.	Does not combine several objects in play	4.50	4.50	5.00	4.75	4.75	4.75	4.87	4.62

NOTE.—The criterion scores were constructed by averaging the scores assigned to the items by each of the sorters. The items were sorted into nine piles with 5, 8, 12, 16, 18, 16, 12, 8, and 5 items, respectively. Items in pile 1 (least characteristic) received scores of 1, and so forth.

[a] The complete items and sorting instructions are available from the authors, Department of Psychology, State University of New York, Stony Brook, NY 11794.

III. SECURITY IN INFANCY, CHILDHOOD, AND ADULTHOOD: A MOVE TO THE LEVEL OF REPRESENTATION

MARY MAIN AND NANCY KAPLAN

University of California, Berkeley

JUDE CASSIDY

University of Virginia

The aim of this chapter is to discuss individual differences in attachment relationships as they relate to individual differences in mental representation, that is, in the individual's "internal working models" of attachment (Bowlby, 1969/1982b, 1973, 1980; Bretherton, in this vol.). We define the internal working model of attachment as a set of conscious and/or un-

We are grateful to the Institute of Human Development, Berkeley, and to the Society for Research in Child Development for funding that made the study of our sample at 6 years possible. In its earlier phases, the Social Development Project was supported by the William T. Grant Foundation, by the Alvin Nye Main Foundation, and by Bio-Medical Support Grants 1-444036-32024 and 1-444036-32025 for studies in the behavioral sciences. The Child Study Center at the University of California was invaluable in its provision of subjects and in the training provided for our observers and examiners. The National Center for Clinical Infancy Programs provided support and assistance to Nancy Kaplan. This project would not have been possible without the direction and assistance provided by Donna Weston and by Bonnie Powers, Jackie Stadtman, and Stewart Wakeling in its first phases. For the initial identification of infants who should be left unclassified—an identification critical to the present study—we gratefully acknowledge both Judith Solomon and Donna Weston. Carol George participated in the designing of the sixth-year project; Ruth Goldwyn served as adult interviewer; and Ellen Richardson served as the child's examiner. The videotapes and transcripts of the sixth-year study were analyzed by Jude Cassidy, Anitra DeMoss, Ruth Goldwyn, Nancy Kaplan, Todd Hirsch, Lorraine Littlejohn, Amy Strage, and Reggie Tiedemann. Mary Ainsworth, John Bowlby, Harriet Oster, and Amy Strage provided useful criticism of earlier versions of this chapter. The overall conceptualization was substantially enriched by suggestions made by Erik Hesse.

conscious rules for the organization of information relevant to attachment and for obtaining or limiting access to that information, that is, to information regarding attachment-related experiences, feelings, and ideations. Previous definitions of individual differences in attachment organization, for example, secure, insecure-avoidant, and insecure-ambivalent, have relied on descriptions of the organization of the infant's nonverbal behavior toward a particular parent in a structured separation-and-reunion observation, the Ainsworth Strange Situation (Ainsworth et al., 1978; Sroufe & Waters, 1977).

Our reconceptualization of individual differences in attachment organization as individual differences in the mental representation of the self in relation to attachment permits the investigation of attachment not only in infants but also in older children and adults and leads to a new focus on representation and language. This conceptualization leads further, to the proposal that the secure versus the various types of insecure attachment organizations can best be understood as terms referring to particular types of internal working models of relationships, models that direct not only feelings and behavior but also attention, memory, and cognition, insofar as these relate directly or indirectly to attachment. Individual differences in these internal working models will therefore be related not only to individual differences in patterns of nonverbal behavior but also to patterns of language and structures of mind.

In that our work connects attachment to representation, it is in keeping with much theoretical work in attachment (Ainsworth, 1967; Bowlby, 1969/1982b; Bretherton, 1980, in this vol.). It poses a departure, however, from the current empirical approach to the study of infant-parent attachment. At the present time, most investigators in our field seek to connect individual differences in security of attachment at 1 year either to differences in infant-parent interaction patterns during the preceding year or to later differences in general functioning and behavior. In contrast to the representational approach presented here, the current approach has remained consistently at the behavioral level.

This chapter constitutes a first report from an ongoing, longitudinal project. In the first phase of the project, infants 12–18 months old were seen independently with each parent in the Ainsworth Strange Situation (Ainsworth et al., 1978). On the basis of the infant's behavioral response to a particular parent in this brief separation-and-reunion situation, each infant was identified as very secure, secure, or insecure in relation to that parent (Ainsworth et al., 1978; Main & Weston, 1981). When the children had reached 6 years of age, we compared early security of attachment to each parent to overall functioning, to reunion behavior, and to aspects of both the parents' and the child's internal working models of attachment. The primary question addressed was, How does early security of infant-parent attachment, as estimated from patterns of infant nonverbal behavior, relate to both the child's and the adult's mental representations of attachment 5 years later?

Our introduction begins with the argument that reunion responses to parents, whether following very brief or major separations, can be seen as indicative of the infant's "view" (Hinde, 1982b) or internal working model of the relationship. Following a review of the Ainsworth Strange Situation procedure and classifications, we consider the apparent meaning of individual differences in reunion response to the parent in this situation. We then draw parallels to reunion responses to parents following major separations. Here we show that, whether a previously secure child avoids the parent following a major separation in a residential nursery or whether a relatively rejected child avoids the parent following a brief laboratory separation, similar detached and hostile responses are likely to be shown by the child in other settings. These observations in themselves suggest that particular types of reunion response indicate particular infant "views," "internal working models," or "states of mind" regarding the relationship with the caregiver and that the internal working model of the relationship with the caregiver should not be conceived as a "sample" of interaction patterns with that caregiver since it can change in the absence of interaction. A particularly striking example of such change is given in the account of a 2-year-old who first welcomed, then avoided a photograph of his mother over the course of a 2-week separation.

Following presentation of our argument for reconceptualizing individual differences in attachment classifications as individual differences in the representation of the self in relation to attachment, we consider what we have learned to date regarding the meaning of (infant-parent) security of attachment in infancy. Here we show that three security classification systems constructed to date are in agreement regarding the identification of security with a single parent-infant interaction pattern indicative of ready emotional access between the infant and the attachment figure, the contrastingly diverse nature of the major patterns of insecurity, and the identification of these diverse but specifiable "insecure" organizations with particular, specifiable forms of the restriction of attention, affect, and behavior. Our working hypothesis is that these restrictions, while generally self-preserving, can be lifted, yielding a secure internal organization.

In Chapter I of this *Monograph,* Inge Bretherton has reviewed the concept of the "internal working model" as developed by John Bowlby. The "internal working model" is a mental representation of an aspect of the world, others, self, or relationships to others that is of special relevance to the individual. This model is an integral component of the attachment behavioral system; it guides appraisals of experience and guides behavior (Bowlby, 1969/1982b, 1973). Like Piaget's object concept, "internal working models" are not merely "pictures" or passive introjections of the objects of past experience. They are active constructions and can be restructured. Reconstruction of early internal working models is difficult, however, since internal working models, once organized, tend to operate outside conscious awareness and resist dramatic change (Bowlby, 1980).

We conclude with a review of previous conceptualizations of the internal working model, adding our own speculations regarding the ways in which stable individual differences in internal working models develop, the ways they may be expected to affect language and thought as well as nonverbal behavior, and circumstances under which change may be expected. In a series of succeeding papers, we will compare and contrast representational aspects of secure, insecure-avoidant, insecure-ambivalent, and insecure-disorganized/disoriented relationships (Main & Solomon, in press). In this chapter, we focus our attention on structural aspects of the apparent internal working model of relationships seen in children and adults who are secure.

Reunion Responses to Parents as Indicative of Internal Working Models of Relationships

Like the acquisition of the concept of object permanence, the acquisition and structure of an individual's model of a relationship must be inferred from observations. The state of infant knowledge reflected in any particular observation may be difficult to clarify, however, so long as that observation is made with the infant in the "object's"/partner's presence. So long as the infant and partner are interacting, the observer may infer that immediate stimulus-response reactions rather than internalized concepts are guiding the infant's behavior.

In Piagetian testing for the concept of object permanence, infants demonstrate their increasing knowledge of the object by changes in their behavior during its absence. Similarly, the acquisition and form of the internal working model of the partner will also be most easily demonstrated to observers by the infant's behavior in the partner's absence. Behavior during separation and at the moment of reunion first following a separation will, therefore, be particularly informative regarding the internal working model of the self and partner.

The Ainsworth Strange Situation: Procedures and classifications based on response to reunion.—The Ainsworth Strange Situation is a brief, structured laboratory observation for parents and infants. Following introductory periods in which the infant is introduced to the room, the toys, and a stranger, the parent twice leaves the room and twice returns to it. There are marked individual differences in infant response to reunion. When the parent returns, some infants seek comfort, proximity, and contact and then gradually and comfortably return to play. Some actively avoid and ignore the parent, turning or moving away. Some show anger and resistance to the parent, a desire for proximity or contact, and an inability to be comforted. These individual differences provide the basis for the classification of infants in terms of Strange Situation behavior. In general, only those in whom the first pattern predominates are called securely attached to the parent (group B in the Ainsworth classification system). Others are called insecure-avoidant (group A) or insecure-ambivalent (group C). There are also subclassifications among infants considered securely attached to the parent. Infants who show some concern during separation, go at once to the parent on reunion, then show some readiness for a return to play are considered very secure (B_3) infants. Those who simultaneously show some aspects of the behavior of insecure infants are termed simply secure with the parent (B_1, B_2, and B_4 infants).

In three white middle-class samples studied to date, security of attachment to mother has been found stable from 12 to 18 or 12 to 20 months of age so long as there are no major changes in life circumstances (see Bretherton, in this vol., for a review of these studies). Main and Weston (1981) found 13 out of 15 infants stable in attachment classification to the father over an 8-month period. At the same time, classifications with the two parents are consistently found independent. An infant who is secure with mother is almost equally likely to be secure or insecure with the father. This finding has been reported now for two American and one North German sample (Grossmann, Grossmann, Huber, & Wartner, 1981; Lamb, 1978; Main & Weston, 1981).

The meaning of reunion responses in children who have experienced major separation from the parent.—The interpretation of infant reunion responses seen in the Ainsworth classification system depended on the interpretation of a previous set of behavior observations that had been seminal to the theory of attachment as developed by John Bowlby (Bowlby, 1973). These were observations of the responses of children in their second and third years responding to placement in institutional settings for "major" time periods, that is, for periods of 2 weeks or more without the support of special caregivers (Robertson, 1953; Robertson & Bowlby, 1952; see also Heinecke & Westheimer, 1966; Robertson & Robertson, 1971).

These investigators showed that major separation from parents at this age alters a child's behavior toward the parent once reunited. Children who had been secure and enjoyed harmonious interaction with the parent before major separation often seemed to be insecure with the parent following the return home. Children who had been left a relatively short time seemed anxious, "clingy," and easily angered. Left for a longer time, children might at first treat the parent as a stranger or at best with an indifference mixed with unpredictable bouts of hostility.

The sign that a malignant reorganization of feelings toward the parent had taken place over the separation was a change in the child's reunion response to the parent. Visited late during separation or brought home following a longer separation, children sometimes responded to reunion with an angry resistance to the parent mixed with proximity seeking. Finally, if the separation lasted long enough, the child actively avoided the parent on reunion, moving away, backing away, or turning away altogether. Thus the earlier proximity-seeking response to reunion had become replaced by avoidance or indifference (Heinecke & Westheimer, 1966). When children had reached the stage of consolidating this avoidant response to reunion, they were observed to be detached and hostile on return to the home environment.

To summarize, major separations seemed responsible for a change in the organization of behavior toward the parent; the sign that these changes had occurred was a change in response to reunion with the parent, that is, from proximity seeking to anger or avoidance; and the angry-ambivalent and the avoidant responses indicating progressive malignant reorganization of relationships in separated children strongly resemble the two major insecure categories identified by Ainsworth in the Strange Situation. We interpret the above as indicative of changes in the child's internal working model in the absence of changes in interaction.

Observations still more relevant to this issue were made by James Robertson and Joyce Robertson, who took "Thomas," 27 months, into their home during a 10-day separation from mother (Robertson & Robertson, 1971). By the Robertsons' report, Thomas was a child who had enjoyed an open and affectionate relationship with both parents. Throughout the separation, Mrs. Robertson repeatedly presented Thomas with a photograph of himself and his mother. At the beginning of the separation, he kissed the photograph and held it tenderly, saying that he liked it. A few days later, he stood back when the photograph was presented, attentively fiddling with an object in his hand and keeping his eyes downcast. Toward the end of the separation period Thomas actively avoided the presented photograph, moving away and turning his back with an anxious expression. He insisted on putting it away from him. Thus the child's response to a pictorially represented "reunion" with the mother changed from proximity seeking to avoidance over a 10-day separation. Since the "behavior" of the photograph did not change over the 10-day period, we are led to presume that what changed was solely the child's internal representation of the relationship. This observation seems to us to be strongly suggestive of the restructuring of an internal working model in the absence of interaction with the caregiver. Specifically, access to a visual reminder of the mother became gradually and actively restricted.

A reconsideration of the Ainsworth Strange Situation: Correlates of the Strange

Situation security classification.—We are now in a position to understand the theoretical and empirical basis for the emphasis on infant reunion behavior in Ainsworth's attachment classification system. Ainsworth's initial observations of infant response to this structured miniature separation situation involved a sample of infants and mothers whose interaction had been observed for a full year in the home environment. Since none of the sample infants had undergone a major separation from the parent, Ainsworth reasoned that differing organizations of relationship had developed on the basis of differing interactive events rather than as a function of major separations.

Ainsworth's examination of infant-mother interaction in the home showed far greater "sensitivity to the signals and communications of the infant" in the mothers of secure infants than in the mothers of insecure infants between 9 and 12 months of age (Ainsworth, Bell, & Stayton, 1971). Mean scores for mothers of "very secure" infants indicated definite sensitivity to infant signals, while scores for mothers of "insecure" infants indicated definite insensitivity. Scores for mothers of "secure" infants fell at scale midpoint.

When the infant cried or approached the mother in the home situation as observed by Ainsworth, mothers of securely attached infants were found responsive and permitting of access. Mothers of insecure-ambivalent infants were found insensitive to signals (e.g., crying) but not notably rejecting (Ainsworth, Bell, & Stayton, 1971). In the Ainsworth study as well as in succeeding studies, mothers of insecure-avoidant infants have been found rejecting of infant attachment behavior as well as insensitive to signals; that is, these mothers often block or reject the infant's attempts toward access (Main, 1981; Main & Stadtman, 1981).

As expected, then, differing responses to reunion with the parent are related to differing events experienced in interaction with the parent. But if different reunion responses indicate different internal working models of relationship, then they should have identifiably differing correlates in behavior observed in other contexts. This should be the case whether the model (reunion response or "view"; see Hinde, 1982b) has originated from major separations or from events experienced in interaction.

Data collected to date are affirming. In general, children who greet the mother actively and positively on reunion in the Ainsworth Strange Situation are found more socially competent, more empathic, and happier than insecure-avoidant and insecure-ambivalent children when observed several years later (see Bretherton, in this vol., for a review). Recently, Sroufe (1983) has reported differences in behavior between nursery school children who had been identified as ambivalent and children identified as avoidant of mother in infancy. In contrast to children who were ambivalent as infants, children avoidant as infants are described as relatively detached, isolated, and hostile in the nursery school setting.

As expected, then, whether the child avoids the parent following a major separation in a residential nursery or following an extremely brief separation in the laboratory, similar detached and hostile responses are seen in other settings. The secure, insecure-avoidant and insecure-ambivalent responses to reunion with attachment figures may be signs of particular working models of relationships, and these particular models may guide behavior in other settings.

The interactions of very secure dyads: Classification in terms of the attachment-exploration balance and in terms of the emotional availability of the parent.—At present there are at least three systems available for the classification of infant-parent attachment. The first, the Ainsworth Strange Situation classification system, has been described above. A second system was devised by Ainsworth and her colleagues for natural or "uncontrolled" home observations of mother and infant in relatively stress-free conditions: this system relies on observation of the infant's ability to use the mother as a "secure base" for exploration of the home environment (Ainsworth, Bell, & Stayton, 1971; see also Waters & Deane, in this vol.). At present, we are developing a third system of classification of dyads in terms of security of relationship, using a structured "Clown Session" involving an unfamiliar adult in a situation initially arousing some apprehension (Main & Weston, 1981). The parent remains with the infant throughout the observation, and the emphasis in this system is on the response of the parent. The system being developed classifies parents in terms of their "emotional availability" (Emde, 1980; Sorce & Emde, 1981) to the infant during this structured and mildly stressful situation.

Classifications of dyads made in terms of the attachment-exploration balance and classifications made in terms of the parent's "emotional availability" show high correspondence to the Ainsworth Strange Situation attachment classifications (e.g., infants with highly "emotionally available" mothers tend to be classified as very secure in the Strange Situation 1 week later, while infants with "emotionally detached" mothers tend to be classified as insecure-avoidant). Security classification systems developed for observation of dyads in differing situations, then, repeatedly place the same dyads within the same categories.

Three main points can be made regarding these three alternative systems for infant security classifications. (1) In each system, there is only one type of interaction pattern or behavior pattern that is readily identified as very secure, while, in contrast, there are several patterns identified as reflective of insecurity. (2) The most striking characteristic of very secure dyads as identified within each system is ease of physical and emotional access between the partners and corresponding ease of movement among the salient features of the environment (cf. Emde, 1980; Waters & Deane, in this vol.). (3) In each of the insecure patterns of attachment, behavior and attention seem constricted in readily identifiable ways. Throughout the Strange Situation, for example, the insecure-avoidant infant attends to the environment and its features while actively directing attention away from the parent. The insecure-ambivalent infant, in contrast, seems unable to direct attention to the environment, expresses strong and sometimes continual fear and distress, and seems constantly directed toward the parent and away from all other environmental features. Similar strong contrasts suggestive of the restriction and direction of attention to particular aspects of the environment are seen as occurring in the home (Ainsworth et al., 1978) and as actively encouraged by the parent in the Clown Session.

Internal Working Models

Early mental representation has always been a central aspect of psychoanalytic theorizing (Fraiberg, 1969). According to A. Freud (1952) and Spitz (1966), an infant's first schemata evolve out of experiences of need fulfillment. Attachment figures are perceived as alternately good or bad, depending on whether they gratify or frustrate infant desires. Only when the infant develops the capacity to maintain an internal schema that is independent of experiences of need fulfillment can he combine the frustrating with the gratifying image and perceive the mother figure as one person.

Object-relations theorists such as Fairbairn (1946) also describe the infants' internal world as peopled by good and bad objects but suggest that the infant possesses a schema of persons as whole or part objects independent of need fulfillment from the beginning. Fairbairn places particular emphasis on the influences that real events experienced with people have on the internal world an infant develops and hypothesizes that an infant's feeling of security depends on the way in which he affectively deals with these internal good and bad objects.

Here, we share the notion that internal models of persons evolve out of events experienced. However, we are interested in exploring the complexities of how different kinds of events lead to different internal representations and how the child actively and continuously constructs his working models of relationships. In this way, we hope to go beyond the notion that events experienced with persons are internalized as simply good and bad objects and to formulate more detailed descriptions of the various models of self-other relationships.

How do internal working models develop? Like memories, they could theoretically be organized out of stimulus-response chains, by association, or by similarity. Bretherton has, however, drawn our attention to recent work suggesting that event schemata (Mandler, 1979), scripts (Schank & Abelson, 1977), or generalized event representations (Nelson & Gruendel, 1981) act as the basic modules of mental representation. This means that what is encoded by and guides the individual is not a concept abstracted out of static environmental features but a generalized representation of the events experienced. In this view, the child's memory is seen as being guided by general event schemata that organize experience in terms of reactions, goal paths, attempts, and outcomes (Mandler, 1983). A young child's knowledge of relationships will then be organized schematically rather than categorically, that is, by actions and action outcomes rather than by the abstraction from the environment of similarities and differences (cf. Werner, 1957). If the child's knowledge of relationships is organized by actions and action outcomes, then the internal working model of the infant-parent relationship will be formed out of a history of the infants' actions, infant-parent interactions, and the fate of the infant's "attempts and outcomes," that is, the fate or outcome of the infant's efforts and intentions to regain the parent even in the parent's absence. The working model of the relationship to the attachment figure will reflect not an objective picture of "the parent" but rather the history of the caregiver's responses to the infant's actions or intended actions with/toward the attachment figure. If this is true, then from the moment at which an animate or inanimate object can be represented there will be individual differences among infants in their internal working models of relationship to the attachment figure.

At what age do infants develop internal working models of attachment relations? Most previous investigators in attachment have presumed that the young infant has generalized and separable internal working models of self and of other and that infants of differing experience put self and other into differing types of relationship only gradually. Only as cognition reaches relatively advanced stages, it is presumed, will children of differing experience develop differing models. In this case, the construction of a primitive working model of a particular relationship as, for example, insecure-avoidant must await a stage of relative intellectual advancement.

Together with Sroufe and Fleeson (in press) we presume instead that even a young infant will have a working model of relationships. Knowledge of self and of other will then be embedded in event-based relationships from the outset (cf. Piaget, 1954). In sum, because a concept of "the attachment figure" apart from the event-relevant relationship between the attachment figure and the young infant does not exist, different relationships will be represented differently from the beginnings of representation.

How do individual differences in internal working models of relationships develop? Given the material reviewed, it seems logical to suppose that the internal working model of the attachment relationship will be organized out of the inner representation of the experienced outcome of actions or plans ("intentions") of particular relevance to attachment. This could lead logically, in terms of conventional cognitive psychology, to an infinite variation in mental representations. We propose instead that, while aspects of each individual's representations of attachment are unique, the essential differences between individuals in representations of particular attachment relationships are finite and can be specified in terms of several central organizations.

This is because we are dealing with a biologically based, that is, largely environmentally stable tendency/"intention" to seek to maintain proximity to a central figure (Bowlby, 1969/1982b). The possible caregiver responses to this infant proximity-seeking intention are finite. To simplify, a caregiver may permit access to the infant who seeks proximity (yielding the secure organization); a caregiver may block access (yielding the insecure-avoidant organization); or a caregiver may permit access only unpredictably (yielding the insecure-ambivalent organization). Finally, because the attachment behavioral system is integrated and balanced in diverse ways with other, for example, exploratory and fear wariness, systems (Bretherton & Ainsworth, 1974; Waters & Deane, in this vol.), these caregiver responses will result in fairly complex and far-reaching systems of attentional and behavioral organization.

There are three presently recognized major organizations of attachment (secure, insecure-avoidant, and insecure-ambivalent), each corresponding to the organizations of caregiver responsiveness identified above. Other patterns of response may yield other major organizations, as yet undiscovered; these too should yield particular, specifiable infant attachment organizations with respect to the caregiver in question. It seems unlikely, however, that there are infinitely many possible caregiver responses to the infant's attempts toward access, and for this reason there may not be infinitely many central organizations, or working models, of attachment.

We are now in a position to provide some definitions of internal working models:

1. Internal working models are mental representations that include affective as well as cognitive components (Bretherton, in this vol.). They are integral components of behavioral systems and play an active role in guidance of behavior (Bowlby, 1980).
2. Internal working models are most likely formed out of generalized event representations (Bretherton, in this vol.).
3. Once formed, internal working models have an existence outside of consciousness as well as a propensity for stability (Bowlby, 1980).
4. The events out of which internal working models of the self in attachment relationships are formed are attachment-relevant events. These models are formed out of the "outcomes" of a rela-

tively environmentally stable (formerly, "instinctive") intention to seek proximity to caregivers (Bowlby, 1969/1982b).

5. Infants whose attempts to gain proximity to the caregiver are consistently accepted will develop different internal working models of relationships than do infants whose attempts to gain proximity are consistently blocked or are accepted only unpredictably. Where access is consistently restricted or admitted only unpredictably, we may expect active reorganization, restriction, and redirection in attention, behavior, and emotional expression.

6. Some type of internal working model of specific relationships may be formed in the first months of life. By the time the infant is 1 year of age, individual differences in Strange Situation behavior with a particular parent may be conceived as reflecting individual differences in the infant's internal working model of a particular infant-parent relationship.

7. Models of relationships do not depend solely on events experienced in the partner's presence. Because event representations are defined to include "attempts and outcomes," they will necessarily include the outcome of, for example, the infant's efforts to gain the caregiver in the caregiver's absence. Thus the internal working model of a relationship may change over the course of the partner's absence.

8. Internal working models of relationships provide rules and rule systems for the direction of behavior and the felt appraisal of experience.

9. Internal working models of relationships also will provide rules for the direction and organization of attention and memory, rules that permit or limit the individual's access to certain forms of knowledge regarding the self, the attachment figure, and the relationship between the self and the attachment figure. These rules will be reflected in the organization of thought and language as it relates directly and indirectly to attachment. Many will be unconscious.

10. In childhood, it is possible that internal working models of relationships can be altered only in response to changes in concrete experience.

11. Following the onset of the stage of formal operations, it is possible that the internal working models of particular relationships established earlier can be altered. This is because these operations may permit the individual to think about thought itself, that is, to step outside a given relationship system and to see it operating (Piaget, 1967).

12. While internal working models show a strong propensity for stability, they are not conceived as templates. They are best conceived as structured processes serving to obtain or to limit access to information.

RATIONALE FOR THE PRESENT STUDY

The project to be described was undertaken in response to our reconceptualization of attachment as representation. The first aim of the project was to test for stability in reunion behavior over a 5-year period. The second aim was to examine individual differences in overall functioning as a function of early security. The major aim was to compare early differences in security of infant-parent attachment to the representational level of speech and behavior in childhood and adulthood. What we hoped to show was that mental processes vary as distinctively as do behavioral processes as a function of differing internal working models of relationships.

Representational processes cannot be witnessed directly. But some efforts toward approximation seem destined to greater accuracy than others. In general, a move to the level of language seems likely to be productive, and one assessment was based on transcripts of child-parent speech during a reunion episode. Here we could ask whether an assessment of discourse alone would show the dyads to be maintaining the same relationships with one another as they did on the nonverbal level 5 years earlier.

We have argued that the representation of a relationship can best be estimated in the absence of the partner. In keeping with this theme, we observed each child responding to presentation of a photograph of the parents (during the parents' absence). Since the photograph could not respond to or control the child's response, the child's response to the photograph could not be simply an example of an interaction pattern being maintained over several years between child and parent.

If children's representations of attachment relationships are constructed out of critical events, then seeking verbal representations of "children's responses" to such events is of interest. Child-parent separation is of critical interest to attachment: we therefore conducted interviews with 6-year-olds, asking both what a pictured child would feel and what a pictured child could do about a separation (Kaplan, 1984).

Finally, we attempted to assess the security of the adult's overall working model of attachment, that is, the security of the self in relation to attachment in its generality rather than in relation to any particular present or past relationship. Here, we could not simply ask adults to verbalize their concepts of relationships since the expressed concept could be affected by its stereotype and could be far from the internal working model actually operating. Therefore, we constructed an adult attachment interview that asked for descriptions of early relationships and attachment-related events and for the adult's sense of the way these relationships and events had affected adult personality (George, Kaplan, & Main, 1984). The interview was transcribed verbatim. Ruth Goldwyn devised a scoring system that permitted use of the full transcript as the basis for inferring the security of the adult's model of the self in relation to attachment. Contradictions and incoherencies of which the speaker seemed unaware were considered as important as views deliberately presented.

METHODS AND RESULTS

Sample.—Forty mothers, fathers, and their 6-year-old children (24 male, 19 firstborn) formed the sample of participants in this 1982 study. The families were drawn from the first wave of subjects studied in the Berkeley Social Development Project (BSDP) sample, a sample of Bay Area families collected over the period 1977–1979 by Mary Main and Donna Weston. Sample mothers were white or Asian; families were college educated and predominantly upper middle class (for more complete sample description, see Main & Weston, 1981). The children's average age at the time of this follow-up study was 69.5 months or just under 6 years of age (SD = 4.34 months).

Each family had been seen in the Ainsworth Strange Situation at 12 months (mother) or 18 months (father) of age. Attachment classifications to both parents had proven stable within this sample; hence differences in infant age at time of observation with mother and father were considered unimportant.

The selection of insecure-disorganized/disoriented infants.—Earlier, we reported that a number of infants in the BSDP sample could not be classified within the Ainsworth system (Main & Weston, 1981). Some seemed insecure but could not be classified in any major category. For others, the "forced" (imposed) classification would have been secure or even very secure. Independent assessments in infancy had suggested, however, that these infants were also insecure with the parent.

Recently, we completed a review of reports of classification difficulties from other studies as well as a review of 36 Strange Situation videotapes that had been left unclassified within our larger (189-family) sample (Main & Solomon, in press). In two cases it was not clear that the child was attached to the parent (the father). The remaining 34 infants could, however, be described by the term "insecure-disorganized/disoriented." "Dazed" behavior on reunion with the parent, stoppage of movement in postures suggestive of depression, confusion, or apprehension, disordering of expected temporal sequences (e.g., strong avoidance following strong proximity seeking), simultaneous display of contradictory behavior patterns (approaching with head averted, gazing strongly away while in contact), incompleted movements, and undirected expressions of affect appeared in these infants.

The majority of these children in our sample had parents who had suffered unusual trauma within their own attachment histories. Because of the similarities in Strange Situation behavior among these children and the similarity between their behavior and that of initially "unclassifiable" infants described in other (particularly, maltreatment) samples, we have proposed that these infants represent a third type of insecurity of attachment to the parent (Main & Solomon, in press). One of the major purposes of the present study was the further examination of children and parents identified as insecure-disorganized/disoriented.

Criteria for sample selection.—The present sample is drawn from project families first seen with infants in 1977. The principal criterion for selection was infant attachment classification with mother at 12 months of age. While a majority of children in the BSDP sample had been judged secure with mother in infancy, we intended this time to invite equal numbers of children who had been judged insecure-avoidant, insecure-disorganized/disoriented, and secure with mother in infancy. Some selection was also made for birth order and sex.

Sixty-nine families qualified for our selection criteria; 11 of these had moved from the Bay Area or left no forwarding address. Fifty-eight families were contacted, and 84.4% agreed to participate. Five of the remaining 49 families were separated or divorced and hence were excluded from the study. The remaining 44 families participated in both the home and the laboratory visits. Some families and individual episodes were lost through equipment malfunction, and reunions and responses to the photograph were not videotaped for the first families who visited the laboratory. Three children were excluded because of illness or recent major separation.

Of the 40 children seen with their parents in the laboratory at 6 years of age, 14 had been classified as secure with mother in infancy, 11 as insecure-avoidant, and 12 as insecure-disorganized/disoriented. For one child the infancy security assessment was available only for father. There were relatively few children classified as insecure-ambivalent in the BSDP sample, perhaps in consequence of stringent infant selection procedures (see Main & Weston, 1981). Two children who were insecure-ambivalent with mother were available and are included out of interest.

Outline of procedures.—Each family was visited in the home, where we obtained information on family changes and child-rearing practices (see Kaplan, 1984). About 1 week after the home visit, the family came to the laboratory for a 2-hour session. Child and parent behavior was videotaped in a playroom. The parents left the playroom for about 1 hour for individual interviews, while the child remained in the playroom with the female examiner (male in two cases).

On arrival at the laboratory, the family was asked to pose quickly for a polaroid photograph. The entire family watched a film of a 2-year-old undergoing a 10-day separation from parents, "Thomas: Ten Days in Fostercare" (Robertson & Robertson, 1967–1972). Parents then left for separate offices for the Adult Attachment Interview.

For the first 15–20 minutes following the parents' absence, the child interacted with the female examiner in a "warm-up" session. Following the warm-up session, the examiner administered the Klagsbrun-Bowlby version (Klagsbrun & Bowlby, 1976) of a separation anxiety interview initially devised for adolescents by H. G. Hansburg (Hansburg, 1972). The family photograph was presented to the child following the separation interview. The child then engaged in free play (sandbox play) until the parent's return. Each reunion lasted 3 minutes; mother-child and father-child reunions were balanced across dyads.

Further details regarding procedures are given together with measures. Specific procedures were closely tied to our measures: both measures and procedures will be most easily understood when presented in conjunction.

Measures.—This study presents seven analyses of attachment-related behavior in 6-year-old children and adults. Each analysis is correlated with the child's Strange Situation classification with mother and with father at 12 and 18 months of age. All measures of child and adult security undertaken are presented; none were dropped from the study.

1. The child's current security of attachment to each parent was estimated from videotapes of the parent-child reunion.
2. Fluency of discourse in each of the parent-child dyads was assessed. This assessment was based on speech transcripts devoid of information about prosody or concomitant nonverbal behavior.
3. The child's overall functioning was assessed from the videotapes of the warm-up sessions.
4. The child's overall emotional openness in discussions of parent-child separations was assessed, using the entire transcript of the separation anxiety interview.
5. The child's ability to deal constructively with parent-child separation was coded from transcribed answers to the question, "What would a child do?" in response to a 2-week separation.
6. The child's videotaped response to presentation of the family photograph was used to estimate the security of the child's relationship to the parents.
7. Each parent was assigned a score for the security implicit in his or her conceptualization of the self in relation to attachment, that is, for the security implicit in the overall working model of attachment. This score was based on study of the entire transcript of an adult attachment interview.

The number of observations, means, and standard deviations for these measures are given in Table 1. There are no significant differences between

TABLE 1

NUMBER OF OBSERVATIONS, MEANS, AND STANDARD DEVIATIONS FOR STUDY MEASURES

MEASURE	MOTHERS			FATHERS		
	N	M	SD	N	M	SD
Child:						
Security on reunion	33	4.51	2.08	34	4.13	2.25
Overall functioning	38	4.90	2.35	38	4.90	2.35
Emotional openness	39	4.25	2.29	40	4.30	2.29
Constructiveness of						
response to separation ...	35	4.57	3.46	37	5.14	3.46
Response to family photo ..	31	4.52	1.96	32	4.62	2.02
Dyad:						
Fluency of discourse	31	4.48	2.57	32	5.53	2.54
Parent:						
Secure attachment	32	5.09	2.11	29	5.12	1.77

mother-child and father-child measures. Intercorrelations among sixth-year study measures were computed separately for mothers and for fathers. The strongest correlation was between the child's security as assessed from videotaped reunion with the mother at 6 and the child's emotional openness as assessed from the verbal transcripts of the Klagsbrun-Bowlby interview ($r = .68, p < .001$).

Reliability.—Eight research assistants blind to early attachment classifications conducted the seven analyses involved in the study. Each worked exclusively from videotapes or transcripts appropriate to her or his phase of the study. None had any knowledge of Strange Situation behavior, and six of the eight assistants had never seen the child in any other segment of the laboratory study. One of the two raters for the child's response to the family photograph had seen other portions of the videotape, but none including the parents. The eighth had seen three of the 40 families while substituting as an examiner. Two assistants who had assessed videotaped behavior also worked on recoded (i.e., unidentifiable) transcribed responses to separation interviews. Interrater reliabilities ranged from .63 (response to the family photograph) to .85 (emotional openness during the separation interview).

Methods of analysis.—In the Results section we present our assessments in terms of nine-point scales. The child or parent receiving a 9 is doing very well on the dimension under consideration (e.g., seems to be extremely secure), while the child or parent receiving a 1 is doing poorly.

For the purposes of the present study, children who were classified as B_3 with the parent are assigned a value of 3, children who were classified B_1 or B_2 a value of 2, and children classified A, C, or D in the infant Strange Situation a value of 1 in terms of security. Because B_4 infants seem to fall between B_3 and C infants in terms of distress and difficulties with exploration and separation, they are also assigned a value of 2 for this study. Each measure of child or adult behavior from the follow-up study is then correlated directly with the presumed degree of early security of attachment. Using the three-point scale described above, we found no relationship between degree of security of attachment to mother and father in infancy ($r = .00$, $p = $ N.S.).

Security of attachment estimated from reunion behavior at 6 years compared with security of attachment to the same parent in infancy.—At the end of the hour-long Adult Attachment Interview, parents were told that we were essentially finished with the study and that the (first) parent could return to the playroom but might have to wait for the other parent. No instructions were given to parents for the reunion "episode," and no emphasis was placed on it. When the second parent entered the room, the examiner, the child, and the other parent had already been playing, waiting, or conversing for approximately 3 minutes.

Children were rated at the very secure end of the nine-point scale if they affectionately and confidently initiated conversation, interaction, or contact with the parent during the 3-minute episode and/or showed eager responsiveness to the parent's remarks (e.g., breaking in to add own observations or comments).

Most children rated at the insecure end of the nine-point scale showed one of two identifiable response patterns (Cassidy & Main, 1984). In one, the child ignored the parent, responding only minimally when addressed and perhaps moving to a distance from the parent. These were most often children who had been judged insecure-avoidant with the same parent in infancy. Other children seemed to attempt to control the parent, either through directly punitive behavior or through anxious, overly bright "caregiving" behavior (inappropriate role reversal). These were most often children who had been judged insecure-disorganized/disoriented with the same parent in infancy.

Figures 1 and 2 present the overall relationships between reunion behavior at 6 years and early security of attachment. The correlation between security of attachment to mother at 1 year and security of attachment to mother at 6 years of age is $r = .76$, $p < .001$. The correlation between security of attachment to the father at 18 months and at 6 years is $r = .30$, $p < .05$.

The sixth-year rating for security with the mother was highly related to other concurrent but entirely independent study measures. The relation to emotional openness in interview was strong ($r = .68$), as was the relation to current overall functioning ($r = .56$), the child's response to the photograph ($r = .50$), and the security of the mother's working model of attachment ($r = .45$). Sixth-year security of attachment to father was substantially

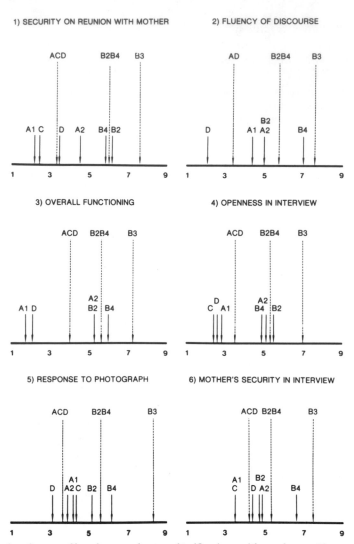

FIG. 1.—Strange Situation attachment classifications with mother at 12 months compared to five child and one adult assessment at 6 years of age. Mean ratings of groups and subgroups on nine-point scales (9 is high).

related to the child's overall functioning ($r = .47$) but bore little or no relationship to the child's representation of attachment (the family photograph or the separation interview). Figure 2 presents the overall relationship between the 18-month and the sixth-year assessments.

Balance, fluidity, and focus in speech between parent and child at 6 years: Discourse fluency compared with security of attachment to the same parent in in-

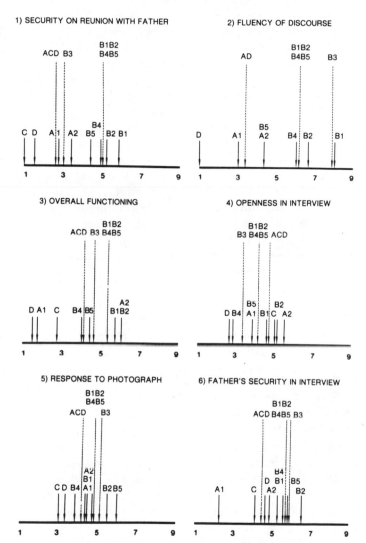

FIG. 2.—Strange Situation attachment classifications with father at 18 months compared to five child and one adult assessment at 6 years of age. Mean ratings of groups and subgroups on nine-point scales (9 is high). (Three infants gave the impression of being secure with father, except for an extreme fear of separation. These infants were given a new subclassification [B5] within the secure group.)

fancy.—We made transcripts of the speech of child, parents, and examiner during each 3-minute reunion. The transcripts were devoid of information about prosody or concomitant nonverbal behavior but contained information about pauses or speaker overlap. Our intention was to remove all cues to emotional tone or status.

The psycholinguistics student who worked with the reunion transcripts (Amy Strage) had no further information of any kind regarding the sample. Working with a general knowledge of categories of infant Strange Situation behavior and the interaction rules developed for the Clown Session, Strage categorized dyads as falling into one of nine discourse categories. Categorization was based on several dimensions of the discourse. A major dimension was fluidity. The discourse was regarded as fluid if the partners answered one another directly and with little pause, while individual speech was regarded as fluid if the person spoke directly, with little evident difficulty in accessing or expressing information. A second dimension was dyadic balance. The discourse was regarded as balanced if neither partner exclusively led or followed the other and if both addressed the partner in a manner that invited further conversation. Three types of focus were distinguished: focus on objects, focus on activities with objects, and focus on relationships. Conversations with the widest range of foci were considered the most desirable.

The nine categories were given a single ordering for fluency of discourse. Dyads placed in the highest category were fluid and balanced in discourse and seemed to range easily in focus. Their conversations had the characteristics of good dialogue. Dyads placed in the lower categories were either restricted or dysfluent in discourse. Dyads who were restricted in discourse had frequent pauses between adult and child conversational turns; topics restricted to impersonal perspective and/or inanimate objects, with limited topic elaboration; and frequent rhetorical questions or empty conversational turns by the parent. These were most often dyads identified as insecure-avoidant in infancy (Strage & Main, 1985). Dyads who were dysfluent in discourse featured disorganization of conversation marked by stumbling and false starts by parent, false starts by child, dyadic focus on relationship-related topics, and parent often passively responding to the child's steering of the conversation. These were dyads identified as insecure-disorganized/disoriented in infancy.

Figures 1 and 2 show the relation between early security of attachment and later fluency of discourse on reunion. The correlation between early security of attachment and later fluency of discourse for mother-child dyads is $r = .63$, $p < .001$. The correlation for father-child dyads is $r = .64$, $p < .001$. The figures show that the discourse fluency of Group B_3 and/or Group B_1 dyads is very high. (Strage was not given Group C dyads; audio malfunctioning had made only one record available.)

Overall functioning related to early security of attachment.—The assessment of overall functioning at 6 years of age was based on 20 minutes of "warm-up" time intended to set the child at ease with the examiner. During this period, the child was asked to make a drawing of her family.

No scale was given to the two raters who worked with this portion of the laboratory session. Each rater was given instructions to rate the child for overall functioning, with some emphasis on the social and emotional aspects of behavior as well as on task orientation. Raters were left to their own interpretations of relatively good versus relatively poor functioning. Each rater viewed each tape several times, then reviewed the entire sample before assigning a final rating. One rater was trained in infant attachment observations, while one was entirely unfamiliar with concepts and measures. Each child was assigned the mean of the two scores given by the two raters. Disagreements were not conferenced.

Figures 1 and 2 present the relationship between overall functioning at 6 years and early security. The correlation with early security of attachment to father is $r = .18$, $p = $ N.S., while the correlation with early security with mother is $r = .46$, $p = .002$.

The 6-year-old's emotional openness in response to pictured separations compared to early security of attachment to each parent.—Following the 20-minute warm-up session, each child was administered the Klagsbrun-Bowlby adaptation of Hansburg's Separation Anxiety Test (Klagsbrun & Bowlby, 1976). This adaptation, made especially for children between 4 and 7 years of age and older, features a series of six photographs of children undergoing separations from the parents. In the mildest of the pictured separations, a parent is saying goodnight to the child. In others, parents are leaving for the weekend, asking the child to play while they talk, or bringing the child to a first day at school. In the most severe, the parents are leaving for 2 weeks. The photographs are stills taken from films and are different for male and female subjects. The children pictured are approximately 4–7 years of age.

The test was introduced approximately as follows: "Parents worry sometimes about what children think when they have to go away for a little while. So we thought we would ask you to tell us what you think a child your age would feel and what a child your age would do when parents go away for a little while." Each picture was then presented with explanation.

Following each of the six pictures, children were asked first what the child in the picture would feel and then what the child in the picture would do on separation. If a child said, "I don't know," or seemed to resist answering, the examiner probed gently until it seemed clear that the child was finished answering or simply did not want to answer. The test was curtailed if the child seemed disturbed by the questions.

The scale for emotional openness drew deliberate parallels between the secure base phenomenon in infancy and the security implicit in emotional openness in 5-year-olds (Kaplan, 1984). Children given high scores for emotional openness seemed to maintain an easy balance between self-exposure and self-containment. They imagined the pictured child as lonely, sad, fearful, or angry during many of the separations and offered reasons for these emotions. These children completed the task with minimal resistance, withdrawal, or stress.

Children given the lowest ratings manifested extremes of several types of insecurity. Some children could not spontaneously express any open-ended feelings and responded to the examiner in a passive way. Some children were silent and overtly depressed; some made irrational responses; and some became disorganized. One child insisted that the pictured child would "feel good" or "feel *nothing*." Simultaneously, she became increasingly hysterical and began hitting a stuffed animal ("Bad lion! Bad lion!"). This child had been classified as insecure-disorganized/disoriented in infancy.

Figures 1 and 2 present emotional openness at 6 years against early security of attachment. Two persons rated all transcripts. The mean of their ratings was used as a final rating; disagreements were not conferenced. The child's emotional openness at 6 was not related to security of attachment to the father ($r = -.15$, $p =$ N.S.). It was strongly related to security of attachment to the mother ($r = .59$, $p < .001$).

The 6-year-old's responses to "What would the child do?" during a 2-week separation from parents compared to early security of attachment to each parent.— According to Bowlby (1969/1982b, 1973), children over time develop "working models" of their attachment figures and the accessibility or inaccessibility of those figures. If the attachment figure has been accessible to the child in real-life situations, the child carries an internal sense of the accessibility of that figure whether or not the figure is actually present at any given moment. An internal model of the attachment figure as accessible is presumed to help the child deal with real-life separations.

Children who were secure as infants might be expected to have internal images of the attachment figure as accessible, while children who were insecure in infancy might lack this image. Children who were secure as infants would then be able to imagine more active ways of dealing with child-parent separations than would children who were insecure as infants (Kaplan, 1984). Following this line of reasoning, a simple scoring system was developed and applied to the child's answers to the strongest of the separation situations, in which parents were portrayed as leaving for a 2-week period: "This little girl's/boy's parents are going away on vacation for 2 weeks; what's this little girl/boy gonna do?" The highest score was given if the child would actively persuade the parents not to leave for their vacation or accomplish the same end through other means. (One secure child suggested just hiding in the back of the car until the parents were launched on the trip.) A high score was also given if the child would express disappointment, anger, or distress directly, with the implication that this might lead to termination of the separation or be communicated to the parent. (Another secure child suggested the pictured child should "cry and stamp her feet.") A slightly lower score was given to the child who would find an apparent alternative attachment figure to stay with, so long as this seemed satisfactory to the child. A middle score was given to the child who would play with objects, but in an imaginative and constructive way that could make herself feel good, and somewhat lower scores were given to unelaborated play. Low scores were given to "I don't know" and to complete silence. The lowest score was given to any response that would result in decreasing the accessibility of the attachment figure. This included killing the self or the parents and locking oneself away. Only one code (the highest or "best" for which the response qualified) was assigned per child.

There was no relation between the level of answer given to this question and security of attachment to the father in infancy ($r = .14$, $p = $ N.S.). There was a strong relation between the level of answer given to this single question and security of attachment to the mother in infancy ($r = .59$, $p = .001$).

The average response for the children who had been B_3 with the mother was close to a constructive response that calls on people. Children who were A_1, C_1, or D with mother in infancy tended on the average to answer that they did not know what the child would do during the 2-week separation, while some gave responses indicating potential or definite harm to self or parents. The Appendix presents the complete answers to the first five examiner queries for children who had been classified as B_3, A_1, C_1, or D with the mother in infancy.

Secure versus insecure responses to presentation of a family photograph compared to early security of attachment to mother and to father.—Following the presentation of the pictures of child-parent separations, each child was shown the photograph of herself with the parents taken earlier. The examiner held the photograph out to the child, saying, "But here is a photograph of yourself and your family, and you see, you are all together." If the child did not take the photograph, the examiner laid it near the child and waited for the child's response. The child was not pressed further.

Two judges who had no familiarity with infant Strange Situation behavior made independent ratings of the child's videotaped response to this situation. The judges were asked to estimate the security of the child's feelings about his or her family, solely from the response to this family picture. Ratings were based chiefly on repeated slow-motion examination of nonverbal behavior. No rating scale was given prior to assessments, but raters were asked to describe the behavior that had led to the assignment of ratings. The ratings presented are averages of the two ratings given. Disagreements were not conferenced.

Children were judged secure in response to the photograph if they readily accepted the photograph, smiled and showed some interest, and let go of the photograph casually following an inspection of a few seconds and/or a few positive comments. Children were considered insecure with respect to the family if they avoided the photograph, refusing to accept it, actively turning from it, or turning it away from them when it was placed near them. These were most often children who had been judged insecure-avoidant with the mother during infancy. Children were also considered insecure in response to the family photograph if they became depressed or disorganized while viewing it; one child, who had been playing cheerfully with the examiner, took on an immediate depressed aspect and bent silently over the photograph for 12 seconds. Children who became depressed or disorganized in response to the photograph were most often children who had been judged insecure-disorganized/disoriented with mother during infancy.

Figures 1 and 2 present the results for the child's response to the family photograph as compared to early security of attachment. Even though father as well as mother is photographed and represented, there is no significant relationship between security of attachment to father and response to the family photograph ($r = .15$, $p = $ N.S.). There is a strong relationship between response to the family photograph at 6 years and early security of attachment to the mother ($r = .74$, $p < .001$).

From this portion of the study we see that it is not necessary to observe "real" interaction between the child and the mother in order to begin to build an understanding of the way in which the child's mind is organized with respect to the relationship. The child's response to an active reminder of the relationship is itself informative.

Security in the adult's discussion of attachment experiences and their influence compared with security of attachment to the same parent in infancy.—The Adult Attachment Interview was designed by Carol George, Nancy Kaplan, and Mary Main to probe alternately for descriptions of relationships, specific supportive memories, contradictory memories, assessments of relationships in childhood, and current assessments of the same experiences and relationships. Parents were asked first to choose five adjectives to describe their relationship to both parents and then to explain what made them choose those adjectives. Later they were asked what they did when they were upset in childhood, whether they had ever felt rejected by parents in childhood, and, if yes, why they now thought their parents behaved as they did. They were asked whether their parents had ever threatened separation, whether there had been any major changes in relationships with parents since childhood, and how they felt about their parents currently. Finally, they were asked how they felt these experiences had influenced their adult personalities. In the analysis of the interview, the judge worked with the interview in its entirety. Any existing contradictions and inconsistencies were carefully examined (Main & Goldwyn, in press).

The Adult Attachment Interviews were rated for security with respect to experiences, ideas, and feelings surrounding attachment. Parents who were rated as secure tended to value attachment relationships, whether with their own parents, with others, or in an abstract sense; to regard attachments and experiences related to attachment as influential on personality; and yet to be objective in describing any particular relationship. Many of these parents recalled favorable early experiences (Main & Goldwyn, in press). Many, however, had had unfavorable attachment-related experiences in childhood, particularly in the form of loss or rejection.

Two other salient characteristics of secure parents were a readiness of recall and an ease in discussing attachment that suggested much reflection prior to the interview and a lack of idealization of parents or of past experiences. When asked about early relationships, one man rated as secure began with, "You've struck a gold mine, actually . . . ," and launched on a history of rejection, loss, abuse, and major separations. His interview responses indicated much prior reflection. When asked the question, "Was there ever a time in childhood when you felt rejected?" this father of a secure son laughed heartily: "If *that* ain't rejection, I don't know what the hell is!"

Parents rated as insecure with respect to attachment lacked the three qualities of adult security listed earlier. At the time of the interview, most fell into one of three major patterns (Main, 1985). In one pattern, the parent dismissed attachment relationships as being of little concern, value, or influence. These were most frequently the parents of insecure-avoidant infants. In a second pattern, the parents seemed preoccupied with dependency on their own parents and still actively struggled to please them. These were most frequently the parents of insecure-ambivalent infants. A third insecure group had experienced the death of an attachment figure before maturity and seemed not yet to have completed the mourning process. These were most frequently the parents of the insecure-disorganized/disoriented infants.

Figures 1 and 2 present the relationship between the security of the adult's apparent internal working model of attachment, as assessed solely from the transcript of the Adult Attachment Interview, and early infant security of attachment. For the mother the relationship to her infant's security of attachment is strong ($r = .62, p < .001$). For father, the relationship is $r = .37, p < .05$.

DISCUSSION

Summary of Results

This chapter is based on a reconceptualization of individual differences in attachment organization as individual differences in the internal working model (mental representation) of the self in relation to attachment. We defined the internal working model of attachment as a set of conscious and/ or unconscious rules for the organization of information relevant to attachment and for obtaining or limiting access to that information, that is, to information regarding attachment-related experiences, feelings, and ideations. This reconceptualization led us to a new focus on investigation of attachment through language and other representational processes.

We first compared individual differences in security of attachment to each parent as assessed in the Ainsworth Strange Situation in infancy (very secure, secure, and insecure) to diverse measures of security, functioning, and representation at 6 years of age. Early security of attachment to mother, but not to father, predicted the child's overall functioning in interactions with a female examiner. We next compared early assessments of security to a given parent to assessments of security to the parent made several years later. We found very strong stability in the child's apparent security on reunion with mother over the 5-year period ($r = .76$) and a weaker but significant stability in apparent security on reunion with the father.

Major findings regarding representation and language were as follows. First, early security of attachment to each parent was highly related to fluency of parent child discourse as evidenced in transcripts of a reunion dialogue. Early security of attachment to mother, but not to father, predicted the child's emotional openness during discussions of "children's responses" to parent-child separations and also predicted whether the child seemed to think a child could take constructive action with regard to a prospective 2-week separation from parents. Early security of attachment to mother, but not to father, also predicted the child's response to presentation of a family photograph. Finally, we used an Adult Attachment Interview to assess the security implicit in the parent's mental representation of the self in relation to attachment. For both mothers and fathers, this security was significantly related to the security of the infant's attachment to the parent 5 years earlier.

Are these results attributable to a single dimension of language competency?— So much of our sixth-year assessment rested on language that it seems possible to question whether individual differences in security of attachment might instead reflect individual differences in some underlying verbal competence. However, several efforts to connect security of attachment to language acquisition and performance have been undertaken with null results (see Bretherton et al., 1979, for review). Moreover, largely nonverbal responses to a family photograph were as strongly related to early security of attachment as were each of the language measures; in addition, responses to this photograph were significantly related to each of the remaining sixth-year measures. Finally, children and adults with different early attachment organizations had predictably differing language organization. The differences were expressed as differing discourse structures (Strage & Main, 1985), not as a shared verbal incompetency. (Similar arguments can be raised regarding an interpretation of these results in terms of a simple underlying dimension of social competence.)

Interpretation of the apparent overriding influence of the mother.—At the outset of this project we expected that the security of the infant's attachment to the father as well as to the mother would be influential in the development of representations of relationships. The unexpected result was that individual differences in early relationships to mother, but not to father, significantly predicted the 6-year-old's responses to the separation interview and responses to the family photograph.

The most likely explanation (although others are possible) lies in the way the children interpreted the task. Our study was deliberately designed to give the child the choice of responding to mother or to father in terms of representation. The child was queried regarding (pictured) responses to the leave-taking of both parents and shown a photograph of the whole family. Given this choice, the child responded as though to the mother. This suggests a hierarchy of internal working models in which the mother often stands foremost, a result that seems in keeping with Bowlby's (1969/1982b) suggestion of hierarchies in the organization of internal working models of attachment figures. We cannot presume on the basis of this study that the relationship with father lacks its own internal model or has disappeared from mental processes. The model may simply have been lower in the hierarchy for the majority of children in our sample.

The Strong Predictability of Behavior Reported in This Study:
"Passive" versus "Active" Accounts of the Predictability
of Behavior and Representation

The magnitude of relationships between early security of attachment and later observations of behavior reported in this study are high for the behavioral sciences. Indeed, they are uniquely high for observations of human behavior made under differing circumstances and across a 5-year period. Our first assessment was based on the organization of the physical movements of an infant's body with respect to that of the parent at 12 months of age. Four of our seven later assessments rested on study of language transcripts bereft of reference to physical movements. What was initially expressed dyadically through the organization of movement was later predictably expressed both dyadically and individually through the organization of language. Maintenance of the security implicit in early relationship structures transcended their modality of expression.

One interpretation of this report would be that the internal working model of the relationship established by the end of the first year of life functions as a "template" of previously unrecognized strength. From this point of view, the template would act as filter for the perception of all succeeding experience and direct all succeeding behavior. An alternative interpretation (espoused by Brim & Kagan, 1980; Brim & Ryff, 1980) would be that no template had been formed but rather that secure versus insecure patterns of interaction had continued over the 5-year period. Child behavior in the laboratory would then be attributable to the child's most recent experience of parent-child interaction.

Note, however, that both theories that would attribute predictability of representation to the early completion of a "template" and theories that would attribute predictability to the child's most recent experiences in interaction with the parent implicitly conceive of the child as a passive participant in the construction and preservation of the internal working model. We propose in contrast that patterns once established are actively self-perpetuating. This proposal is in keeping with the most basic tenets of psychoanalysis (Freud, 1940; Greenberg & Mitchell, 1983; see esp. Sullivan's descriptions of "security operations," Sullivan, 1953) and certainly with Bowlby's proposal that internal working models, once established, have a propensity towards stability (Bowlby, 1980). Sroufe and Fleeson (in press) have recently summarized and reviewed arguments for the self-preserving nature of early relationships, adding as well recent supportive evidence stemming from their own studies.

Our work has led us to the specific hypothesis that rules for the direction of attention and behavior serve actively and repeatedly to restrict and perhaps in some cases to distort the types of information that may be made available, either through memory or through attention to the immediate environment. Each internally or externally originating signal that is potentially disruptive to the system is not merely blocked from perception (as in the template theory) but must be actively countered by perceptual and behavioral control mechanisms. Supporting evidence will be offered within the succeeding sections.

Security and Representation: Security in Infancy, Childhood, and Adulthood

Security in infancy.—Earlier, we reviewed the characteristics of very secure dyads as observed in infancy. First, very secure dyads were characterized not by static features but rather by ease of movement within the physical environment and ease of access between the partners (cf. Emde, 1980; Waters & Deane, in this vol.). The parents of very secure infants made no effort to focus the infant's attention either on themselves and away from the environment or vice versa. In consequence, the attention of secure infants and their parents seemed to flow freely, permitting shifts in attention and emotional expression across a range of situations. In contrast, we noted that, in the case of insecure attachment, attention, emotional expression, and behavior seemed restricted or rule bound in predictable and specifiable ways. Here we look for parallel characteristics in the later mental representations of secure infants and their parents.

Evidence for active dyadic cooperation in the maintenance of secure versus insecure relationship structures.—As opposed to the reunion episodes of the Ainsworth Strange Situation, in which the behavior of the parent is controlled, our own reunion situation was left unstructured. In this unstructured reunion situation, dyadic cooperation in the maintenance of particular relationship structures was notable and unrestrained. The parents of the secure, "initiating" children entered the room with confidence, easily overriding any signals of reserve, while the parents of the "controlling/ caregiving" (disorganized) children often appeared embarrassed or flustered immediately on entrance. In two cases parents of avoidant children failed to address the child throughout the 3-minute period.

The active efforts of the dyad to construct and to preserve a particular relationship structure could also be seen in speech transcripts taken from the reunion episodes, transcripts that provided us with information regarding sheerly mental aspects of the preservation of particular forms of relationship. In secure dyads, topics of conversation were free ranging and balanced and discourse showed ease of access between members of the dyad. Insecure dyads, in contrast, were restricted in the topic of their speech—the parents of avoidant infants concentrating on objects and activities, the parents of disorganized/disoriented infants focusing on relationships and feelings. Parents as well as children, in short, invited the continuation of the major structure of the relationship. Through discourse as well as through nonverbal behavior, dyads maintained their organization.

Mental aspects of security in 6-year-olds.—The secure 6-year-olds seemed to have free ranging access to affect, memory, and plans, whether in forming speech in conversation with the parent or in discussing imagined situations relevant to attachment. Early in the reunion, they confidently initiated proximity or interaction. Speech flowed readily without false starts or pauses.

These children seemed at ease in exploring feelings during the separation interview and had ideas (interestingly unique to each child) regarding constructive interactions that a child might take in response to a projected 2-week separation from the parents. In response to presentation of a family picture, these children seemed pleased but casual.

For children who had been insecure with mother in infancy, in contrast, varying types of restriction seemed to preserve differing organizations of information and attention. Restrictions differed according to whether the child had been judged insecure-avoidant or insecure-disorganized/ disoriented with mother in infancy. In almost every assessment presented, children who had initially been judged insecure-avoidant showed an avoidant response pattern at 6 years of age. They directed attention away from the parent on reunion, attending to toys or to activities; responded minimally (although politely) when addressed; and sometimes subtly moved away from the parent. They seemed ill at ease in discussing feelings regarding separation and typically "did not know" what a child might do in response to an expected 2-week separation from the parents. They actively avoided, refused, or turned around and away from the presented photograph of the family.

Children who had been judged disorganized-disoriented in infancy showed a distinctly differing response pattern. Behavior on reunion with the parent was controlling, being either directly punitive or inappropriately role reversing (caregiving). Discourse was dysfluent. Questioned regarding children's responses to child-parent separations, many of these children became distressed, silent, irrational, or occasionally self-destructive. Presented with the family picture, they became depressed or disorganized.

Mental properties of security in adulthood.—We have already discussed the readiness of recall and apparent ease in discussing attachment experiences that characterized the parents of the secure infants. The most striking mental property of very secure parents was, however, their coherency in discussing their attachment history and its influence. These parents seemed particularly at ease in the integration of positive with negative aspects of expression and feeling.

In the parents of secure babies, unfavorable attachment experiences seemed to have been considered and integrated into mental process long before the interview took place. If unfavorable aspects of early relationships to parents were to emerge, they often emerged in the first description of early relationships and then were subject to a coherent discussion. At the same time, negative events were typically placed in context. One B_3 mother who had been strongly rejected by her family laughed at our initial query regarding the nature of her early relationships and asked, "How many hours do you have? Okay, well, to start with, my mother was not cheerful, and I can tell you right now, the reason was that she was over-worked" (Main & Goldwyn, in press).

Although as speakers the parents of insecure infants gave us information regarding negative experiences and processes, from the viewpoint of the adults themselves the information seemed to us unintegrated and perhaps not fully recognized as part of a coherent whole. Contradictions and inconsistencies in the organization of information appeared in their records.

Particular forms of incoherency seemed to characterize parents of infants in the differing insecure groups. Some parents of insecure-avoidant infants were striking for an incoherency that took the form of a contradiction between the semantic (general) and episodic (specific) descriptions of the parents, as the father who described his mother as "excellent," "a fine relationship," but remembered in response to specific probes being afraid and unable to tell her when he had broken his hand. This contradiction between the picture of the parent as almost ideal and specific memories denoting strong loneliness or rejection characterized a number of the parents of the insecure-avoidant infants (Ainsworth, personal communication, 1982; Main & Goldwyn, in press). Another characteristic was the frequency and strength of their insistence on an inability to recall the period of childhood.

For parents of the insecure-disorganized/disoriented infants, incoherency sometimes took the form of persistent, repeated positive-negative oscillations in viewpoint; apparent irrationality; and refusal or inability to remain with the topic of the interview, sometimes losing track of the topic or question.

All parents in our sample were questioned regarding their early attachment history and its influence. Because parents of secure as well as insecure infants sometimes reported histories of rejection or traumatic experiences, including early loss of attachment figures, we are led once more to the hypothesis that access to information and the coherent organization of information relevant to attachment may play a determining role in the creation of security in adulthood.

SIGNIFICANCE

We discuss the significance of the present chapter in terms of the potentials for linkage between attachment and other fields contingent on the development of these new methods; the practical and theoretical significance of the development of the new, insecure-disorganized/disoriented attachment category; and the potential for understanding parents previously termed "insensitive" (e.g., inaccessible or rejecting) in terms of their own histories and present representations.

1. *The import of methods of assessment of attachment at older ages.*—Perhaps the most obvious application of the development of methods of assessment for attachment at older ages is to clinical work in child and adult psychology and psychiatry. It has long been presumed that the parent's representation of his or her own life history shapes the way in which the infant is conceptualized and, concomitantly, the way in which the infant is treated (Freud, 1940; Fraiberg, Adelson, & Shapiro, 1975; Miller, 1981), but to date only anecdotal reports have been available. Ours are the first systematic studies affirming this presumption (see Main, in press; Main & Goldwyn, in press).

The newly available assessment of adult attachment status should permit others to follow. A particularly intriguing use of these new methods would be in tracing changes in the representation of life history over the course of (child or adult) clinical treatment.

The development of methods of assessment of attachment for children and adults may also yield fruitful results for students investigating the concept of the self and for investigators working within personality. Recently, Cassidy has reported strong relationships between sixth-year attachment status and individual differences in self-concept in a Charlottesville sample (Cassidy, 1985). In a doctoral dissertation involving University of Virginia freshmen, Roger Kobak (1985) reports very strong relationships between adult attachment status and "mental health" status as described independently by peers using the California Q-sort for adult personality.

Other uses of the new methods may be less obvious. First, as most psychologists and psychiatrists are aware, connections between the psychological and physiological aspects of disease and disease process are increasingly being discovered. Connections between attachment processes and psychoimmunology have now been reported in several studies by Reite and his colleagues (e.g., Laudenslager, Reite, & Harbeck, 1982). Our knowledge of the psychological contribution to disease process may be considerably increased by the new potential for classification of adult attachment status.

Second, the new methods of assessment should be of interest to workers in psycholinguistics and to students of social aspects of discourse. The strong overlap between attachment classifications as assessed by nonverbal methods in infancy and discourse classifications discovered 5 years later suggests new anchors for the study of individual and dyadic differences in speech patterns (Strage & Main, 1985). Knowledge of the attachment status of adult speakers may provide psycholinguists with new bases for systematic studies of the ways language is used to communicate and/or to censor information regarding feelings and relationships (to and from the self as well as the attachment partner).

Finally, the Adult Attachment Interview, as well as the child separation interview, can be put to use in other cultures. Thus, the methods presented may be used in anthropological research studies where the Strange Situation may be either difficult to conduct or difficult to interpret. These methods may also be of assistance in determining whether differences in distribution from the U.S. norms for infant Strange Situation attachment classifications (recently reported in North German, Japanese, and Israeli samples) have similar or diverse meanings from that established in our own culture (Grossmann et al., in this vol.; Miyake et al., in this vol.; Sagi et al., in this vol.).

2. *The insecure-disorganized/disoriented classification.*—Study of the development of infants judged insecure-disorganized/disoriented in infancy was one of the primary aims of the present study. At 6 years of age, these

children seem to form a single, coherent group—controlling or subtly caregiving toward the parent on reunion but depressed, disorganized, and intermittently irrational in thought processes in other situations. The existence and identification of this group of infants is of practical as well as humane import. To begin with, the "forced" or "imposed" classification for half the disorganized/disoriented infants in our sample was secure. Had we failed to identify these infants as insecure in infancy, our power to predict future functioning on the basis of early attachment status would have been much reduced. In addition, some of the maltreated infants previously puzzlingly classified as "secure" in the Ainsworth Strange Situation (see Main & Solomon, in press, for a review) may in fact have been disorganized/disoriented.

Our discovery of the D category of infant Strange Situation behavior rested on an unwillingness to adopt the "essentialist" or "realist" position regarding the classification of human relationships. It was based on the presumption that both individuals and relationships are unique and that they have a higher "reality" than any classification system can fully encompass. We suggest that the understanding of behavior at the representational level as well as at other levels will best be served by leaving the study of behavior classification open to a continuing dialectic between our knowledge of an individual's history and careful descriptions of behavior in particular, structured situations (Main & Solomon, in press). This process may lead to the discovery of new classifications at the representational as well as the behavioral level.

3. *The parents of insecurely attached infants: "Insensitive to infant signals" or incoherent in the representation of attachment?*—Observations of the parents of insecurely attached infants as compared to the parents of securely attached infants have repeatedly shown relative insensitivity or unresponsiveness to infant signals and communications (Bretherton, in this vol.). In the present study, conducted 5 years after the Strange Situation, we report a powerful ($r = .62$) link between infant security of attachment and the security implicit in the mother's internal working model of herself in overall relation to "attachment experiences, feelings, and ideations" as determined in the Adult Attachment Interview.

Security in adulthood can now be provisionally identified as the ability to integrate existing information relevant to attachment; where this integration is possible, the parent is likely to exhibit "sensitivity to infant signals." This ability need not be stable for any given individual; indeed, this definition allows for shifts in both the parent's and the infant's attachment status. Malignant changes in life circumstances relevant to attachment may be at least temporarily difficult to integrate with other attachment-relevant information, yielding the implied downward shifts in maternal sensitivity and distinct shifts in infant attachment status reported in some high-risk poverty samples (Vaughn et al., 1979). Positive changes in life circumstances should correspondingly increase the "ability to integrate existing information relevant to attachment," leading to increased sensitivity to infant signals and positive shifts in infant attachment status.

Parental "insensitivity" to infant signals, then, may originate in the parent's need to preserve a particular organization of information or state of mind. Attachment-relevant signals originating externally from the infant and internally from memory may be similar in the "rules" they evoke for parents who are insecure in terms of their own internal working models of attachment. The need to restrict or reorganize attachment-relevant information, whether it originates internally or externally, may result in an inability to perceive and interpret the attachment signals of the infant accurately and, in some cases, in an active need either to alter infant signals or to inhibit them. To summarize, where the parent's own experiences and feelings are not integrated, restrictions of varying types are placed on attention and the flow of information with respect to attachment. These restrictions appear in speech in the form of incoherencies and in behavior as insensitivities.

Directions for Future Studies

"Rules" preserving particular internal working models of attachment: Descriptive or prescriptive?—We have claimed that what accounts for the stability and predictability of attachment representation is the self-preserving nature of the internal working model (particularly, internal working models that are restrictive or incoherent and insecure in type). To date, this claim rests merely on the predictability of "representational" behavior patterns from the early organization of nonverbal behavior toward the attachment figure. Thus the insecure-avoidant infant turns away from, moves away from, and ignores the parent within the Strange Situation and 5 years later turns away from representational reminders of the parent. In discourse with the child, the parent focuses on objects and activities, asks rhetorical questions, and offers (as does the child) little opportunity for turn taking or topic elaboration. Finally, during the Adult Attachment Interview, the parent of the avoidant infant tends to state that she is unable to recall the events of childhood and/or dismisses or devalues those events as likely influences. Selective inattention to potential cues eliciting attachment or reminding of relationship seems to be a rule preserved by both partners over the 5-year period (see Bowlby, 1980; Main & Weston, 1981, for discussions of selective inattention in avoidance). This is rule-bound behavior in terms of predictability and regularity. But are these merely predictable regularities, or are they internally directed "rules," rules that are prescriptive for the individual who attempts to preserve a particular organization of information?

One way to test for the possible prescriptive nature of these "rules" is to attempt to violate them. In the case of studies employing the photograph, we might observe children of differing attachment organization as we instruct them to violate their "rules" for dealing with these representations. Thus, insecure-avoidant children might be instructed to gaze directly at the photograph for a long period of time (as insecure-disorganized/disoriented children do typically). Insecure-disorganized/disoriented children might, in contrast, be instructed to glance at the photograph only briefly, then drop it on the floor (as insecure-avoidant children have been observed to do). If such treatment of the photograph produces the troubled responses we expect in children in these insecure groups, we would have some evidence for the prescriptive, self-preserving nature of these "rules." If, on the other hand, these instructions are carried out without difficulty, the "rules" would appear to be mere regularities.

An interesting theme that runs throughout our study is that of differences in the presence of "rules" appearing to guide behavior in secure versus insecure dyads and individuals. In studies of the speech transcripts made during reunion episodes, we noted strikingly stylized turns of speech within the insecure dyads and even within each subclass among the moderately secure dyads (i.e., B_1, B_2, and B_4 dyads). Of all dyads studied in speech transcripts, the very secure dyads were the most difficult to identify through particular "rules" or stylistic turns of speech (Strage & Main, 1985). Indeed, the rule used for identifying the B_3 dyad was to identify the dyad as belonging to the secure group overall and then to identify the dyad as B_3 because of the lack of stylistic features or rules identifying it with any other secure subgroup organization. In sum, the very secure dyads were the dyads most free of predictable, "rule-like" regularities and patternings in discourse.

Some further support for this intriguing possibility is found in the positive but "casual" treatment of the photograph by 6-year-olds who had been secure with mother as infants. We would predict that "very secure" children could without difficulty either turn away and drop the family photograph or continue to gaze at it for long periods.

The question of sensitive periods in the formation of internal working models of attachment.—As noted earlier, our presumption (with Bowlby, 1973) is that, at any point in time, relationship-related forms of behavior are guided simultaneously by internal working models and by ongoing interaction patterns preserving of those models of attachment. Our data are insufficient to determine whether models acquired as a function of early attachment-related events are particularly resistant to change. The mother-child interaction pattern changed for so few children in our sample over the 5-year period that our data cannot provide an answer.

The new measures we have developed for assessing child-parent attachment patterns at older ages will, however, make the critical tests possible. Researchers wishing to address this issue can now examine behavior at older ages as a function of security of mother-child attachment assessed at several time periods. By repeatedly observing the same dyads with respect to security of attachment, researchers can, for example, compare the mental representations and school behavior of children who were insecure with mother in infancy but are secure at 6 with children who were secure with mother at both time periods.

The need for studies investigating sources of change.—The present study would be both destructive and unethical in its implications and/or its implementation if it led to the labeling or identification of any individual in terms of his or her presumably unalterable early and "primary" internal working models of attachment. First, in disseminating the results of this study, it is important to note that very strong predictability was achieved only when we compared early security of attachment to attachment-related behavior and representation 5 years later. Early security of attachment to the mother had only a moderate relationship to the child's overall functioning in a nonstress situation.

Furthermore, in this first study of early attachment in relation to representation we deliberately worked with a stable, upper-middle-class sample and deliberately included in our follow-up study only those families who had not suffered events known to have major malignant impact on attachment organization. This was a necessary first step in delineating the way in which patterns of attachment and representation develop in undisturbed circumstances. While replications of this study with similar samples in other locations are clearly in order, there is both an ethical and a scientific necessity to begin simultaneously on studies that trace and investigate sources of change, for example, in samples undergoing major shifts in life circumstances.

Although we have reported strong relationships between our infancy and our sixth-year assessments, the retrospective reports available from the Adult Attachment Interview suggest possibilities for change once the child has reached the stage of formal operations. This stage permits the child to see the operations of whole systems, to place herself within those systems, and to imagine possibilities that have not yet been experienced (Piaget, 1967). As noted previously, a number of adults were considered to be secure in their internal working models of relationships despite unfavorable early experiences. Interestingly, many of these recalled a period of rebellion during adolescence. For those concerned with change as well as stability in representation, adolescence may provide a particularly fruitful area for further study.

APPENDIX

CHILDREN'S RESPONSES TO "WHAT WOULD A CHILD DO?"
DURING A 2-WEEK SEPARATION FROM PARENTS:
RESPONSES TO FIRST FIVE QUERIES[1]

Responses of All 6-Year-Old Children Classified B₃ with Mother in Infancy

Child 1.—Cry. [Giggles.] *Cry?* [Nods yes.] *Why's she gonna cry?* Cause she really loves her mom and dad. *Cause she really loves her mom and dad?* Mm. *What else is she gonna do?* Play a little bit.

Child 2.—She's gonna, um, stay up until she gets tired. *Mm.* And she's gonna cry. *Mmm.* And she's gonna get a flu. *The flu!* Yeah. *Uh-oh.* And she's gonna get dressed in the morning with that dress on all the time.[2]

Child 3.—She's gonna be happy. *She is?* Mmm. *For the whole 2 weeks?* Yes.

Child 4.—Go outside. *Go outside? And do what?* . . . Play soccer. *Play soccer? What's he gonna do for 2 weeks while his mom and dad are gone?* Do everything. *Do everything that he normally does?* Yeah.

Child 5.—Runaway. *Gonna runaway?* And leave the car there. *Leave the car there?* And leave a sign on it saying, "I'm running away." *Mm. Tell em. Where's he gonna go?* I don't know. *He's gonna go away?* Probably gonna catch a bus . . . and tell him to take him to San Francisco . . . and he can get to the cable cars and ride to the wharfs . . . he has money.

Child 6 (B₂).—He might . . . Well, he might need someone to stay with him. Like if the car, like if the car has some batteries . . . he might not know the store to get them. He might not know how much they cost. *Mm. So what's he gonna do?* Don't know. *Hm?* I don't know. *Any ideas what he could do?* Don't think, I don't, well . . . he could go to his friend's house, and their mom—if their mom and dad are going out, he might, he might just like ask them to see if they would come with him . . . *I see. Get some other grown-ups to help him?* [Nods yes.]

Responses of All 6-Year-Old Children Classified A₁ with Mother in Infancy

Child 1. He's gonna go with his mom and dad. *Gonna go with his mom and dad maybe?* Yeah, and shitbag.

Child 2.—I don't know. *What could he do?* I don't know! *Any ideas?* Ow. Ow. [High voice through toy horse.] No, I don't. *No?* Wheww. Sit up lion.

Child 3.—[Shrugs shoulders.] *Hm? Why don't you take a guess. Her mom and dad are going away for 2 weeks.* [Silence.] *What do you think she might do when they leave?* [Silence.] *Know what she feels like doing?* [Shakes head no.]

Child 4.—Runaway. *Runaway? Where's she gonna run to?* I don't know. *You don't know. What else do you think she might do?* I don't know. *Don't know? You have any ideas?* No.

---

[1] The children's responses are printed in roman type, the experimenter's in italic.
[2] The "dress" is a pictured going-away present from the parents.

Child 5.—Nothing! *Nothing?* I don't know. *What will she do for 2 weeks while her mom and dad are gone?* I don't know. *No guesses?* Nnn.

Responses of All 6-Year-Old Children Classified C with Mother in Infancy

Child 1 (C_1).—Chase them. *Chase who?* Their dad and mom in his new toy car—he's psssshh—run right off. *Then what's gonna happen?* And then he's gonna, then he is gonna . . . toss a bow and arrow and shoot them. *Shoot his mom and dad?* Yeah. If he wants to, maybe.

Child 2 (C_2).—I don't know. *Well, that's a long time. I mean a lot, you can do a lot in 2 weeks. What is this little girl gonna do?* I don't . . . *Two weeks—that's a long time.* [Silence.]

Responses of All 6-Year-Old Children Disorganized with Mother in Infancy

Child 1.—I don't know.

Child 2.—Run away. *She's gonna run away?* Yeah. Now could we play?

Child 3.—Probably gonna hide away. *Gonna hide away?* Yeah. *Then what's gonna happen?* He'll probably get locked up in his closet. [Forced giggle.] *Locked up in his closet?* Yeah, I was locked up in a closet.

Child 4.—I don't know. *Have any ideas about what he might do?* Shakes head no. *Or what he feels like doing?* He might feel like kicking the car. *Mm.* Got mad at em. *Feeling mad?* That all I can think of.

Child 5.—Mmmm, I don't know. *Any guesses?* Mm . . . *Ideas for what he could do?* Nope.

Child 6.—Gonna go somewhere. *Gonna go somewhere? Is she gonna go by herself?* [Shrugs shoulders.] *Hm? Can you tell me more about that?* [Shakes head no.] *No? Where do you think she'll go?* [Shrugs shoulders.] *She just feels like going somewhere?* [Nods yes.]

Child 7.—Nothing. *Nothing?* Yeah. *What's that like?* Just do nothing. Not playing. *Not playing?* Yeah. *For 2 whole weeks?* Yeah.

Child 8.—Nothing. *Just do nothing?* Yeah. *For 2 whole weeks?* Yeah, it doesn't matter! *Doesn't matter—2 weeks do nothing.* Yeah, cuz it's just a picture. *Mm. Just a picture.* And it's not real.

Child 9.—[Interview curtailed, child seemed distressed.]

Child 10.—[Interview curtailed, child seemed distressed.]

Child 11.—Um . . . do you think. *What do you think she might do while her mom and dad are gone?* [Silence.] *What do you think?* I don't know. *Don't know? Take a guess, huh?* [Sighs.] *What do you think she'll do while her mom and dad are gone?* [Shakes head no.]

Child 12.—Play all day. *All day. What's he gonna do for 2 weeks while they are gone?* Play, probably. *Hm?* Play. *Probably with the car?* Wonder if they got the house . . . wonder if he has the house keys. *Hm.* Can't get in.

ADAPTATION, MALADAPTATION, AND INTERGENERATIONAL
TRANSMISSION: INTRODUCTION TO PART 3

The term "adaptation," in relation to attachment theory, has been used in at least three major ways (Ainsworth, 1984): in the phylogenetic sense, in the ontogenetic sense, and in the developmental mental health sense. This indiscriminate use of the same term for different processes has led to some confusion.

"Adaptation" in the phylogenetic sense refers to the survival advantage that certain behavior patterns and physiological structures confer on organisms. For example, attachment behavior is believed to predispose an infant not to stray too far from a protective figure and to seek that figure when danger threatens. In this sense "adaptation" is a normative concept. The ontogenetic sense of "adaptation" takes the phylogenetic sense for granted. As Lorenz (1965) and others have pointed out, phylogenetic predispositions are not necessarily rigid but can be adapted to specific environmental conditions (e.g., an animal that habitually grows a winter coat in a cold climate may not do so in a hot climate). Although ontogenetic adaptations often yield survival advantage, they do not do so under all conditions. They may, moreover, foreclose future optimal development. This brings us to the meaning of "adaptation" in the developmental mental health sense. Like the concept of physical health, developmental mental health is a highly evaluative concept. What is being evaluated is adaptation to current conditions with regard to assumed long-term consequences for optimal psychological/social development. Note that this use of the term "adaptation" replaces the older, equally evaluative terms "adjustment" and "maladjustment."

The six chapters in this part discuss the child's adaptation to a variety of caregiving arrangements, using the term "adaptation" both in the ontogenetic and in the developmental mental health sense. Vaughn, Deane, and Waters (Chap. IV) consider two issues in adaptation, the immediate and the more long-term effects of entry into day care. The major short-term effects of entry into high-quality day care (assessed with the Q-sort presented in Chap. II) seemed to be not on security of attachment but on interaction with adults other than the mother and on object manipulation. The findings from the second study were more provocative. Children's performance on a joint problem-solving task with mother at 24 months was evaluated in terms of maternal work status and the children's attachment classification at 18 months. In this disadvantaged sample, securely attached children whose mothers had not returned to work by 18 months showed the highest levels of enthusiasm and persistence. Secure and insecure children whose mothers returned to work early (before 12 months) performed more poorly and received scores similar to those of the insecure no-work children. In Chapter V, Dontas, Maratos, Fafoutis, and Karangelis describe 7–9-month-old infants' transition from institutional to maternal care. At Mitera Babies' Center (Athens) adoptive mothers are encouraged to take over their infants' care from a nurse gradually, during a 2-week adaptation period. There is evidence that the infants have begun to form attachments to the adoptive mother before they leave the center. Although the long-term consequences of gradually easing adoptive mothers into their new role are unknown, the short-term effects seem benign in comparison to responses to adoption reported by Yarrow (1967). Chapters VI and VII discuss attempts to predict later patterns of maladaptation from insecure attachment patterns at 12 months. The first study (Erickson, Sroufe, & Egeland) was based on children from disadvantaged families in Minnesota, the second (Bates, Maslin, & Frankel) on children from middle-class two-parent families in Indiana. The Minnesota study reports strong evidence that links insecure attachment at 12 and 18 months with behavior problems in the preschool at 4½–5 years of age (high levels of dependency on adults, poor peer interaction skills, noncompliance, hostility, giving up easily, and withdrawing). In the Indiana study many of the theoretically predicted relationships among maternal interaction variables at 6, 13, and 24 months and Strange Situation classifications at 12 months were obtained. However, a behavior-problem questionnaire filled out by mother and preschool teachers at 3 years bore almost no relation to earlier attachment security. The best predictors of mothers' ratings of behavior problems were earlier maternal perceptions of infant temperament and of infant management problems. A different set of factors (but not security) was related to secondary caregivers' perception of behavior problems. Reasons for the discrepancy between the findings of Chapters VI and VII may be due to the Minnesota mothers' inadequate social support (especially absence of father figures) as well as to the greater stability in their children's attachment patterns (only children classified similarly at 12 and 18 months were included in the study). Chapter VIII considers attachment patterns in maltreating families. Schneider-Rosen, Braunwald, Carlson, and Cicchetti report data on attachment in samples of abused/neglected children at 12, 18, and 24 months. At all three ages, over two-thirds of the infants were classified as insecurely attached in the Strange

Situation, with insecure-avoidant patterns being more frequent at the later ages. The authors discuss these ontogenetic adaptations as precursors for possible maladaptative (in the mental health sense) coping with later developmental tasks. They also discuss possible reasons why some of the abused infants show secure reunion patterns in the Strange Situation. Rather than assuming that some infants are invulnerable, the authors propose a transactional model in which patterns of attachment are seen as the outcome of many enduring and transient compensatory and potentiating factors. In the concluding chapter of Part 3, Ricks considers the intergenerational transmission of parental behavior. Two major domains of study are reviewed, effects of separation and disruption in the family of origin and parental acceptance as related to secure attachment in the next generation. Studies reviewed by Ricks show that parents who idealized their own rejecting parent were likely to have insecurely attached children. By contrast, parents who were able to forgive a rejecting parent and/or to speak coherently about an unhappy childhood tended to have securely attached children.

The processes underlying continuities in adaptation from infancy to childhood and from one generation to the next are likely to be representational: the internal working model that an individual constructs of self and attachment figures becomes part of the personality structure and thus influences later relationships. In most cases, the effect is adaptive in the developmental mental health sense. In some cases the effect is disastrous. However, in some of these disastrous cases, reorganization in the internal model of the relationship may break the intergenerational cycle. Thus attachment theory comes to conclusions very similar to those of recent psychoanalytic thinking (see Fraiberg et al., 1975).

I. B.

IV. THE IMPACT OF OUT-OF-HOME CARE ON CHILD-MOTHER ATTACHMENT QUALITY: ANOTHER LOOK AT SOME ENDURING QUESTIONS

BRIAN E. VAUGHN

University of Illinois at Chicago

KATHLEEN E. DEANE
EVERETT WATERS

State University of New York at Stony Brook

Over the past 30 years there has been a dramatic increase in the employment of mothers outside the home. Hoffman (1979) cited statistics compiled by the Department of Commerce indicating that more than one-third of all women in the United States with children under 3 years of age were working on at least a part-time basis. By 1990 this figure is estimated to increase to 75% of mothers with young children (Urban Institute, 1980 [cited in Belsky, Steinberg, & Walker, 1982]). The large-scale entry of mothers into the work force has helped focus a strong research interest on potential effects of nonmaternal, out-of-home care on the intellectual and emotional development of these infants and young children (see reviews by Belsky & Steinberg, 1978; Clarke-Stewart & Fein, 1983; Rutter, 1981). With respect to cognitive growth, there is a current consensus that no deleterious (or enhancing) effects can be directly attributed to out-of-home care per se

The research reported here was supported in part by a Biomedical Research Support Grant from the Campus Research Board, University of Illinois at Chicago, to Brian E. Vaughn. The authors also acknowledge the gracious help of the parents, teachers, and staff of the Stony Brook Nursery School and the Chicago Circle Children's Center, from which the subjects of Study 1 were drawn. Data for Study 2 were provided by Byron Egeland from the Minnesota Mother-Infant Interaction Project, which has been supported by grant MC-R-274016-01-0 from the Maternal and Child Health Service of the Department of Health, Education and Welfare.

(Belsky & Steinberg, 1978; Gunnarson, 1978; Kagan, Kearsley, & Zelazo, 1978). However, research on the emotional development of very young children in out-of-home care has yielded more controversial (and often contradictory) results; consequently, no widely accepted consensus has emerged (see Rutter, 1981).

Though the available data do not support the pessimistic speculations of some child welfare experts from the 1950s (e.g., Baers, 1954) concerning the emotional development of young children whose mothers are working, over the past decade several researchers have reported results suggesting that infants and young children in out-of-home day care may be at greater risk for problems associated with infant-mother attachment than are comparable groups of children who do not enter day care for the first 2–3 years of life (e.g., Blehar, 1974; Schwartz, 1983; Schwarz, Strickland, & Krolick, 1974; Vaughn, Gove, & Egeland, 1980). The question of a relationship between day-care experience and quality of the child-mother attachment was first addressed by Blehar (1974), who compared the behavior of young children (24 or 36 months) who had recently started day care to that of home-reared children, using Ainsworth's Strange Situation procedure (see Ainsworth et al., 1978). She reported that day-care children were more likely than home-reared children to exhibit behavior during the reunion episodes of the Strange Situation characteristic of infants described as "insecurely attached" (Ainsworth et al., 1978). Blehar concluded that the routine daily separations occasioned by day care could lead to anxiously toned attachments in 2- and 3-year-old children. She further suggested that the style of reunion behavior characteristic of her younger day-care group (i.e., avoidance of the mother at reunion) was indicative of a more profound effect on attachment quality than was the case for the 3-year-olds who tended to appear angry with their mothers at the reunions.

Not surprisingly, the Blehar (1974) study proved to be very controversial, and many attempts at replication were subsequently published (e.g., Brookhart & Hock, 1976; Doyle, 1975; Moskowitz, Schwarz, & Corsini, 1977; Portnoy & Simmons, 1978; Ragozin, 1980). Although none of the replication studies reproduced Blehar's procedures and measurements exactly, in each the child's responses to separation from and reunion with the mother were observed. In most of the studies, some behavioral differences between the day-care and the home-care groups were found. However, none reported significant differences relevant to attachment quality. The results of these replication attempts prompted several reviewers (e.g., Belsky & Steinberg, 1978; Clarke-Stewart & Fein, 1983; Rutter, 1981) to offer qualified conclusions that the effects of day care on the attachment quality of 2- and 3-year-old children may have been exaggerated.

While there is a qualified consensus that out-of-home care has only minor effects on the attachment behavior of 2- and 3-year-olds, an increasing number of infants and younger toddlers are being placed in out-of-home care, and data relevant to the attachment quality of these very young children are only beginning to accumulate (e.g., Farber & Egeland, 1982; Kagan et al., 1978; Schwartz, 1983; Vaughn et al., 1980). Interestingly, two of these recent studies (i.e., Schwartz, 1983; Vaughn et al., 1980) have used and scored the Strange Situation procedure in the same manner as Blehar (1974) did in her original study. In both studies, infants starting out-of-home care prior to their first birthdays were more likely to show avoidance of their mothers in the reunion episodes of the Strange Situation than were home-reared controls. These results stand in contrast (with Blehar's original study) to the bulk of the literature describing effects of out-of-home care on child-mother attachment. In order to reconcile these differences and to place them in appropriate perspective, it is necessary to digress briefly from the issues surrounding day care per se and to discuss the currently accepted uses and limitations of the Ainsworth Strange Situation.

Methodological Issues in the Assessment of Attachment Quality

Attachment quality versus attachment behavior.—Ever since Ainsworth and Wittig (1969) presented their standardized procedure for eliciting patterns of attachment behavior of 12-month-old infants in response to a mildly (but cumulatively) stressful experience, the Strange Situation (or some variant of the procedure) has become the single most widely used technique for studying the social attachments of infants and toddlers. A large body of literature has shown that the classifications of attachment quality derived from the procedure have substantial concurrent and predictive validity (see Ainsworth et al., 1978; Joffe & Vaughn, 1982; Waters & Sroufe, 1983). As a result of the demonstrated utility of the Strange Situation classifications and ratings, the procedure has become de facto *the* attachment situation.

Age-appropriate assessment.—Although the ethological-organizational viewpoint has proven itself in the arena of competing ideas (see Joffe & Vaughn, 1982; Waters & Sroufe, 1983), it would be incorrect to assume that all the important questions regarding attachment formation, maintenance, and assessment have been resolved. For example, though the Strange Situation procedure has been shown to yield stable assessments of attachment quality over the late infancy period (e.g., Main & Weston, 1981; Vaughn et al., 1979; Waters, 1978), there are neither reliability nor validity data for the procedure when it is used with children over the age of 20 months. Research on older children's responses to brief separations (e.g., Maccoby & Feldman, 1972; Marvin, 1972) suggests that, by 24 months of age, such separations are not especially distressing. Since it is assumed that the Strange Situation allows for observation of the organization of attachment behavior while the infant is under stress, these data suggest that the procedure may not allow for valid assessments of attachment quality in older children. At the very least, it seems that the criteria for assigning subjects to one of the three classification groups should be modified for children older than about 20 months. This limitation on the interpretation of older toddler's responses in the Strange Situation has prompted at least one research team to seek an alternative method for measuring attachment security for children over 20 months of age (Waters & Deane, in this vol.).

The issue of age-appropriate assessment is very important for the interpretation of the results from many of the out-of-home care effects studies because the majority of such studies (e.g., Blehar, 1974; Moskowitz et al., 1977; Portnoy & Simmons, 1978; Roopnarine & Lamb, 1978) used as subjects children older than 20 months. The Strange Situation behavior of the children in these studies may well be of only limited use for evaluating individual differences in attachment quality.

Standardized assessment.—In addition to the limitations of children's age, further reservations concerning interpretation of Strange Situation behaviors must be made when the procedure is substantially altered. For example, Waters et al. (1979) were unable to discriminate between anxious/avoidant and anxious/resistant infants when responses to only one separation and reunion were observed (secure infants were, however, adequately distinguished). In other studies (e.g., Brookhart & Hock, 1976; Cochran, 1977), the separation-reunion sequences have been done in the homes of the subjects. Since infants are not expected to experience distress due to brief separations from their caregivers in the familiar environment of the home, it should come as no surprise that such observations offer little or no insight into the organization of the infants' attachment behaviors.

Unfortunately, many of the studies on the effects of out-of-home care (e.g., Kagan et al., 1978) have significantly modified the Strange Situation procedure. Further, instead of using the qualitative behavioral ratings and/or the classifications of attachment quality developed by Ainsworth and her associates, most of the studies have compared day-care to home-reared children in terms of the frequencies of specific behaviors (e.g., Cummings, 1980; Farran & Ramey, 1977; Kagan et al., 1978; Ragozin, 1980; Ricciuti, 1974). Since psychometrically unreliable data (see Masters & Wellman, 1974; Waters, 1978) are unlikely to be valid, the results of these studies probably do not reflect on the individual differences construct of attachment articulated by Ainsworth (e.g., Ainsworth et al., 1978). Consequently, even those studies whose subjects were in the age range more appropriate for the Strange Situation procedure (e.g., Brookhart & Hock, 1976; Doyle, 1975; Kagan et al., 1978; Ricciuti, 1974) have been compromised by the use of assessments with unknown validity. Interestingly, when the standard Strange Situation procedure, the interactive scales, and the classification criteria have been employed at appropriate ages (e.g., Schwartz, 1983; Vaughn et al., 1980), significant and interpretable effects of out-of-home care on attachment quality have been reported.

Methodological Limitations in Day-Care Studies

Selection of comparison groups.—In addition to the general methodological problems associated with using nonstandard assessments at ages for which even the standard Strange Situation procedure has not been validated, most of the presently available research on day-care effects is limited by the use of between-group designs (i.e., comparisons of "treatment" groups with home-reared control children). By implication, home-reared and day-care samples are assumed to be comparable on most demographic and psychological characteristics save the out-of-home care experience. Observed differences between groups are then attributed to rearing condition. Unfortunately, when data testing the assumption of group equivalence are gathered (e.g., Hock, 1980; Roopnarine & Lamb, 1978; Vaughn et al., 1980), differences between the groups prior to "treatment" have often been reported. Thus much of what we presently believe about the impact of day-care experience on attachment comes from studies using nonequivalent control group designs.

Range of assessments.—Most studies of attachment and out-of-home care have assessed the effects in terms of Strange Situation classifications, ratings of a limited range of interactive behaviors either in the procedure itself or in a similar context, or frequencies of a few specific behaviors in brief laboratory observations (e.g., Blehar, 1974; Cummings, 1980; Ragozin, 1980; Schwartz, 1983). Any of these represents a relatively narrow range of assessment on a topic with such broad implications. Classification as secure or anxious in the Strange Situation is surely one significant and well-validated approach to studying the impact of out-of-home care on attachment quality; however, the Strange Situation classifications (i.e., secure, avoidant, resistant) are highly specific to a single dimension of individual differences in infant-parent relationships. If the day-care experience had significant effects on dependency, sociability, or specific areas of interactive or exploratory behavior but not on security, these would be overlooked in a study employing only the Strange Situation. Additionally, the avoidant/secure/resistant (A, B, C) categories yield unequal marginal distributions, and effects large enough to be extremely important, in view of the number of infants/children who might be affected, could, nonetheless, be too small to be statistically significant in samples of 30–60 subjects.

Assessment in terms of specific behaviors, especially distress and exploratory behavior, can be broader than emphasis on security alone, but it also introduces a variety of problems. First, while it may be of interest to know whether out-of-home care has any effects at all, the issue for public policy is whether it poses risks or offers any advantages over the longer term. That is, significant effects are not enough; they need to be interpretable. Unfortunately, single categories of behavior (based on time-sampling procedures) used in the research on day care have not been independently validated as correlates or predictors of problems in any domain of social/ emotional development. Of course, even in the absence of external validation, some effects might justify caution, or encouragement, if assessments occur in ecologically valid contexts and could be evaluated with reference to other types of assessment. For the most part, these conditions have not been met in day-care research (though see Clarke-Stewart, 1982, for changes in the status quo).

Summary of Limitations for Attachment/Day-Care Studies

The preceding discussion suggests that many of the questions concerning effects of out-of-home care on individual differences in attachment quality for children over 24 months of age cannot be resolved given the available empirical data. Indeed, we speculate that most of the data are irrelevant to issues derived from the ethological-organizational perspective in early emotional bonds (and associated individual differences). In brief, this area of research is plagued by problems associated with inadequate measurement (e.g., Blehar, 1974; Kagan et al., 1978; Ragozin, 1980), with nonequivalent control groups, and with a limited range of assessments in restricted ecological contexts (e.g., Blehar, 1974; Cochran, 1977; Doyle, 1975). Finally, only a very limited number of studies afford the opportunity to evaluate possible changes in attachment quality or attachment relevant behaviors that might be associated with entry into out-of-home care (e.g., Roopnarine & Lamb, 1978; Vaughn et al., 1980).

Research Strategies for Evaluating Effects of Out-of-Home Care

Having argued at some length that most of the presently available data on day care and attachment quality are not adequate to address questions derived from the ethological-organizational perspective, we feel obliged to present alternative research designs and data analytic strategies. In the remaining sections of this chapter we present the results of two studies that illustrate these alternative approaches. Study 1 describes behavioral changes associated with entry into a high-quality, part-time nursery school program in a sample of 10 24- to 36-month-old boys. A major purpose of this study was to establish the feasibility of a within-subjects, home observational design that other researchers could employ in a wide range of (larger) samples, ages, and out-of-home care experiences. Study 2 presents a reanalysis of data originally published by Farber and Egeland (1982). Farber and Egeland followed longitudinally the three groups of subjects originally described by Vaughn et al. (1980) and compared their performances in a set of problem-solving tasks when the children reached 24 months of age. Consistent with Vaughn et al. (who did not report significant differences in the proportions of securely and anxiously attached infants across their out-of-home care and home-care groups), Farber and Egeland found only a few 24-month variables to discriminate among the home-reared and the out-of-home care groups. Study 2 follows up on the results reported by Farber and Egeland by analyzing the 24-month variables within each of the work-status groups.

Both Study 1 and Study 2 are presented primarily as illustrations of what we believe to be appropriate strategies, from both design and data analytic standpoints, for examining the potential impact of out-of-home care on attachment quality. Both studies have particular theoretical and methodological advantages and limitations and, for these reasons, serve our illustrative purpose well. However, neither study is presented to demonstrate conclusively effects (or the absence of same) of out-of-home care on attachment quality. Study 1 employs a within-subjects design to examine both the immediate (i.e., during the first 2 weeks after entrance into nursery school) and the longer-term (i.e., 2–3 months postentry) effects on a wide range of attachment and other behaviors. Since the subjects are beyond the age at which the Strange Situation has been validated, all attachment data come from extended home observations followed by completion of the Attachment in Infancy Q-set (Waters & Deane, in this vol.). Generalizations from Study 1 are limited as a result of the relatively small sample size and gender bias (all subjects are boys) and by the fact that the subjects are drawn from a high-quality, university-sponsored program. The emphasis in Study 2 is on sequelae of infant-mother attachment. The attachment assessments for subjects in this study were done at appropriate ages, and the measures selected for analysis here were chosen because they have been shown to be predictable from earlier attachment quality (e.g., Gove, 1982; Matas et al., 1978). At issue in this study is whether the expectable continuity of adaptation from attachment security to the emergence of autonomy by the end of the second year (see Sroufe, 1979; Waters & Sroufe, 1983) is changed for children receiving out-of-home care. The primary limitations on Study 2 concern the nature of the sample. These children are from a larger sample believed to be at "social risk" (Egeland, Deinard, & Sroufe, 1977), and some of them have had less than optimal out-of-home care experiences (see Vaughn et al., 1980); consequently, these groups are not representative of many infants/toddlers in out-of-home care. Despite these limitations, we believe that both studies presented here do serve as effective illustrations of the types of research that is required before firm and generalizable conclusions about the effects of out-of-home care can be made.

STUDY 1

Method

Subjects

The subjects in the study were 10 males from intact middle-class families. The mean age of the subjects at the first assessment was 2-5 (range 2-3–2-10). All the children's fathers were in graduate school or employed; one mother lived on campus and attended graduate school, and none of the mothers had undertaken full-time employment since the child's birth.

Preschool Program

The subjects were registered for a preschool program organized by the Developmental Psychology Program at the State University of New York at Stony Brook. The program consists of four classes, two for older toddlers and two for 3-year-olds. The program is staffed by a doctoral level developmental psychologist, four certified preschool education teachers, and student aides. Three children in the study attended the program three times a week for 2¾ hours; seven attended twice a week for the same period. Nine of the subjects attended older toddler classes; one attended a 3-year-old class. Between 10 and 14 children were enrolled in each class. The adult/child ratio averaged 1:4.

The curriculum implemented in each class divided the day into directed instruction, child-initiated activities, and free play. Teachers and aides encouraged each child to remain constructively occupied; they assisted when asked or where appropriate; and they commented and encouraged prosocial interaction during these activities. The classroom teachers employed verbal instruction and occasional time-out to control disruptive behavior.

Measures

The behavior of each subject was assessed in terms of the attachment behavior Q-set described by Waters and Deane (in this vol.). The Q-set consists of 100 items that assess the attachment, exploration, and related behavior in the home and other naturalistic settings. Unlike many Q-sets, the items refer more specifically to behavior than to trait constructs. Each

117

item consists of a brief descriptive title and a specification of relevant behaviors and contexts. The content of the item set can be summarized as covering eight domains: attachment-exploration balance, response to comforting, affect, social interaction, social perception, object manipulation, dependency, and endurance. The Q-set has been used successfully with children aged 12 months to 4 years. Observer agreement and agreement between observers and parent Q-sorts have consistently ranged between .6 and .9 for each child observed, and the items have been judged equally applicable to assessment with either parent.

Design

Q-sort descriptions were obtained for each child at three different points in time. The first observations occurred within the month prior to the child's first preschool attendance. The second observations (made independently by new observers) occurred during the first 2 weeks in which the child attended preschool. The third round of observations (again made independently by a different pair of observers) took place after 10–12 weeks of preschool attendance. The observation schedule was arranged to insure that the three assessments of each child were conducted blindly and that each observer contributed approximately equal numbers of Time 1, Time 2, and Time 3 observations.

Procedure

Q-sort descriptions of each subject were provided by two observers at each of the three assessments. Each observer made two 3–4-hour visits to the subject's home on the following schedule: Observer 1 visited once; Observer 1 and Observer 2 made a joint visit; and Observer 2 made a second visit. The purpose of this schedule was to insure that the Q-sort data reflected behavior over more than a single day and to minimize the effects of individual observer characteristics on the data. During each visit the observer(s) sat quietly in the home, responded but did not initiate interaction with the child, and encouraged the mother not to adjust her schedule or activities because of the visit. The observers accompanied the mother and child on any excursions from the home. The observers were instructed not to discuss their observations with each other. The purpose of the joint visit was to enable the person who had previously visited the family to introduce the second observer. This kind of transition from one observer to the other significantly reduces the imposition that introduction of six different observers might otherwise involve.

The observers described each subject by sorting the 100 Q-set items into nine piles, from most characteristic to least characteristic. The number of items placed in each pile conformed to a standard distribution (5, 8, 12, 16, 18, 16, 12, 8, 5). Items in the most-characteristic pile were assigned a score of +4; items in adjacent piles were less characteristic of the subject and were assigned scores of +3, +2, and +1. Items in the center pile were neither characteristic nor uncharacteristic of the subject and were scored 0. The 16, 12, 8, and 5 items in the adjacent piles were scored −1, −2, −3, and −4. The five items scored −4 were most uncharacteristic of the child in question. The two observers' scores on each item were averaged for the analyses presented below. The reliability of the averaged Q-sort descriptions of each subject was computed by correlating the sets of scores assigned by the two sorters and applying the Spearman-Brown formula. The mean reliability across all the assessments was .82.

Results and Discussion

The effects of day-care attendance on attachment and related behavior were assessed by performing pairwise t test comparisons between the mean scores for each item (Time 1 vs. Time 2; Time 2 vs. Time 3; and Time 1 vs. Time 3). While this procedure seems appropriate in order to maximize statistical power in a small sample and in the context of a demonstration project in a sample where very few large effects were expected, MANOVAs, ANOVAs, and more conservative post hoc tests would presumably be employed in research designed to test substantive effects in larger samples. In addition, Waters & Deane (in this vol.) describe a number of other analytic strategies that can be applied to Q-sort data in larger samples. The items for which comparisons across time periods reached a $p < .10$ criterion are presented in Table 1.

Twenty-nine out of the 100 items showed significant effects across at least one of the time intervals. Since this analysis involved a large number of items and a large number of statistical tests, the items showing significant effects were organized according to the content areas mentioned above in the description of the Q-set. Not only does this serve to summarize the results, but it also enables us to determine whether the significant effects are randomly distributed throughout the item set, as might be expected if the results were due to chance.

In brief, the most evident effects of day-care attendance occurred during the first weeks of adjustment to out-of-home care. The majority of the effects were on items related to object manipulation and social interaction. The children learned a wide variety of new activities during their first weeks in day care, and the parents allowed them to practice and share these activities at home. As a result, a greater proportion of the child's time was devoted

TABLE 1

Attachment Q-Set Items Showing Changes over Time

Content Areas	Item Means			Probability Levels		
	Time 1	Time 2	Time 3	Time 1 vs. Time 2	Time 2 vs. Time 3	Time 1 vs. Time 3
Object manipulation:[a]						
Babbles or talks when playing alone	1.2	.3	1.5	.05	.02	...
Gross motor control is smooth and coordinated	2.0	2.8	2.0	.05	.04	...
Prefers realistic play	1.7	.4	.6	.07	...	...
Is attracted to novelty rather than familiarity	.4	1.7	.8	.00	.07	...
Is creative with objects or social roles in play	.2	.1	1.0	...	.06	...
Fine motor manipulation is skillful	1.0	2.5	2.2	.00	...	.01
Combines several objects in play	-.01	.7	1.0	...	...	.08
Social interaction:[b]						
Approaches adult to interact	1.5	2.3	1.5	.07	.09	...
Prefers female adults	.1	.3	-.3	...	.08	...
Shares willingly	2.1	2.2	1.1	...	.06	.06
Is indifferent to observer's invitations to play	2.8	-1.3	-1.1	.02	...	.05
Initiates interaction with familiarized adults	2.8	1.4	2.0	.03	...	...
Imitates adult's behavior	1.5	.5	.9	.02	...	...
Child's observations and requests are often difficult to understand	.5	-.4	-.9	...	...	.05
Endurance:[c]						
Sleeps on a regular schedule	.9	-.2	-.8	.04	...	...
Sleeps lightly	-.5	-.05	-.2	.07	...	...

Dependency:[d]					
Cries to prevent separation	.0	-.8	-.7	.05	...	...
Is independent with most adults	2.3	1.8	1.5	...	...	.06
Rarely asks for help	-.3	.4	-.9	...	.05	...
Accepts adult's attention to others	1.3	1.5	.4	...	.04	.06
Social perception:[e]					
Is responsive to distress in adults	-.6	-.2	.3	.10	...	...
Expects adult will be unresponsive	-2.4	-1.2	-1.4	.05	...	...
Response to comforting:[f]					
Is bolder and more confident to play when adult is nearby	-.6	.2	-.4	.10	...	...
Accepts adult's assurances when wary in unfamiliar settings	.5	.7	.2	...	.04	...
Attachment/exploration balance:[g]					
Bouts of exploration and play away from the adult are brief	-1.3	-.09	-.4	...	...	.10
Proximity/exploration cycles are evident in ½–1-hour observations	1.4	.7	.4	...	...	.04
Affect:[h]					
Laughs easily with observer	2.6	1.5	1.8	.02	...	.07
Easily distracted from distress	.9	.1	1.1	...	.03	...
Is not wary of new objects	-.2	.7	.5	.05	...	.04

[a] Seven out of 14 items (50%) show significant changes in at least one test.
[b] Seven out of 18 items (40%) show significant changes in at least one test.
[c] Two out of six items (33%) show significant changes in at least one test.
[d] Four out of 14 items (28%) show significant changes in at least one test.
[e] Two out of eight items (25%) show significant changes in at least one test.
[f] Two out of nine items (22%) show significant changes in at least one test.
[g] Two out of twelve items (18%) show significant changes in at least one test.
[h] Three out of 19 items (15%) show significant changes in at least one test.

to object play immediately after preschool attendance than it was in the weeks before (e.g., 46, 49, 59, 99, 100). Most of the increase in the children's approach to adults from Time 1 to Time 2 (e.g., 5, 21, 91) was judged to arise from approaches to show, share, or ask for help from the observer at Time 2. Most of these effects returned to the pre-preschool level after 10–12 weeks of adaptation to out-of-home care. The decrease in sharing and reduced interest in observers' invitations to play are more likely to reflect repeated exposure to the observers than any negative effect on social interaction per se.

There were very few effects on items most obviously related to the child's attachment relationship with the mother. There was some evidence of minor sleep disruption during the first weeks of preschool (60, 67), but this recovered. Although the duration of exploration away from the mother increased (12, 24), there were no negative effects on items that would imply negative effects on the security of the attachment relationship (e.g., easily becomes angry at the parent). There were no negative effects on responses to comforting or affect during interaction with the mother after 10–12 weeks of adaptation to preschool. This summary indicates that the major effects of out-of-home care in this sample were on exploratory behavior and social interaction with adults other than the mother. It also indicates that the effects were not randomly distributed across content areas, as might be expected if they were merely artifacts of the large number of items and statistical tests. Thus short-term effects on exploratory behavior and social interaction and an absence of effects on attachment behavior may well represent generalizable findings for similar samples in similar day care.

The importance of this research lies in demonstrating the feasibility of within-subjects home observational designs for research on day care and attachment. This study highlights the importance of assessing both immediate and longer-term effects of out-of-home care and the importance and feasibility of assessing a wide range of behaviors across several contexts. While Q-sort data are not equivalent to direct observation and time sampling of specific categories of behavior, Q-sort data can afford economical research designed to indicate what the answers to important questions will be like and how resources should be deployed in more detailed observational studies.

STUDY 2

As with Study 1, the analyses of the following study were not initiated in order to establish widely generalizable effects of out-of-home care. The heterogeneity of day-care experiences for this sample effectively precludes such generalization. Rather this study was conceived and presented as an illustration of how a knowledge of infant-parent attachment histories can help in the interpretation and explanation of day-care effects when these are found.

Method

Subjects

The subjects for this study were 90 mothers and their 24-month-old children, who represent all the original 104 mother-child pairs from the Vaughn et al. (1980) study returning for testing at 24 months of age. In the original study, groups had been formed on the basis of the infant's age at the time the mother returned to work/school and placed him or her in out-of-home care (an "early work" group placed prior to 12 months, a "late-work" group placed between 12 and 18 months, and a "no-work" group receiving in-home care by the mother through the first 18 months of life). Of 34 early work, 18 late-work, and 52 no-work subjects, 32, 17, and 41, respectively,[1] were seen again at 24 months of age. Data collected during the first year of the larger longitudinal project (Egeland et al., 1977) were used to evaluate the possibility that mothers returning to work/school prior to the infant's 18-month anniversary were in some way demographically or psychologically different from mothers of infants not using out-of-home care. There were few meaningful or significant differences between the three groups, with the single exception that mothers using out-of-home care were less likely than mothers who did not use such care were to have the support of an adult male living in the household.

Infant care in the work groups was most frequently provided by an adult female, often a relative or friend of the infant's mother in the other person's home. Vaughn et al. (1980) noted that changes in the care arrangements were common, with at least 80% of the subjects experiencing a change in the substitute caregiver. Though the care arrangements were varied, and changes in such arrangements were common, they suggested that such arrangements typified the out-of-home care settings most often used by lower socioeconomic status populations.

Measures

Attachment assessments.—All the infants were observed at both 12 and 18 months in the Ainsworth Strange Situation. All the 12-month Strange Situa-

[1] An additional five child-mother pairs from the no-work group were tested at 24 months, but the infant had been placed in an out-of-home setting between 18 and 24 months. Data from these pairs were not analyzed for this report.

123

tion procedures were videotaped and coded at a later point in time by two coders working independently; two additional coders independently classified the infants at 18 months. Rater agreement for the classifications (i.e., secure, anxious/avoidant, and anxious/resistant) was 89% at 12 months and 94% at 18 months. All coding of the Strange Situations was done without knowledge of the mothers' work status and without knowledge of the present uses of these data.

Compliance and problem solving at 24 months.—When the children reached 24 months of age, the mother-child pair returned to the laboratory for additional assessments following the protocol described by Matas et al. (1978). An initial period of free play (10 mins.) was followed by a compliance task (mother was asked to have her child pick up and put away all the toys with which he or she had been playing) that lasted for 6 minutes. Two global measures were rated from this task, a rating of the mother's effectiveness in setting limits and structuring the setting for the child and a rating describing the overall experience of the child during the task. Immediately following the cleanup task, the experimenter introduced a set of problem-solving tasks. A series of four "tool-use" tasks developed by Charlesworth and Fitzpatrick (1979) and modified for the present purpose by Matas et al. (1978) were used as the "problems" requiring solution. As each task was brought into the room by the experimenter, she instructed the mother to let the child start the task and try to solve it on his or her own and then to "give any help he or she needs" in order to solve the problem successfully.

The first two tasks are known to be well within the difficulty level of an average 24-month-old child (Charlesworth & Fitzpatrick, 1979) and were included in the battery as warm-up items. The remaining two problems consisted of fitting two sticks together end to end to retrieve a prize from a large Plexiglas tube and using a wooden block to weight/balance a lever such that a cup (containing candy pieces) attached to the opposite end of the lever protrudes through a hole in a large Plexiglas box. These two tasks are extremely difficult for 24-month-old children and require the active assistance of the mother in order for the average 24-month-old child to reach a successful solution.

All 24-month compliance and problem-solving procedures were videotaped and coded by independent raters at a later point in time. Coders for the 24-month procedures were blind to the 12- and 18-month Strange Situation classifications. Some of them were aware, unavoidably, of the mother's work status. However, these coders were unaware of the purposes and design of the present study, and we are confident that knowledge of mother's work status had no effect on the frequency counts or ratings made. The behaviors of the children and their mothers observed during the last two problem-solving tasks were coded using a variety of measures (including frequency counts of specific behavioral categories and more global ratings of the qualities of maternal and child behavior) developed by the staff of the longitudinal project (see Egeland et al., 1977). Additionally, these behaviors were rated according to several of the criteria described by Matas et al. (1978). Capsule definitions of the 24-month variables are presented below in Table 2. Looking at Table 2, it can be seen that these variables refer not only to the specific characteristics associated with task performance (e.g., persistence and endurance) but also to the modulation of affect, both with respect to the tasks and with respect to the use of the mother as a resource to help the child solve the problem tasks.

Design

Our initial purpose in this study was to compare the sequelae of individual differences in infant-mother attachment for children experiencing routine daily separations from the mother during that period when primary attachment bonds are thought to be forming and becoming consolidated (Bowlby, 1969/1982b) to sequelae for children reared at home by their mothers. Previous analyses of these data (i.e., Farber & Egeland, 1982) have shown that the 24-month variables do not distinguish among children when they are grouped solely on the basis of mothers' work status; however, those analyses did not group subjects on the basis of attachment classifications.

Our own analyses of these data proceeded in two steps. First, we made comparisons between the children identified as secure and those identified as insecure (i.e., collapsing across the anxious/avoidant and anxious/resistant categories) within each of the three work-status groups. All comparisons made in this first series of analyses used the t test with appropriate degrees of freedom. At the second step in our analyses, we used the 24-month variables found to discriminate between the secure and the insecure children (from step 1) to compare the work groups within attachment classification group. That is, 24-month scores for all securely attached children were compared across the three work-status groups. Then the 24-month scores for all insecurely attached children were compared across work groups. These comparisons were carried out using one-way analyses of variance with a priori contrasts for early work versus no-work and late-work versus no-work groups. Finally, post hoc tests compared scores for the two out-of-home care groups.

---

[2] Though not reported here, separate analyses of the 24-month variables, grouped by 12-month Strange Situation classification, yielded substantial replication of the findings presented in this chapter. The interested reader may contact Brian E. Vaughn (Department of Psychology, University of Illinois at Chicago, Chicago, IL 60680) for details.

TABLE 2

MEANS OF 24-MONTH VARIABLES BY ATTACHMENT CLASSIFICATION AND WORK GROUP

VARIABLE DEFINITION	WORK GROUP	SECURE		INSECURE		t VALUE
		M	SD	M	SD	
		MATERNAL VARIABLES				
1. Directives—total number of task-oriented verbalizations (suggestions, commands, etc.) given by mother during problem-solving tasks	Early	68.8	33.6	53.5	28.7	−1.34
	Late	63.3	52.0	52.3	24.2	−.57
	None	48.4	26.9	59.0	32.0	1.09
	F value	1.89[a]		.18		
2. Rating of maternal effectiveness in organizing and directing the child during the cleanup task	Early	4.3	1.3	4.5	1.1	.52
	Late	3.3	1.3	3.8	1.8	.65
	None	3.9	1.5	3.9	1.3	−.04
	F value	N.S.		N.S.		
3. Summary rating of maternal effectiveness for all problem-solving tasks	Early	2.9	1.0	3.0	1.1	−.35
	Late	2.8	1.0	2.3	1.1	.79
	None	3.4	1.0	2.5	1.0	2.87***
	F value	2.76*[a,b]		1.22		
		CHILD VARIABLES				
1. Bayley MDI from 24-month testing	Early	100.6	16.0	103.6	21.3	−.59
	Late	103.4	12.4	107.4	24.9	−.71
	None	104.9	19.1	97.1	21.6	1.30
	F value	N.S.		N.S.		
2. Total time for problem-solving tasks (mins.)	Early	11.8	6.9	13.4	5.9	.70
	Late	11.3	7.8	11.8	4.6	−.18
	None	9.4	6.0	13.0	4.7	1.90**
	F value	N.S.		N.S.		

			Proportion Scores			
3. Proportion of directives with which child complies	Early	.60	.19	.58	.17	.58
	Late	.65	.24	.59	.20	.52
	None	.66	.23	.56	.21	1.29
	F value[c]	N.S.		N.S.		
4. Proportion of directives opposed by child	Early	.22	.20	.14	.10	1.35*
	Late	.14	.13	.14	.15	.04
	None	.07	.07	.25	.19	-4.59****
	F value[c]	6.32***[a,b]		2.61*[d]		
5. Proportion of directives in which the child says no	Early	.10	.11	.07	.08	.86
	Late	.06	.02	.08	.13	-.46
	None	.05	.10	.11	.13	1.60*
	F value	N.S.		N.S.		
6. Proportion of directives ignored by the child	Early	.19	.11	.24	.19	1.15
	Late	.17	.10	.25	.09	1.69*
	None	.22	.13	.21	.11	.37
	F value	N.S.		N.S.		
			Frequency Variables			
7. Number of times child asks mother to help in the problem-solving tasks	Early	3.1	3.5	4.4	4.2	-.85
	Late	2.0	1.8	7.2	4.6	2.62***
	None	3.3	2.7	6.3	4.9	2.61***
	F value	N.S.		N.S.		
8. Number of times child expresses frustration in the problem-solving tasks	Early	3.5	2.8	5.9	5.5	1.54*
	Late	3.8	5.7	4.6	4.0	-.29
	None	1.4	2.1	6.9	12.2	1.74**
	F value[c]	3.40***[a,b]		.21		
9. Frequency of aggressive behavior directed toward the mother during the problem-solving tasks	Early	.33	.72	.29	.83	.17
	Late	.33	.82	.67	1.1	-.62
	None	.25	.70	.87	1.6	1.80*
	F value	N.S.		N.S.		

TABLE 2 (Continued)

VARIABLE DEFINITION	WORK GROUP	SECURE		INSECURE		t VALUE
		M	SD	M	SD	
10. Number of times child whines during the problem-solving tasks	Early	6.3	5.8	6.7	8.0	-.17
	Late	7.0	10.8	13.6	14.3	-.95
	None	4.3	5.8	11.5	12.8	2.58***
	F value	N.S.		N.S.		
				Rated Variables		
11. Overall positive affect for the problem-solving tasks (lower scores indicate more positive affect)	Early	4.2	1.1	3.9	1.3	.60
	Late	4.0	1.5	4.7	1.0	1.08
	None	3.7	.80	4.9	.92	4.36****
	F value[c]	1.00		3.18[d]		
12. Overall negative affect for the problem-solving tasks (lower scores indicate less negative affect)	Early	4.2	2.0	3.7	1.8	.76
	Late	3.6	1.7	4.4	2.0	1.08
	None	2.7	.90	4.3	2.3	3.08***
	F value[c]	4.90**[a]		0.52		
13. Dependency	Early	3.1	1.9	3.0	1.9	.19
	Late	2.3	1.5	3.8	1.6	2.00**
	None	2.9	1.5	3.5	1.7	1.28
	F value	N.S.		N.S.		
14. Noncompliance with maternal directives during problem-solving tasks	Early	3.9	1.5	3.4	1.5	.96
	Late	2.8	1.5	3.3	1.4	-.83
	None	2.6	1.1	3.8	1.6	-2.73***
	F value[c]	5.38***[a]		.31		
15. Overall level of frustration in problem-solving tasks	Early	3.1	2.0	3.5	2.0	-.62
	Late	2.8	2.2	3.4	1.4	-.78
	None	2.2	1.4	3.3	2.2	2.03**
	F value	N.S.		N.S.		

	Mean	SD	Mean	SD	
16. Persistence in problem-solving tasks					
Early	2.4	1.1	2.8	1.1	-.96
Late	3.5	1.1	3.0	1.2	.89
None	3.4	1.0	2.4	1.0	3.06***
F value[c]	4.57**[a]		.97		
17. Child's capacity to cope with the problem-solving tasks					
Early	3.5	1.7	3.5	.00	...
Late	4.8	1.5	3.1	1.7	2.11**
None	4.3	1.7	3.2	1.6	1.88**
F value	N.S.		N.S.		
18. Child's enthusiasm toward the problem-solving tasks					
Early	7.1	2.8	7.3	2.4	-.16
Late	8.5	2.7	7.6	2.2	.74
None	9.4	2.2	7.7	2.5	2.44***
F value[c]	4.25**[a]		.12		
19. Anger shown during the problem-solving tasks					
Early	2.4	1.5	3.1	1.6	-1.27
Late	2.6	1.9	3.4	1.7	-.96
None	2.0	1.4	3.2	2.0	-2.05**
F value	N.S.		N.S.		
20. Summary profile based on rating scales (dependency to enthusiasm, lower scores are more optimal)					
Early	2.9	1.2	3.0	1.0	-.34
Late	2.2	1.5	3.2	3.6	-1.60*
None	2.1	1.0	3.2	.9	3.22***
F value[c]	2.04[a]		.83		
21. Summary rating of the child for all problem-solving tasks					
Early	2.9	1.2	3.5	1.0	-1.54*
Late	3.6	1.2	2.9	1.3	1.23
None	3.9	1.1	2.8	1.2	3.72****
F value[c]	4.56**[a]		1.61[d]		

RATINGS OF MOTHER-CHILD INTERACTION

	Mean	SD	Mean	SD	
1. Mother-child interaction in the cleanup session					
Early	3.8	1.3	3.5	1.3	.56
Late	3.0	1.3	2.9	1.4	.09
None	3.3	1.0	2.9	1.4	1.24
F value	N.S.		N.S.		

TABLE 2 (Continued)

VARIABLE DEFINITION	WORK GROUP	SECURE		INSECURE		
		M	SD	M	SD	t VALUE
		RATINGS OF MOTHER-CHILD INTERACTION				
2. Overall quality of interaction during the problem-solving tasks	Early	3.2	.8	3.2	.9	.00
	Late	2.9	1.3	2.6	1.3	.51
	None	3.6	.9	2.5	1.1	3.67****
	F value[c]	2.20[b]		1.72[d]		

NOTE.—One-tailed tests used to evaluate significance of t values.

[a] No-work group significantly different from early work group on post hoc tests at $p < .10$.

[b] No-work group significantly different from late-work group on post hoc tests at $p < .10$.

[c] Interaction significant at $p < .10$ for 3 (work group) × 2 (attachment) ANOVA.

[d] Early work group significantly different from no-work group on post hoc tests at $p < .10$.

* $p < .10$.

** $p < .05$.

*** $p < .01$.

**** $p < .001$.

Results and Discussion

The children were classified as securely or insecurely attached on the basis of their 18-month Strange Situation assessments.[2] The means for the secure and insecure children within each work group and the results of the *t* tests for the individual 24-month variables are presented in Table 2.

Within-work-group differences.—The results presented in Table 2 are both dramatic and provocative. Of 25 separate comparisons between the secure and the insecure children, none reached the .05 probability level for subjects in the early work group, suggesting the possibility that changes in the quality of the child-parent relationship had occurred between 18 and 24 months. Neither maternal nor child behaviors distinguished between the (formerly) secure and insecure children from this work group. Further, three of the four categories showing a trend toward significant differences actually favored the insecure children. That is, children identified as secure at the 18-month assessment exhibited more oppositional behaviors in the face of maternal directives (from mothers who gave more of such directives) than did the children previously identified as insecure. Consistent with these behavioral differences, the formerly secure children were also rated as having had a less optimal experience during the problem-solving tasks than the insecure children. Though the magnitude of the differences here is not large, these results stand in contrast both to the normative data with these procedures (Matas et al., 1978) and to the results of the other two work-status groups.

In the late-work group, five tests yielded significant differences ($p <$ .10). Securely attached children in this group ignored a smaller proportion of maternal directions, asked for mother's help less frequently, and were rated as less dependent on their mothers and as better able to cope with the stresses of the problem-solving tasks. Finally, the summary profile scores were significantly lower (more optimal) for the securely than for the insecurely attached children from this group. Though only a few of the comparisons yielded significant differences in this work-status group, we note that the number of subjects is relatively small and that greater mean differences were required to reach significance than in either of the other work-status groups. Unlike the early work group, the few differences found in this work-status group are consistent with the notion of continuity in adaptation proposed by Matas et al. (1978).

Contrary to the results for the early- and late-work groups, the analyses within the no-work group yielded numerous significant differences between children identified as securely versus insecurely attached. In this group, secure children were less likely than insecure children to behave in an oppositional way, to say no, to whine, or to display frustration behaviors in the face of maternal directives. In addition, the secure children were less likely than their insecure counterparts to ask for mother's help. These securely attached children were rated as more persistent, as better able to cope with the stress of the problem-solving procedure, as showing more positive affect (and less negative affect) during the procedures, and as being more enthusiastic in approaching the problems. Further, the secure children were rated as less noncompliant, frustrated, and angry than the insecure children were. Finally, mothers of securely attached children were rated as being better able to structure and control the situation for the child. Probably as a result of both child and mother characteristics, children identified as secure received more optimal ratings for the quality of the "experience," and they tended to complete the series of tasks in less time than the insecure children in this work-status group did.

Between-group differences within attachment classifications.—The results reported above indicate that there were few significant or meaningful sequelae of attachment quality for the children in the early- and late-work status groups. One possible interpretation of these results is that the effects of out-of-home care are seen only for insecurely attached children, whose scores on the 24-month variables improve relative to what might have been expected had these insecure children received no "treatment," thus attenuating differences between the classification groups. This hypothesis was tested by contrasting the three work-status groups within both attachment classification groups (i.e., secure and insecure) for the 20 variables yielding significant group differences in the initial round of t tests.

These results are also presented in Table 2. For the children who had been identified as secure at 18 months, eight of the ANOVAs and a priori contrasts proved to be significant. In all cases, the direction of the difference favored the no-work group, and in all cases, the early work group was found to be significantly different from the no-work group. Secure children from the no-work group were rated as more enthusiastic, especially for the most difficult tool-use task, and were seen as more persistent than the other secure children. They were less frequently oppositional to mother's directives and rated as less noncompliant and negative than the children from the early work group. Mothers of these children were rated as being better able than other mothers to structure the tasks for their children. Very likely as a result of these differences, the children in the no-work group were rated as having had a more positive experience in the problem-solving tasks. Post hoc comparisons between the early- and the late-work groups yielded no significant differences. Overall these analyses suggest that secure attachments were predictive of positive adaptations only for the no-work group.

Similar analyses over the same variable set, with the group of insecurely attached children, yielded only two significant results (favoring the early work group). The pattern of results for the secure and insecure groups

[3] At the suggestion of one reviewer.

suggested the possibility of a significant work group by attachment-category interaction. A supplementary 2×3 factor ANOVA[3] revealed interactions at $p < .10$ for 10 variables (see Table 2, n. c).

The primary purpose of this study was to examine the sequelae of individual differences in infant-mother attachment for children experiencing routine daily separations (occasioned by out-of-home care) during the first 18 months of life. Sroufe (e.g., 1979) has argued persuasively that continuity of adaptation quality over the period from 12 to 24 months is the norm of development, with securely attached infants receiving more optimal scores on the variables measured at 24 months. The data presented in Table 2 suggest that the patterns of continuity characteristic of both middle- and lower-SES groups (Matas et al., 1978; Gove, 1982) are absent in the two work groups studied here. This discontinuity is most clear for the early work group, in which none of the 24-month variables significantly distinguished between formerly secure and insecure children. The mean values on the 24-month variables for the late-work group consistently fell between those for the other two groups and were not usually significantly different from either of them. These results offer compelling evidence that out-of-home care during the period when primary attachments are forming and becoming consolidated is associated with deviations in the expected course of emotional development (as this is assessed by our procedures) for the children in this sample.

While the results of the first set of analyses suggest that children receiving out-of-home care during the first 18 months of life experience discontinuities in emotional development, they cannot directly address questions concerning the effects of out-of-home care on the quality of social/emotional functioning. In our second series of analyses, comparing the three work-status groups within attachment classification, we were able to consider these possible effects. These results clearly indicate that the formerly secure children from the early work group received ratings on the problem-solving tasks that were less optimal than the scores for secure children from the no-work group were, with scores for the children in the late-work group falling between the two extremes. No interpretable differences were found when the three work-status groups were compared for the insecure children.

These data lead to the conclusion that effects of out-of-home care were felt primarily by the formerly secure children in the early work group and to a lesser extent by secure children in the late-work group. By comparison to the secure children from the home-care group, these children showed a deterioration in the quality of adaptation over the period from 18 to 24 months. Indeed, by 24 months the formerly secure children in out-of-home care were no longer distinguishable from the insecure children. These results complement and extend the interpretations offered by Farber and Egeland (1982) for this sample by indicating that relation(s) between attachment and out-of-home care are interactive rather than static over the period from infancy to toddlerhood. The results also highlight the fact that, in this economically disadvantaged sample, optimal adaptations were achieved by the children who were both secure in their attachments and cared for at home during the first 2 years of life.

General Discussion

These two studies suggest several substantive and methodological points. First, they provide evidence that out-of-home care can have both immediate and longer-term effects on the behavior of young children. The results of Study 1 indicate that entry into a high-quality, part-time nursery school program can be associated with immediate changes in young children's behavior observed in the home. Interestingly, the large majority of these behavioral changes are not conceptually related to attachment security. Thus, the data from Study 1 converge with the current consensus regarding effects of out-of-home care on attachment security; that is, such effects are minor and transient. On the other hand, the results of Study 2 suggest that the expectable sequelae of attachment (see Waters & Sroufe, 1983) may be disrupted for out-of-home care children.

This seeming discrepancy between the interpretations of results for the two studies illustrates a second substantive point. That is, the effects of out-of-home care will likely differ depending on the age of the child at the onset of out-of-home care. In Study 2, the effects on attachment sequelae were seen primarily in the early work group (i.e., those infants starting out-of-home care prior to their first birthday). The secure children from the late-work group were not found to be significantly different from the no-work secure children in the 24-month problem-solving tasks. This finding of age-specific effects for out-of-home care is consistent with the results of Schwarz et al. (1974), who reported elevated levels of noncompliance and aggression in preschool children who had been in day care since infancy. This finding is also reminiscent of Blehar's (1974) conclusion that more severe and enduring effects of day care are found in groups starting such care at early ages.[4]

In addition to addressing substantive issues concerning the effects of out-of-home care on the behavior and quality of adaptation of young children, these studies serve to illustrate design and data analytic strategies

---

[4] Though the spirit of our conclusion is consistent with Blehar's in suggesting that early out-of-home care may be associated with later problems in the child-mother relationship, our data do not support her assertion that such care will influence attachment quality (and possibly other domains of functioning) if it is initiated between 2 and 3 years of age. Indeed, those children starting out-of-home care between 12 and 18 months of age were not significantly different from the home-care controls at 24 months.

necessary for appropriate interpretation of the results obtained. In Study 1, a short-term repeated-measures design was used to evaluate changes in the home behavior of young boys entering a regular preschool program for the first time. That significant, meaningful changes in the behavior of these children at home were observed and described in this small sample suggests the feasibility of similar designs in other day-care studies. The results of Study 1 also suggest that the attachment behavior Q-set will be a useful (and age-appropriate) tool for the assessment of individual differences relevant to attachment security for children beyond 20 months of age. Study 2 also illustrates the uses of age-appropriate assessment; however, the defining issues from the 24-month problem-solving tasks are related less to attachment security and more to autonomy and exploration. Though the emergence of autonomy/independence is seen as having a foundation in the attachment relationship (Sroufe, 1979; Waters & Sroufe, 1983), the 24-month tasks are not thought of as attachment assessments per se. Nonetheless, these tasks and measures provide a means of examining the current status of the emotional bond between the 24-month-old and the caregiver, a means that would not be afforded by recording the child's responses in the Strange Situation.

The last point of discussion concerning the results of Study 2 has both methodological and substantive implications for studying the impact of day care. These data suggest that research designs assuming only main effects attributable to treatment condition (out-of-home care experience) will not yield significant results. The results of analyses presented here show that effects of out-of-home care can only be understood when the interaction of attachment history and nonmaternal care experiences are considered together. In this study, no "treatment" effects were found for the children earlier classified as anxiously attached; all groups of anxiously attached children were characterized by somewhat maladaptive behavior in the 24-month tasks. On the other hand, marked "treatment" effects were noted for the secure children, with formerly secure children from the early work group receiving less optimal scores on the 24-month measures than their home-care counterparts did. Unfortunately, the implication drawn from these data must be that the out-of-home care experiences characterizing this sample are not associated with optimal parent-child relationships as the children grow and mature.

V. EARLY SOCIAL DEVELOPMENT IN INSTITUTIONALLY REARED GREEK INFANTS: ATTACHMENT AND PEER INTERACTION

CLEO DONTAS

Corfu General Hospital

OLGA MARATOS

Aghia Children's Hospital

MARIA FAFOUTIS AND ANTIGONE KARANGELIS

Mitera Babies' Center

Normal social development is believed to take place in widely varying ethnic and socioeconomic settings that include most possible permutations of nuclear and extended families (e.g., Whiting & Child, 1953). Several important studies of the 1940s, 1950s, and 1960s (e.g., Goldfarb, 1943; Skodak & Skeels, 1949; Spitz, 1946) concluded, however, that normal personality and cognitive development is adversely affected by rearing in institutional settings. In this chapter we hope to demonstrate that under certain conditions institutionally reared infants *can* develop normally, in the sense that they are able to form attachments to key caregivers and to distinguish familiar from unfamiliar peers. In addition, these infants are capable of forming bonds with new primary caregivers.

The research described here was conducted at the Mitera Babies' Center in Athens. The center has been in operation since 1955. At any one time it houses approximately 100 infants from about the fifth day after birth until placement with adoptive parents or until their natural mothers can take them home. The center's ultimate aim was "to create a system within which

The authors would like to thank Professor Doxiades and the staff of Mitera Babies' Center for their encouragement and cooperation.

children born without families and whose care must be undertaken by some institution or organization might enjoy full, normal development" (Mitera Babies' Center, 1975, p. 8). One of the center's goals was to provide consistent mothering by a limited number of caregivers.

Most of the infants' natural mothers are young and unmarried or living in social circumstances that would make it difficult for them to bring up their infants. The center offers them material and social assistance both before and after giving birth. Although the infants reside in the center from birth, the mothers generally decide within the first 5–6 months whether they will give the babies up for adoption or whether they can manage to raise them on their own. Thus the majority of infants leave the center by 5 or 6 months, but a considerable number remain at Mitera during the second half of the first year. In a few cases, older infants or toddlers (who are hard to place or whose natural parents have not yet been able to settle their future) are eventually placed in foster care or in other institutions. Nearly all the adoptive parents are childless couples in comfortable social and financial circumstances who have undergone a long waiting period and consideration by the social services department. Before the adoptive parents may leave with their new baby, they must spend a 2-week adaptation period at Mitera to give them an opportunity to become accustomed to each other.

From the age of 1 month on (when they leave the newborn unit) infants are brought up in one of eight pavilions with 10–12 other infants. In each pavilion a baby's crib is always in the same spot in one of four cubicles shared with other infants. The nursing staff remains as constant as possible in each of the pavilions and consists of two head nursery nurses and three or four student "nursery nurses"[1] during waking hours. An effort is made to assign infants to the primary care of one nurse for their entire stay. Extremely unresponsive infants are assigned to the exclusive care of one nurse for several weeks. They may even move out of the pavilion during that period.

The relatively limited number of caregivers and peers with whom each infant is brought up and the optimal child-staff ratio means that the infant is not obliged to make continual transitions to new attachment figures, which could lead to a state of detachment and the inability to enter into new loving relationships (Bowlby, 1973). The type of care provided at Mitera can be defined as closer to "multiple mothering" than to traditional institutional care, where all the staff care for all the infants. Most infants observed in the second half of the first year seem comfortable with any of their pavilion

---

[1] The term "nurse" will be used hereafter. In fact, all the caregiving staff have graduated from the 3-year nursery-nurse training course at Mitera, which lays equal emphasis on psychological development, psychometrics, and psychiatry as on more traditional nursing subjects. Graduates are usually employed as day-care teachers if not as nursery nurses at Mitera.

nurses but appear specially attached to one (or two) nurses only. They do not indiscriminately seek affection and toys from strangers or nurses from other pavilions, as do many institution-dwelling infants (Dennis & Najarian, 1957; Spitz, 1946).

One period during which an infant's experience at Mitera may be considered as less than optimal is the first month of life. Newly admitted 5-day-old infants, separated at birth from their natural mothers, reside in the center's newborn unit for about a month before going to their pavilion. It is possible that the early separation, as well as a month-long stay in a quiet and rather unstimulating environment with several caregivers, may not facilitate subsequent dyadic relationships. In fact, one study at Mitera showed that the presence of a sole caregiver from birth on affects infants' performance on one dimension (Organizational Processes: State Control) of the Neonatal Behavioral Assessment Scale as early as 9 days of life (Maratos et al., 1982). It is not clear how this relates to subsequent development or whether deleterious effects may result from such early experiences before infants settle in their pavilion.

Previous research at Mitera on psychomotor development using Illingworth's version of the Gesell Developmental Scales has established that infants brought up at Mitera develop well within the normal age range (Karangelis, 1959). In fact, Mitera infants were precocious in the first trimester. A slight but growing lag in development made its appearance from the fourth trimester on, when the setting at Mitera may no longer be adequate to stimulate continued normal development. Alternatively, it may be that only hard-to-place infants were left at the center. It is also the general opinion of the staff that difficulties in social development, such as a high incidence of insecure attachments, begin to appear in the fourth trimester. Thus efforts are made to have most infants settled in their families by 5 months if possible and by age 1 year at the latest.

When an adoptive family is found for an infant, a 2-week adaptation period is required of the parents. This requirement exists in order to give parents and infants time to become accustomed and attached to each other and to acquaint the parents with the baby's eating, sleeping, and toilet habits. The parents typically arrive at the center when the baby wakes and spend the whole day in the pavilion or gardens. Day by day they assume more of its care. If a harmonious relationship between the new parents and the infant has not developed within that time, the adaptation period is lengthened or the matching of the baby with the specific parents is reconsidered. This 2-week period seems sufficient to ease the parents into their new role, and most 6–12-month-olds seem attached to their new parents by the end of the period.

An infant's stay at Mitera will typically involve close contact with the other children in the pavilion.[2] Unfortunately, there is little information on peer relations among institutionally raised infants, in sharp contrast with the wealth of knowledge on their attachment to and separation from adults (e.g., Bowlby, 1969/1982b; Rutter, 1972). Pilot observations and questionnaires did not reveal any notable peer attachments in infants below 1 year, but the few 3- and 4-year-olds left in the center often show very intense attachments to one of their peers.

Two studies are reported here. The first study was designed to explore whether 7–9-month-olds at Mitera would begin to form an attachment to the adoptive mother during the 2-week adaptation period. The objective of the second study was to compare 5–12-month-old infants' social interaction with familiar and unfamiliar same-age peers and, more specifically, to find out whether we could document peer attachments at this age.

STUDY 1

Maratos designed Study 1 to see whether infants who were already attached to a favorite nurse could transfer their allegiance to an adoptive mother within a 2-week adaptation period and to evaluate the infants' growing attachment to the new mother by examining infant exploratory and attachment behaviors in mother's presence (approach, physical contact, and distance interaction) as well as in her absence and during stranger encounters. Research up to the last decade focused primarily on indirect indices of attachment: fear of strangers and separation protest (Dontas, 1977). Ainsworth (1967, 1973) was among the first to criticize this approach. More recently, Ainsworth and her colleagues began to study the infant's ability to use the mother as a secure base and to describe patterns of attachment (Ainsworth et al., 1978).

Method

Sample.—Fifteen infants (eight female and seven male) between 7 and 9 months of age were studied. Pilot observations showed they had already formed attachments to specific nurses at the time when adoptive parents were being selected for them.

Procedures and data reduction.—The infants were observed twice. The first observation was conducted with their favorite nurse, before they were

[2] An infant resides in a particular pavilion with the same 10–12 children until his departure; changes occur only as some children leave for their new homes and new infants take their places.

introduced to the adoptive mother. During the second observation, at the end of the adaptation period 2 weeks later, the infants were seen with their adoptive mothers.

The experimental situation was a modification of Ainsworth's Strange Situation (Ainsworth et al., 1978), with Episode 7 (infant and stranger) omitted and each episode lasting 5 minutes, as opposed to the usual 3 minutes. The infants and their nurses or adoptive mothers were observed through a one-way mirror in a small room with two chairs, a crib, a cupboard, and four toys on the floor. During each 5-minute episode, 30 seconds of observation alternated with 30 seconds of recording, for a total of 5 observation and 5 recording periods. Intercoder agreement ranged from 85% to 92%.

Results

Five-point scales were constructed to assess intensity of attachment to the adoptive mother or nurse as indicated by looking at, vocalizing, smiling, seeking proximity, and clinging; separation anxiety as expressed by a variety of distress reactions (crying, whimpering, rocking, etc.); stranger reactions as expressed by avoidance and distress reactions; and exploration, including all behavior directed toward inanimate objects in the environment (looking around, touching toys, playing with toys, moving toward toys, and moving about). The frequency and duration of each behavior were noted.

Results of t tests for related samples showed that infants obtained significantly higher scores on the attachment scale with their adoptive mother than with their favorite nurse, $M = 3.90$ vs. 3.26, $t(14) = 3.12$, $p < .001$. In addition, the infants obtained higher scores on the separation anxiety scale when they were left by the adoptive mothers than when they were left by the favorite nurse, $M = 3.76$ vs. 3.26, $t(14) = 2.93$, $p < .02$.

With respect to stranger reactions, infants scored significantly higher on stranger anxiety when observed with the adoptive mother than with the favorite nurse, $M = 3.06$ vs. 2.40, $t(14) = 2.37$, $p < .05$. Although infants explored somewhat less in the presence of the adoptive mother than in the presence of the favorite nurse, the difference did not reach statistical significance ($M = 2.86$ vs. 2.54).

Discussion of Study 1

It may be concluded that the infants had indeed begun to form an attachment to the adoptive mother during the 2-week adaptation period at Mitera. When the behavior of the infants toward the adoptive mother was compared with their behavior toward the favorite nurse 2 weeks earlier, they scored higher with their adoptive mother on three of the four scales. This includes the scale assessing attachment behavior directly (the attachment scale) and the two scales that we considered to be indirect measures of attachment (the stranger reaction and separation anxiety scales).

It is noteworthy that the infants scored relatively low on the stranger reaction scale and relatively high on the separation anxiety scale. This may be characteristic of infants living in institutions. That the infants showed more intense stranger reactions and separation anxiety when tested with the adoptive mother than with the favorite nurse may indicate that the infants felt less secure with the new mother. This is also a possible explanation of the lower (although not significantly so) exploration scores with the adoptive mother. The reason for the lower scores was that the infants spent more time on the adoptive mother's lap than on the lap of the favorite nurse. The adoptive mothers who were very new to their role were perhaps not yet capable of serving as an effective secure base for their babies' exploration, although they were able to serve as a safe haven when the infants felt anxious. Our interpretation is supported by findings from a study by Feldman and Ingham (1975) in which infant behavior to mother and a 1-hour acquaintance was compared in the Ainsworth Strange Situation. One-year-olds were unable to use the new acquaintance as a safe haven. That the infants at Mitera sought physical contact with their mother in a modified Strange Situation therefore suggests to us that the attachment process was well on its way, even though the infants were somewhat more clingy with their new attachment figure.

STUDY 2

The value of peer interaction in childhood is generally acknowledged. Experience with peers is considered essential for certain aspects of socialization, that is, the control of aggression or the acquisition of sex-role behaviors (Hartup, 1970). The importance of experience with age-mates during infancy has not been extensively studied in the past (Bridges, 1932; Maudry & Nekula, 1939), although this situation is now being remedied (e.g., Eckerman & Whatley, 1977; Mueller & Brenner, 1977; Mueller & Vandell, 1978; Ross & Kay, 1980; Vandell, 1980). The link, if any, between the development of infant-mother attachment and peer attachments in infancy is also largely unexplored. This area would seem to be of great interest, especially for those concerned with infants lacking the customary opportunities for the development of a secure bond with a mother figure.

A classic study of six orphans in World War II documents young children's ability to form attachments to each other in the absence of any tie to an adult (Freud & Dann, 1951). These children had been together in the same concentration camp since infancy, with no consistent adult care. They eventually arrived together in England at about age 4, where they were cared for and studied. Although they were completely indifferent to adults, they were extremely loving of each other, forming a close-knit group with no evidence of jealousy or hostility. They refused to be separated for any activity and for even the shortest period of time. Their attachment to each other was intense, seeming to compensate (though not optimally) for the absence of early mothering.

Somewhat more recently, Heinicke and Westheimer (1966) observed that children admitted to day-care centers and hospitals showed much less distress when they were accompanied by a sibling than did children left alone. This was true even when the sibling was quite young and therefore unable to act as a mother surrogate. While it is established that the adult to whom an infant is attached can provide him or her with a sense of security in a strange or threatening environment, we are now discovering that another young child can also do so.

Even under normal rearing conditions, infants can develop simultaneous attachments to adults and children. Schaffer and Emerson (1964) found that, by 18 months, attachment relationships had developed between a substantial number of infants and persons other than the mother (siblings, neighbors' children) even though the mother was the primary caregiver for all.

These findings raise the question whether the developmental course of infant-peer relationships resembles that of infant-mother attachments. Although we know that infants distinguish their mothers from strangers somewhere between 2 and 14 weeks of age and that they show fear of unfamiliar adults between 7 and 10 months (e.g., Schaffer & Emerson, 1964), no comparable age ranges have been determined with respect to unfamiliar infants. So far, research on infants' responses to infant and child strangers in the first and second year of life provides evidence only for friendly reactions (Lenssen, 1975; Lewis & Brooks, 1974).

Study 2 was designed by Dontas and Karangelis to answer the following questions. Do infants between 5 and 12 months show fear of a strange infant or attachment to a very well known peer? Do they behave differently toward a known versus an unknown peer, and are there any age differences in their behavior?

Method

Sample.—Sixteen infants between 5 and 12 months were studied. They came from six of the pavilions at the Mitera Center, and many of them took part in Study 1 as well because both research projects were conducted during the same period. The eight younger infants (four boys, four girls) were 5–8 months old, with a mean age of 7 months; the eight older infants (four boys, four girls) were 9–12 months old, with a mean age of 10 months 11 days.

Procedures and data reduction.—Each subject was observed twice, once with a familiar peer from the same pavilion and once with an unfamiliar peer from a different pavilion. The peers were always within 2 months of each other's age. The two observations for each child took place no more than 7 days apart. The sequence of conditions (familiar, unfamiliar peer) was alternated randomly for the infants. The infant's own nurse brought him or her to the same observation room used for Study 1. The nurses were instructed not to initiate interaction. They were observed from behind a one-way mirror.

The following infant behavior categories were scored: looks at other infant, moves toward infant, smiles, touches infant (active contact), vocalizes, excited movements/bouncing, imitates infant, unhappy expression, whimpers/cries, rocks/sucks thumb, looks at toy (own or other infant's), takes other's toy, moves toward toy (own or other infant's), plays with/touches toy (own or other's), and resists when other infant grabs toy. The infant dyads were observed for 10 minutes, using a time-sampling technique. Thirty seconds of observation alternated with 30 seconds of recording. Interobserver reliability was between 78% and 90%.

Results of Study 2

Planned comparisons by t test were carried out, testing separately for differences in the behavior of older and younger infants during encounters with familiar and unfamiliar peers.

We obtained no statistical differences in the comparison of the younger infants' behavior toward familiar and unfamiliar peers. This was not true for the older infants, however. Older infants looked at the familiar peer less, $M = 4.4$ vs 7.8, $t(7) = 3.37$, $p < .02$, touched the familiar peer less, $M = 1.0$ vs. 2.0, $t(7) = 2.93$, $p < .03$, played with the same toy as the familiar infant more, $M = 6.6$ vs. 3.3, $t(7) = 3.32$, $p < .02$, took the familiar peer's toy away more often, $M = 3.1$ vs. 1.6, $t(7) = 2.65$, $p < .05$, and bounced up and down more with the familiar peer, $M = 3.6$ vs. 1.7, $t(7) = 2.35$, $p < .05$, in contrast to their behavior with unknown peers.

There was no statistical difference in the behavior of the older and younger children to the unfamiliar peers, but a number of differences were found in comparisons of the younger and older children's behavior to the familiar peer. The older infants shared a toy with the familiar peer more often than the younger infants did, $M = 6.6$ vs. 2.3, $t(14) = 3.88$, $p < .01$.

The older infants also took a toy from the familiar peer more often, $M = 3.1$ vs. .6, $t(14) = 2.50$, $p < .05$, looked at the familiar peer more frequently, $M = 8.1$ vs. 2.5, $t(14) = 4.42$, $p < .001$, and moved toward the familiar peer's toy more often, $M = 4.6$ vs. .9, $t(14) = 2.67$, $p < .05$.

Discussion

None of the experimental observations of the infants' interaction with same-age peers revealed to us behavior as emotionally intense as the attachment behaviors they directed toward their adult caregivers. Nor did the infants show any obvious fear of unfamiliar infants comparable to the fear infants demonstrated when faced with a strange adult (illustrated by an extremely low incidence of distress during the encounter with the unfamiliar peer). Younger infants did not behave differently with familiar and unfamiliar peers, although they certainly differentiated between familiar and unfamiliar adults, tending to avoid the latter or at least to watch them intently. One possible explanation for these findings is that the course of infant-peer relationships does not resemble that of infant-caregiver attachments. Alternatively, the onset of a capacity for peer relations may occur at a much later age, even among infants who are so intimately acquainted with each other.

Older infants did discriminate strange from familiar peers: they appeared to explore the strange infant more (visually and tactually) but engaged in more toy play with a familiar peer. Their bouncing behavior suggests that they were more excited or happier with the familiar peer, but there was no evidence of fear of the strange infant. These findings indicate the beginnings of cooperation and synchronization in infants' interactions with familiar peers.

Our findings do not support Maudry and Nekula (1939), who found older infants prone to quarrel over possessions and only just beginning to show some cooperation. We found, like Maudry and Nekula, that peer interaction in the older infants was mediated by mutual interest in toys but, in contrast to them, noted little negative affect during the few struggles over toys (see also Vandell, 1980).

We did not find much in the experimental situation, however, to support our initial hypothesis that peer relationships play a compensatory role in institutionally raised infants under 1 year who have had the opportunity to become attached to adults. Pilot questionnaires and observations prior to this study had revealed that most of the infants we tested interacted much more with the older infants and children in their pavilion than with the same-age peers we selected as their partners. Even so, at the end of the experimental situation, when some infants became distressed as the nurses left them alone, we noted occasional efforts by a partner to comfort his or her infant peer by vocalizing, patting, and even kissing the crying infant's foot.

GENERAL DISCUSSION

The infants observed at the Mitera Center in the above research projects showed none of the possible devastating results of institutionalization: depression, marasmus, detachment, or indiscriminate attention seeking. Even young infants of 7–9 months of age were attached to adults and seemed capable of becoming attached to a new figure. The development of a new attachment relationship seems quite feasible even in the short period of 2 weeks. This supports Schaffer (1963), who found that one 12-month-old, after a 37-week separation, showed attachment behavior to his mother on his third day at home. Unfortunately, it was not possible to study the actual process of becoming attached to a new figure in infants at Mitera. Therefore we do not know whether the new relationship with the mother was in any sense equivalent to the waning relationship with the favorite nurse or how soon the infant would demonstrate an exclusive attachment to the mother and indifference to the nurse. Certainly, when the mother happened to be absent during the adaptation period, the infants accepted interaction and care from their old nurse. It is also possible that the infants developed qualitatively different relationships with their mothers later on when they were assured of her exclusive attention, as they never could be with their favorite nurse.

Bretherton (1980) has hypothesized that "requiring a young child to reorganize his security-regulating system continually around new principal figures may finally make the child unwilling to engage in this task yet again . . . leading . . . to the inability to form a loving relationship with anyone" (p. 206). This may be the main reason why infants remaining at Mitera beyond the age of 1 year and occasionally until 3 or 4 years of age develop problems in relationships with adults. Changes in staff and therefore in principal attachment figures become inevitable over that length of time, and some children may eventually become unable or reluctant to enter into new attachment relationships.

It is worth noting that older children at the center often have very intense relationships with a peer. Perhaps the fact that their emotional needs could not be satisfied by adults lead them to form peer attachments. Thus the compensatory role of peer relationships may arise only in cases of failures of relationships with adults, that is, when infants lack attachments to adults (as in Freud & Dann, 1951) or in early childhood when a child has had several disrupted relationships with adults and finds it difficult to establish new ones. It would therefore be useful to create opportunities for the development of stable peer relationships in institutions or other nonfamily-care settings, especially for those who will remain in institutional care or who are not likely to be given opportunities to establish stable ties with adults until after infancy.

This could be accompanied by retrospective research or case studies of infants who eventually develop strong peer attachments in order to examine the outcome of their relationships to other salient figures in their social environment. A further area of study is the outcome of intense peer relationships in later life, when children are eventually placed with a family. Kibbutz studies in Israel have shown that relationships among kibbutz-reared children last into early adulthood (e.g., Shepher, 1971). Whether such relationships facilitate or hinder other interpersonal relations (e.g., if a child is adopted without his or her favorite peer) is an unanswered question.

Stevens's (1968) impression of Mitera infants, about 10 years prior to the present studies, was that "intensity and duration of the primary attachment are correlated negatively with ease of transfer to a secondary object at the time of adoption" (p. 26). It would seem that all our subjects managed this transfer of allegiance, yet the clinical picture of these and slightly older infants during the adaptation period showed hints of the ambivalence they must have been experiencing. The infants occasionally became distressed when old and new attachment figures were present together, even though nurses were generally tactful and trained to bow out of such situations. Sometimes the infants appeared to show angry rejection of their nurses or clinging, anxious behavior with their new mothers. We do not know how much their behavior reflected the probable upset of their nurses at losing them or their mothers' eagerness to feel wanted and needed, but they gave the impression of being under some stress.

Transitions from one attachment figure to another have not been systematically studied, nor are there any data relating the quality of an infant's attachment to a foster mother to the ease with which he or she forms an attachment to an adoptive mother or to the type of relationship that eventually develops between infant and adoptive mother. We are in agreement with Bretherton (1980) that, with today's more mobile and divorce-prone society, some separations are inevitable and that field research needs to be conducted on infants' separations, on the formation of new attachments, and on whether possible ill effects may be mitigated by opportunities for peer attachments.

VI. THE RELATIONSHIP BETWEEN QUALITY OF ATTACHMENT AND BEHAVIOR PROBLEMS IN PRESCHOOL IN A HIGH-RISK SAMPLE

MARTHA FARRELL ERICKSON, L. ALAN SROUFE,
AND BYRON EGELAND

University of Minnesota

Bowlby (1969/1982b, 1973, 1980) has eloquently described how an infant's relationship with the primary caregiver lays the groundwork for later social-emotional development. The patterning of the early attachment relationship is the foundation on which later representational models of self and attachment figure are constructed. Such models strongly influence the ways in which a child relates to others, approaches the environment, and resolves critical issues in later stages of development. In Bowlby's words, a person who has formed a secure attachment "is likely to possess a representational model of attachment figure(s) as being available, responsive, and helpful and a complementary model of himself as at least a potentially lovable and valuable person" (Bowlby, 1980, p. 242). The securely attached child, with positive expectations of self and others, is more likely to "approach the world with confidence and, when faced with potentially alarming situations, is likely to tackle them effectively or to seek help in doing so" (Bowlby, 1973, p. 208).

In contrast, infants whose emotional needs have not been consistently or adequately met come to view the world as "comfortless and unpredictable; and they respond either by shrinking from it or doing battle with it" (Bowlby, 1973, p. 208). Bowlby proposes that disturbances of the attachment

This research was supported in part by grants from the Maternal and Child Health Service of the Department of Health, Education, and Welfare (MC-R-270416-01-0) and the William T. Grant Foundation. We wish to acknowledge the excellent cooperation we have received from the staff at the Child and Youth Project, Minneapolis Public Health Clinic.

147

relationship are the main cause of psychopathology characterized by chronic anxiety or distrust, placing children doubly at risk. First, they render the child less able to cope with later adverse experiences, and, second, they increase the likelihood that the child will behave in such a way as to bring about more adverse experiences (Bowlby, 1982a).

Erikson (1963), Mahler (Mahler, Pine, & Bergman, 1975), and Sander (1975) have provided theoretical frameworks that complement and extend Bowlby's. These theorists emphasize that the resolution of issues or crises during earlier developmental stages paves the way for optimal adaptation during subsequent periods. For example, infants who have successfully negotiated the issue of "basic trust," "symbiosis," or "focalization" (all counterparts to Bowlby's secure attachment) are better prepared to move forward toward more autonomous functioning. Their ability to explore the environment and to evolve new patterns of interaction and communication within the safety of the child-caregiver relationship promotes greater self-reliance during the toddler period. Likewise, toddlers who have negotiated the movement toward autonomous functioning in the context of parental support can face an ever widening world with increasing confidence and enthusiasm. Mastery of object skills, confident expectations concerning others, and a history of positive social exchanges all promote successful peer relations during the preschool period. Thus, beginning with attachment issues in infancy, each developmental period sets the stage for how the child adapts to the developmental tasks of the next period (Sroufe, 1979).

Such coherence of individual development applies not only to optimal patterns of adaptation but to maladaptive patterns as well. Thus pronounced difficulties with impulse control, aggression, and other antisocial behaviors, prolonged emotional dependency, and extreme difficulty in relating to other children may be linked to adaptational failures during earlier periods when the major developmental issues were attachment and autonomy.

The empirical base for these theoretical propositions began with Ainsworth's method for assessing the quality of infant-caregiver attachment—the Ainsworth Strange Situation procedure (Ainsworth et al., 1978). Individual differences assessed using Ainsworth's procedure have predicted various aspects of functioning at subsequent ages. Securely attached infants were found to be more cooperative at 22 months with mother and another adult (Main, 1973), more enthusiastic, persistent, affectively positive, and compliant in problem solving at age 2 (Matas et al., 1978), more socially competent with peers at age 3½ (Waters et al., 1979), and more ego resilient at age 5 (Arend et al., 1979).

The studies cited above have used middle-class families in which relationships and life circumstances tend to be stable and continuity of development is found with relative ease. The Minnesota Mother-Child Interaction

Project, from which the data presented in this chapter are derived, involves families from a lower socioeconomic background, where life circumstances are less stable and less continuity of development might be expected. With this sample of 267 socially and emotionally at-risk mother-child pairs, secure attachment also has been found to predict later competent functioning. Securely attached infants have been reported to be more sociable as toddlers (Pastor, 1981) and more compliant at age 2 with their mothers and at 4½ years with preschool teachers (Erickson & Crichton, 1981; Erickson, Farber, & Egeland, 1982), to have better self-control in the preschool (Egeland, 1983), and to be less dependent on preschool teachers (Sroufe et al., 1983). A special laboratory preschool for a selected subsample of children from the Mother-Child project afforded a unique opportunity to explore the roots of maladaptation and competence through an extensive, detailed study of these 40 children. The results of this project (Sroufe, 1983) provided striking evidence of the importance of a secure attachment to a child's competent functioning in subsequent years. Children securely attached as infants were found to be more ego resilient, independent, compliant, empathic, and socially competent; they had greater self-esteem and expressed more positive affect and less negative affect than did children who were anxiously attached as infants.

Furthermore, this study yielded some tentative evidence that helped to elucidate the often subtle differences between children exhibiting anxious/resistant (or ambivalent) and anxious/avoidant patterns of attachment in infancy. On the basis of teachers' descriptive statements about the children, independent coders were able to classify children as having been avoidant or resistant with notable accuracy. Consistent with theoretical predictions, children who had exhibited anxious/avoidant patterns of attachment in infancy were described by teachers as hostile, socially isolated, and/or disconnected (psychotic-like) in the preschool setting. This represents the defensive posturing one would predict for a child with an attachment figure who is rejecting, emotionally unavailable, or perhaps depressed. Such a child has difficulty relating to others and carries an underlying anger that he or she has not learned to express directly. Children who had been anxious/resistant in infancy were described by preschool teachers as impulsive and tense and/or helpless and fearful, patterns that are hypothesized to be the result of ambivalent/inconsistent or over-involved caregiving.

The study presented in this chapter is an extension of the Sroufe (1983) study to include an additional 56 subjects from preschools and day-care centers throughout the metropolitan area. By necessity, this extended study sacrifices some of the breadth and detail allowed by the relatively controlled setting of the laboratory school; but this study allows us to test the predictive power of early attachment in more natural, less ideal circumstances and across a variety of preschool settings.

In this study we wanted to test the hypothesis that children who were anxiously attached would be more likely to have behavior problems in preschool and to determine if the particular pattern of anxious attachment related to specific problem behaviors in the preschool. We also examined the exceptions to the predicted relationship. Specifically, we sought to identify child, parental, interactional, and environmental factors that account for behavior problems in preschool children who were securely attached at 12–18 months and factors that account for competent functioning among children who earlier had been anxiously attached.

METHOD

Subjects

A sample of 267 mothers was selected from primiparous pregnant women seen at the Minneapolis Public Health Clinic and considered to be at risk for later caretaking problems. Risk factors included low socioeconomic status, low educational level (41% had not completed high school at the time of baby's birth), age ($\overline{X} = 20.5$, range = 12–34), lack of support (62% single at the time of baby's birth), chaotic living conditions, and a high degree of life stress. Eighty-six percent of the pregnancies were unplanned. Eighty percent of the mothers were white, 13% were black, and 7% were Hispanic or Native American. Fifteen percent of the children were of mixed racial background.

At 4½–5 years of age, 96 of the children (52 boys, 44 girls) were observed in preschool. Forty children attended a special laboratory school at the University of Minnesota Institute of Child Development. (That school and the children who attended it are described in detail in Sroufe, 1983.) Fifty-six other children attended preschools or day-care centers throughout the Twin Cities metropolitan area. The findings presented in this chapter are based on these 96 children.

Procedure

Assessments of mother-child interaction.—To assess quality of attachment, all children were videotaped at 12 and 18 months with their mothers in the Strange Situation (Ainsworth et al., 1978). Infants were classified as anxious/avoidant (Group A), securely attached (Group B), or anxious/resistant (Group C).

At 24 months the children were videotaped with their mothers in a series of four tool-using problem-solving tasks to assess how mother and child were working together during this period of emerging autonomy. In each task a small toy or treat was visible inside a clear Plexiglas container but was accessible to the child only if he or she used a tool in a specific way to retrieve the prize. The last two tasks were too difficult for a 2-year-old to solve without help. The mother was instructed to help her child when she felt she needed to. These tasks were designed to tax the child in order to assess how the child makes autonomous efforts to solve the problems as well as how the child uses the mother for support and guidance in a potentially frustrating situation. Assessments of the mother focused on the emotional support she provided and the clarity, quality, and careful timing of the assistance she offered her child in these problem-solving tasks. Children were rated on a five-to-seven-point scale on the following dimensions: dependency on mother, noncompliance with maternal directions and suggestions, frustration and anger (toward mother and toward the environment in general), persistence in attempting to solve the problems, effectiveness of strategies used to cope with the challenges and frustrations of the situation, and enthusiasm for the tasks. Three-point scales provided global measures of positive and negative affect expressed by the child.

When the children were 42 months old, the mother-child pairs were observed in four tasks that were difficult enough to require that the mothers use some teaching strategies to enable the child to complete the tasks. In the first task, the child was asked to construct copies of a large wooden block, using smaller blocks of various shapes. In the second task, the mother asked the child to name as many things with wheels as he or she could think of. The child was required to place colored shapes in the correct spaces on a matrix in the third task. The final task involved using an Etch-a-Sketch to trace a maze drawn on its screen. Mothers were rated on seven-point scales on supportive presence (the warmth and encouragement provided to the child), respect for the child's autonomy, structure and the firmness and consistency of limit setting, hostility toward the child, quality of instruction (e.g., clarity of directions, timing of cues), and the overall sense of confidence conveyed by the mother's behavior toward her child in this situation. Children were rated, also using seven-point scales, on the following variables: persistence, enthusiasm for the tasks, anger/negativity (toward the mother and/or the environment in general), compliance with maternal suggestions and directions, reliance on mother for help and encouragement, affection for mother, avoidance of mother, and general quality of experience for the child in this situation. Mother and child both were rated by two observers whose scores were added together, yielding scores ranging from 2 to 14. In cases where observers disagreed by two or more points, ratings were decided by conference and/or a third observer.

Assessments of environmental influences.—When the children were 30 months of age, observers visited the home and completed the Caldwell

(1979) HOME Inventory, which assesses the quality of the home environment and the degree of stimulation provided for the child. This inventory assesses the mother's responsiveness to her child, avoidance of restrictions in the environment that might impede the child's development, organization of the home environment, provisions of age-appropriate play material, degree of the mother's involvement with the child, and opportunities for the child to engage in a variety of activities.

When their children were 30, 42, and 48 months old, mothers completed the Life Events Scale (Egeland, Breitenbucher, & Rosenberg, 1980). This scale rates the occurrence of 44 events typically considered to be stressful. Items deal with such things as financial problems, moving, divorce, increased arguments with a friend or relative, chemical use, and illness or death in the family.

Based on interview data gathered from the mothers when their children were 18, 24, 30, 42, and 48 months old, ratings were made of the quality of emotional support and help with parenting available to the mother from husband, friends, and relatives. Interview data also was used to classify mother's primary relationship as intact (living with steadily from the time the child was 18 to 48 months of age) or not intact.

Assessments of mother.—To obtain an estimate of mother's intellectual functioning, the following three subtests from the Wechsler (1981) Adult Intelligence Scale were administered to the mothers when the children were 48 months old: comprehension, similarities, and block design.

At the same time, the mothers completed the Profile of Mood States Inventory (McNair, Lorr, & Droppleman, 1971), which yields measures of the mother's perceived tension, depression, anger, vigor, fatigue, and sense of confusion or bewilderment; the Institute for Personality and Ability Testing (IPAT) anxiety scale (Cattell & Scheier, 1963); and a self-report depression scale (Radloff, 1977).

Child assessments.—To assess the child's cognitive functioning the Bayley (1969) Scales of Infant Development were administered to the children when they were 24 months old. At 42 months they were given the Preschool Language Scale (Zimmerman, Steiner, & Pond, 1979), which assesses auditory comprehension and verbal expression and yields an overall language quotient.

Preschool assessments.—When the children were 4½–5 years old, they were observed in their preschool or day-care setting on at least two days in a variety of teacher-directed and free-play activities. Using seven-point scales, observers rated the children on the following dimensions: agency (how confidently and assertively the child approaches tasks and classroom activities), ego control (how the child monitors impulses and modulates his or her responses to stimuli in the preschool environment), dependency on teachers for support and nurturance, social skills in the peer group, positive affect, negative emotional tone, and compliance with teachers' directions and suggestions. All coders were blind to attachment history.

To provide more specific information about behaviors typically exhibited by these children in preschool, and particularly to identify children who were seen by their teachers as having behavior problems, a teacher or childcare provider completed the Preschool Behavior Questionnaire (Behar & Stringfield, 1974). This measure consists of 30 items often associated with socioemotional problems in young children. The teacher was asked to check for each item: (1) does not apply (scored one point); (2) applies sometimes (two points); or (3) certainly applies (three points). Teachers also completed the 31-item Behavior Problem Scale written by our staff (Erickson & Egeland, 1981), using the same format as was used for the Behar and Stringfield measure.

RESULTS

The Preschool Behavior Questionnaire (Behar & Stringfield, 1974) and our own Behavior Problem Scale were factor analyzed separately, yielding five major factors for each of these measures. The major factors of the Preschool Behavior Questionnaire were as follows: (1) hostility (items loading heavily on this factor included fights, bullies, is irritable, kicks, and hits); (2) hyperactivity/distractibility (squirming, inattentive, poor concentration); (3) gives up, cries easily; (4) nervous habits (twitches, bites nails); and (5) worried, unhappy. On the Behavior Problem Scale the major factors included (1) exhibitionistic/impulsive (verbally aggressive with peers, shows off, is impulsive); (2) withdrawal (little interest, passive, tired, does not play); (3) repetitive movements, self-abuse; (4) shy, anxious (shy, overly fearful, clings); and (5) sulks, does not accept criticism, tantrums.

Comparison of Attachment Groups on Preschool Measures

One-way analysis of variance, with Student-Newman-Keuls post hoc comparisons, was used to compare anxious/avoidant, anxious/resistant, and securely attached children on the seven preschool rating scales and on the factors derived from the Preschool Behavior Questionnaire and our own Behavior Problem Scale. These analyses included only those children whose attachment classification remained the same from 12 to 18 months. Results are presented in Table 1 and are described here.

Anxious/resistant infants were rated by observers in preschool as being less agentic (confident, assertive) and as having poorer social skills than securely attached infants. Anxious/avoidant children were rated by observers as being more dependent on teachers and having poorer social skills

TABLE 1

MEAN SCORES FOR STABLE ATTACHMENT GROUPS ON PRESCHOOL VARIABLES

	Anxious/ Avoidant (N = 10)	Secure (N = 40)	Anxious/ Resistant (N = 10)	F Value	p	Contrast
Conferenced observers' ratings:						
Agency	3.90	4.50	3.20	3.43	.04	B > C
Ego control	3.90	4.35	4.50	.66	.52	...
Dependency..........	4.10	2.70	2.90	3.86	.03	A > B
Social skills...........	3.20	4.05	3.10	3.66	.03	...
Positive affect	4.20	4.73	4.20	.88	.42	...
Negative emotion......	3.60	2.53	2.10	2.32	.11	...
Compliance	4.30	5.58	5.60	3.53	.04	...
Preschool Behavior Questionnaire (factors):						
Hostility	.25	−.15	−.71	3.36	.04	A > C
Hyperactive inattentive	.11	−.16	.28	1.56	.22	...
Gives up, cries.........	.59	−.24	.13	4.29	.02	A > B
Nervous habits	−.27	−.02	.32	1.31	.28	...
Worried, unhappy	.02	−.12	−.12	.10	.91	...
Total	53.00	41.26	44.45	6.25	.003	A > B, C
Behavior-problem scale (factors):						
Exhibitionistic, impulsive	.66	−.23	−.39	5.32	.008	A > B, C
Withdrawal	.95	−.05	.35	4.00	.02	A > B
Repetitive movements, self-abuse	−.04	−.08	−.15	.09	.92	...
Shy, anxious	.26	−.01	.52	1.45	.24	...
Sulks, tantrums........	.05	−.16	−.39	.76	.47	...
Total	49.50	40.29	41.73	6.82	.002	A > B, C

than securely attached children. Even though the post hoc comparisons were not significant, the anxious/avoidant children were less compliant with teachers' instructions and rules and expressed more negative emotion (e.g., whining, pouting, angry outbursts) in the classroom than both anxious/resistant and securely attached children.

The analyses based on the teachers' ratings indicated that anxious/avoidant children were more withdrawn and gave up more easily than securely attached children. These children were seen by their teachers as more exhibitionistic and impulsive than children in the other attachment groups and as more hostile than anxious/resistant children. Anxious/avoidant children received higher total scores on both the Preschool Behavior Questionnaire and our Behavior Problem Scale than either anxious/resistant or securely attached children, suggesting more and varied behavior problems in that group.

Behavior-Problem Groups

From the 96 children observed in preschool, three groups of children with behavior problems were identified: acting out ($N = 17$; 11 boys, six girls), withdrawn ($N = 7$; three boys, four girls), and attention problems ($N = 3$; all boys). A group of children virtually free from behavior problems and functioning competently in preschool ($N = 22$; 12 boys, 10 girls) was selected from the same sample. Because a high-risk sample such as ours tends to have a high incidence of behavior problems, we chose not to use a predetermined cutoff point (e.g., one standard deviation above the mean) for selecting these groups. Such a procedure would have excluded some children who clearly do have behavior problems. Instead, selection was based on the scores children received from their teachers on specific items from the Preschool Behavior Questionnaire (Behar & Stringfield, 1974) and the Behavior Problem Scale (items that loaded most heavily on factors relevant to these behavior problems) and was corroborated by observers' ratings on the seven-point scales (agency, ego control, etc.) described earlier.

Children in the acting-out group were described on the checklists by their teachers as disobedient, inconsiderate, easily irritated, verbally aggressive with peers and/or adults, and fighting with or bullying other children. Observers rated them as noncompliant, often high on negative emotion, and usually low on social skills. Withdrawn children were described by teachers as passive, showing little interest in their surroundings, usually not engaging in play, and sometimes daydreaming. Observers rated these children notably low on agency, social skills, and positive affect. Children in the attention-problem group were characterized by their teachers as squirmy, inattentive, and having poor concentration. Although their teachers saw them as impulsive, they were relatively obedient, cooperative, and nonaggressive with peers and adults.

Children for whom there was any doubt as to the presence or absence of behavior problems were not included in any group. For example, a child who received a 3 ("certainly applies") on only one item relevant to the acting-out pattern and several 2's ("sometimes applies") was included only if observers' ratings strongly suggested problems (e.g., a compliance rating of 4 or below and a negative emotion rating of above 4 on a seven-point scale). Or if a child received mostly 1's and some 2's on selected checklist items, suggesting an absence of behavior problems, but ratings from observers suggested a lack of competence (e.g., unduly high dependency, very low social skills), that child was not included in the well-functioning group. Thus children in the behavior-problem groups were seen by both teachers and observers as functioning poorly in the preschool setting, and children in the well-functioning group were viewed by both teachers and observers as being free of behavior problems.

Attachment Classification in Infancy and Membership in Behavior-Problem Groups in Preschool

Chi-square analysis of these combined behavior-problem groups by attachment classification at both 12 and 18 months was significant ($p = .001$ and $.04$, respectively; for children whose attachment classification was the same at 12 and 18 months, $p = .01$) and confirmed the hypothesis that children who were anxiously attached were more likely to have behavior problems in preschool. Of particular interest was how accurately preschool group membership was predicted for children who were classified as anxiously attached at both 12 and 18 months (stable anxious), children who were securely attached at both times (stable secure), and children who were classified as secure at one time and anxious the other (mixed). Results of this analysis are not surprising. Of 16 stable anxiously attached children, only two were in the well-functioning group in preschool. In contrast, 15 of 22 stable secure children were in that group. And for children with mixed classification, preschool group membership was hard to predict: four of 10 were in the group without behavior problems. When analyzed separately by sex, the results were the same.

Factors Accounting for Exceptions to the Predicted Relationship between Attachment and Preschool Behavior

While the results thus far clearly indicate the importance of quality of attachment as a predictor of behavior in preschool, we were interested in examining the exceptions to the predicted relationship: Why did some securely attached children show behavior problems in preschool ($N = 8$), and why did some anxiously attached children appear competent in preschool ($N = 6$)? Specifically, we wanted to determine which child, parental, interactional, and environmental factors account for behavior problems in children who were securely attached and which factors account for competent functioning among the anxiously attached children. First, securely attached children with behavior problems (acting out, withdrawn, and attention problems were combined) and securely attached children without behavior problems were compared on a number of variables assessed when the children were 18, 24, 30, 42, and 48 months of age. Then anxiously attached children with and without behavior problems were compared on these same measures. (In order to have groups large enough for analysis, attachment groups were based on classification at 18 months.) Results are presented in Tables 2–4 and are described here.

Mother-child interaction.—Patterns of interaction in the 24-month tool-using tasks and the 42-month teaching tasks were important in accounting for differences between securely attached children with and without behavior problems and anxiously attached children with and without behavior problems (Table 2). Among securely attached children, those with behavior problems tended ($p = .06$) to express more negative affect at 24 months, and their mothers provided less support and encouragement ($p = .02$) as the children attempted the problem-solving tasks. In the 42-month teaching tasks, mothers of securely attached children with behavior problems gave less clear and structured directions, were less firm and consistent in setting limits, and were judged to be less confident in their ability to deal effectively with their children. The behavior-problem children expressed less affection and were more avoidant of their mothers in the teaching task situation than were securely attached children without behavior problems. The overall quality of experience in the teaching tasks tended to be poorer for the behavior-problem group than for the children without behavior problems.

Among anxiously attached children (anxious/resistant and anxious/ avoidant combined), those who did not have behavior problems in preschool had tended to look more enthusiastic in the 24-month tool-using tasks but otherwise did not differ from the behavior-problem group at age 2. Ratings of maternal behaviors in the 2-year tool tasks did not discriminate between groups. However, there were significant differences among groups on all maternal behaviors and most child behaviors in the 42-month teaching situation. Mothers of anxiously attached children who did not have behavior problems were more respectful of the child's autonomy; were more supportive; provided clearer structure and firm, consistent limits; were less hostile; provided clear, well-timed instruction; and seemed confident that they could work with the child in this situation. These children were persistent in their attempts to solve the tasks, were compliant with their mothers' instructions, expressed affection for their mothers, and had a generally positive experience with their mothers in this setting.

Environmental influences.—Comparison of children with and without behavior problems suggests that the degree of stimulation provided in the home, as measured by the Caldwell HOME Inventory, is important in accounting for group differences (Table 3). The securely attached children who had behavior problems in preschool came from homes where fewer age-appropriate play materials were provided than were provided to securely attached children without behavior problems. Mothers of these children also were less involved with their children in the home. Among securely attached children there were no differences between children with

157

TABLE 2

COMPARISON OF CHILDREN WITH AND WITHOUT BEHAVIOR PROBLEMS: MOTHER-CHILD INTERACTION VARIABLES

VARIABLE	SECURELY ATTACHED (18 Months)				ANXIOUSLY ATTACHED (18 Months)			
	With Behavior Problems ($N = 8$)	Without ($N = 16$)	t Value	p	With Behavior Problems ($N = 19$)	Without ($N = 6$)	t Value	p
24-month tool using:								
Maternal:								
Support	3.60	5.15	2.58	.02	3.78	4.40	−.85	.41
Quality of assistance	3.80	4.53	1.50	.15	3.87	4.20	−.48	.64
Child:								
Dependency	3.80	2.53	−1.46	.16	3.53	3.67	−.16	.88
Noncompliance	3.60	3.00	−.75	.46	3.79	2.83	1.29	.21
Frustration	3.40	2.40	−1.01	.33	3.53	3.17	.36	.72
Persistence	2.80	3.33	.77	.45	2.47	2.50	−.05	.96
Coping	4.00	4.27	.30	.77	3.26	3.67	−.50	.62
Enthusiasm	8.60	8.64	.03	.98	6.79	9.00	−1.83	.08
Positive affect	1.80	1.71	−.25	.81	2.33	2.00	1.17	.25
Negative affect	1.60	1.07	−2.06	.06	1.78	1.67	.21	.83
42-month teaching tasks:								
Maternal:								
Respect for autonomy	9.43	11.06	1.70	.10	8.50	11.33	−2.85	.009
Supportive presence	7.86	10.38	1.86	.08	7.17	10.83	−2.79	.01
Structure/limits	9.14	11.31	2.17	.04	8.94	12.00	−2.49	.02
Hostility	3.14	2.75	−.57	.57	4.39	2.00	2.62	.02
Quality of instruction	7.71	11.50	3.45	.002	7.33	11.50	−3.18	.004
Confidence	7.86	10.94	2.31	.03	7.17	10.83	−2.61	.02
Child:								
Persistence	9.14	11.13	1.69	.11	7.28	10.67	−2.64	.02
Enthusiasm	8.00	10.06	−1.42	.17	6.83	9.00	−1.58	.13
Negativity	5.00	2.75	−1.51	.17	4.83	2.50	1.54	.14
Compliance	9.14	11.31	1.57	.13	7.28	10.50	−2.12	.05
Reliance on mother	6.86	6.25	−.57	.58	8.61	6.33	1.62	.12
Affection for mother	6.43	9.00	2.27	.03	6.50	9.83	−2.41	.03
Avoidance of mother	3.57	2.38	−2.90	.009	4.22	2.67	1.17	.25
Experience in session	8.14	10.56	1.94	.07	6.89	10.67	−3.14	.005

TABLE 3

COMPARISON OF CHILDREN WITH AND WITHOUT BEHAVIOR PROBLEMS ON ENVIRONMENTAL VARIABLES

Measure/Variable	Securely Attached (18 Months)				Anxiously Attached (18 Months)			
	With Behavior Problems	Without	t Value	p	With Behavior Problems	Without	t Value	p
Caldwell HOME Inventory:								
Responsivity of mother	9.00	8.75	-.26	.80	7.89	10.00	-1.35	.19
Avoidance of restrictions	3.86	3.75	-.09	.93	3.83	4.60	-.88	.39
Organization of environment	4.86	5.33	1.63	.12	5.17	5.60	-.89	.39
Provision of play material	8.43	10.93	3.09	.006	8.56	12.20	-2.70	.01
Maternal involvement	3.29	5.20	2.50	.02	3.28	5.60	-3.68	.001
Opportunity for variety	1.57	1.87	.46	.65	.78	.40	.80	.43
Total	31.00	35.60	1.54	.14	29.50	38.40	-2.13	.05
Life Events Scale:								
30 months	9.88	7.75	-.91	.39	11.26	12.33	-.34	.74
42 months	10.33	6.69	-1.27	.22	9.47	7.40	.70	.49
48 months	7.75	7.00	-.39	.70	7.40	6.00	.80	.44
Quality of emotional support available to mother:								
24 months	4.29	4.86	.77	.45	3.56	4.50	-1.21	.24
30 months	4.38	4.47	.14	.87	3.72	4.33	-.93	.36
42 months	4.14	4.47	.46	.65	3.63	4.33	-1.09	.29
48 months	3.88	4.40	.89	.39	3.13	4.67	-2.67	.02

159

TABLE 4

COMPARISON OF CHILDREN WITH AND WITHOUT BEHAVIOR PROBLEMS ON MOTHER AND CHILD VARIABLES

MEASURES/VARIABLE	SECURELY ATTACHED (18 Months)				ANXIOUSLY ATTACHED (18 Months)			
	With Behavior Problems	Without	t Value	p	With Behavior Problems	Without	t Value	p
Maternal measures:								
Age	20.63	21.19	.29	.77	20.74	20.33	.25	.81
Education	11.63	12.56	.93	.36	11.63	11.00	.88	.41
WAIS (3 subtests)	37.00	35.06	−.29	.78	30.00	35.25	−1.07	.30
Profile of mood states:								
Tension	10.33	6.63	−1.15	.26	8.53	9.00	−.20	.85
Depression	7.67	6.25	−.35	.73	6.80	4.40	.74	.47
Anger	6.33	7.00	.08	.94	7.21	5.80	.40	.70
Vigor	19.17	16.19	−1.15	.26	16.53	14.33	.76	.46
Fatigue	7.17	9.50	.73	.47	7.67	5.67	.69	.50
Confusion	7.83	3.94	−2.95	.008	7.00	5.50	.71	.48
Depression inventory	11.83	9.63	−.57	.58	13.27	10.00	.86	.40
IPAT anxiety	39.00	27.81	−1.88	.07	43.25	34.20	1.32	.20
Child language and DQ:								
Bayley scales—24 months	92.29	111.88	2.56	.02	94.16	110.67	−1.97	.06
Preschool language scale:								
Auditory	100.71	123.00	2.22	.04	102.00	120.80	−2.09	.05
Verbal	105.57	119.25	1.19	.25	98.20	122.40	−3.02	.007
Language	103.29	121.88	1.81	.08	100.27	121.80	−2.86	.01

behavior problems and children without problems on scores on the Life Events Scale at 30, 42, or 48 months. Nor were there differences on the quality of emotional support available to the mother from husband, relatives, and friends. Chi-square analysis of securely attached children with and without behavior problems by groups whose mothers were involved in stable and unstable relationships approached significance ($\chi^2 = 2.56$, $p = .11$). Of 11 children whose mothers lived with the same man from the time the child was 12–48 months of age, nine did not have behavior problems and two did. For securely attached children whose mothers were not involved in an intact relationship over that time period, six had behavior problems and six did not.

Among anxiously attached children with and without behavior problems in the preschool, results were similar. Anxiously attached children who did not have behavior problems came from homes rated by observers on the Caldwell HOME Inventory as providing age-appropriate play materials and characterized by a high degree of involvement between mother and child. A significant difference also was found on the total score for the Caldwell HOME Inventory. Anxiously attached children without behavior problems came from more stimulating home environments. Life Events scores did not discriminate between anxiously attached children with and without behavior problems. Quality of support available to mother at 24, 30, and 42 months did not discriminate among groups, but at 48 months mothers of children without behavior problems were judged to have more support from family and friends. Chi-square analysis of anxiously attached children with and without behavior problems by groups whose mothers had intact relationships (living with the same man from the time the child was 12–48 months of age) and those who did not was significant ($\chi^2 = 6.40$, $p = .01$). Of four children whose mothers had intact relationships, only one had behavior problems. There were 20 anxiously attached children whose mothers did not have intact relationships, and 17 of those had behavior problems in preschool.

Maternal measures.—Mothers of children with and without behavior problems did not differ significantly as to age or level of education (Table 4). Nor were there significant differences between behavior-problem groups and children without behavior problems on mothers' scores on three subtests from the Wechsler Adult Intelligence Scale (Wechsler, 1981). Among securely attached children only the "confusion" score on the Profile of Mood States Inventory discriminated between mothers of children with and without behavior problems. Mothers of children with behavior problems reported more feelings of confusion, bewilderment, and disorganization than did mothers of children who did not have behavior problems. And mothers of securely attached children with behavior problems tended to score higher on the IPAT anxiety scale ($p = .07$) compared to mothers of securely attached children without behavior problems. Among anxiously attached children there were no significant differences on maternal measures.

Child language and developmental quotient.—For both securely and anxiously attached children there were significant cognitive differences between children with behavior problems and those who had no problems. Children without behavior problems obtained significantly higher scores on the Bayley Scales of Infant Development (Bayley, 1969) at 24 months and on the Preschool Language Scale (Zimmerman et al., 1979) at 42 months than did children who had behavior problems in preschool.

DISCUSSION

As predicted, children who were anxiously attached as infants functioned more poorly in preschool than did children who were securely attached. That these differences were evident across such varied preschool settings and during relatively brief periods of observation makes these results even more powerful. Anxious/avoidant children differed most strikingly from the secure infants. They were observed to be highly dependent, noncompliant, and poorly skilled in social interaction with peers. Teachers described them as hostile, impulsive, giving up easily, and withdrawn. These children generally presented a picture of extensive and varied behavior problems in preschool.

While anxious/resistant children were similar to securely attached children on some measures (e.g., compliance rating, "worried" factor), these children also were functioning poorly. They lacked agency and the confidence and assertiveness necessary to engage the preschool environment effectively. And like the avoidant children, they tended to be incompetent in interactions with peers. While few of the post hoc contrasts showed significant differences between the avoidant and resistant children on individual variables, the results do suggest some differences that are consistent with theoretical predictions and the findings of the earlier study (Sroufe, 1983) mentioned in the introduction to this chapter. High scores on the hostility factor and the noncompliance rating scale fit the predicted pattern for anxious/avoidant children, while low agency ratings and high scores on the distractibility factor are consistent with the pattern of passivity and inattentiveness predicted for resistant children.

Some differences noted in the earlier study (Sroufe, 1983) with the subsample of 40 children were not evident in this study and possibly are a function of the relatively limited observation of the 56 children in the community preschools. The 40 children attending preschool classes at the university were made up exclusively of children from the Mother-Child project. Positive affect ratings did discriminate between anxious and secure children in the laboratory school but did not discriminate among attachment groups for the total preschool sample of 96. And most notably, both anxious/resistant and anxious/avoidant children were found to be more dependent than securely attached children in the subsample of 40, while among the total sample of 96 children in this study who attended preschool only the anxious/avoidant were rated as more dependent. It is important to note here that the 40 children in the university preschool were observed daily for more than 6 weeks and that dependency was assessed with a variety of measures, whereas the only measure of dependency in this study was a rating based on two observations. Dependency can be manifested in many ways, and we believe that a more comprehensive assessment would have revealed dependent patterns of behavior in the resistant children in this larger sample as well. Generally, we do not feel that children with histories of avoidant attachment are more (or less) poorly functioning than those with histories of resistant attachment. Rather we feel that they will manifest different kinds of problems, in different ways, being more or less obvious in different contexts.

When groups of children who clearly had behavior problems were identified on the basis of teachers' ratings on behavior checklists and corroborated by observers' ratings, the predictive power of attachment classification was demonstrated most dramatically. Among the well-functioning groups, 16 of 22 had been securely attached. The majority of children in all three behavior-problem groups had been anxiously attached as infants. Both avoidant and resistant children were represented in all problem groups (acting out, attention problems, withdrawn), with no apparent tendency for either attachment group to fall into a particular problem group. This is not too surprising given the relatively broadly defined behavior-problem groups (and given the fact that avoidant and resistant children differed little on the single variables assessed in preschool). And it does not preclude the likelihood that the behaviors have different meaning or intent among resistant children than among avoidant children. For example, we might expect that the withdrawn behavior of avoidant children represents a psychological disconnection from others, whereas the resistant children's withdrawal would stem from passivity, weakness, or tearfulness.

Even though there is a strong relationship between quality of attachment and behavior problems in preschool, there are some exceptions. There were six anxiously attached children at 18 months who were competent in preschool, and there were eight securely attached children who had behavior problems in preschool. We examined certain child and mother characteristics, environmental stimulation, and life circumstances in an attempt to account for these exceptions. The results of the examination of change between quality of attachment at 18 months and functioning in preschool must be considered as tentative due to the small sample sizes. Nevertheless, some coherent patterns did emerge. Among both securely attached and anxiously attached children, those without behavior problems were, on the average, functioning better cognitively than were children with behavior problems. It is likely that brighter children have an advantage in coping with the preschool environment. And perhaps brighter children tend to be easier for mothers to deal with effectively, thus eliciting better caretaking. But intelligence does not insure healthy functioning, nor does lower cognitive ability preclude healthy functioning. There were children of a wide range of cognitive ability in the behavior-problem groups and in the group without problems. We must look at other variables to explain further these differences in preschool behavior.

Children who were securely attached but presented behavior problems in preschool had mothers who appeared to be less effective in helping them negotiate subsequent stages of development. These mothers were less supportive of their children's efforts to solve problems at 24 months. They did not provide the warmth and encouragement their children needed to cope with a challenging, potentially frustrating situation. When engaging their children in a series of educational tasks at 42 months, they again failed to provide support and encouragement, and they were ineffective as teachers. They did not structure the tasks well, and they did not let the child know what was expected. Nor did they set firm, consistent limits when the child deviated from the task. While the securely attached children without behavior problems did not differ at 2 years from those with behavior problems, by 42 months they were less affectionate and more avoidant of their mothers.

At home at 30 months, securely attached children with behavior problems lacked age-appropriate play materials, and their mothers interacted with them less than mothers of children without behavior problems interacted with their children. When these children were 4 years old, their mothers reported feeling confused, bewildered, and disorganized. Perhaps these mothers were able to meet the needs of an infant but did not have the resources to cope with the ever-changing demands of the maturing, individuating child.

Among anxiously attached children with and without behavior problems, there were no differences on either the mother or the child variables at 24 months, but by 42 months they were remarkable. Mothers of children without behavior problems were respectful of children's autonomy, allowing the child to explore and attempt the tasks without maternal intrusion. They were warm and supportive, structured the tasks carefully, provided well-timed cues to help the child, and set firm, consistent limits but without being hostile. The mothers of anxiously attached children without behavior problems in preschool were confident that they could deal effectively with their children. The children were persistent in their efforts to accomplish the tasks, compliant with their mother's instruction, and affectionate toward mother. As with securely attached children, the anxiously attached children without behavior problems came from homes where appropriate play materials were provided and mothers were involved actively with their children. These homes provided the stimulation necessary to foster healthy development. For anxiously attached children, emotional support available to mother from family and friends was important in accounting for differences between children with and without behavior problems. Mothers of children without behavior problems had better support when their children were four years old, and they were more likely to be involved in an intact, primary relationship, living with the same man from the time the child was 18–48 months of age. There were no differences between anxiously attached children with and without behavior problems on the occurrence of stressful life events.

In conclusion, quality of attachment at 12 and 18 months is a strong predictor of behavior in the preschool at age 4½–5. That the child's experience with the attachment figure leads to expectations that influence the way the child organizes his or her behavior throughout the first 5 years of life is demonstrated clearly here. Furthermore, quality of attachment is an assessment of the quality of care and support provided in the first year of life (Ainsworth et al., 1978; Grossmann et al., in this vol.) and, as such, is also a predictor of subsequent care. We assume, in most cases, continuity of care and support across time, continuity that serves to perpetuate the expectations and the behavioral organization the child developed during the attachment phase. Thus, in cases where the outcome changes (that is, the quality of the child's adaptation or behavioral organization does not fit the predicted pattern), we expect that there were changes in the quality of care and support. The findings here provide some evidence to support that expectation. Where securely attached children developed behavior problems, there was a pattern of inadequate maternal care and support at subsequent stages of development. And where anxiously attached children became well functioning by preschool, their mothers were sensitive and responsive to the special needs of their children at later stages.

It appears that both securely and anxiously attached children who are competent in preschool have mothers who are sensitive to the demands of the task for the child at a particular age. At 2 they were aware of the child's need for emotional support, and they understood the requirements necessary for the child to succeed. At 42 months they were aware that, in order for the child to succeed, the situation needed to be structured and limits needed to be set in an appropriate fashion. The relationship between attachment and outcomes in preschool is obviously complex. One major factor that may make the anxiously attached child less vulnerable to later maladaptation is mother's emotional support and overall sensitivity. Even though the mothers of anxiously attached children apparently did not provide the support necessary to foster a secure attachment, the support they provided to the child from 24 to 42 months, accompanied by a stable family environment and improved support to the mother from family and friends, was enough to move the child toward healthy functioning in the preschool.

This does not lead us to conclude that effects of early experience are erased, even for this minority of subjects who changed substantially. Rather we would expect that children with early maladaptation, whose lives have improved, remain differentially vulnerable, at least for a time. Likewise we would expect that securely attached infants who are later showing maladaptation would rebound quickly should life supports again improve. This is a matter for ongoing research.

VII. ATTACHMENT SECURITY, MOTHER-CHILD INTERACTION, AND TEMPERAMENT AS PREDICTORS OF BEHAVIOR-PROBLEM RATINGS AT AGE THREE YEARS

JOHN E. BATES, CHRISTINE A. MASLIN, AND KAREN A. FRANKEL

Indiana University

The central goal of the study reported here was to identify antecedent characteristics of the child and family that best predicted behavioral/ emotional problems at 3 years of age. In prior work (Bates & Bayles, 1984; Bates, Olson, Pettit, & Bayles, 1982; Lee & Bates, 1984; Lounsbury & Bates, 1982; Olson, Bates, & Bayles, 1984; Pettit & Bates, 1984) we have written extensively about mother-infant interaction, temperament, and intellectual functioning and about their interrelationships across development. What we learned from these prior findings will form the basis for interpreting patterns of relationships among our predictor and outcome variables in the present study.

As a first step toward answering our central question, we considered how the important index of attachment security related to several of the mother-child relationship measures that had been included in our previous studies. As a second step, we examined relationships of attachment security to other child characteristics, such as difficult temperament and sociability. Finally, we approached our central question more directly by considering how all these variables jointly predicted behavior problems at age 3 years.

This research was partly supported by NIMH MH28018 and a Biomedical Research Support Grant (USPH RR 7031) to Indiana University. The authors are grateful to the families who participated and to others who made vital contributions: for training on procedures, L. A. Sroufe and B. Vaughn; for major contributions throughout the project, K. Bayles and G. Pettit; for help with data collection, C. Arnett, J. Doughman, K. Erickson, M. Gingerich, E. Liesmann, D. Palmer, and J. Schmidt; for data analysis help, R. Church- ward, S. Meit, D. Pfenninger, T. Rowlison, A. Schnaufer, and T. Rizzo; and for useful comments on earlier drafts, J. Belsky and B. Vaughn.

This stepwise approach was based on the dominant theoretical models in personality development.

Current models emphasize that individual differences in children's personality and social competence are the product of a variety of factors, including heredity, perinatal influences, and social factors (Bell, 1979; Parke & Asher, 1983; Rutter, 1979; Sameroff, 1982; Schwartz, 1979; Thomas, 1981). The present study includes both biological factors (e.g., temperament) and social factors (e.g., mother-infant attachment). We would not claim to have achieved "pure" measures of either. However, we felt that our study might help discriminate between operational concepts that are and are not useful in charting the development of individual differences. Before describing the study in more detail, we will therefore summarize what models of personality development and recent empirical findings, including our own, have to say about the major constructs around which this study was designed.

Mother-Child Relationship

Mother-child relationship variables are central in models of personality development. We considered three widely used kinds. First, warm, involved, educative behaviors have clustered together in a number of studies of infants and mothers. This complex of interaction behaviors has been found to be coherent across development and associated with child verbal-cognitive development in the second year (Bates et al., 1982; Bradley & Caldwell, 1980; Clarke-Stewart, 1973; Cohen & Beckwith, 1979; Olson et al., 1984; Pettit & Bates, 1984).

A second construct, conceptually related to the first, is attachment security (Ainsworth et al., 1978). Ainsworth et al. demonstrated that early maternal warmth and responsiveness predicted the infant's later ability, following the stress of separation, to reestablish supportive contact with the mother and to resume exploration. Social indicators of competence, including the effectiveness of toddler-mother interaction in solving difficult problems, as well as children's efficacy in both the achievement and the social tasks of nursery school, have been predicted by early attachment security (see Sroufe, 1979, 1983).

A third kind of parent-child construct especially relevant to behavior problems is control. A dimension of child "trouble" behavior combined with reactive control appears by 13 months of age and is quite stable to 24 months (Bates, Pettit, & Bayles, 1981). Positive maternal control, for example, suggesting child activities or offering choices, has been observed at the same ages (see Schaffer & Crook, 1979). The classic findings of Baumrind (1967) suggest that a combination of positive parental behaviors and firm, effective control is concurrently associated with the best adaptations in preschoolers. However, it is not yet established that control styles at early ages are predictive of behavior at later ages.

Temperament

A second element in current models of personality development is temperament. Temperament traits are usually defined as cross-situationally and developmentally stable behavior tendencies with strong, inborn, biological roots (Goldsmith & Campos, 1982; Plomin, 1983; Rothbart & Derryberry, 1981). The dominant measures of child temperament have been parent reports, especially on questionnaires but also in interviews. Empirical evidence from a wide array of parent-report temperament scales suggests that temperament ratings reflect both objective child characteristics and subjective characteristics in the rater (e.g., see Bates & Bayles, 1984), although the proportions of variance explained by these components remains small.

The three temperament constructs that seemed especially useful for our purposes were sociability, difficult temperament, and activity level. Sociability, or extraversion, concerns an open versus a timid approach to new people and novel experiences. The validity of this construct has been shown by both parent-report (e.g., Bates & Bayles, 1984; Olson, Bates, & Bayles, 1982) and laboratory measures of sociability (Garcia Coll, Kagan, & Reznick, 1984; Wilson & Matheny, 1983), and it appears that there may be a genetic contribution to such traits (Plomin, 1983). Low sociability might be expected to be related to internalizing-type behavior problems, especially if it is assumed that constitution is a component of anxiety characteristics (e.g., Eysenck & Eysenck, 1978). The second construct, difficult temperament, was originally invoked by Thomas, Chess, and Birch (1968), who assigned it a potentially important role in the development of behavior problems. In the present study, the difficult temperament factor centers on the frequent and intense expression of negative affect (Bates, Freeland, & Lounsbury, 1979).

Another important dimension of temperament is activity level. Variations in preschoolers' activity level have some stability over time and generalize to other personality and social adjustment measures (Buss, Block, & Block, 1980; Campbell, Szumowski, Ewing, Gluck, & Breaux, 1982). However, it has not been well established that such variations have their roots in comparable behaviors in infancy, and external validation of early parent reports of activity level is generally lacking (e.g., Wilson & Matheny, 1983).

Perceived Management Problems

Early perceptions of behavior problems constitute a third set of useful predictor variables. We have measured mothers' perceptions of difficulties in controlling their 13- and 24-month-olds (Bates & Bayles, 1984; Olson et al., 1982). We suggest that this may represent a variable with constitutional components, like temperament.

Stress

A final predictor category is the concept of environmental stress. Studies have suggested that family stress such as divorce and marital discord predict the appearance of behavior problems in middle childhood (Emery, 1982; Hetherington & Martin, 1979), although there is of course no a priori assurance that a given family stress index will be totally independent from the other elements. For example, marital discord could partly result from a difficult to manage child.

Behavior-Problem Outcome Measures

At age 3 years, we assessed child behavior problems as perceived by parents and secondary caregivers. Ideally, we would have added our own observations. However, the most socially relevant definition of behavior problems is based on the social perceptions of teachers and families. Research (e.g., Lobitz & Johnson, 1975) has usually found the social perception criterion of clinical referral to be more closely associated with parent-report checklists than with objective observations.

METHOD

Subjects

Families in the vicinity of a town of 50,000 were recruited on the basis of birth announcements when their infants were near 6 months of age. The size of the sample ranged from approximately 160 at age 6 months to approximately 120 at age 3 years. The N's for the various analyses fluctuate because of attrition over the years of the study (primarily due to moving out of town) and because the multivariate analyses included only subjects who provided each of the measures included in the particular set of analyses. Also, the second half of the sample received several additional procedures that the first half did not. Preliminary analyses suggested no systematic differences in demographic or a variety of other characteristics in the families who dropped out as compared to those who continued. With minor fluctuations, depending on the particular analysis, the children were evenly divided on sex and being firstborn or later born. Parent occupation levels were 14% upper middle, 70% middle, and 16% working class. Subjects were paid for participation in the evaluations that took place when the infants were 6, 13, and 24 months of age.

Procedures

For the sake of brevity, we will give an overview of procedures here but will describe many of the specific scales in conjunction with the results.

Age 6 month procedures.—(*a*) Home visits: Mother-child interaction was assessed at home during two 3-hour visits by specially trained women using electronic event recorders for molecular coding. Observers also used the Caldwell HOME scales to record impressions of mothering qualities and the appropriate Infant Characteristics Questionnaire (ICQ) scales (see below) for impressions of child characteristics (as in Bates et al., 1979). The home measures and their factor dimensions and sequential indexes are defined in Bates et al. (1982). (*b*) Laboratory: The subjects visited the laboratory once for the Bayley test of infant mental development and an interview concerning family adjustments since the baby's birth (yielding the social support score used in the current analyses and in Bates et al., 1982) and once for a videotaped face-to-face play procedure. The play involved three 3-minute segments: play with infant in high chair, unresponsive mother, and return to play. Qualities of interaction were scored on dimensions theoretically relevant to the development of attachment, for example, maternal responsiveness to infant cues (see Kiser, Bates, Maslin, & Bayles, 1983, for details). (*c*) Maternal questionnaires: At age 6 months mothers completed the ICQ (Bates et al., 1979) and, in the second half of the sample, the Revised Infant Temperament Questionnaire (RITQ) (Carey & McDevitt, 1978). Mothers completed the Jackson (1974) Personality Research Form, from which we used only the social desirability scale for the current study.

Age 13 month procedures.—(*a*) Home visit: There was one 3-hour home visit, with procedures very similar to those at 6 months, yielding home observation factors and HOME scales, as described by Pettit & Bates (1984). (*b*) Laboratory: There was one visit to the laboratory for the Bayley test for the whole sample and, for the second half of the sample ($N = 74$), a separate visit to an unfamiliar room for the Strange Situation assessment of attachment (Ainsworth et al., 1978). We received training in procedure and scoring technique from L. A. Sroufe and B. Vaughn as well as help in establishing reliability. For 68 dyads, attachment security could be confidently

171

judged, yielding 66% secure, 13% anxious/avoidant, 16% ($N = 11$) anxious/resistant, and 5% split classifications (showing characteristics of both avoidant and resistant attachments). For six dyads, it was not possible confidently to score Strange Situation behavior because of either problems with the procedure or lack of fit between infant behavior and attachment patterns specified by Ainsworth et al. (1978). For the sake of simplifying the analytic task in the current project, we converted the standard attachment classifications to a three-point scale of attachment security. This is based on the common practice of combining avoidant (A) and resistant (C) infants into one group for comparison with the securely attached (B) group and on the argument advanced by Ainsworth et al. (1978, p. 235) that the B_3 subgroup shows the optimal level of security. In creating the scale, avoidant and resistant infants were assigned the score of 1; B_1, B_2, and B_4 infants were assigned the score of 2; and B_3 infants were assigned the score of 3. This index was then used in correlational analyses.[1] (c) Maternal questionnaires: Mothers completed two questionnaires, a 13-month version of the ICQ and a new research instrument, the Maternal Perceptions Questionnaire (MPQ) (Olson et al., 1982).

Age 24 month procedures.—(a) Home visits: There were two 3-hour home visits during which mother-child interaction was assessed at 6 and 13 months. However, the new Post-Observation Questionnaire (POQ) was filled out by the observer (Olson et al., 1982) instead of the HOME scales, and the Peabody Picture Vocabulary Test was given at the end of the second visit. In addition to the factors of behavior codes (see Olson et al., 1984, for details), we also used probabilities computed across three-step behavior-code sequences. The sequences involved various kinds of child trouble, mother control, and child conflict versus comply codes (see Lee & Bates, 1984, for details). For further analysis these sequential probabilities were reduced to five relatively independent factors (described below, in conjunction with the results) and also reduced to a single sum of the probabilities across all 17 sequences. (b) Laboratory visits: On a laboratory visit, the Bayley test was administered. In the second half of the sample, the Matas et al. (1978) mother-child problem-solving tasks were videotaped for a subsample of 48 dyads and scored in ways similar to Matas et al. In the current study we use the problem-solving factors found by Frankel and Bates (1984). (c) Maternal

---

[1] We selected the correlational approach over analysis of variance primarily for convenience in interpreting a large network of correlations and for its greater power (Hays, 1963) to detect expected effects. We also used the points on the attachment security scale as groups for analyses of variance and found a pattern of effects similar to that yielded by correlations but less often reaching significance. We also examined a large number of analyses of variance using the traditional A/B/C classifications and conclude that the ordinal scale yields a generally similar pattern of results (see Frankel & Bates, 1984; and Maslin, 1983).

questionnaires: Mothers completed the 24-month version of the ICQ (details available from the authors)[2] as well as the 24-month version of the MPQ (Olson et al., 1982).

Age 3 year procedures.—Shortly after the child's third birthday we mailed the parents questionnaires. The questionnaires included the Behar (1977) Preschool Behavior Questionnaire (PBQ), the Faschingbauer (1974) short form of the MMPI, the Spanier (1976) Dyadic Adjustment Scale, and two instruments not applied to the current study. We also asked mothers for the name of an adult outside the immediate family who knew the child well. We sent Behar questionnaires to 97 secondary caregivers and received responses from 70. Of these, 40% were teachers, 27% relatives (usually grandmother or aunt), and 30% baby-sitters or family friends.

RESULTS AND DISCUSSION

Data will be reported in three sections, corresponding to the major research questions of the study. In the area of early social development there are few measures whose meanings are well established. Therefore it is necessary to explore the validity of both operational measures and the constructs that inspired them.

Attachment Security and Mother-Child Relations

Our first question was whether in our sample and with our measurement system attachment security would imply the same kinds of mother-child interactions as reported in the Ainsworth et al. (1978) and Grossmann et al. (in this vol.) studies. We examined data from home and laboratory observations prior to, concurrent with, and subsequent to the attachment assessment. These data are the focus of three separate reports (Frankel & Bates, 1984; Kiser et al., 1983; Maslin, 1984) and are summarized here.

Antecedents of attachment security in home interaction.—First, we will summarize the significant correlations between the three-point attachment scale and mother-infant interaction at age 6 months. These were neither strong nor pervasive, averaging about .23 ($df = 64$, $p < .05$, one-tailed). However, the findings are worthy of note because they fit some key expectations that are based on prior interpretations of our home observation variables and the few prior studies of the antecedents of attachment security. Most important was the correlation between the attachment scale and mother Affectionate Contact ($r = .24$, $p = .03$), the one home observation factor we had designated a priori as relevant. We had no prior expectations for the other

[2] See n. 3 below.

four mother factors tested, and none had a significant correlation with attachment. We did correctly predict, however, that maternal responsiveness indexes would correlate with attachment: both the mother's quickness to respond to the infant's distress with a high-level intervention (e.g., pick up as opposed to distal vocalization) and the proportion of the infant's potential social elicitations to which the mother responded within 6 seconds correlated significantly ($r = -.22$, $p = .04$; $r = .22$, $p = .04$, respectively) with the attachment scale. Three of six HOME scales had significant or borderline-significant correlations with attachment: mothers of infants later judged securely attached tended to score higher on organization of the environment ($r = .32$, $p = .01$), emotional and verbal responsiveness ($r = .18$, $p = .07$), and involvement ($r = .18$, $p = .07$), which assesses direct stimulation of cognitive development (see Bates et al., 1982). While these correlations support Ainsworth et al. (1978), their smallness may indicate either that generalizability of the link between early maternal warmth and responsiveness is limited or that our measures are not equivalent to Ainsworth's sensitivity ratings. We also examined the relationship among several factors of infant behavior, including amount of fussing and crying and attachment security, and found no significant correlations. Ainsworth et al.'s (1978) findings led us to expect that infant crying would differentiate attachment groups; however, this was not the case in our sample.

Antecedents of attachment security in face-to-face play.—The face-to-face play results (detailed in Kiser et al., 1983) offer additional support to the Ainsworth model of the origins of attachment security. Discriminant function analysis gave a modest but theoretically interpretable pattern of results. Positive mutuality in play and maternal interest in initiating play bouts both predicted secure attachment. There was also a tendency for infants who were to be securely attached to be calmer than other infants in facing a noninteractive mother in the second segment. This may indicate infant comfort in the mere presence of the mother and expectancy of availability. Babies who were to be secure also, however, showed relatively greater negative affect in the following, "reunion" segment. The reason for this is not clear, but perhaps the distress was due to violation of an expectancy of closer interaction than our experimental procedure allowed.

Concurrent home interactions and attachment.—There were some modest but theoretically appropriate links between the attachment security scale and the 13-month home observation. The average r was .23 ($p < .05$, one-tailed). Mother Teaching (composed of six codes for showing and naming things, asking questions, and positive comments about the baby's actions), infant Object Communication (point out, bring object, comply with positive request), and mother Affection and Caregiving (affection, social-expressive speech, physical needs caregiving) correlated with the attachment scale ($r = .22$, $p = .04$; $r = .27$, $p = .01$; and $r = .20$, $p = .05$, respectively). The five remaining home observation factors (see Pettit & Bates, 1984) did not correlate with the attachment scale. The four HOME scales scored at this age, Emotional and Verbal Responsivity, Avoidance of Restriction, Provision of Play Materials, and Maternal Involvement, also did not correlate with attachment security.

Attachment and subsequent home interaction.—At age 24 months, we found further evidence that attachment security at 13 months describes, to a modest degree, transsituational, enduring qualities of the mother-child relationship. The average significant *r* for this data set was .27 (*p* < .05, one-tailed). Interestingly, we found that attachment security did not predict variables we regarded as close counterparts of the maternal affection and verbal communication variables at 6 and 13 months (mother Verbal Stimulation and Affection/Play). However, variables pertaining mainly to the harmony of the dyads' handling of child independence versus control issues were predicted. The control-issue correlations were expected on the basis of Londerville and Main (1981), Main et al. (1979), and Matas et al. (1978). Specifically, secure attachment predicted lower mother Negative Control (prohibition, scolding, restraining, etc., *r* = .24, *p* = .04), although not the child counterpart, Trouble. Insecure attachment predicted child resistance to maternal control for one of the five conflict sequence composites, Conflict after Restrain or Physically Punish (*r* = .33, *p* = .01), but not for conflict after other forms of maternal control responses to child trouble stimuli. The postobservation rating factor Reciprocal Interaction, an index of smooth mutuality, composed of mild mother control, acceptance of child explorations, reciprocal interactions, and pleasant, mature child behavior, was predicted by attachment security (*r* = .24, *p* = .04). Five other postobservation composites and six other molecular code factors were not predicted by attachment security.

Attachment and subsequent laboratory interaction.—In accord with Matas et al. (1978), attachment security predicted lower scores on the main factor in the 24-month laboratory problem-solving interactions, Negative and Conflictual Task Interaction (*r*[40] = −.34, *p* = .03). This factor includes the key ratings of maternal quality of assistance and supportive presence and child percent of compliance to mother commands as well as global and molecular ratings of child noncompliance to mother directives, anger/aggression, and time off task. The other five problem-solving factors did not correlate significantly with attachment security. These results replicate Matas et al. (1978), although we do not find as extensive an array of relationships between problem solving and attachment security. In addition, for the first time to our knowledge, we extended the generalizability of the Matas et al. assessment to mother-child interactions at home. As detailed in Frankel and Bates (1984), we found that the problem-solving factors were predicted by 6-, 13-, and 24-month home observation factors describing both verbal interaction and child trouble/mother control.

In summary, the answer to our first question, whether attachment security at 13 months has the same implications in our study as in the few prior studies, is a qualified yes. The correlations with other mother-child indexes were weak and far from pervasive but probably not merely due to chance. The correlations most strongly expected were found in both home and laboratory assessments at 6, 13, and 24 months. On the basis of the attachment security literature and our prior findings of stability and external validity in our home observation and problem-solving measures (e.g., Olson et al., 1984; Pettit & Bates, 1984) we conclude that the attachment security measures and our other home and laboratory measures represent valid constructs.

Attachment Security and Temperament

The second question, whether behavior in the Strange Situation assessment bears any relation to child characteristics that could be called temperament, was answered by correlations between attachment and temperament measures. The basis for expecting such relations has recently been debated (Chess & Thomas, 1982; Goldsmith & Campos, 1982; Sroufe & Waters, 1982). In computing correlations we used the attachment security scale as well as Strange Situation behavior ratings (proximity seeking and avoiding and contact maintenance and resistance in the reunion episodes). We measured temperament via both parent and observer ratings at ages 6, 13, and 24 months.

Antecedent ratings.—At 6 months none of the four ICQ scales, including the main, difficultness factor, correlated significantly with the attachment security scale at or beyond the criterion for all correlations in this section ($p = .05$, two-tailed). This was also the case for the Carey and McDevitt Revised Infant Temperament Questionnaire, nine separate scales and its summary measure of difficultness. These findings support Sroufe (1983) in his contention that attachment classification transcends temperament differences in children.

However, while the overall ratings of attachment security were uncorrelated with temperament, there were four temperament measures (both RITQ and observer measures) that predicted infant contact maintenance in the reunion episodes in understandable ways. However, these are not crucial here.[3]

Concurrent temperament ratings.—At 13 months, babies rated by their mothers on the ICQ as low in social responsiveness, that is, unexcitable and not much liking to play with people, tended to have less secure attachments

[3] A more detailed summary of these results is available from John E. Bates, Department of Psychology, Indiana University, Bloomington, IN 47405.

($r[63]$ = .37, $p <$ .01). Unresponsive infants were also more likely to resist contact in the second reunion (r = .35, $p <$ .01). The remaining three mother ICQ factors at 13 months were not significantly correlated with Strange Situation behaviors. Ratings on the four MPQ factors did not significantly correlate with attachment security but did show some modest correlations with Strange Situation reunion behavior ratings. Two MPQ scales, Sociability and Unresponsive to Mother, and examiner's impression of fear during the Bayley test were related to contact maintaining in the Strange Situation in easily interpretable ways: babies seen as outgoing and fearless by their mothers and the Bayley examiner and babies seen by their mothers as lacking interest in them all made less effort to maintain contact (details are available from the authors).

Subsequent temperament ratings.—None of the 24-month ICQ or MPQ variables had notable correlations with the attachment security scale, but contact maintenance during reunion did predict several conceptually relevant, mother and observer 24-month scales, for example, the MPQ index of stranger fear, Unsociable (r = .41, $p <$ .01). Further details on these findings are available from the authors.

In summary, the data suggest that Strange Situation classifications are mostly independent of both mother- and observer-perceived temperament measures. However, some infant temperament measures were modestly correlated with specific reunion behavior ratings during the Strange Situation. Of these, infant contact maintenance had the most notable pattern of correlations with child characteristics rated at 6, 13, and 24 months of age.

Antecedents of Behavior Problems at Age 3 Years

Having considered the network formed by attachment, mother-child interaction, and temperament measures at 6, 13, and 24 months, we now ask how these various indexes predict perceptions of behavior problems at 3 years of age. Our approach involved a systematic sifting of the data. We examined (1) multiple regressions and accompanying bivariate correlations within a set of conceptual domains, (2) a set of multiple regressions with predictors selected from all domains on the basis of the results of the set 1 analyses, and (3) tests of a limited number of hypothesized, multiplicative effects to see whether interactions between key predictors might contribute to the account of behavior-problem outcomes.

Predictor Domains

We sorted the predictor variables into eight conceptual domains. This sorting was aided by prior explorations of relationships and nonrelationships among a number of the variables of current interest. Especially important were (1) a second-order factor analysis of mother perception variables across development and examination of these variables' correlates with more objective indexes, reported by Bates and Bayles (1984), and (2) factor analyses and cross-time correlations of home observation measures reported by Bates et al. (1982), Lee & Bates (1984), Olson et al. (1984), and Pettit & Bates (1984). Despite notable convergences between mothers and independent observers (e.g., Bates & Bayles, 1984), in general it is clear that the observational and mother-report data are far from equivalent.

The predictor domains and their defining variables are listed in Table 1. Domains 1–4 represent concepts that our prior analyses (see above) have established as factorally coherent, stable across development, and having at least modest amounts of overlap between various kinds of observer ratings and parental questionnaire ratings. The domains are the following: (1) negative emotion—pertains to difficult temperament; (2) unadaptability/unsociability; (3) activity management problems scores, which concern the dimension of child exploratory action and mother reactive control (it is not now clear whether this pertains to the temperament construct of activity level); (4) verbal development, which pertains to affectively warm, educative communication, and child verbal-cognitive development; (5) attachment security and reunion behavior ratings; (6) problem-solving factors summarizing mother-child interactions in the Matas et al. (1978) tasks; (7) family stress, which refers to indexes of the strains and resources of the family; and (8) sex of child, the final predictor. According to prior studies of behavior problems, boys would be more likely than girls to develop behavior problems, especially of the acting-out sort.

Outcome Variables

For behavior-problem outcome data at age 3 years we used Behar PBQ ratings by mothers and, in a subsample, the ratings of secondary caregivers. The content of the three Behar scales is crucial to interpretation of the regression analyses. Anxious refers to fretfulness, fear of novelty, speech problems, and passivity. In contrast, Hostile involves aggression and active conflict with both peers and adults. Hyperactive, a very short scale, describes restlessness and inattentiveness but not aggressiveness. The weak correlations between the perceptions of mothers and secondary caregivers ($r[68]$ = $-.03$, $.16$, $.25$, for the Anxious, Hostile, and Hyperactive scales, respectively) make it worth contrasting the meaning of behavior problems for the two different perspectives. The correlations were modest to moderate among the three PBQ factors for mothers ($r[12]$ = $.47$, $r[13]$ = $.35$, $r[23]$ = $.50$) and for secondary caregivers ($r[12]$ = $.39$, $r[13]$ = $.15$, $r[23]$ = $.26$).

Regressions within Predictor Domains

An overview of the results of the first-level regressions will be presented first. The main focus here will be on the overall prediction success of each domain. A more detailed consideration of particular predictors will be presented in the next section. Given the emphasis on attachment in this chapter, we were inclined to report the predictions by attachment variables first. However, attachment variables, especially attachment security, were largely uncorrelated with the behavior-problem outcomes. Therefore we will discuss the more successful predictors before considering attachment. As can be seen in Table 2, early mother perceptions were the most successful predictors of later behavior problems. This was especially so for outcome ratings by the mothers themselves. This could be attributed to consistency in the subjective aspect of maternal perception alone. However, on the basis of the pattern of results, the validational evidence concerning mother reports (above), and supplemental analyses concerning possible influences due to mother personality, we would argue that the predictiveness of the early mother reports has substantive meaning. First, mother reports of negative, fearful reactions to novelty predicted only the Anxious scale, consistent with the content of the outcome scale, and reports of early activity management problems predicted only the acting-out behavior problems, also consistent with scale content. Difficult temperament predicted each of the kinds of behavior problems. This is consistent with the prior interpretations that difficultness contains a component of aversive demandingness, which pertains in theory to acting-out behavior problems (Bates et al., 1979; Lee & Bates, 1984; Lounsbury & Bates, 1982).

In considering the extent to which the link between difficultness and behavior-problem perceptions represents a negative bias in the mother, we note that the ICQ difficultness scales are relatively low in overlap with indexes of a general response bias (Bates & Bayles, 1984). Further multiple regression analyses suggested that maternal defensiveness and social desirability bias did not account for the links between difficultness and the two acting-out scales of the PBQ. However, correlations between difficultness, the PBQ Anxious scale, and mother self-reported anxiety, defensiveness, and social desirability allowed us to hypothesize that anxious mothers are more likely to have anxious children (for both environmental and genetic reasons); as infants these children may express their proneness to anxiety via difficult temperament (Bates & Bayles, 1984).

In the attachment domain, attachment security did not predict later behavior problems, unlike the findings reported by Sroufe (1983) and by Erickson et al. (in this vol.). This is not a critical nonreplication: Sroufe's team assessed a sample with many more than the usual numbers of insecurely attached children and based PBQ scores on extensive observations in

TABLE 1

PREDICTOR VARIABLES BY CONCEPTUAL DOMAIN

	VARIABLES		
DOMAIN	Observational	Mother Perception	
1. Negative emotion	Infant Fussy (6)	ICQ Fussy-Difficult (6)	
	Infant Socially Demanding (13)	ICQ Fussy-Difficult-Demanding (13)	
	Child Negative Emotion (24)	ICQ Difficult (24)	
	Observer ICQ Difficult (6)	RITQ Difficult (6)[a]	
	Observer ICQ Difficult (13)		
2. Unadaptability/unsociability	Bayley Fear Composite (6)	ICQ Unadaptable (6)	
	Bayley Fear Composite (13)	ICQ Unsociable (13)	
	Bayley Fear Composite (24)	ICQ Unadaptable (13)	
	Observer ICQ Unadaptable (6)	ICQ Negative Adaptation (24)	
	Observer ICQ Unsociable (13)	MPQ Unsociable (13)	
	Observer ICQ Unadaptable (13)	MPQ Unsociable (24)	
	Observer ICQ Negative Adaptation (24)	RITQ Approach + Adaptability (6)[a]	
3. Activity Management	Infant Persist + Mother Manage (13)	ICQ Persistent (13)	
	Child Trouble + Mother Restrict (24)	ICQ Unstoppable, Noncuddly (24)	
	Conflict Sequence Sum (24)	ICQ Irregular (24)	
	POQ Pleasant, Nonirritating Child (24)	MPQ Compliant, Mature (24)	
	POQ Maternal, Non-Punitiveness (24)	RITQ activity (6)[a]	

4. Verbal development	Mother Affectionate Contact + Object Stimulation – Come and Go + HOME Involvement (6)
	Mother Teaching + Infant Object Communication + HOME Involvement (13)
	Mother Verbal + Response to Speech + Child Speech + POQ Mature Child Communication (24)
	Bayley MDI (24)
	Peabody vocabulary (24)
	MPQ Language Competence (13)
	MPQ Language Competence (24)
5. Attachment (13)[a]	attachment security scale
	proximity seeking[b]
	contact maintenance
	proximity avoidance
	contact resistance
	crying
	...
6. Problem solving (24)[a]	Negative-Conflictual Task Interaction
	Dependency
	Say No to Mother, Ask E's Help
	Ignore Mother Directives
	Overcontrolling Mother, Frustrated Child
	...
7. Family stress	Parent Occupation Status (6)[c]
	Life Events Score (24–36)[d]
	Marital Satisfaction Spanier Total (36)
8. Sex of child	

NOTE.—Factor-based composite names are capitalized; numbers in parentheses refer to age in months; and composites are formed by adding standardized scores of first-order composites.
[a] Variable measured only in second half of sample.
[b] This and next three variables are summed over reunions 1 and 2.
[c] Represents higher of two parents = upper middle, 2 = middle, and 3 = lower SES.
[d] A weighted index of stressful events (e.g., death, major illness, or job loss) reported in phone contacts at 18 and 24 months.

TABLE 2

MULTIPLE CORRELATIONS FROM FIRST-LEVEL REGRESSION ANALYSES

	PBQ Rater					
	Mother			Secondary Caregiver		
PREDICTOR DOMAIN	Anxious	Hostile	Hyperactive	Anxious	Hostile	Hyperactive
A. Negative emotion:						
1. Observation	...ᵃ	...	...	...	...	...
2. Mother perception (excluding RITQ)	.33**	.44*****	.41*****	.35*	...	...
3. Mother perception (including RITQ)	.46**	.46**	...	...	...	...
B. Unadaptability/unsociability:						
1. Observation	.37**	...	...	...	...	...
2. Mother perception (excluding RITQ)	.35**	...	...	...	.54*****	...
3. Mother perception (including RITQ)	...	...	...	...	.57**	...

	(1)	(2)	(3)	(4)	(5)	(6)
C. Activity management:						
1. Observation	...	...	...	...	...	...
2. Mother perception (excluding RITQ)	...	.48*****	.42****	...	...	...
3. Mother perception (including RITQ)	...	.54***	.45*	...	...	...
D. Verbal development:						
1. Observation	...	...	...	.45**	...	.44*
2. Mother perception	...	...	.24*	...	...	...
E. Attachment	.48**	.49**	...	...	...	...
F. Problem solving	...	.46*	...	...	...	...
G. Family stress:						
1. SES and Spanier	...	.23**	...	.36***	.35**	...
2. SES, Spanier, and life events	...	...	...	.44*	.57*****	...
H. Sex of child	...	...	.18[b]**	...	.30[b]***	...

[a] Only significant or borderline R's are lsted.
[b] Boys rated higher.
* $p \leq .18$.
** $p \leq .05$.
*** $p \leq .01$.
**** $p \leq .005$.
***** $p \leq .001$.

183

a research preschool rather than mother ratings. Furthermore, Sroufe's sample contained many more multiproblem families (e.g., single mothers, welfare families, and familes with legal problems) than our sample. We can presume that an anxiously attached infant in Sroufe's sample had fewer chances for compensatory relationships, for example, with a warm, supportive father, compared to a similar infant in our sample. One attachment-domain variable in our study, proximity seeking during reunions, did contribute to a significant multiple correlation in predicting behavior problems. The nature of its link to behavior problems will be considered in the second-level regressions.

In general, early home observation variables did not combine to predict the outcome perceptions of mothers very well. Rather, maternal ratings of anxious and acting-out behavior problems at 3 years of age were predicted by earlier (conceptually related) perceptions of temperament and activity management problems. On the other hand, secondary caregivers' ratings of anxious and hyperactive problems were related to earlier observation measures (less verbal-educative interaction with the mother and lower scores on verbal-cognitive test performance). Secondary caregivers' ratings of hostile problems were predicted by prior maternal perceptions of unadaptability and unsociability. The secondary caregiver pattern is similar for teachers, friend/baby-sitter, and relatives. The finding that poor verbal development predicted secondary caregiver's perceptions of behavior problems was expected on the basis of prior studies (e.g., Richman, Stevenson, & Graham, 1982). Perhaps the secondary caregivers see behavior problems because the low verbal children are relatively unresponsive to secondary caregivers' efforts to positively engage them and to set limits.

A final point to emerge from the first-level regressions is that boys were seen by their mothers as having very slightly more Hyperactive problems than girls, again analogous to the findings of Richman et al. (1982). Secondary raters saw boys as having a few more Hostile problems than girls. On the basis of studies of older children, we might have predicted a more pervasive sex effect. However, prior research has found small sex differences at young ages (Richman et al., 1982).

In broadest overview, the first-level regression analyses suggest that most of the domains had some modest but generally interpretable links with the behavior-problem outcomes. Early mother perceptions were generally better predictors than direct observations of mother-child interactions.

Second-Level Regression Analyses

On the basis of the first-level regressions, the best predictors were selected for a set of second-level regressions. Selection was based on least trend-significant bivariate correlations between the predictor and criterion and on overlap between the predictor and criterion after controlling for overlap among predictors. Thus some predictors were selected as representatives of their domain despite the multiple r for their set being nonsignificant. Some variables, despite relatively large bivariate correlations with outcome measures, were omitted or combined with other predictor measures because they were too similar to other predictors and did not make a sufficiently large independent contribution. For these reasons and in order to maintain a larger N for analyses, no RITQ scales were included in the second-level analyses, even though several RITQ scales did make modest, conceptually appropriate predictions of behavior problems.

Although common practice, selecting best predictors may provide inflated estimates of explained variance, capitalizing on sample-specific correlations. We took steps to reduce predictor variable overlap within domains, guided by our prior findings, but not all collinearity was eliminated. Nevertheless, we saw the second-level analysis as a useful distillation and felt that we could avoid the worst excesses of overinterpretation. As can be seen in Table 3, most of the second-order multiple correlations were significant. Not all the predictors made independent contributions, and the regression equations of the whole sample analysis did not always correspond to those of the attachment/problem-solving subsample analysis. However, overall the data suggest that there are interesting meanings in the behavior-problem scales. For each behavior-problem outcome variable, we will present the results for the whole sample first and then those for the subsample that participated in the attachment and problem-solving assessments. As mentioned above, the attachment-domain results were not striking enough to be featured first.

1. *Anxious.*—As can be seen in Table 3, mothers' perceptions of Anxious problems were best predicted both by ICQ difficult temperament (i.e., frequent negative emotion, summed over 6–24 months) and by 24-month MPQ unsociability, an index of fear versus approach responses to new people. These links are consistent with the Behar PBQ concept of anxious problems. An attachment behavior index was also a significant predictor—infants who did not seek proximity to their mothers after separation were more likely to be seen as high on Anxious problems 2 years later. The link here may be that low proximity seeking represents a passive response to stress, an aspect of the Anxious scale.[4]

The secondary caregivers' perceptions of Anxious problems were predicted by a different set of variables than those predicting mother percep-

[4] It may be noted that in the attachment subsample analysis, the relative beta weight of the difficultness sum decreases from what it is in the whole sample. This is due not to overlap between difficultness and proximity seeking but rather to a higher overlap between difficultness and unsociability in the subsample ($r = .41$) rather than in the whole sample ($r = .16$).

TABLE 3

SECOND-LEVEL REGRESSIONS: PREDICTIONS OF 3-YEAR BEHAVIOR PROBLEMS WITH BEST PREDICTORS FROM FIRST-LEVEL REGRESSIONS

	Dependent Variable	
	Mother-perceived Anxiety	Secondary Caregiver–perceived Anxiety

A. Whole sample	($N = 109$)
	$r = .41$
	$p = .000$
	Beta weights:
	  a. Difficultness ($6 + 13 + 24$–month ICQ) = .24***
	  b. Unsociable (24-month MPQ) = .23**
	  c. Fear (6-month Bayley) = .14
		($N = 62$)
		$r = .58$
		$p = .002$
		Beta weights:
		  a. SES = .39***
		  b. Language (24-month MPQ) = −.20*
		  c. Difficultness (6-month ICQ) = −.20
		  d. Difficultness (6-month Observer ICQ) = −.12
		  e. Irregular (24-month ICQ) = −.12
		  f. Verbal Development (supercomposite, 6 month)[a] = −.10
		  g. ICQ Negative Adaptation (24 month) = .09

B. Attachment subsample	($N = 52$)
	$r = .61$
	$p = .000$
	Beta weights:
	  a. Unsociable (24-month MPQ) = .41***
	  b. proximity-seeking, reunions $1 + 2$ = −.35***
	  c. Fear (6-month Bayley) = .18
	  d. Difficultness ($6 + 13 + 24$–month ICQ) = .12
		($N = 39$)
		$r = .82$
		$p = .000$
		Beta weights:
		  a. proximity avoidance reunions $1 + 2$ = .44***
		  b. SES = .40***
		  c. Difficultness (6-month ICQ) = −.35***
		  d. Language (24-month MPQ) = −.26**
		  e. Irregular (24-month ICQ) = −.20*
		  f. Verbal Development (supercomposite, 6 month)[a] = −.12
		  g. Difficultness (6-month Observer ICQ) = −.10
		  h. Negative Adaptation (24 month ICQ) = .08

	Mother-perceived Hostility	Secondary Caregiver–perceived Hostility
A. Whole sample	($N = 88$) $r = .58$ $p = .000$ Beta weights: a. Persistent (13-month ICQ) + Unstoppable (24-month ICQ) = .40*** b. Difficultness (6 + 13 + 24–month ICQ) = .23** c. marital satisfaction (3 years) = .15 d. Observed conflict sum (24 month) = .10	($N = 57$) $r = .67$ $p = .000$ Beta weights: a. Unsociable (13 + 24–month MPQ) = −.68*** b. Negative Adaptation (24-month ICQ) = .63*** c. SES = .32** d. Difficultness (13-month Observer ICQ) = .17 e. Verbal Development (supercomposite, 6 month)[a] = −.07 f. sex of child = −.03
B. Attachment subsample	($N = 52$) $r = 66$ $p = .068$ Neither Attachment behavior (crying and proximity seeking) nor Problem Solving (Reject Mother Suggestion, Seek E's Help) adds significant variance	($N = 33$) $r = .74$ $p = .014$ Neither Attachment behavior (proximity seeking) nor Problem Solving (Reject Mother Suggestion, Seek E's Help, and Overcontrol and Frustration) adds significant variance

	Mother-perceived Hyperactive	Secondary Caregiver–perceived Hyperactive
A. Whole sample	($N = .90$) $r = .55$ $p = .000$ Beta weights: a. Persistent (13-month ICQ) = .28** b. Pleasant, Responsive Child (24-month Observer POQ) = −.23 c. Difficult (6 + 13 + 24–month ICQ) = .21* d. Difficult (24-month Observer ICQ) = −.18	($N = 59$) $r = .41$ $p = .006$ Beta weights: a. vocabulary (24-month Peabody) = −.39*** b. Difficult (13-month Observer ICQ) = −.05

TABLE 3 (*Continued*)

	Dependent Variable	
	Mother-perceived Hyperactive	Secondary Caregiver–perceived Hyperactive
	e. Language (13 + 24–month MPQ) = − .17* f. Compliant, Mature (24-month MPQ) = − .12 g. observed conflict sum (24 month) = .11 h. sex of child (1 male, 2 female) = .09	
B. Attachment subsample	(N = 52) r = .51, N.S. Attachment behavior (contact maintenance) did not add significant variance	(N = 33) r = .37, N.S. Problem Solving (Negative, Conflictual Interaction) did not add significant variance

NOTE.—N's are variable due to listwise deletion of subjects with any missing data and the varied sets of variables in each of the analyses.
[a] Defined in Table 1, pt. 4.
* $p \leq .1$.
** $p \leq .05$.
*** $p \leq .01$.

tion on the Anxious scale, as seen in Table 3. In the prediction equations, the beta weight for family occupation status (SES) overshadowed the beta weight for the observed stimulation of verbal development. However, the bivariate correlation between SES and outcome ($r = .40$) was only very slightly greater than the correlation between the verbal-educative composite and outcome ($r = -.36$). This finding, in conjunction with the overlap between SES and the verbal-educative composite ($r = -.39$) and the significant beta for the fairly objective 24-month MPQ Language Development, suggests that it is really the lower encouragement of verbal development of lower-class families and the slow verbal development of lower-class children that predict secondary caregivers' later perceptions of anxiety, not SES per se. This is consistent with the speech difficulty item on the Anxious scale. However, we cannot say whether slow verbal development makes for anxious adaptation in the presence of secondary caregivers or whether both verbal development and anxiety are by-products of an underlying, experiential process.

The analysis of secondary caregivers' Anxious ratings in the attachment subsample showed that, the more an infant avoided proximity in the reunions of the Strange Situation, the more likely that child would be seen as having anxiety problems by the secondary raters 2 years later. Assuming that anxious behavior problems have some overlap with the construct of dependency, this finding partially converges with the Sroufe (1983) finding that anxious attachment (partly based on observed proximity avoidance) predicts high dependency on nursery school teachers. The secondary caregiver analyses, especially in the attachment subsample, also suggest that the bearing of early temperament on secondary raters' Anxious ratings was essentially the opposite of what it was for mothers' ratings: easy and biologically regular infants were more likely to be seen by secondary caregivers as anxious than were difficult and irregular infants, especially in this subsample. The reason for this relationship may be similar to the interpretation we suggested above for the prediction by proximity seeking—a child with low emotionality and high rhythmicity may be seen by outsiders as passive and unresponsive (cf. Thomas et al., 1968).

2. *Hostile.*—As with the Anxious scale, it appears that the antecedents of aggressive behavior problems depend on who is rating the Hostile scale. Mothers' Hostile ratings were predicted best by early perceptions of management problems and by difficultness. As explained in connection with the first-level regressions, these links are quite consistent with prior thinking. However, secondary caregiver ratings of high aggression were predicted best by lower family occupation class and by the contrast of MPQ Unsociability and ICQ Negative Adaptation to Change. The large, opposite-sign beta weights for the latter two predictors represent a suppressor effect. The two predictors have a moderately high correlation with each other ($r = .65$) but

have modest correlations of opposite signs with the criterion. Both predictors were retained because the contrast makes conceptual sense. Negative Adaptation to Change refers to rejection of change or variety in general, and it is understandable that a child who has this tendency might be seen by a comparative outsider as hostile. Unsociability, on the other hand, refers specifically to fear of versus approach to new people, an analogue to extraversion or lack of social fear, a variable seen as a component in acting-out disorders (e.g., Eysenck & Eysenck, 1978).

The attachment and problem-solving variables did not add significantly to the prediction of the Hostile scale for either kind of rater. The much less expensive mother report measures were a good substitute for the attachment measures in predicting later perceptions of hostile behavior.

3. *Hyperactive.*—In contrast to the quite different patterns of predictors for mothers versus secondary raters on the Anxious and Hostile scales, there was some similarity on the Hyperactive scale. Both mothers and secondary raters saw children whose language development had been slow as more likely to have hyperactive problems at age 3 years, although it was the mother's prior MPQ rating of language development that was (modestly) predictive of her own Hyperactive scale and the Peabody vocabulary score that was (moderately) predictive of the secondary rater's scale. It would be useful to know whether these links represent the slow language development of temperamentally restless, inattentive children or whether the slow language development and the factors that underlie it somehow make the child more prone to later hyperactivity. Our early measures did not allow us to evaluate these possibilities. For the mother Hyperactive ratings only, early ICQ perceptions of management problems and difficult temperament also made significant contributions to the prediction equation. This parallels the findings for the Hostile scale and supports the common view that aggressive and hyperactive problems have some aspects in common.

To summarize what did and did not predict the maternally perceived behavior problems at age 3 years: early mother perceptions predicted in conceptually appropriate ways, observer indexes of verbal development and attachment behavior also predicted to a modest degree, but attachment security and most of the other observational measures did not. Secondary caregivers' behavior-problem perceptions were usually predicted by different antecedents than those of mothers. Secondary caregiver ratings were best predicted by SES-related verbal development measures and mother reports of adaptability and sociability.

Tests for Interaction Effects

A number of writers have suggested that important effects in development may involve nonlinear, interactive relationships between predictor variables (e.g., Denenberg, 1979). However, our analyses suggested the contrary—the simpler, linear additive models are sufficient. We tested several specific nonlinear models suggested by prior literature and plausibility.[5] First, we tested an approximation of the Crockenberg (1981) finding that high irritability in the infant interacts with poor mother social support to predict later attachment security. Second, we evaluated the possibility that difficult temperament might result in behavior problems especially in families where there is a low marital satisfaction. A third model reasoned that difficult boys might be more likely to have behavior problems than difficult girls. Fourth, we asked whether attachment security, even though it did not directly predict later behavior-problem ratings (above), might predict them at high levels of marital stress. Finally, we searched for a difficultness by attachment interaction. We tested the models with multiple regression analyses, using both effect coding (i.e., creation of a new independent variable vector by multiplication of two original, hypothetically interacting variables' vectors) and dummy coding (i.e., creating new predictor terms descriptive of the separate cells of a two-way design [Kerlinger & Pedhazur, 1973]). The analyses essentially failed to support the nonlinear models. Although such effects may be found in other research, we would, for now, emphasize additive models' parsimony.

CONCLUSIONS

The current study suggests a number of useful conclusions. First, the data give a limited validation of prior interpretations of attachment security. According to Sroufe (1983) and others, attachment security grows from maternal warmth and responsiveness; it is not related to early temperament of the infant, but it does predict adaptive problem solving in the toddler-mother dyad. However, in our study the degree of overlap between attachment security and the other relevant measures was consistently small. Some proportion of this nonoverlap must be due to measurement error in attachment security and the other indexes. However, the measurement-error problem could not be the major explanation because the generalizability of observational variables was good. Likewise idiosyncrasies of our sample should not be too important because the sample was a typical demographic cross-section. The remaining explanation is that observation measures of the Ainsworth tradition tap different aspects of mother-child relations than do those of the behavior coding tradition from which our measures derived. Ainsworth-type measures might be especially sensitive to subtle and idiosyn-

---

[5] These analyses were performed through the help of Tom Rizzo. Additional details are available from the authors.

cratic interaction events that indicate conflicted feelings. Our own, more molecular behavior codes might be especially sensitive to the events marking a verbal, educational orientation and relatively insensitive to the signs of conflicted motives in the mother. The complementarity of the two might prove useful.[6]

Second, another conclusion of the present study addresses the role of temperament in attachment. Temperament indexes did not predict major attachment classifications. However, temperament measures did predict ratings of contact maintenance during the reunion episodes of the Strange Situation. The correlations may be due to a temperamental basis in infant emotional reactivity and stress reactions to strangers, but the cause of the correlation might also lie in subtle parent-child interaction processes.

Third, counter to original expectation, attachment security did not predict the behavior-problem outcomes. We mentioned some possible reasons for this above, centering on the relatively healthy families in our study and possible compensatory processes for insecurely attached infants. Another explanation concerns the limitations of our age 3 year outcome measure: if we were to use more socially relevant outcome diagnoses, for example, based on behavior at age 9 years rather than at 3 years, attachment security might be predictive.

Fourth, although attachment at 12 months did not predict behavior problems at 3 years, other variables explained substantial amounts of variance in the multiple regression analyses. Mothers' perceptions of their infants and toddlers were the strongest predictors of the PBQ. Perceptions of negative reactions to new people (unsociability) and frequent displays of negative affect (difficultness) predicted later maternal ratings of anxious behavior problems, while early activity management problems and difficultness predicted hostile behavior problems. How do these early perceptions arise? We have argued above that the perception does reflect some objective reality, possibly constitution or possibly parent personality influences on the parent-child process. How is it that early characteristics come to predict later problems? The linkages between early social fear or distaste for new people and early activity management difficulties and their corresponding behavior disorders seem relatively straightforward. However, how the difficult temperament scales come to predict both anxious and acting-out disorders is probably more complicated. Perhaps anxious disorders are predicted by the hypothetical irritability component of difficultness (Bates, 1983), while acting-out disorders are predicted by a need-for-stimulation

[6] We are currently evaluating Ainsworth-type measures in home observations in a small subsample of 4-year-olds and their families from our longitudinal sample (Pettit & Bates, 1983), making a detailed narrative record, with special focus on describing family conflict events, and then rating a set of clinically derived scales concerning family adaptations.

component plus a learned or innate tendency to display aversive behavior when bored.

Also of interest, finally, are the ways secondary caregivers' perceptions of behavior problems and their antecedents differ from those of parents. It appears that secondary caregivers may tend to see anxiety in some lower-class children who have been slow in communication development and who have avoided an attachment figure when under stress; and they may regard as hostile some lower-class children who have previously been negative in adaptation to new situations in general but relatively fearless in dealing with new people.

In conclusion, we have found a network of measures of the very young child and the family environment with both coherence and differentiation. A subset of these measures was moderately successful in predicting perceived behavior problems at age 3 years. Of course, one would expect some shrinkage in predictive power if the same variables were tested in a new study. However, for the present, it appears that we have made progress toward finding a battery of measures that could eventually be useful in identifying children at risk for early behavior problems.

VIII. CURRENT PERSPECTIVES IN ATTACHMENT THEORY: ILLUSTRATION FROM THE STUDY OF MALTREATED INFANTS

KAREN SCHNEIDER-ROSEN, KAREN G. BRAUNWALD,
VICKI CARLSON, AND DANTE CICCHETTI

Harvard University

INTRODUCTION

While much of the current work on attachment is based on Bowlby's observations of clinical populations of infants, it is ironic that it is only recently that investigators have begun to study the quality of attachment in atypical populations of infants (e.g., Cicchetti & Serafica, 1981; Crittenden, 1981; Egeland & Sroufe, 1981a; Gaensbauer & Harmon, 1982; Schneider-Rosen & Cicchetti, 1984; Serafica & Cicchetti, 1976). The study of atypical populations has implications for our current theories of normal development and for our understanding of the integrative nature of advances in the cognitive, social, and emotional domains (see Cicchetti & Schneider-Rosen, 1984, for a review). Furthermore, the examination of qualitative differences in the nature of the attachment relationship in atypical populations can help

This investigation was supported by grant no. 90-C-1929 from the National Center on Child Abuse and Neglect, Administration for Children, Youth, and Families, and by grant no. 1-ROI-MH37960-01 from the National Institute of Mental Health. The authors are grateful for the support and encouragement of James Harrell, Aeolian Jackson, and Cecelia Sudia of the National Center of Child Abuse and Neglect and Thomas Lalley of the National Institute of Mental Health. We would like to thank the social workers of the Massachusetts Department of Social Services and the Massachusetts Society for the Prevention of Cruelty to Children. We thank J. Lawrence Aber for his helpful comments on an earlier version of this chapter, and we wish to express our appreciation for the help and support of Judy Bigelow, Ellen Bressler, Ann Churchill, Laura Damson, Valerie Johnson, Carol Kottmeier, Carol Marquez, Margaret Schubert, Liz Tingley, and Jody Wilinski.

to highlight and refine some of the critical theoretical issues that are relevant to the construct of attachment.

The investigation of infants who have been maltreated provides a unique opportunity for examining the relative importance of extremes in the caregiving environment presumed to influence subsequent attachment behavior. The chaotic, disorganized home setting in which many maltreated infants are reared and the inconsistent or abusive patterns of care provided for them place maltreated infants at risk for suffering from the negative consequences of "caretaking casualty" (Sameroff & Chandler, 1975). In particular, the extreme fluctuations in stressful life circumstances that tend to characterize those home environments where maltreatment occurs provide the appropriate framework within which the effect of such stress on the activation of the infant's attachment behavioral system may be examined (Cicchetti & Rizley, 1981; Egeland et al., 1980; Garbarino & Gilliam, 1980). Furthermore, variations in the capacity to deal with stressful experiences may influence the organization of attachment behaviors within the infant-caregiver dyad and the stability of the attachment relationship. In middle-class families with stable environments, attachment classifications have been found to be highly constant over time. However, there is a broad consensus that changes in patterns of care during infancy and early childhood can lead to changes in the attachment relationship (Thompson, Lamb, & Estes, 1983; Vaughn et al., 1979; Waters, 1983). Accordingly, it is important to identify the conditions that either promote stability or bring about change in a relationship that exists in dynamic transaction with a multitude of sociocultural and environmental influences.

The study of an atypical population, such as maltreated infants, makes it necessary to consider the many environmental variables that may influence the quality of the caregiving process and the nature of the attachment relationship. The maltreated infant may develop certain organized modes of responding to the caregiver that would serve to reduce the likelihood of subsequent abuse and/or neglect. Similarly, the maltreating caregiver may adopt certain styles of child rearing that would minimize the degree of contact with the child or serve to fulfill certain necessary and basic functions without incorporating any emotional or affectionate involvement. The maintenance of this pattern of interaction could, in fact, remain stable. On the other hand, certain characteristics of the infant, the caregiver, and/or the environment may change the nature of the interactive process. As a consequence, attempts to predict the stability or instability of attachment classifications over time need to take into account those situational factors that could interfere with the relative consistency in the dyad.

Furthermore, it becomes critical to determine exactly what is being assessed when one evaluates the organization of attachment behaviors in a population of maltreated infants. Inherent to this issue is a shift in focus

195

from a concern with the relatively enduring or transient nature of attachment in general to a more specific concern with the meaning of attachment behaviors as they are either continually reorganized or maintained in a stable pattern, in relation to environmental stressors or demands. Because the infant's behavior will vary in its form and function as new cognitive, affective, and social skills emerge and become integrated with earlier modes of responding, it is necessary to consider qualitative differences in manifest behaviors as reflecting unique patterns of adaptation at a particular age.

In the present investigation the following hypotheses will be examined in an attempt to address these theoretical issues: infants who were maltreated will be more likely to manifest an insecure attachment relationship with their caregivers than will a matched comparison group of infants who were not maltreated; when examined over time, the quality of the attachment relationship between maltreated infants and their caregivers will be more likely to show instability in attachment classifications than will that of nonmaltreated infants with their caregivers. The examination of these predictions is essential to an understanding of the quality of adaptation or maladaptation in infants who have been maltreated in an effort to identify the relationship between abuse and/or neglect and the infant's socioemotional development. It will have implications for theoretical formulations with regard to the nature and importance of the early attachment relationship. Furthermore, the exploratory examination of qualitative differences in the attachment relationship in maltreated infants and their caregivers may provide insight for identifying ways in which contemporary theory and data may be translated into strategic and maximally potent intervention strategies.

METHODS

Subjects

The sample consisted of maltreated and nonmaltreated infants who represent part of a larger sample of children being studied in the Harvard Child Maltreatment Project, an ongoing longitudinal investigation of the etiology, transmission, and sequelae of child maltreatment (Cicchetti & Rizley, 1981). All the infants in the study came from families with lower-class status as defined by several critical demographic variables.

There were three groups of infants. The 12-month-old group included 35 infants (17 males, 18 females) ranging in age from 11 months, 24 days, to 16 months, 4 days, with a mean age of 12 months, 28 days. Seventeen (nine males, eight females) of the 35 12-month-old infants were maltreated; 18 (eight males, 10 females) constituted the comparison group at this age. The

18-month-old sample consisted of 53 infants (27 males, 26 females) with a mean age of 18 months, 30 days, and a range from 17 months, 21 days, to 21 months, 3 days. Twenty-six of these infants (14 males, 12 females) were maltreated; 27 (13 males, 14 females) were included in the comparison group. The 24-month-old group consisted of 60 infants (32 males, 28 females) ranging in age from 23 months, 5 days, to 28 months, 23 days, with a mean age of 25 months, 1 day. Twenty-eight of the infants (14 males, 14 females) in this age group were maltreated; 32 (18 males, 14 females) constituted the comparison group. All the infants who were included in the maltreatment groups at the three different ages were maltreated while living with one or both of their natural parents.

Due to the longitudinal nature of the Harvard Child Maltreatment Project, there was a sample of infants who had been seen at two different ages (i.e., 12 and 18 months or 18 and 24 months). Thus, while the data were examined cross-sectionally at the three ages, data from this subsample of infants were analyzed longitudinally. Twenty-four of the 12-month-old infants (10 maltreated, 14 comparison) were also seen at 18 months and were included in the 18-month-old group. Thirty-two of the 18-month-old infants (16 maltreated, 16 comparison) were seen at 24 months of age and were included in the 24-month-old sample.

All the families of the maltreated infants were being monitored by either the Department of Social Services of the Commonwealth of Massachusetts or the Massachusetts Society for the Prevention of Cruelty to Children and met Massachusetts legal criteria requiring protective services. Operationally defined inclusion and exclusion criteria were employed to place infants in the maltreated group. Inclusion criteria for the maltreated infants consisted of a legal record of abuse and/or neglect filed on the family with the Department of Social Services, which was corroborated by an interview with the family's protective service worker. Exclusion criteria for the infants included any physical condition or organic brain damage that might indicate an unusual characteristic of the population of maltreated infants that these infants represent.

A careful review of statewide protective service families, by the Department of Social Services, and statewide demographics of families receiving Aid to Families with Dependent Children (AFDC) indicated remarkable similarities between the two groups. Therefore recruitment of comparison families was aimed at families receiving AFDC support. This was accomplished through the use of advertisements in welfare offices, newspapers, and neighborhoods. Children with organic brain damage or physical impairment were excluded, and careful screening procedures were employed to insure that there was no history of protective service involvement in these homes as documented by an interview with parents prior to participation in the study.

Fifty-five of the 56 families where maltreatment had occurred, and all the comparison families, were receiving welfare support in the form of AFDC. While the families where maltreatment had occurred tended to have more children in the home, there were no significant differences between the two groups in the number of adults in the home and the highest grade in school the mothers had completed. In addition, maltreatment and comparison families were matched on household prestige ratings (Nock & Rossi, 1979). These scores capture a greater degree of variation among families in socioeconomic status than is possible by the use of gross conventional measures of social class such as the Hollingshead-Redlich Two-Factor Index of Social Position (see Mueller & Parcel, 1981).

Types of Maltreatment

In the past, investigators of child maltreatment have failed to distinguish between the various forms of maltreatment experienced by the children in their samples and have assumed that the different forms would have uniform effects on development. The recent evidence that various types of maltreatment may have different impacts on the child's development (Egeland & Sroufe, 1981b) requires a consideration of the potential interaction between the form of maltreatment experienced and the developmental subsystem most at risk at a given stage of life. To this end, it is essential that investigators employ specific and clearly delineated methods by which the types of maltreatment experienced by their subjects may be identified. In this investigation, the social worker of each of the families where maltreatment had occurred was interviewed with a modification of the 92-item checklist of specific incidents and conditions of maltreatment that was developed and validated by Giovannoni and Becerra (1979). Each item on the checklist has assigned to it a severity rating ranging from 1 to 9. These ratings are the averages of ratings made by 149 practicing protective service social workers. Checklist items were grouped into four categories: physical injury, emotional mistreatment, physical neglect, and sexual abuse. If children had one or more items in a category, they were considered to have experienced that category of abuse. Fifty-three percent of the infants ($N = 21$) were judged by their social workers as having experienced more than one of the four types of maltreatment. Thirty-three percent ($N = 13$) of the maltreated infants had experienced physical injury. Forty-eight percent ($N = 19$) had been emotionally mistreated, and 75% ($N = 30$) were either living in an inadequate physical environment or experiencing parental failure to provide (the two categories commonly referred to as neglect). No child had been sexually abused.

Procedure

The infants and their mothers were brought to the laboratory for the 2-hour experimental session. During the visit, a specified protocol of measures was administered. The initial assessment was the Strange Situation (Ainsworth et al., 1978), which was employed to examine the quality of the attachment relationship between the infant and the caregiver.

In the classification of the 18- and 24-month-old infants included in this sample, it was necessary to make modifications in the scoring criteria since the available descriptions for assignment into the three attachment categories were originally devised for younger infants. A framework was developed for characterizing patterns of attachment at each age that considered age-appropriate alterations in the overt manifestations of the interactive behaviors of proximity seeking, contact maintenance, avoidance, resistance, search, and distance interaction. Moreover, the organization of behaviors was considered in terms of the behavioral systems activated by the Strange Situation—attachment, affiliative, fear/wariness, and exploration (Bretherton & Ainsworth, 1974). Accordingly, single behaviors that could serve more than one system (e.g., moving toward mother in stranger's presence could be both an attachment and a wary behavior) and the sequential activation of more than one system (e.g., offering an object to the stranger [affiliative] followed by retreat to the mother [attachment]) were considered in the context of ongoing activity. The infant's developing repertoire of more advanced modes of responding to the environment was integrated into this scheme. The emerging capacities for verbal communication, autonomous functioning, independent exploration, affiliation with unfamiliar adults, emotional control, and flexibility were considered. The pattern delineated for the 12-month-old sample is based on the empirical work of Ainsworth et al. (1978). The patterns at 18 and 24 months were developed for purposes of classifying the population of infants included in this investigation.[1] The attachment classifications were made by independent trained coders who were blind to the group membership of the infants. Infants were assigned to one of the three attachment categories: securely attached (group B) or insecurely attached and either anxious/avoidant (group A) or anxious/resistant (group C). Interrater reliability for attachment classifications was 89% at 12 months, 90% at 18 months, and 92% at 24 months of age. For those cases where there was disagreement, videotapes were reviewed by the raters together, and consensual agreement was reached through discussion.

---

[1] Space constraints prohibit the inclusion of the classification system. A copy may be obtained by writing to either Karen Schneider-Rosen, Department of Psychology and Social Relations, Harvard University, Cambridge, MA 02138, or Dante Cicchetti, Department of Psychology and Psychiatry, University of Rochester, Rochester, NY 14627.

RESULTS

Quality of Attachment at 12 Months

In the 12-month-old sample of maltreated infants ($N = 17$), 29% ($N = 5$) were classified as having an anxious/avoidant (group A) attachment with their mother, 29% ($N = 5$) were classified as securely attached (group B), and 42% ($N = 7$) were classified as having an anxious/resistant (group C) attachment with their mother. In contrast, among the nonmaltreated sample of 12-month-old infants ($N = 18$), 11% ($N = 2$) were classified as anxious/avoidant (group A), 67% ($N = 12$) were classified as secure (group B), and 22% ($N = 4$) were classified as anxious/resistant (group C). The maltreated group had a higher percentage of insecurely attached infants (71%) than did the nonmaltreated group (33%).

Within the maltreated group, the proportion of securely attached (group B), anxious/avoidant (group A), and anxious/resistant (group C) infants was significantly different from the proportions of 70%, 20%, and 10%, respectively, that were expected on the basis of prior research (Ainsworth et al., 1978), $\chi^2(2) = 21.27$, $p < .001$. Within the nonmaltreated group, there was no significant difference between the percentage of infants falling into each category and that which was expected, $\chi^2(2) = 3.43$, $p > .05$.

Quality of Attachment at 18 Months

In the 18-month-old sample of maltreated infants ($N = 26$), 46% ($N = 12$) were classified as anxious/avoidant (group A), 23% ($N = 6$) were classified as secure (group B), and 31% ($N = 8$) were classified as anxious/resistant (group C) in their attachment to their caregivers. Among the nonmaltreated group of infants ($N = 27$), 7% ($N = 2$) were classified as anxious/avoidant (group A), 67% ($N = 18$) were classified as secure (group B), and 26% ($N = 7$) were classified as anxious/resistant (group C). The maltreated group had a higher percentage of insecurely attached infants (77%) than did the nonmaltreated group (33%).

The proportion of maltreated infants falling into the three groups was significantly different from that which was expected, $\chi^2(2) = 28.28$, $p < .001$. There was an unusually high proportion of anxious/avoidant (group A) infants (46%) in this group. The proportion of nonmaltreated infants falling into the A, B, and C categories was also significantly different from that which was expected, $\chi^2(2) = 9.03$, $p < .05$. It is apparent that the percentage of securely attached nonmaltreated infants (group B) (67%) is comparable to the 70% that was expected. However, the percentage of anxious/resistant (group C) infants (26%) exceeds the 10% that was expected, while the percentage of anxious/avoidant (group A) infants (7%) is lower than the 20% that was expected.

Quality of Attachment at 24 Months

In the 24-month-old sample of infants, an analysis of the attachment classifications in the maltreated group (N = 28) revealed that 46.5% (N = 13) were classified as anxious/avoidant (group A), 32% (N = 9) were classified as secure (group B), and 21.5% (N = 6) were classified as anxious/resistant (group C). In contrast, among the nonmaltreated sample (N = 32), 9% (N = 3) were anxious/avoidant (group A), 66% (N = 21) were secure (group B), while 25% (N = 8) were anxious/resistant (group C). The maltreated group had a higher percentage of insecurely attached infants (68%) than did the nonmaltreated group (34%).

Within the maltreated group, the proportion of anxious/avoidant (group A), securely attached (group B), and anxious/resistant (group C) infants was significantly different from the expected proportions, $\chi^2(2)$ = 19.17, $p < .001$. The difference in the proportion of nonmaltreated infants falling into each of the three groups was also significant, $\chi^2(2)$ = 9.1, $p <$ .05. Again, it is evident that the percentage of nonmaltreated infants who were classified as secure (group B) (66%) is comparable to the 70% that was expected. However, the percentage of anxious/resistant (group C) infants (25%) was particularly high, while the percentage of anxious/avoidant (group A) infants (9%) was particularly low; this is the same pattern that was observed in the sample of 18-month-old nonmaltreated infants.

Stability of Attachment Classifications

The Harvard Child Maltreatment Project is an ongoing longitudinal study. Hence, 44 infants had participated in more than one assessment in the Strange Situation. An inspection of the data for these longitudinal infants permits preliminary statements about the stability of the attachment relationship in maltreated and comparison infants.

As seen in Table 1, 29 infants, 12 maltreated and 17 comparison, were observed in the Strange Situation at 12 and 18 months. In the maltreatment group, five infants were classified in the same group at both 12 and 18 months, while 13 of the nonmaltreated infants obtained the same classification across this time period. Cohen's (1960) index of nominal scale agreement ($\hat{\kappa}$) was computed and used to test the stability of group classifications of both the maltreated and the comparison group of infants (see Fleiss, Cohen, & Everitt, 1969). It is computed by correcting the observed rate of agreement (same classification at both ages) for the rate of

TABLE 1

STABILITY AND CHANGE IN ATTACHMENT CLASSIFICATIONS
FROM 12 TO 18 MONTHS AND FROM 18 TO 24 MONTHS

	A	B	C
	18-Month Attachment Classification		
Maltreated infants:			
12-month attachment classification:			
A	2	0	1
B	2	1	2
C	1	1	2
Comparison infants:			
12-month attachment classification:			
A	0	2	0
B	0	9	2
C	0	0	4
	24-Month Attachment Classification		
Maltreated infants:			
18-month attachment classification:			
A	7	0	2
B	2	1	1
C	2	2	2
Comparison infants:			
18-month attachment classification:			
A	0	1	0
B	2	11	2
C	0	2	5

agreement expected by chance alone. The $\hat{\kappa}$ for the maltreated group was not significant ($\hat{\kappa} = .15$, $z = .82$, $p > .05$), indicating that this group did not manifest a significant level of stability in attachment classifications from 12 to 18 months. Of the seven maltreated infants who shifted classifications, four securely attached infants changed to an insecure relationship (two A's and two C's), two insecurely attached infants shifted into another insecure group (one A to C and one C to A), and one anxious/resistant 12-month-old shifted to a secure relationship at 18 months.

In contrast, the comparison group of infants showed significant stability in attachment classifications across the 6-month period ($\hat{\kappa} = .53$, $z = 2.69$, $p < .03$). Nine of the 13 infants who remained in the same attachment group were securely attached. Out of the four infants who shifted, two infants changed from the secure to the anxious/resistant group, while two went from the anxious/avoidant to the secure group.

As shown in Table 1, 42 infants, 19 maltreated and 23 comparison, were observed at 18 and 24 months in the Strange Situation. The maltreated group did not show significant stability of attachment classifications across the 6-month period, with nine infants shifting classifications ($\hat{\kappa} = .22$, $z = 1.34$, $p > .05$). Three securely attached 18-month-olds developed an insecure relationship at 24 months (two A's and one C). In addition, two maltreated infants changed from the anxious/resistant group to a secure attachment, while four infants changed from one insecure group to the other across the two assessments (two from A to C and two from C to A). Of the maltreated infants who received the same attachment classification at both assessments, one was rated as securely attached at 18 and 24 months, while nine infants remained in the same insecure group on both occasions (seven anxious/avoidant [group A] and two anxious/resistant [group C]).

Of the 23 comparison infants, 16 obtained identical attachment ratings at both assessments. Of these, 11 manifested consistently secure relationships, while five exhibited anxious/resistant (group C) relationships. The comparison group manifested significant stabilty across the 6-month period ($\hat{\kappa} = .40$, $z = 2.29$, $p < .05$). For the seven infants who changed classifications, four securely attached infants became insecure (two A's and two C's), while three insecurely attached infants (one A and two C's) developed a secure relationship with the mother.

Type of Maltreatment

The maltreatment severity ratings described above were employed in order to examine the relationship between type of maltreatment and security of attachment. The highest severity rating within each of the four categories was taken as each child's score for that category. To test for differences between the securely and insecurely attached maltreated children on these four variables, t tests were employed. None of the tests were significant.

DISCUSSION

The Relationship between Early Maltreatment and Attachment

The finding that a greater proportion of maltreated infants in each of the three age groups was insecurely attached is in accordance with the predictions based on attachment theory (Ainsworth, 1980; Bowlby, 1969/1982b). In the analyses that were conducted at each of the three age periods, a consistent finding emerged within the maltreated group. It was found that the distribution of maltreated infants into the three major attachment categories differed significantly from the expectations based on prior research with nonclinical samples.

In contrast, within the comparison sample of infants there was no significantly different distribution from that which was expected at 12 months. However, both at 18 and at 24 months, while significantly different distributions were obtained, the difference was found in the percentages falling into the two insecure groups. There were fewer infants in the anxious/avoidant category and more infants in the anxious/resistant category than was expected. It should be noted, though, that the percentage of infants falling into the secure group was comparable to the percentage found in earlier studies. The interpretation of these interesting results awaits further research. However, the results of the present study indicate that the attachment system in maltreated infants is especially vulnerable to disruption over the first 2 years of life.

Quality of Attachment and Type of Maltreatment

Theoretical formulation (Ainsworth, 1980) and previous empirical work (Crittenden, 1981; Egeland & Sroufe, 1981b; George & Main, 1979) have suggested that the type of maltreatment experienced by an infant may have different effects on specific developmental systems. Accordingly, while it was predicted that there would be more insecure attachments within the maltreated group in general, it was expected that those infants who were physically abused would be more likely to be classified as anxious/avoidant (group A), while those infants who were neglected or emotionally mistreated would manifest an ambivalent and anxious/resistant (group C) attachment relationship with the caregiver (see Ainsworth, 1980). In this study, the type or combination of types of maltreatment experienced by each infant were carefully identified. However, no clear relationships between the quality of attachment and the type of maltreatment emerged within any of the three age groups.

A number of explanations may be offered to account for these puzzling results. They may be due to the heterogeneous nature of the sample, as 53% had experienced multiple forms of maltreatment. Furthermore, 75% of the infants had been neglected, either as the sole type of maltreatment experienced or in conjunction with other types of maltreatment. The predominance of one type of maltreatment may serve to obscure any more specific associations that may exist between the type of maltreatment and differences in the quality of attachment. Finally, there is the possibility that the infant experienced undetected types of maltreatment that had not been reported to the protective service workers.

The Effect of Multiple High-Risk Factors on Developmental Outcome

It has been suggested that membership in the lower class exerts as much of a deleterious effect on later child development as does a history of abuse (e.g., Elmer, 1977). The study of maltreatment in a lower-class population provides a unique opportunity to examine this claim because of the necessity of employing matched comparison families of lower socioeconomic status. In this study of qualitative differences in attachment, the percentages of securely and insecurely attached comparison infants are comparable to those found in Ainsworth et al.'s (1978) study of 12-month-old middle-class infants, in Waters's (1978) study of 18-month-old middle-class infants, and in Vaughn et al.'s (1979) group of 18-month-old lower-class infants as well as in Schneider-Rosen and Cicchetti's (1984) sample of 19-month-old nonmaltreated lower-class infants. These data refute Elmer's (1977) claim that lower-class membership will inevitably lead to deviant developmental outcomes.

It therefore becomes possible to clarify the comparative impact of a history of maltreatment and the risk status associated with cultural-environmental factors on specific developmental systems. While both the maltreated and the comparison infants in this study were subject to environmental stress (e.g., that associated with lower-class membership), the maltreated infants experienced additional stress in the infant-caregiver transaction in the form of maltreatment. Thus, each risk factor, that is, maltreatment and lower-class status, must be considered independently. These findings demonstrate that the use of appropriate comparison groups when investigating multiple high-risk factors will allow for the determination of the potency of varying environmental factors that impinge on the development of the high-risk infant. Furthermore, it allows for the examination and identification of those developmental systems that seem to be most vulnerable to manifesting deviations in outcome.

The Use of Alternative Pathways in the Resolution of Developmental Tasks

An increase in the percentage of maltreated infants who manifested anxious/avoidant (group A) attachments was observed cross-sectionally from 12 to 24 months of age. At 12 months of age, 29% of the maltreated infants were classified as anxious/avoidant in their attachment relationships. In contrast, in the 18- and 24-month samples, 46% and 46.5%, respectively, of the maltreated infants were classified as anxious/avoidant. This observed pattern may represent an increasingly organized effort on the part of the maltreated infant to cope with the inconsistent and problematic nature of the relationship with the caregiver.

It is important to consider that infants may develop an avoidant relationship with their caregivers as a result of different maltreatment experiences. In some cases, developing cognitive sophistication and social skills, more advanced modes of communicative functioning, and an increase in mobility may enable intentional avoidance of interaction with an abusive caregiver, thereby decreasing the number of potentially threatening experiences (i.e., physical or emotional abuse). In other cases, neglected infants may adopt an avoidant pattern of attachment. This may represent a more passive, as opposed to an intentional, response to the repeated failure of the caregiver to fulfill the infant's emotional or physical needs. Thus the infant's avoidance may be viewed as an organized mode of responding to aberrant caregiving patterns and is adaptive in this respect.

Recent theoretical work has tended to focus on the optimal resolution of the salient task of developing an attachment relationship with the caregiver and has described the secure pattern as that which promotes competence (Ainsworth, 1972, 1982; Sroufe et al., 1983; Sroufe & Waters, 1977; Waters & Deane, 1982). However, the examination of maltreated infants illuminates the variability and range of behavioral outcomes that may emerge. For example, the avoidant solution may lead to modifications in the attachment-exploration balance such that independent exploration with active attempts to ignore the caregiver during exploration will prevail but proximity seeking may be activated under conditions of relatively extreme stress. The predominance of autonomous exploration and the tendency actively to ignore the caregiver may be associated with failure to exploit the caregiver as a partner in the learning process. However, the adaptive significance of the patterning of attachment behaviors adopted by the avoidant infant needs to be considered independently of the expectations for what may be the "optimal" or most competent solution (i.e., achieving a secure attachment relationship) of this developmental task. It therefore becomes important to distinguish between a behavioral outcome that is typically defined as competent (i.e., secure attachment) and an outcome that may be adaptive for the maltreated infant (i.e., avoidance of the caregiver).

A central question for developmental theory then becomes whether the use of alternative pathways for resolving stage-salient tasks predisposes the infant to current or subsequent adaptation or maladaptation across behavioral domains (i.e., cognitive, social, emotional). Qualitative differences in attachment may be related to behavioral outcome in other developmental domains. For example, associations between language and attachment were found in a population of 25-month-old maltreated and nonmaltreated toddlers (Gersten, Coster, Schneider-Rosen, Carlson, & Cicchetti, in press). Securely attached toddlers showed higher levels of linguistic performance.

Thus the predominance of insecure attachment relationships among the maltreated group was associated with relatively less advanced communicative performance, suggesting that the adaptive resolution of the attachment relationship for the maltreated child (i.e., anxious/avoidant) does not necessarily promote concurrent adaptive resolution of other developmental issues.

It is also important to examine the adaptation of the avoidant maltreated infant over time in order to establish the manner of resolution of subsequent developmental tasks beyond that of establishing and consolidating an attachment relationship with the primary caregiver during the first 2 years of life. The use of alternative pathways in the successful resolution of one developmental task may predispose the toddler toward the use of alternative pathways in later tasks, such as the mastery of the peer world, thereby making the toddler more vulnerable to manifesting difficulties in accomplishing subsequent tasks in a competent or adaptive manner.

*Processes Associated with Qualitative Differences
in the Attachment Relationship*

The examination of a population of maltreated infants may help to ascertain the conditions under which one would expect to find stability or change in the quality of the attachment relationship. Rather than attempting to determine whether qualitative differences in attachment reflect a general pattern of organized behavior that has been established over time or whether they represent the current mode of interaction within the dyad, the focus should be redirected toward specifying those factors that could influence the relative stability of the attachment relationship. Because this population of infants is being reared in an environment in which there is a great deal of stress (e.g., Egeland et al., 1980; Garbarino & Gilliam, 1980) and a reduced likelihood of experiencing consistent care, it is critical to examine the quality of attachment over time in order to understand the dynamic nature of the transaction between the infant, the caregiver, and the environment.

In the current investigation, an analysis of the two longitudinal samples revealed that the comparison infants manifested significant stability in the quality of attachment with the caregiver, while the maltreated group did not. Forty-one percent of the maltreated infants and 69% of the comparison infants maintained the same attachment classification from 12 to 18 months of age; 53% of the maltreated infants and 69% of the comparison infants were classified in the same attachment groups at 18 and 24 months of age. These data shed light on the unexpected finding that some maltreated infants form secure attachment relationships with their caregivers. Rather than assuming that these infants represent a resilient group who are invulnerable to the negative impact of early maltreatment, a longitudinal examination of the results indicates that this would be a premature conclusion. Of the five maltreated infants who had a secure attachment relationship at 12 months of age, four shifted to insecure attachment classifications by 18 months (two A's, two C's). Likewise, three of the four securely attached 18-month-old infants developed an insecure attachment relationship by 24 months (two A's, one C). It is evident from these data that, as a group, insecurely attached maltreated infants tend to remain insecurely attached across time, while securely attached maltreated infants tend to shift into the insecure groups over time. Conversely, securely attached comparison infants are more likely to remain secure across assessments. These results suggest that the early secure relationship in maltreated infants may be influenced by multiple environmental factors that may interfere with the maintenance of a secure attachment to the caregiver. Furthermore, they underscore the need more carefully to isolate those critical features that may characterize the transaction between the infant and the environment.

Increasingly in the disciplines of developmental psychology and developmental psychopathology, more sophisticated models of the relationships among parent, child, and environmental factors are being employed (see Belsky, 1980; Sameroff, 1982). Cicchetti and Rizley (1981) have proposed a transactional model to account for risk factors on three dimensions (caregiver, child, and environment) that are related to the etiology and intergenerational transmission of different types of maltreatment. It is possible to extend this model and use it to explain the processes that may lead to specific developmental outcomes. In particular, if one attempts to identify those conditions that maintain stable attachment relationships or precipitate alterations in the consistency of these relationships over time, the model represents a useful framework for identifying the salient factors associated with each potential outcome. Accordingly, this model provides a way of conceptualizing stability or change in attachment not only in a population of infants at risk (e.g., maltreated infants) but in all infant-caregiver dyads.

The scheme for characterizing the process leading to different developmental outcomes in the attachment system is shown in Table 2. The factors associated with each outcome (i.e., secure or insecure attachment relationship) are classified into two broad categories: potentiating factors, which increase the probability of manifesting an insecure attachment with the caregiver, and compensatory factors, which increase the likelihood of achieving a secure attachment relationship. Transient factors refer to those influences that are fluctuating and relatively short-lived, whereas enduring factors represent more permanent attributes or conditions.

Within this model, potentiating factors include the enduring influence of vulnerability factors and the transient influence of challengers. Vulnera-

TABLE 2

FACTORS ASSOCIATED WITH QUALITATIVE DIFFERENCES IN THE ATTACHMENT
RELATIONSHIP (Temporal Dimensions)

	IMPACT ON THE ATTACHMENT SYSTEM	
	Potentiating Factors	Compensatory Factors
Enduring factors......	Vulnerability factors: Enduring conditions in the caregiving environment that decrease the harmony of interaction and the quality of care	Protective factors: Enduring conditions that promote harmonious interaction between the infant and the caregiver and maintain responsive, sensitive, and continuous care
Transient factors......	Challengers: Transient but significant factors that increase the probability of inconsistent or inadequate care being provided for the infant	Buffers: Transient conditions that protect the infant against experiencing negative consequences that could result from temporary disruptions in quality of care provided
Outcome..........	Insecure attachment	Secure attachment

bility factors refer to those relatively enduring characteristics of the caregiving environment that interfere with the establishment of a harmonious pattern of interaction within the dyad. These factors may be psychological in nature (e.g., personality attributes in the caregiver or the infant such as high levels of anger or hostility or manifest forms of psychopathology), situational (e.g., poor physical environment, poverty, crowding, or social isolation), sociological/cultural (e.g., specific child-rearing practices or techniques of socialization), or biological (e.g., physical deviations or temperamental characteristics of either the infant or the caregiver that introduce difficulties to the child-rearing environment). Challengers represent more transient factors that could potentiate an insecure attachment relationship. Stressful life experiences such as a significant loss, changes in family situation, marital or child-rearing difficulties, or physical injury or severe illness could introduce a transient challenge to the caregiving system and interfere with the quality of care provided to the infant. Maltreatment experiences are clearly potentiating factors. Depending on the circumstances under which maltreatment has occurred, it is possible to conceive of its influence as being either enduring or transient.

The compensatory factors that increase the likelihood of achieving a secure attachment relationship within the dyad include both the enduring influence of protective factors and the transient impact of buffers. Protective factors represent conditions that may be psychological in nature (e.g., sensitive responsivity of the caregiver, resiliency to stress, adaptability to changing life circumstances, good coping mechanisms, and problem-solving skills), biological (e.g., good temperament, good physical health, and resistance to illness), situational (e.g., good physical environment and economic stability), or sociological/cultural (e.g., a history of good parenting and good socialization techniques). These protective factors may be present in the infant, the parent, or the caregiving environment and promote harmonious interaction within the dyad. Buffers are relatively transient in nature but may serve to protect the infant or the caregiver during periods of unexpected stress. When circumstances occur that challenge the quality of care provided to the infant, buffers such as a supportive network of family and friends, the availability of additional caregivers or of day-care facilities may reduce the negative consequences that could result from temporary disruptions in the caregiving environment. Maltreatment may not necessarily exert a deleterious effect on the attachment system if the presence of protective factors or buffers is sufficient to override the experience of abuse and/or neglect.

This model represents a framework within which one may account for the possibility of developing a secure or an insecure attachment relationship as manifested at any specific point in time. Implicit in the model is the assumption that the quality of attachment represents neither enduring nor transient influences alone but rather a multiplicity of factors that need to be considered in combination with one another in order to account for and adequately explain the process whereby a specific developmental outcome may be achieved. The present investigation has illustrated the necessity of considering the transaction among child, caregiver, and environmental influences that must be examined in order adequately to account for current adaptation, as well as stability or change over time, in the quality of the attachment relationship. While the recognition of these multiple factors that exist in transaction with one another reaffirms the intricate nature of the developing attachment system, it simultaneously challenges researchers to extend future empirical investigations to embrace this broader theoretical conceptualization.

IX. THE SOCIAL TRANSMISSION OF PARENTAL BEHAVIOR: ATTACHMENT ACROSS GENERATIONS

MARGARET H. RICKS

University of Massachusetts, Amherst

The idea that an individual's childhood relationships with parents affect later close relationships, including adult love relationships and parent-child relationships, is central to Freud's developmental theory. This idea has continued to play an important role in psychoanalytic theory and is prominent in psychoanalytically oriented work (e.g., Benedek, 1949; Berger & Kennedy, 1975; Bettelheim, 1967; Fraiberg et al., 1975; Giovacchini, 1970; LaBarre, Jessner, & Ussery, 1960, Winnicott, 1965).[1]

The view that there is intergenerational continuity in the quality of parental behavior is also explicit in Bowlby's theory of attachment (Bowlby, 1979). However, it is only very recently that empirical studies guided or influenced by attachment theory have been conducted in this area. Two bodies of research relevant to the question of intergenerational continuity of attachment quality will be presented here: studies documenting the effects of separation or disruption in the family of origin and studies in which parents reported on their childhood attachments. This research will be interpreted within a theoretical perspective derived from Bowlby (1969/1982b, 1973, 1980), Epstein (1973, 1976, 1979), and Epstein and Erskine (1983).

The author wishes to thank Donna Noyes for her help in some of the research discussed here and Alan Sroufe, Seymour Epstein, Brian Vaughn, and Per Gjerde for their comments on earlier drafts of this chapter.

[1] Page limits prohibit more than this acknowledgement of the significant contributions made by psychoanalytic work and by sociological studies to the study of parental behavior across generations. A bibliography is available from the author, Department of Psychology, University of Massachusetts, Amherst, MA 01003.

MODELS OF SELF AND MODELS OF ATTACHMENT FIGURES

Although Bowlby's primary concern has been with attachment and Epstein's with the self-concept, the theories overlap in major ways. Bowlby (1969/1982b, 1973, 1979, 1980) postulated that children build representational models of their attachment figures and that these representational models are complementary to the representational model they build of themselves (see Bretherton, in this vol., for a detailed review). According to Bowlby (1979), a child whose parents are available and supportive will construct a representational model of self as able to cope but also as worthy of help. Conversely, a child whose parents are consistently lacking in responsiveness, who threaten abandonment or who actually abandon the child, will tend to build a representational model of self as unworthy and unlovable (see also Adam, 1982).

These ideas are compatible with Epstein's personality theory, which, like Bowlby's theory, has close ties to Freudian theory. According to Epstein (1973, 1976, 1979), the self-concept is best seen as a self-theory that consists of hierarchically organized major and minor postulates inductively derived from emotionally significant experience. The self-theory is part of a theory of reality (of self and world) that each individual constructs in the course of development. An example of a major postulate is "I am loveworthy." An example of a minor postulate is "I look good in pink." Epstein suggests that major postulates concern relatively universal human domains (in which everyone should form a postulate) and are highly integrative (global rather than specific). Because major postulates are formed early in life, subsequent experience is assimilated into the existing postulates. With development, they become anchored in a broad network of associated major and minor postulates. Therefore major postulates are highly resistant to change.

A personal theory of reality has three related functions: to maximize a person's pleasure-pain balance through the foreseeable future, to assimilate the data of experience coherently, and to maintain a favorable level of self-esteem. When the theory fulfills all three functions, the individual experiences a predominance of positive affect. However, when it does not, when any of the three is compromised, the experience is dysphoric. The intensity of an emotion (pleasant or painful) is a function of the hierarchical order of the postulate at stake. Epstein argues that a personal theory of reality, like a scientific theory, can be evaluated on the dimensions of extensivity, parsimony, empirical validity, internal consistency, and testability. Personal theories and scientific theories, he claims, change in much the same way: sometimes gradually, through invalidation of minor postulates, and sometimes more drastically, through invalidation of major postulates (for compatible views, see Eckblad, 1981; Parkes, 1971; Piaget, 1981). Since invalidation of a major postulate provokes strong anxiety and disorganization, a person threatened with invalidation of a major postulate may guard against painful reorganization of the self-theory by selectively excluding relevant information from awareness (cf. Bowlby, 1980).

One of the most basic postulates in an individual's self-theory concerns self-esteem (Epstein, in press). Like Bowlby, Epstein argues that self-esteem is largely a function of childhood relationships with parents. The person with high self-esteem, "in effect, carries within him a loving parent, one who is proud of his successes and accepting of his failures." In contrast, "the person with low self-esteem carries within him a disapproving parent who is harshly critical of his failures" (Epstein, 1980, p. 106). Low self-esteem conflicts with one of the three major functions of the reality theory (to maintain a favorable level of self-esteem). Nevertheless, the requirements of one of the other functions (to assimilate the data of experience coherently) may, under some circumstances, lead a person to maintain low self-esteem, despite the conflict this engenders.

The theoretical perspective adopted here, an integration of Bowlby's and Epstein's theories, rests on viewing representational models of attachment relationships as systems of postulates in an individual's conceptual system. Broad generalizations regarding attachment figures are likely to be major postulates. An advantage of viewing models of attachment relationships in this manner is that Epstein's theory directly addresses the growth and transformation of personal theories of reality. This allows us to be much more specific about continuity and change in attachment-related postulates and therefore makes Bowlby's representational models of attachment figures and self more amenable to research. For example, taking Epstein's perspective, one would predict that individuals who incorporate experiences related to anxious attachment into major postulates in their theory of reality would seek to maintain coherent conceptual systems by validating these postulates through recreating similar experiences in subsequent attachment relationships. As Epstein (in press) points out, even an unpleasant but predictable world is preferable to a chaotic one. A postulate such as "I am not loveworthy," which appears, from the outside, to be maladaptive, a source of misery and of unsatisfying attachment bonds, has the advantage of organizing experience. The person holding such a postulate will therefore interpret the behavior of others in accord with the postulate, may even provoke others to behave in congruence with the postulate, and will resist evidence contrary to the postulate (see also Bowlby, 1979). Epstein's theory thus helps to explain why continuity should be expected but also helps to explain certain cases of change. Empirical and conceptual work on change in major postulates has important implications for intergenerational transmission of attachment relationships and is considered in more detail in the concluding section of this chapter.

RESEARCH ON ATTACHMENT ACROSS GENERATIONS

Methods of Study

There are two basic methodological problems in the study of attachment across generations. One concerns the measurement of relationships; the other involves the problem of gathering the necessary information across lengthy time spans.

The question of how best to capture the important aspects of relationships is a formidable one (Hinde, 1976, 1979, 1982a). The considerable research activity that followed Ainsworth and Wittig's (1969) introduction of the Strange Situation procedure for assessing infant-caregiver relationships attests not only to the lively interest in such relationships but also to the productive enthusiasm of researchers when they find a good measure of an important construct. Further progress toward other theory-based assessments of attachment relationships has been made by Main et al. (in this vol.) and by Waters and Deane (in this vol.).

A second problem facing those who attempt to study intergenerational transmission of attachment quality is the time span involved in studying parental behavior across generations. The obvious methods involve either reliance on retrospective reports or require very long term prospective studies. As a great deal of recent research in cognitive psychology has vividly illustrated, recall of past events does not necessarily involve a veridical reading off of those events but rather may include complex processes of reconstruction. Recall of the past may be affected by present cognitive structures (Piaget & Inhelder, 1973), by mood (e.g., Bower, 1981), and by a variety of contextual factors of both the past and the present (e.g., Loftus, 1979). Piaget and Bowlby actually had a series of fascinating discussions on the influence of the past on the present, taking as their starting point Freud's position that early structures are never quite destroyed. As Piaget recounts it: "We fundamentally agreed on the problem of relations between an individual's past experience and current organization. I had understood that Bowlby does not consider, as did Freud in certain passages, that we are fixed in the past and that there is necessarily regression into the unconscious during the utilization of this past, but rather that the past is continuously reorganized according to present needs and present structures" (Piaget, 1960, p. 91). Although a parent's reconstruction of the past may guide present behavior, the question must still be asked whether childhood memories closely reflect actual childhood, as experienced at the time, or whether the accuracy, consistency, and accessibility of memories of childhood are significantly affected by changing circumstances in an adult's life. Can we estimate the accuracy of adult recollection of childhood relationships? Schaefer and Bayley (1967), using data from the Berkeley Growth

Study, found no significant correlations between adult retrospective accounts of parental behavior in infancy (birth to 3 years) and actual observations. However, 11 of 12 correlations between adult retrospective accounts and data from interviews with the parents regarding their actual parental behavior completed when the subjects were adolescents (aged 9–14 years) were significant. Field (1981) questioned 60 adults in the Berkeley Guidance Study about their recollections of childhood when they were 59–80 years of age. Reports of childhood experience had been obtained when they were young adults. While the findings showed considerable consistency in memories of childhood from early to advanced adult years, there were also wide individual differences in the consistency of recall (see also Block, 1969b). Some clinical reports suggest that loss of memory for the affect associated with maltreatment in childhood is linked to reenacting childhood experience in the second generation (Fraiberg et al., 1975). In the absence of sufficient research on factors affecting the stability and accuracy of adult's recollection of childhood, it will be important to include measures of defensiveness, internal consistency, and dimensions describing the cognitive quality of the memories.

It might appear that the problem of continuity could be solved by longitudinal studies across two generations. However, such longitudinal studies have their own problems. Collecting data on parent-child relationships across two generations requires at least 30 years. Such a long span introduces a number of problems. It is unlikely, for example, that data collected over 30 years would be gathered in the same conceptual and methodological framework, and it would almost certainly not be gathered by the same group of researchers. Even the most attractive theory and methods available in 1985, for example, are likely to be modified by the year 2015. Thus by the time the second generation data were in, one might find the earlier measures unsatisfactory. The longitudinal approach that might appear ideal is therefore not without inherent problems.[2]

There are two little-explored approaches to the problem of cross-generational continuity in attachment that hold considerable promise. Each has the advantage of avoiding reliance on retrospective reports while involving less time than longitudinal studies across generations. These are studies of intragenerational concordance and studies of three generations concurrently. Concordance, a measure borrowed from twin studies, is a comparison of the variation within and between pairs of siblings. This approach rests

[2] In 1959, Bronson, Katten, and Livson published a study of patterns of authority and affection in two generations, based on ratings made from the Berkeley Guidance Study files. Results showed little evidence of similarity across generations. There are, as the authors acknowledge, a number of reasons to question the implications of these results. These problems were largely due to the difficulties of very long term longitudinal studies discussed.

on the largely untested assumption that parents in the family of origin behaved similarly toward the siblings studied (Plomin, 1981). Nonetheless, in the only intragenerational study of parental behavior published, McGlaughlin (1981) found considerable concordance between pairs of sisters in their attitudes toward and behavior with their children from 12 to 30 months of age. However, as McGlaughlin (1981) points out, the similarity in sisters' parental behavior need not be ascribed to shared early experiences but could be due to current shared experiences. Investigations of three generations simultaneously have examined dependence (Fu, Hinkle, & Hanna, 1983) and other aspects of family ties across generations (Cohler & Grunebaum, 1981; Kell & Aldous, 1960). Because these approaches have not been tested in intergenerational attachment research, they will not be further considered here.

Intergenerational research especially relevant to attachment theory has focused on two areas of study: separation or disruption in the family of origin and detailed recollections by parents of childhood relationships with their own parents. The separation and disruption studies, which were all conducted in Britain, will be discussed first.[3]

Separation and Disruption

Frommer and O'Shea (1973a, 1973b) conducted a series of interviews with English mothers over the course of their infant's first year of life. The interviews focused on mothers' problems in raising their infants. The research is reported in two papers. In the first, separation from parents in the family of origin was found to be related to problems in parenting (Frommer & O'Shea, 1973a). "Separation" was defined simply by the mother's answer to the question "Were you separated from one or both of your parents before the age of 11?" Nothing was known regarding the cause or duration of separation. The second report showed that separation in the family of origin was also associated with later marital problems and with depression in the mothers (Frommer & O'Shea, 1973b). As the authors acknowledge, parenting difficulty could not be attributed to the experience of childhood separation alone.

A series of reports by Hall, Pawlby, and Wolkind suggest that the effects obtained by Frommer and O'Shea might have been due to disruption of the family of origin rather than solely to the experience of separation (Hall & Pawlby, 1981; Hall, Pawlby, & Wolkind, 1979; Pawlby & Hall, 1980; Wol-

[3] There are a number of interesting differences between British and American research on intergenerational continuity. Americans are relative newcomers to the field. American research focuses on the quality of relationships (perhaps because of the impact of the work of Ainsworth, Sroufe, and their colleagues), while British research focuses on separation, loss, and disruption (see Rutter & Madge, 1976).

kind, Hall, & Pawlby, 1977). A mother was classified as coming from a disrupted family of origin if, before the age of 16, her parents had divorced or separated, if one or both of her parents had died, or if she had been cared for away from both parents for 1 month or more of her childhood. Separation was defined as care away from both parents for less than 1 month before the age of 16.

The study included 233 women from an inner-city area of London. Eighty-one of the women were initially included in an observational study that deliberately included a high proportion of women thought to be vulnerable to parenting problems. Parenting measures reported included home observations at 20 weeks, language testing at 27 months, and laboratory testing and observations at 3½ years.

Disruption, whether alone or in conjunction with separation from the parents, was an important determinant of parental behavior in the next generation. Mothers from disrupted families of origin were less likely than mothers from nondisrupted families to engage in close, stimulating, and contingent interaction with their infants at 5 months. They talked to, looked at, and touched the infants less. They also responded less to the infants' fretful and positive vocalizations. In addition, mothers from disrupted families of origin spent more time in a different room than the baby. Later, as preschoolers, children whose mothers came from disrupted families had impoverished language skills when compared to children whose mothers had not experienced disruption of their own families. What appeared to be associated with nonoptimal caretaking behavior was the disruption of early attachment relationships, due to divorce, death, or long-term separation from parents rather than the experience of short-term separation from parents without disruption.

In the larger sample, which included interviews of over 200 women, disruption of the family of origin was also associated with being unmarried and being a teenage mother. These two variables have been linked to disruption in the family of origin in a large number of other studies (see Rutter & Madge, 1976, for a review).

Rutter, Quinton, and Liddle (1983) compared the early childhood experience of parents who had serious family difficulties, defined as having had a child taken into the care of the local government twice, with a control group of similar socioeconomic status. The multiple problems found in families with children in care were almost always associated with serious childhood adversities on the mother's part. For example, one-quarter had been in care themselves as children (vs. 7% of the controls), and 40% had been separated from their parents as a result of "discord" or "rejection" (vs. 14% of the controls). Rutter, Quinton, and Liddle conclude that serious parenting problems in the context of widespread family difficulties rarely arose in the absence of such previous childhood adversities.

In a second study (Quinton & Rutter, in press), institution-reared women were compared with non-institution-reared women from the same inner-city London area. Poor parenting (globally characterized) was more likely to occur in the institution-reared group and was also more likely when marital support was lacking. Mothers who were institution reared were more likely to lack marital support. That is, they were more likely to be unmarried or to have married men with problems and to have a poor relationship with them.

The conclusion to be drawn from these studies is that maternal problems with child rearing are not associated with relatively brief separation experiences if these are not also accompanied by family disruption. Difficulties are, however, related to serious disruptions in the family of origin (due to death, separation, or divorce). Experience of family disruption in childhood is also related to later marital status and to marital disharmony. A simple route from childhood experience to later parental behavior cannot therefore be inferred from the available literature on disruption.

The studies just reviewed are consistent with Bowlby's and Epstein's views regarding the relation between an individual's construction of a self-theory and the individual's relationships with parents. However, the studies on loss and disruption have not attempted to gain access to the parent's representational models of attachment relationships. Several studies have done just that, but for mothers only. These studies are presented in the next section.

Child-Mother Attachment as Related to the Quality of the Mother's Childhood Relations with Parents

Findings from three studies will be discussed. For all these studies at least two sets of information are available: an assessment of the child's attachment to the mother at 12 or 18 months and detailed reports of maternal recollections of childhood attachments based on interviews or questionnaires. These studies were conducted in the context of larger projects at Minnesota, Berkeley, and Amherst.

The Minnesota project.—Morris (1980, 1981) drew on the Sroufe and Egeland sample to investigate maternal history as related to child outcome measures (see Sroufe, 1983, for a review of other findings from this project). Thirty-six mothers from a project involving 267 economically disadvantaged mothers were selected for participation. Child outcome measures included Strange Situation assessments at 12 and 18 months and performance in a problem-solving task at 2 years of age. A 160-item interview designed to obtain information regarding crises in childhood, relationships in mother's family of origin, the mother's current relationship with her mother, and her current social support network was administered to mothers when their children were 2 years old.

Morris found that scores on scales derived from the interviews (marital harmony, relationship to mother, relationship to father, role reversal, and home milieu) were all in the predicted direction but that no single scale was significantly related to outcome measures. However, when two clinically trained judges reviewed the interviews to predict child outcome, one judge was highly successful in assigning children to the correct attachment class (31 of 36 correctly assigned). This judge used criteria that stressed the quality of the relationship to the mother, the quality of the home milieu, the presence of severe crisis, and the mother's sense of how she dealt with these crises. The second judge made his predictions solely on the amount of crisis in the mother's history modified by current support network. These criteria were less successful than those used by the first judge but did predict outcome combined across the Strange Situation and problem-solving assessments.

It is important to note that there were some striking misses. Morris indicates that some of the mothers whose histories were characterized by sexual abuse, role reversal, unhappy parents, and a hostile home environment did well on the three mother-child outcome variables. The opposite also held. Some mothers who reported harmonious families of origin, little or no crisis, and plentiful support nonetheless did not do well on outcome measures.

The Berkeley project.—A recent intergenerational study of attachment was conducted by Main and Goldwyn (in press). These investigators administered the Berkeley Attachment Interview to 30 mothers who had participated in a larger study of early social development (see also Main et al., in this vol.). The infants had been assessed in the Ainsworth Strange Situation with their mothers at 12 or 18 months. The attachment interview was conducted when the children were 6 years old.

The mothers were first asked to choose five adjectives that best described their relationship to both parents and to explain the reason for their choices. They were then asked to respond to a number of more specific questions such as "When you were upset in childhood, what did you do?" Other questions concerned memories of being held for comfort, of feeling rejected by parents in childhood, and of reasons for the parents' behavior. The interviewer also asked the mothers about parental threats of separation in childhood, about major changes in the relationship with parents since childhood, and about feelings regarding the current relationship with parents.

The interview transcripts as a whole were rated for descriptions of rejection by mother in childhood, for idealization of a rejecting mother, for anger toward mother now, for insistence on inability to recall childhood (regardless of how many memories were actually produced), and for overall coherence.

Main and Goldwyn report that the infants' avoidance of the mother in the reunion episodes of the Ainsworth Strange Situation was significantly correlated with interview ratings of the mother's rejection by her mother in childhood, with insistence on inability to recall childhood events (regardless of how many memories were actually produced), and with idealization of a rejecting mother. However, if the mother expressed anger and resentment about rejection by her mother in childhood, and if her discussion about attachment issues was coherent, her infant was unlikely to have avoided her on reunion in the Strange Situation. Main and Goldwyn describe one mother whose recollection of her unhappy childhood was exceptionally coherent. She had not idealized her rejecting parents but had forgiven them. This mother had the least avoidant infant in the sample.

The Amherst project.—Another intergenerational study of attachment was conducted by Ricks and Noyes (Ricks, 1982, 1983; Ricks & Noyes, 1984; Tronick, Ricks, & Cohn, 1982). Most of the findings from this study have not been published elsewhere and will therefore be reviewed in somewhat more detail than the data from the Minnesota and Berkeley projects. On the basis of Epstein's personality theory and Bowlby's attachment theory, it was predicted that both mother's self-esteem and her memories of childhood relationships would be related to the infant's security of attachment as assessed in the Strange Situation. Self-esteem has been shown to have global and widespread relationships with an individual's behavior. Substantial data links low self-esteem to feelings of anxiety, inhibition, and dependent affiliation and high self-esteem to feelings of spontaneity, integration, and autonomous affiliation (Burns, 1976; Epstein, 1973, 1976; O'Brien, 1981). High self-esteem should, then, be associated with sensitive and responsive mothering.

Twenty-eight mother-infant pairs, living in stable, middle-class families participated in this study. All mothers and their infants were seen in the Strange Situation when the infants were 1 year old. In addition, each mother was given two Likert-type questionnaires, the O'Brien-Epstein Self-Report Inventory (O'Brien, 1981), and the Mother-Father-Peer Scale (Epstein, 1983).[4] Questionnaires were completed at home to allow mothers time and privacy and to remove, as much as possible, any biases connected with the mother's experience in the laboratory. The Self-Report Inventory is a measure of general self-esteem (the degree to which a person reports that he likes himself and feels he is a person of worth vs. having a low self-opinion) and of eight evaluative realms of the self-concept, including self-control,

---

[4] Unpublished tests and manuals available from Seymour Epstein, Department of Psychology, University of Massachusetts, Amherst, MA 01003.

power over others, likability/loveworthiness, competence, morality, body image, body appearance, and body functioning. A defensiveness scale measures the extent to which respondents are likely to bias their answers toward gaining social approval. Examples of items on the self-report inventory include, "I am a great big nobody" (general self-esteem), and, "I feel as if nothing I do is very good" (competence).

The Mother-Father-Peer Scale includes dimensions of acceptance-rejection (by mother, father, and peers), independence/overprotection (by mother and father), and defensive idealization (of mother and father). Examples of items on these scales include, "When I was a child, my mother could always be depended on when I really needed her help and trust" (mother acceptance), "When I was a child, my mother often said she wished I'd never been born" (mother rejection), and, "My mother was close to a perfect parent" (defensive idealization). Epstein has found that adult report of mother acceptance in childhood is more highly correlated with sense of loveworthiness in adulthood (measured on the Epstein Mother-Father-Peer Scale and the O'Brien-Epstein Self-Report Inventory, respectively) than with any other of a wide range of personality variables assessed, including ego strength, neuroticism, introversion, and so on (Epstein, 1983). This is fully consonant with Bowlby's (1973) view on the reciprocal relation between an individual's representational models of self and of parents.

Ricks and Noyes found, as predicted, that mothers of securely attached infants had higher self-esteem scores and reported more positive recollections of childhood relationships with their mothers, fathers, and peers than did mothers of anxiously attached infants. Table 1 shows the relationship between the quality of infant attachment and mothers' reports of childhood relationships. The results on mothers' recollections of childhood acceptance by their own mothers were particularly strong; there were very few cases of overlap between mothers of secure infants and anxious infants. There was no difference between the two groups on the defensiveness scale (on the Self-Report Inventory) and no difference on the mother idealization scale, but mothers of securely attached infants tended to idealize their fathers more than did mothers of anxiously attached infants. Whether or not these mothers are able to tell us accurately what their childhood relationships were like, these results suggested that mothers of anxious infants felt less accepted by their parents than did mothers of securely attached infants.

In a follow-up investigation, Ricks (1983) conducted a study of 44 mothers and their 4–5-year-old preschoolers. All had been seen in the Ainsworth Strange Situation at 1 year of age, and 20 of them were included in the study reported above. Mothers were interviewed about their childhood experience, current relationships, and life stress (Cochrane & Robertson, 1973). They also completed the Mother-Father-Peer questionnaire (Epstein, 1983) and the revised O'Brien-Epstein Self-Report Inventory. Child out-

TABLE 1

MOTHER'S RECOLLECTION OF CHILDHOOD RELATIONSHIPS RELATED
TO INFANT ATTACHMENT

| | INFANT ATTACHMENT CLASSIFICATION | | | |
| | Secure (N = 12) | | Anxious (N = 12) | |
MOTHER-FATHER-PEER SCALE SCORES	M	SD	M	SD
Mother:				
Encouragement of independence*	3.14	.88	2.38	.66
Overprotection**	1.60	.77	2.53	.83
Encouragement total[a]***	9.17	9.52	−3.58	5.62
Acceptance***	3.46	.72	2.44	.85
Rejection**	.63	.54	2.29	.61
Acceptance total[a]***	23.25	6.55	3.42	4.44
Idealization	1.62	1.18	1.83	.54
Father:				
Encouragement of independence*** ...	2.99	.64	1.88	.77
Overprotection	1.67	1.09	2.05	.50
Encouragement total[a]***	7.58	10.96	−3.25	5.46
Acceptance***	2.96	.89	.81	.76
Rejection	1.06	1.01	.49	.23
Acceptance total[a]***	16.25	12.10	3.08	5.85
Idealization*	1.44	.77	.77	.37
Peers:				
Acceptance***	2.98	.90	1.87	.42
Rejection	1.40	1.00	1.69	.45
Acceptance total**	15.75	15.22	1.83	5.34

[a] Scores for the individual scales (i.e., encouragement of independence, overprotection, acceptance, rejection, and idealization) represent mean ratings of all items on the scale. Total scores are sum scores. Encouragement total was derived by subtracting the summed ratings of all items on the overprotection scale from the summed ratings of all items on the encouragement of independence scale. Likewise, acceptance total was calculated by subtracting the summed ratings on the rejection scale from the summed ratings on the acceptance scale.

* $p < .05$ (by t test).
** $p < .01$ (by t test).
*** $p < .005$ (by t test).

come measures included self-esteem, social competence (Waters et al., in press), and perceived competence (Harter, 1982, 1983) as well as laboratory observations of the child, both alone and interacting with the mother in a referential communication task.

Although child outcome and parenting quality measures were wide ranging, the major findings of the study can be conveyed by focusing on the relationship of mother's childhood recollections and self-esteem with a single outcome measure, the child's emotions rating. The emotions rating was a composite of two independent raters' observations of the child at three different points in the laboratory visit; four negative and three positive emotions were rated at each point. The rating was, thus, an aggregated measure of the child's affective state, with higher scores indicating more positive and lower scores more negative emotional behavior. A number of results indicate the validity of the emotions rating. Children who, as infants, had been securely attached (B_3) in relation to the mother had higher (more positive) emotions ratings than did children who had been anxiously attached to the mother in infancy (A and C). Those intermediate in security of attachment (B_1, B_2, and B_4) fell in-between. The emotions rating was significantly positively correlated with concurrent maternal behavior (composite ratings of support and pleasure in interaction with the child); it was significantly negatively correlated with scores on family stress intervening between the infant and preschool assessments.

In contrast to findings from the infant study, in the preschool follow-up both maternal defensiveness (on the Self-Report Inventory) and idealization of mother and father (on the Mother-Father-Peer Scale) were significantly related to earlier attachment classification of the infant. Mothers of infants seen as anxious were more defensive and more likely to idealize their parents than were mothers of infants seen as secure. The intermediate group fell in-between, and all contrasts were significant. Defensiveness (regarding the self) and idealization (of parents) are interesting in their own right. When, additionally, defensiveness or idealization was viewed as a potential suppressor and controlled for in correlations between maternal self-report scores and child outcome variables, a number of significant relationships emerged. With the relevant distortions partialed out, mothers' self-esteem and mothers' recollections of childhood were significantly related to the children's emotions ratings outcome. As in the infant study, in the preschool follow-up study mothers' acceptance from their own mothers in childhood was the strongest predictor of child outcome.

Results from the interview showed that mothers of children who had been anxiously attached at 1 year and who fared poorly as preschoolers were also likely to report that their own mothers (the childrens' grandmothers) were currently unhappy. In line with the findings from the Minnesota and Berkeley projects, a few mothers in the Amherst study reported recurrent changes of attachment figures through loss or disruption yet had children who had been securely attached and were doing well as preschoolers. These mothers, like those described in the other two studies, appeared to have successfully reworked childhood issues in their teenage years or to have had strong support systems. When good child outcome was associated with a maternal history of disruption or rejection, the mothers lived in stable marriages and had positive self-esteem. They often had exceptionally strong ties to their husband's families.

Although insistence on inability to remember childhood was not specifically investigated (as it had been by Main and Goldwyn), the mothers who spontaneously mentioned loss of memory of childhood events had histories of abandonment or rejection. For example, one mother described herself as having "blanked out" much of her childhood, saying that, even when her brother reminded her of specific events in their shared and harsh childhood, she herself could not remember the events.

A few mothers in the Ricks (1983) preschool study fit the pattern of forgiveness described by Main and Goldwyn (in press). In the Ricks (1983) study, the avenue toward forgiveness involved taking an autonomous stance toward the parent. For example, one mother reported that she accepted her own mother only after refusing to pay for her mother's third divorce. Previously, she had acceded to such demands. Another mother, who felt that her parents were extremely difficult to please and that she and her siblings had "been destroyed" by them, said, nonetheless, "It's hard to be mad at them; my parents did what they thought was best. Only recently did I tell my parents to 'quit bossing me around.' Before, I would always do what they told me." These cases are especially relevant to Epstein's discussion of the postulate "I must please mother," a postulate that is clearly maladaptive when the mother cannot be pleased. It seems that abandoning this postulate was a major influence in these two cases; both women had infants classified as securely attached.

PATHWAYS TO CROSS-GENERATIONAL EFFECTS IN ATTACHMENT

The actual findings reported here (summarized in Fig. 1) are consistent with the theoretical perspective presented in the first section of this chapter. It should be noted, however, that these data can be taken only as an indirect confirmation of Bowlby's hypothesis because they link infant attachment classification to the parent's concurrent model of early attachment relationships rather than to past representational models. For example, Main (Main & Goldwyn, in press; Main et al., in this vol.), Morris (1980, 1981), and Ricks (Ricks, 1982, 1983; Ricks & Noyes, 1984) have all documented significant relationships between a mother's retrospective recollections of childhood attachments and a mother's ability to serve as a secure base for her child, assessed in the Ainsworth Strange Situation. In addition, Ricks (1983) and Ricks and Noyes (1984) have documented relationships between the security of infant-mother attachment and maternal self-esteem (current model of self). Similar relationships have been found in other studies not directly tied to the attachment tradition. For example, self-esteem has been related to perceived parental acceptance in childhood by Medinnus and Curtis (1963), to regard for others in adulthood (Burns, 1976; Epstein, 1976), and to parental behavior and attitudes (cf. Belsky, 1984).

In addition to findings linking retrospective views of childhood attachments to later parental behavior, a number of intergenerational links between quality of early attachment experience and quality of later marital relations have been documented. Frommer and O'Shea (1973b) and Wol-

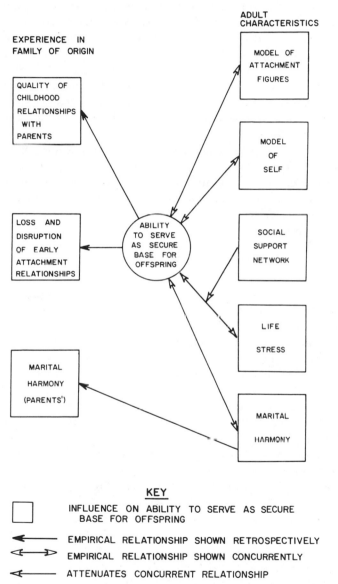

FIG. 1.—Influences on a parent's ability to serve as secure base for offspring

kind et al. (1977) found that separation or disruption of primary attachment relationships in childhood predicted later marital disharmony or marital status. A host of studies not directly tied to the attachment tradition have further shown concurrent associations between marital harmony and quality of parental behavior (e.g., Sherefsky & Yarrow, 1976). Crockenberg (1981) also found that a good social support network—often provided by members of the extended family—predicts the security of the infant's attachment to the mother and buffers the effects of life stress. Finally, an extensive review by Rutter and Madge (1976) supports the view that marital harmony in the first generation is related to marital harmony in the second. These findings corroborate Bowlby's assertion that the quality of early attachments will influence later adult-adult as well as parental relations. However, the causal relations among the personality, marital, and parental variables need further empirical clarification.

Prospective data on the influence of childhood relationships on eventual parental behavior—and hence on the quality of infant-parent attachment in the next generation—are still lacking. The concurrent links presented in Figure 1 are increasingly well supported in the research literature. The evidence reviewed here compellingly indicates that the quality of a mother's caregiving behavior is strongly related to her memories of childhood relationships. The same result has now been established through multiple methods (two quite different interviews and a questionnaire) and across samples differing in important respects. Yet however well substantiated the retrospective link, one cannot assume the prospective truth. That is, even though a parent's memories of childhood may be concurrently related to parental behavior, the memories may bear little resemblance to actual childhood experience. Although unlikely in this extreme form, we know that memory is reconstructive, mood related, context cued, and selective. Further studies on the validity and on individual differences in the validity (cf. Block, 1969b) of retrospective accounts of childhood are needed, as are long-term longitudinal studies.

Another important task for the future is that of tracing the integration of representational models of attachment across multiple relationships; it will be important to investigate the pathways of cross-generational effects on parental behavior for males and females separately and in relation to their own mothers and fathers (see Bretherton, in this vol.).

Sources of Discontinuity

Although continuity of key aspects of parental behavior across generations may be the rule, each of the studies discussed here has reported clear exceptions to the rule. Cases in which parents are able to provide secure bases for their children despite their own malignant childhood experience are particularly informative. Epstein's theory suggests that there are lawful processes through which change in the basic postulates of a representational model of attachment occurs. First, change occurs through significant emotional experience. Thus although a parent may consciously wish not to treat her children as she was treated, Epstein's theory would suggest that it is difficult to act on this wish without experience having altered the underlying representational models of self and others. Emotionally significant experience may or may not provoke conceptual change, depending on individual differences and situational factors, but such change is unlikely to occur in the absence of emotion. Second, if postulates regarding attachment bonds are acquired through internal representations of experience in early attachment relationships, then it is reasonable to suppose that change occurs through three major types of emotionally corrective experience in relationships: through change within the same early relationships across time, through repeated experience in other relationships that disconfirm earlier acquired models, and through especially strong emotional experience within a single relationship that, similarly, disconfirms earlier postulates. Since models of self and others are complementary, reflected appraisals from others that differ from childhood appraisals are particularly significant. Epstein suggests that the implicit logic behind naturally occurring changes in self-esteem is as follows: "I admire this person; he likes and respects me. Then maybe I am a worthwhile person myself; after all, I respect his judgment."

Reorganization or change in attachment-related postulates may be especially likely at particular points in the life span. A number of researchers have suggested that adolescence offers special opportunities for reorganization (Main & Goldwyn, in press; Main et al., in this vol.; Morris, 1980, 1981; Sroufe & Fleeson, in press). With the advent of formal operations, an individual who has suffered in childhood from any of the conditions leading to anxious attachment may profit from the ability to manipulate hypotheticals. Establishment of relationships outside the family of origin may alter existing attachment-related postulates. The birth of a child seems to be another time of reorganization. For example, mothers in the Amherst infant study often spontaneously discussed their own childhood relationships in relation to what they hoped for their infants (see also Belsky, 1984; Osofsky & Osofsky, 1984).

Although research on intergenerational continuity has made considerable strides in a short period of time, a number of rather thorny problems remain. However, the area is rich in complexity for the researcher, made all the more tantalizing by the potentially enormously fruitful applied implications of understanding intergenerational continuity and discontinuity in the quality of attachment relationships.

**PART 4
CROSS-NATIONAL STUDIES OF
ATTACHMENT IN INFANCY**

CROSS-NATIONAL STUDIES OF ATTACHMENT IN INFANCY: INTRODUCTION TO PART 4

Attachment is universal. But are patterns of attachment universal, especially patterns of attachment assessed in the Ainsworth Strange Situation? The three studies presented in this section attempt to provide preliminary answers to this question. In all three studies most infants observed in the Strange Situation could be satisfactorily classified according to Ainsworth's instructions, although the distribution of secure (B), avoidant (A), and resistant (C) patterns departed significantly from U.S. norms. This suggests that it may not be legitimate to interpret Strange Situation classifications in other cultures as they are interpreted in the United States. However, only extensive cross-cultural data on parent-infant interaction in the home and in other contexts will provide clarification on this issue.

Grossmann, Grossmann, Spangler, Suess, and Unzner (Chap. 10) are the first investigators to make a serious attempt at replicating Ainsworth's Baltimore study (Ainsworth et al., 1978). Like Ainsworth, they conducted lengthy home observations of mother-infant interactions before observing the infants in the Strange Situation. The correlational patterns among maternal and infant interactive behaviors observed in North German homes and the correlations of early maternal sensitivity to later Strange Situation classifications support the Baltimore findings. At the same time, one-half of the North German infants were classified as insecure-avoidant (group A), as contrasted with about one-quarter of the U.S. infants, even though maternal sensitivity ratings for group A in North Germany resembled those for group B_1/B_2 mothers in the Baltimore study. Grossmann et al. argue that the A classification in North Germany may not indicate an underlying rejecting maternal attitude but may be linked to the culturally valued early encouragement of independence. But does classification in group A have no implications in North Germany? This question can also be asked about Israeli kibbutz infants (Sagi, Lamb, Lewkowicz, Shoham, Dvir, & Estes, Chap. 11). A larger than expected number of kibbutz infants, when observed in the Strange Situation with mother, father, and metapelet, were classified as group C (insecure-resistant). For many of these infants the Strange Situation procedure had to be curtailed after the first separation because of inordinate distress. The authors reason that this distress was due to the infants' inexperience with strangers. However, the nighttime caregiving arrangements at the kibbutz could also explain the infants' feelings of insecurity (the metapelet did not sleep in the same house as the infants and had to be summoned by an intercom system if an infant cried at night). It is noteworthy that Israeli city infants in day care who formed the comparison group did not differ from U.S. samples in terms of the proportion of secure versus insecure classifications, although they did differ in the proportion of insecure infant-mother attachments classified as insecure-resistant (group C). In studying infant attachment in Japan, Miyake, Chen, and Campos (Chap. 12) also obtained more group C classifications than is usual in the United States. The authors, like Sagi et al., explain the infants' level of separation distress on the basis of inexperience with nonfamily baby-sitters. However, C classification could also be predicted from temperament assessments and maternal interactive behaviors.

The three studies in this section raise legitimate questions but cannot yet give definitive answers about patterns of attachment and the meaning of Strange Situation classifications in other cultures. None of them fully addresses the question as to what the important individual differences in attachment patterns might be in their culture. To make further progress in this area, we will have to study culture-specific ideals of healthy adult functioning in relation to patterns of parent-child interaction, to parental representations (internal working models) of attachment relationships, and to culturally valued child-rearing practices. An obvious strategy is to compare cultures that are very different from one another (as different as the Balinese and the Tikopia described in Chap. 1). However, this may not be necessary. Chapters 10 and 11 suggest that a more efficient strategy may be to compare distinct subgroups within a larger culture. For example, the preponderance of group A attachments was observed only in North Germany, not in South Germany. The very high proportion of C attachments was observed only in Israeli kibbutz infants, not in city infants. It appears that we may be able to learn much about culture-specific variations in attachment patterns by comparing groups that live in the same country but differ widely in terms of their shared belief systems.

I. B.

X. MATERNAL SENSITIVITY AND NEWBORNS' ORIENTATION RESPONSES AS RELATED TO QUALITY OF ATTACHMENT IN NORTHERN GERMANY

KARIN GROSSMANN, KLAUS E. GROSSMANN, GOTTFRIED SPANGLER,
GERHARD SUESS, AND LOTHAR UNZNER

University of Regensburg

The study presented here is a cross-national partial replication of Ainsworth's Baltimore project (Ainsworth et al., 1978). Like Ainsworth and her colleagues, we conducted home visits throughout the first year and then observed infants and their mothers in the Strange Situation at 12 months. In addition, we used the Neonatal Behavioral Assessment Scale (NBAS) to assess the infants as newborns.

Our longitudinal study was conducted in Bielefeld, North Germany. In our home observations we focused on infant crying and maternal responsiveness, on behaviors relevant to close bodily contact, and on infant responses to brief everyday separations and reunions. All these behaviors were found by Ainsworth et al. (1978) to be closely linked to the development of different patterns of infant-mother attachment. We also used Ainsworth's maternal sensitivity scale to make global ratings of maternal behavior during the infant's first year and correlated these ratings with infant attachment patterns in the Strange Situation. In addition, we tried to ascer-

This research report is based on three diplom theses submitted by the third, fourth, and fifth authors to the University of Regensburg, Department of Psychology. The research was supported by a grant from Stiftung Volkswagenwerk to K. E. Grossmann. We wish to thank our many helpers: the late Dr. P. Lachenicht and the staff of the Sankt Franziskus Hospital in Bielefeld for their generous cooperation; H. Als for coming to Bielefeld to conduct NBAS training; I. Bretherton for establishing reliability between the ratings of some Bielefeld and Baltimore narrative reports. Jutta Ermshaus and Elisabeth Heimesaat helped with NBAS assessments and the home visits; Ulrike Fuchs served as an additional home observer; and Gisela Bokaemper and Margret Steierberg coded the narrative reports patiently and accurately.

tain whether infant interactive style as assessed by the NBAS (Brazelton, 1973) might be a useful independent predictor of Strange Situation classification at 12 months of age.

Much attachment research, whether conducted in the United States or elsewhere, is based on the Strange Situation developed by Ainsworth and Wittig (1969) as a standard procedure for assessing the quality of infant-mother attachment. It is often forgotten, however, that the validity of this procedure is based on 14–16 lengthy home observations of mother and infant, summarized in Ainsworth et al. (1978). For example, in the Baltimore study, mothers of infants with avoidant reunion responses during the Strange Situation at 12 months were rated low on sensitivity to infant signals during home visits conducted during the last quarter of the first year. By contrast, mothers whose infants sought proximity to and contact with them during reunion episodes of the Strange Situation were rated high on sensitivity to signals.

Our longitudinal study is the first attempt to use Ainsworth's methodology in an attempt to replicate the systematic relationships between the quality of mother-infant interactions at home and Strange Situation classifications obtained in the laboratory (Ainsworth et al., 1978). In virtually hundreds of studies it was tacitly assumed that infant behavior patterns in the Strange Situation can be explained with reference to the interaction patterns documented for 23 Baltimore mothers and their infants. This occurred despite the fact that Ainsworth herself cautioned that "adequate validation of our Strange Situation procedure as a test of infant-mother attachment will require a series of replicatory studies with different samples" (Ainsworth et al., 1971, p. 19).

Ainsworth's Baltimore project emphasized the maternal contribution to the quality of infant-mother interaction and hence to the quality of infant-mother attachment. However, as Hinde (1976) pointed out, the quality of an interaction depends on the reciprocal meshing of both partners' behaviors. In a number of recent studies the infant's contribution, in terms of a readiness to respond to social interaction, has been assessed by means of the NBAS (Brazelton, 1973). This scale documents individual differences in behavioral and interactive style during the first few days of life. According to Brazelton, Als, Tronick, & Lester (1979), the NBAS allows for an evaluation of the infant's capacities along dimensions that are thought to be relevant to the infant's developing social relationships. Indeed, several studies have shown that individual differences documented by the NBAS are predictive of infant-mother attachment classification, assessed in the Strange Situation at 1 year. For example, Egeland and Brunnquell (1979) reported that, in their economically disadvantaged sample, infants' orienting ability was the third best predictor of adequate versus inadequate care (after two maternal variables). For the same sample, Waters, Vaughn, & Egeland

(1980) found that lower neonatal scores on motor maturity and regulation were associated with insecure-resistant attachment at 12 months (see also Bretherton, in this vol., for a review of this literature).

In sum, our longitudinal study was designed to address the following questions:

1. Do mothers in Bielefeld and Baltimore show similar patterns of sensitive mothering, despite the potential effects of different cultural norms on maternal child-rearing attitudes and practices?
2. Is the distribution of Strange Situation classifications (secure vs. avoidant and resistant) comparable to U.S. samples?
3. Is maternal sensitivity as good a predictor of Strange Situation classifications at 12 months in Bielefeld as it was in Baltimore?
4. Does the infants' interactive behavior during the NBAS predict maternal sensitivity at 2, 6, and 10 months and Strange Situation classifications at 12 months?
5. If significant differences between the Bielefeld and Baltimore samples are found, what would be the most likely explanation for them? Under the assumption that the ethological foundation of attachment theory is valid, how could cultural demands and practices operate to yield the observed differences?

In our preliminary observations, we gained the general impression that there are strong demands for self-reliance on German infants, in the sense that mobile infants are discouraged from staying too close to the mother (Grossmann & Grossmann, 1981a). Such demands have not been documented for U.S. infants, and U.S. researchers have not found it necessary to create a special category to describe such parental requests (e.g., Clarke-Stewart, 1973; Lytton & Zwirner, 1975; Stayton et al., 1971). Moreover, we felt that North German mothers' demands for self-reliance were not linked to other forms of maternal rejection in any obvious way, despite the fact that mothers denied the infant close bodily contact on a number of occasions. If such culturally determined practices were to result in the avoidant patterns of reunion behavior in the Strange Situation, would that imply the same kind of nonoptimal infant-mother attachment for the North German infants as for the Baltimore infants? In other words, are children who do not show the B patterns of reunion behavior in the Strange Situation psychologically troubled, no matter whether they were rejected or whether they were trained to be self-reliant, even if perhaps somewhat prematurely?

In her paper on attachment theory and its utility in cross-cultural research, Ainsworth (1977, p. 64) suggested that "we have every reason to believe that different infant care practices and patterns of maternal behavior have differential effects in shaping the nature of the infant-mother relationship. If different societies have different practices and different patterns of mother-infant behavior, crosscultural comparisons will supplement within group comparisons in throwing light upon the development of qualitative differences." However, in order to confirm whether the Strange Situation procedure is a valid test of infant-mother attachment in another culture, three important aspects of the development and assessment of mother-child relationships have to be considered: direct assessments of naturalistic mother-child interactions at home, the role of the infant's contribution to the interaction, and the role of cultural expectancies and demands in mother-infant interaction patterns.

On the basis of systematic correlations with the quality of mother-infant interaction in the home, the normative Strange Situation reunion pattern observed in U.S. infants is held to indicate secure attachment. Moreover, of the three subgroups of securely attached infants, the pattern termed B_3 (the largest of the eight subgroups identified by Ainsworth) is considered to index optimal security. In agreement with theoretical considerations linking a secure attachment to close bodily proximity, high emotional involvement, and communicative competence (Ainsworth et al., 1971), the B_3 pattern has been implicitly treated as the natural pattern. Hinde, however, has refuted any implications of nature's intention to establish an "idyllic" relationship (Hinde, 1982a). Indeed the B_3 pattern would be judged by many German parents as that of a spoiled or immature toddler. The Strange Situation, as a specific observational procedure using a 1-year-old's behavior pattern in the laboratory as a basis for classifying the quality of attachment to parents, may not do sufficient justice to the meaning of similar behavior patterns in other cultures.

We hope that, by identifying dynamic stabilities of developing relationships, we may uncover culturally guided emotional and behavioral priorities. This may lead to an understanding of how patterns of interaction become integrated into relationships under specific cultural expectations.

METHOD

Subjects

Fifty-four mothers and their healthy full-term newborns (27 boys, 27 girls) participated. The mothers and fathers were asked for their consent prior to the birth of the infant. Fifty-two percent of the infants were firstborns. Their mean birth weight was 3,490 grams (SD = 398 grams), their mean Apgar score at 1 minute was 9.6. At 5 minutes, all infants had an Apgar score of 10.

The families lived in stable conditions without major socioeconomic changes. Only three mothers planned to go back to work after the baby was born, and only one of them had a full-time job. Fifty-three percent of the families were lower middle class; they differed widely, however, with respect to number of children (range 1–5), parents' education (69% of the fathers had completed 9 years of school as well as 3 years of apprenticeship), fathers' occupation (unskilled to academic), and maternal age (range 18–42 years).

Neonatal Assessments

Procedure.—The NBAS was administered three times to each infant (on day 2 or 3, on day 5 or 6, and on day 8 or 9). Mothers and infants were customarily discharged from the hospital on the tenth day after delivery. Two infants could only be tested twice (one mother-infant pair was discharged on the seventh day, and for one infant the pediatrician advised us not to administer the NBAS during the first 3 days). The choice of the specific day was made according to the circumstances in the nursery: days of major disturbances or of medical examination and innoculations were avoided. Four conditions had to be met before an infant was examined: the preceding rest period of the infant had not been unduly disturbed, at least 1½ hours had passed since the last feeding, the infant had taken the normal amount of milk at the last feeding, and body temperature in the morning had been normal.

The examination took place in a small, quiet, dimly lit, warm room where the examiner was alone with the infant. The main examiner (first author), who carried out about 50% of the assessments, was trained to 90% reliability by Heidelise Als. Two additional examiners were trained by the first author. Interrater reliability between the three examiners of this study was repeatedly checked and kept at the 90% level throughout the 3 months of testing.

Data integration and analysis.—The test results were factor analyzed with Varimax rotation. For each testing day, two factors emerged that were consistent with other data: Orienting ability, composed of NBAS test variables 5–10, and Irritability, composed of NBAS variables 16–19, 24, and 25. For the longitudinal analysis presented here, the mean sum of the scores for all three assessments was computed for each infant. By rank ordering the factor scores and dividing the group at the median, each infant was assigned to the following categories: above or below average in orienting ability and above or below average in irritability (detailed results are reported in Grossmann & Grossmann, in press).

Home Visits

Procedure.—Of the 54 families observed in the hospital, 49 were included in the longitudinal study. To approximate the procedures used in the Baltimore study (Ainsworth et al., 1978), each family was visited three times during the first year, that is, when the infants were 2, 6, and 10 months old. These ages corresponded to the first quarter, to mid-term between the second and third quarters, and to the fourth quarter data in the Baltimore study. For five families the 2-month visit had to be omitted because the families were on vacation or moving. Two observers were present during each visit. The 2-hour visit included an interview conducted in accordance with the guidelines of Ainsworth's Uganda study (Ainsworth, 1967) and a 45–60 minute intensive observation by both observers.

Each of the visits was audiorecorded. In addition, both observers (only one during the interview period) took written notes describing maternal and infant behaviors relevant to attachment, but the infant's interactions with other persons were also included. Immediately after the home visits the observers compared their notes and wrote a very detailed 15–20 page version of their observations. The written narrative reports, supplemented by the audiorecordings, formed the data base.

The first two observers (the first and second authors) trained themselves in the above recording procedures by conducting a pilot study with six families for 1 year. During the main investigation there were three additional observers who learned the method by serving as the third observer for three visits.

Data integration and analysis of the 10-month home visits.—The initial analysis of the 10-month narrative reports was made by the fourth and fifth authors (see Suess, 1981; Unzner, 1981), who had not participated in the home visits. Instructions reported in Ainsworth et al. (1972) were used in this analysis. The following behaviors were coded: infant crying and maternal responsiveness, behaviors relevant to close bodily contact, and the infants' responses to their mothers' comings and goings. For the analysis of infant crying and maternal responsiveness the following information was extracted from the 10-month home-visit data:

1. Number of crying episodes, differentiating between intensive crying and unhappy vocalizations.
2. Length of crying episodes, assigned to five categories from very short (1–5 seconds) to very long (over 1 minute).
3. Situation, contrasting caretaking routine with routine-free interaction.
4. Mother's reaction to infant crying according to nine categories: pickup, touch or pat, verbal or playful interaction, routine interactions such as feeding or changing diapers, offering a toy or a pacifier

without further interaction, just checking what happened, removing the source of distress, angry reactions such as rough handling or scolding, and other reactions.

5. Mother's responsiveness according to three categories: prompt reaction, delayed reaction, and ignoring.
6. Effectiveness of mother's interventions, noting which interventions stopped the infant's crying.
7. Effectiveness of the mother's responsiveness, noting the average number of interventions a mother needed to stop the infant's crying.

In similar fashion, maternal and child behaviors relevant to close bodily contact and behaviors relevant to the mother's comings and goings were tabulated. Interrater reliability for the 30 analyzed behaviors ranged between 78% and 100%, with a mean of 90.4%.

In addition, the same 10-month narrative reports were coded sentence by sentence by two trained students, using the object of action, the mood, form, or other quality of the action, and/or the relatedness of the action to previous action. The German adaptation of the coding system, based on systems used by Caldwell (1969), Lytton and Zwirner (1975), and Roper and Hinde (1978), was undertaken by the first author. The system was adapted for computer analysis by the third author (Spangler, 1981, 1982).

Finally, maternal sensitivity to infant signals and maternal cooperation versus interference were rated according to Ainsworth's scales.[1] Reliability coefficients were .96 and .99, respectively, and the raters never differed by more than one point. After establishing reliability, one rater applied the sensitivity scale, the other the cooperation scale, to the whole narrative report for each visit. Reliability of the use of these rating scales was checked again by Inge Bretherton, a co-worker of Mary Ainsworth in her Baltimore study. Being of German origin, she rated six of our home-visit reports, and our raters had the opportunity to rate five sets of the Baltimore fourth-quarter narrative reports. Interrater reliability was .92. The maximum difference was two points, but this occurred only once. With this reassurance, the 2- and 6-month visits were also rated for maternal sensitivity, again avoiding having the same rater judge the same family twice.

For the comparisons of the Bielefeld and Baltimore mother-child pairs, all behavior categories were standardized to 1 waking hour of the child. Due to the fact, however, that the Bielefeld families were visited only once during the fourth quarter, not all behaviors occurred in all families. In order to test for relationships between these behaviors and maternal sensitivity despite low frequency of occurrence, we grouped the mothers into two categories:

[1] For a description of the scales, see Ainsworth et al. (1971, 1978). The scales have been made available to us by Mary Ainsworth and were translated into German by the first and second authors. For the German version of the sensitivity scale, see Grossmann (1977).

sensitive mothers (those scoring 5 and higher) and insensitive mothers (those scoring 4 and lower). If significantly more sensitive mothers or infants of sensitive mothers showed the specific behavior at least once, it was concluded that this behavior was positively related to maternal sensitivity.

The Strange Situation

At 1 year of age, the Ainsworth Strange Situation procedure was carried out with the 49 children and their mothers. At 18 months, 46 children were seen in the Strange Situation with their fathers. Their attachment relationship was classified according to the prescribed criteria by Mary Main (Ainsworth et al., 1978). The results have been published (Grossmann et al., 1981).

RESULTS

Mother-Infant Interaction Patterns at Home

Behaviors relevant to infant crying and maternal responsiveness.—At 10 months (see Table 1) all children showed distress at least once, but 11 children never cried longer than 5 seconds. Six children had long crying episodes of more than 1 minute during the visit.

All but one mother reacted promptly to the infant's crying at least once, but at the same time 41 mothers also ignored at least one unhappy vocalization. Ignoring or not responding was also dependent on the intensity of the infant's distress signals. There was only one mother who ignored all five of her child's distress signals.

The types of interventions the mothers used to comfort the children or to relieve their distress were very diverse. Mothers picked up the child in about 25% of the crying episodes. In 75% of the crying episodes the mothers tried other interventions: diverting the child by offering a toy or pacifier, interacting verbally or playfully with the child, which usually implied that the mother at least acknowledged the child's distress, offering food, or changing the diaper. Even angry or annoyed reactions occurred, although such negative reactions were observed in only six mothers. Picking up the infant was the most common maternal reaction to crying, but in only 5% of all crying episodes was it the first. Instead, other kinds of interactions (31.2%) and attempts to divert the child (22.7%) were seen more often as the first reaction. Because these behaviors were usually not very effective, some mothers picked up their child within the next five reactions. If they did, the crying episodes were most likely to stop (Spangler, 1981).

Most mothers needed more than one intervention to soothe the child

TABLE 1

INFANT CRYING, MATERNAL RESPONSIVENESS, AND EFFECTIVENESS OF INTERVENTIONS DURING THE 10-MONTH HOME VISIT

Behavior	N	M (per Waking Hour)	SD	Effectiveness (%)
Infant crying:				
Frequency of distress vocalizations	49	7.5	5.5	...
Frequency of intensive crying	37	2.4	3.7	...
Duration of crying (sec.)	49	68.8	13.7	...
Episodes lasting 0–5 sec.	49	4.9	3.0	...
Episodes lasting 5–15 sec.	38	1.2	1.5	...
Episodes lasting 15–60 sec.	14	.3	.7	...
Episodes lasting more than 60 sec.	6	.2	.6	...
Maternal responsiveness:				
Prompt reactions (%)	48	63.7	25.7	...
Delayed reactions (%)	26	10.1	14.2	...
Ignored episodes (%)	41	26.0	21.2	...
Maternal interventions to % of crying episodes:				
Picks up	43	22.3	19.9	50
Touches, pats	19	3.3	9.0	14
Vocalizes, interacts	35	16.1	15.6	37
Feeds, changes diapers	28	9.8	14.7	34
Offers toy, pacifier	35	19.6	30.5	36
Enters room	3	.5	2.2	0
Removes noxious stimulus	18	6.1	10.6	29
Reacts angrily	6	4.9	9.4	46
Other types	38	20.2	17.2	37

($M = 3.4$). Therefore the effectiveness of the various interventions was also assessed (see Table 1). As predicted by attachment theory, close bodily contact was the most effective intervention, and 34 of the 49 mothers used it at least once. Interestingly, from the standpoint of distal communication in mother-child interaction at 10 months, other interventions were also quite successful. Later we offer an explanation of the mothers' use of noncontact intervention strategies in spite of the fact that almost all of them experienced the greater effectiveness of close bodily contact in ending their child's distress.

Frequency and duration of the infant's crying episodes were closely related to maternal responsiveness. About half the mothers ($N = 22$) never ignored the crying of their infants during the visit: these infants cried significantly less often and for shorter periods (chi-square test, $p < .01$), and these mothers needed significantly fewer interventions to calm their child (chi-square test, $p < .01$), that is, they were more effective.

Mothers' general effectiveness in calming their infants (proportion of effective interventions) differed greatly. Four mothers were almost never effective, and seven mothers were always effective, most mothers being 30%–40% effective. In those crying episodes that ended quickly, close bodily contact was used more often than was diverting. It is worth mentioning that verbal empathy with the child proved to be ineffective if it was not combined with close bodily contact. Closeness in mind is surely not enough for a 10-month-old infant to relieve his or her distress.

Behaviors relevant to close bodily contact.—During the 10-month home visit, all mothers picked up their child at least once. The mothers held their infants for an average duration of 6 minutes per hour (range ½ minute to almost 20 minutes). This is not surprising in view of the fact that, by 10 months, 39 of the children could creep or crawl well, and the others tried to move. The children wanted to be on the floor trying their new skills. Long holding episodes occurred almost exclusively when the child was fed or when mother and child played a social game as the child sat on the mother's lap. Routine care was the most frequent reason for picking up the child, but once on mother's lap, playful interactions ensued in one-quarter of the episodes.

Except for five mothers, all engaged at least once in playful behavior while picking up or holding the infant. However, fewer than half the mothers showed any sign of tenderness while holding the infant. This may be due to the time of day. Visits took place during the more playful afternoon and not at bedtime or during sickness.

The children initiated few pickups during the 10-month home visit. Only half the children showed this behavior at all. In 93% of all pickup episodes contact was initiated by the mother. In 22% of these episodes the pickup event interfered with the child's ongoing activity for no obvious reason. We may conclude that at 10 months most children preferred to play or explore on their own at home and that even the relatively small amounts of close bodily contact during playtime were in general not demanded by the child. This is also reflected in the children's reactions to being picked up. Although 44 infants reacted positively or ambivalently at least once, in only 30% of the episodes could the observers detect any emotional reaction at all. A positive reaction occurred only slightly more often than an ambivalent one, that is, the child may have been happy to be picked up but at the same time appeared to be annoyed at being disturbed in his activity. Likewise, being put down again produced protest from the infants in only 17% of the episodes. All children went on playing after being put down at least once. With respect to the issue of reinforcing dependency behavior or acknowledging and answering the infants' communications appropriately, we can confirm Ainsworth's finding (Answorth et al., 1972) that infants who showed positive reactions to being picked up tended not to protest when being put down again ($r = .52, p < .001$).

There were great individual differences in the behaviors of mothers and infants. Except for a few general behaviors, not all mothers or infants showed all varieties of attachment behavior, as Ainsworth has also noted for her Uganda and Baltimore samples (Ainsworth et al., 1972).

Correlating the crying variables with the infants' responses to close bodily contact, we found that infants who cried a lot tended to react negatively to being picked up and put down ($r = .30, p < .05$). Mothers who ignored their infants' crying also tended to get negative reactions when they picked them up or put them down ($r = .40, p < .01$).

Infants' responses to their mothers' comings and goings.—Because the visit lasted only about 2 hours, not many leave- and enter-room episodes were recorded. Forty-six mothers left at least once, but only six mothers left and returned more than 10 times. Maternal greeting behaviors and infant crying responses to maternal departure occurred infrequently, illustrating that mothers' coming and going in the home is a familiar phenomenon for 10-month-old infants to which they do not pay very much attention. The frequency with which the mother left and returned to the room was unrelated to either crying or greeting behavior in the infant.

Comparison of Mother-Infant Interaction Patterns at Home: The Baltimore and Bielefeld Studies

Maternal interactive behaviors.—Table 2 shows those maternal interactive behaviors that are directly comparable for the Baltimore and the Bielefeld studies. The comparison is based on the fourth-quarter home visits in the Baltimore study and the 10-month home visit in the Bielefeld study. Table 2 also shows relationships of these maternal behaviors with the global mater-

TABLE 2

Maternal Interactive Behaviors during the Fourth Quarter as Related to Maternal Sensitivity in the Baltimore as Compared to the Bielefeld Study

Maternal Behavior	Baltimore Sample ($N = 23$)		Bielefeld Sample ($N = 49$)	
	M	Relates to Sensitivity	M	Relates to Sensitivity
Responsiveness to infant crying:				
Ignoring of crying (episodes/hour)	1.8	+*	1.7	+*
Unresponsiveness to crying (min/hour)	2.1	−*	10% of episodes	−*
Behavior relevant to separation/reunion (%):				
Acknowledging baby when entering room	28.0	+*	37.0	+
Behavior relevant to close bodily contact (%):				
Pickups in which mother behaves affectionately	16.0	+*	5.1	+*
Pickups that are abrupt or interfering	12.9	−*	22.1	−*
Holding time in which mother is tender	15.0	+	5.2	0
Time of inept holding	7.4	−	.0	0
Holding time occupied with routines	23.4	−*	11.1	−*
Sensitivity vs. insensitivity to signals	4.7		4.5	
Cooperation vs. interference	5.8	+*	4.7	+*

* $p \leq .05$.

nal sensitivity ratings during the fourth quarter or the 10-month visit. Remembering that we made only one 2-hour home visit during the fourth quarter, the results show that the frequency of behaviors per hour differed but that the associations with maternal sensitivity were the same for both samples. However, the overall pattern of bodily contact seems to be significantly different for the two samples. Although the total duration of holding per waking hour of the 10-month-old infant was about the same (360 sec. in Baltimore, 342 sec. in Bielefeld), the mean duration of holding episodes was only about half as long in our sample (120 sec. vs. 58 sec.). Thus the Bielefeld children were picked up twice as often as, but for shorter periods than, the Baltimore children. In addition, the Bielefeld mothers were less tender, less careful and affectionate while holding the infant in their arms; they were more interfering, but they also behaved less ineptly while holding the infant. The difference in percentage of time occupied with routines may be due to the fact that, during our 2-hour visit, the mother avoided routines in order to be sociable. The Baltimore visits lasted approximately 4 hours and usually included a feeding.

The relationships between maternal interactive behaviors and ratings of maternal sensitivity at 10 months confirm Ainsworth's findings: mothers rated as sensitive responded more promptly and ignored their infants' crying less often than mothers rated as insensitive. Sensitive mothers needed fewer interventions to soothe the child and picked up their crying infants more often. All mothers with a sensitivity rating of 6 and above responded with close bodily contact to the infant's intensive crying. Sensitive mothers interfered less often with the activities of their infants when they picked them up, and they behaved more affectionately when the infant was in their arms. They were also less occupied with routines while holding their infants. All these differences are significant at $p < .05$ or less using chi-square tests. Finally, as in the Baltimore study, maternal sensitivity and cooperation ratings were highly correlated ($r[21] = .81$ for Baltimore and $r[47] = .76$ for Bielefeld, $p < .001$ for both).

Infant interactive behavior.—Table 3 compares infant interactive behaviors at home during the fourth-quarter visits in Baltimore and the 10-month visits in Bielefeld. It also shows relationships of infant behaviors to maternal sensitivity ratings.

Bielefeld infants communicated less than Baltimore infants. They cried less when their mother left the room and greeted her less often when she reentered. Bielefeld infants responded less often, either positively or negatively, to being picked up and put down, and they initiated pickup less often.

Despite these quantitative differences, infant interactive behavior and maternal sensitivity show the same correlational patterns as in the Baltimore sample. The infants of sensitive mothers cried less than infants of insensitive mothers, they sought close bodily contact more often, and they responded

245

TABLE 3

Infant Interactive Behaviors during the Fourth Quarter as Related to Maternal Sensitivity in the Baltimore as Compared to the Bielefeld Study

Infant Behavior	Baltimore Sample		Bielefeld Sample	
	M	Relates to Sensitivity	M	Relates to Sensitivity
Crying:				
Frequency of crying (episodes/hour)	4.1	–	7.5	–*
Duration of crying (min/hour)	4.6	–*	1.2	–*
Response to mother's comings and goings (%/hour):				
Crying when mother leaves room	18.0	–*	6.7	–*
Following when mother leaves room	49.8	+*	14.5	+
Positive greeting when mother enters	33.0	+*	18.2	–
Behaviors relevant to body contact (%/hour):				
Positive response to being picked up and held	26.0	+*	13.3	+*
Negative response to being picked up and held	13.0	–*	5.7	–*
Nonnegative response to being put down	63.2	+*	36.9	+*
Negative response to being put down	31.0	–*	16.9	–*
Initiation to pickup	18.4	+*	6.7	+*
Initiation of put down	3.5	–	5.5	+
Sinking in as a form of contact behavior	.18	+*	.4	+
Active contact behaviors	.25	+*	1.2	+

* $p \leq .05$.

more promptly to being picked up and protested less often when being put down again. Because mothers' comings and goings were so rare during the Bielefeld 10-month home visit, not all the tests reached statistical significance, but the direction of association is generally the same as in the Baltimore study.

Thus we can now claim that we are referring to the same behavior patterns as Ainsworth (Ainsworth et al., 1978) when we speak of maternal sensitivity to infant signals and communications.

Strange Situation Classifications as Related to Maternal Sensitivity

The Ainsworth Strange Situation procedure yielded the same patterns of reunion behavior with the 49 North German mother-child pairs as with the 23 mother-child pairs of the Baltimore sample. However, the distribution of the patterns was different. Forty-nine percent of the North German children showed the avoidant pattern of reunion behavior toward their mothers (group A) compared to 26% in Baltimore. Only 33% sought close bodily proximity or contact with the mother on her return (group B) compared to 57% in the Baltimore sample. Within group B, Ainsworth's largest subgroup was group B_3 (39%), whereas in Bielefeld the largest subgroup was group B_2 (20%). Finally, 12% of the Bielefeld infants, compared to 17% of the Baltimore infants, responded ambivalently to their mothers' return (group C; see Grossmann et al., 1981). Interestingly, a replication of the Strange Situation with 51 12-month-olds and their mothers in South Germany (Regensburg) yielded a distribution more similar to that in the United States (Escher-Graeub & Grossmann, 1983).

As regards maternal sensitivity, it turned out to be highly stable across the first year ($r_{2/6} = .61$; $r_{6/10} = .58$; $r_{2/10} = .50$, using Spearman rank correlations, $p < .001$, for all three visits). All scale points were used in making the ratings, although a score of 9 (very sensitive) was given only once during a 2-month visit. A score of 1 (very insensitive) was given twice during each of the three visits.

Figure 1 shows the mean maternal sensitivity ratings by Strange Situation subgroups for the three fourth-quarter home visits of the Baltimore sample and for the 2-, 6-, and 10-month visits of the Bielefeld sample. The mean for all three Bielefeld visits combined is also included. The number of infants in each subgroup is shown on the left. Both similarities and differences between the samples are noteworthy.

In the Baltimore sample, the mean fourth-quarter maternal sensitivity score of group B mothers differed by almost four points from the mean of group A mothers and by more than four points from group C mothers. In our sample, the mean difference between group B and group A mothers at

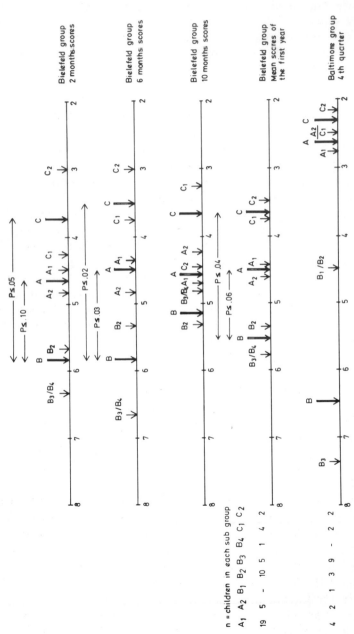

Fig. 1.—Mean maternal sensitivity ratings by Strange Situation groups and subgroups for the Bielefeld sample (at 2, 6, and 10 months for the first year) and for the Baltimore Sample (fourth-quarter visits).

2 months was only one point ($p < .10$) and two points between group B and group C mothers ($p < .05$). At 6 months, the differences between the groups in our sample were 1.3 points ($p < .03$) and 2.3 points ($p < .02$), respectively. For the mean of the 2-, 6-, and 10-month visits combined, the difference between the group B and group A mothers was again one point ($p < .06$), but group B mothers differed from group C mothers by almost two points ($p < .01$). Despite the small group differences, the data support Ainsworth's findings: Bielefeld infants who were classified as securely attached in the Strange Situation procedure have had more sensitive mothers during the first year than infants who had been classified as insecurely attached. There are, however, some conspicuous differences between the Baltimore and the Bielefeld samples.

1. The mean sensitivity ratings of the group B mothers in Bielefeld was markedly lower at the 10-month home visit ($M = 5.1$) than at the previous visits ($M = 5.8$). The means of group A and group B mothers were no longer significantly different (see Fig. 1) because the overlap of the scores in the two groups became quite large. At 10 months only six of the 16 group B mothers had sensitivity scores of 7 or above, but so had seven of the 33 non-B mothers. Five of the 16 group B mothers had sensitivity scores of 3 and below, as compared to 12 of the 33 non-B mothers.

2. The mean sensitivity ratings of the group A mothers in Bielefeld was always about midway between the values for the group B and group C mothers, whereas in Baltimore the sensitivity scores of the group A and group C mothers were almost indistinguishably low. Figure 1 shows that the mean sensitivity score of the 24 group A mothers in Bielefeld was the same as that of the four Baltimore mothers whose infants were classified as B_1 or B_2. In other words the mean score of our group A mothers was two points above the mean score for the Baltimore group A mothers.

3. Maternal sensitivity as rated from the 10-month visit only was not significantly related to the infants' attachment classifications at 1 year in the Bielefeld sample. The range of mean sensitivity ratings for all subgroups had shrunk to two points (3.7–5.7) on the nine-point scale (see Fig. 1), although the range of individual ratings remained the same as for the previous visits.

4. Sensitivity ratings for the five mothers of subgroup B_3 (in Bielefeld one-third of group B, in Baltimore two-thirds of group B) changed dramatically between 6 and 10 months. These had been the most sensitive mothers when their infants were 2 and 6 months old. By 10 months they had become almost as insensitive as group A mothers. In contrast, group B_2 mothers, the largest B subgroup in Bielefeld, had relatively stable mean sensitivity ratings during the whole year.

The increase of the mean sensitivity score of the two C_2 mothers is due to the extreme increase in sensitivity of one of these mothers. At the 10-

month visit, the infant was slightly ill, and the mother was very concerned and highly responsive. The observers agreed that this high sensitivity seemed an exception rather than a true increase from the last visit due to the special circumstances.

Neonatal Behavioral Assessment Factor Scores and Attachment Classification at 1 Year of Age

In Bielefeld we found significant relationships between the orienting ability of the newborn as assessed by the NBAS and the attachment classification of the infant to his mother at age 1. No comparable neonatal assessments for the Baltimore sample are available.

In the relatively unchanging hospital environment where the Bielefeld mothers and infants stayed during the entire 9-day assessment period, the three NBAS assessments yielded consistent results (see Grossmann & Grossmann, in press). Three different criteria were used to ensure that the Bielefeld sample was indeed a healthy group of newborns: a low frequency of NBAS scores evaluated as worrisome by the a priori clustering suggested by Brazelton et al. (1979); indices for healthiness (Aleksandrowicz & Aleksandrowicz, 1975), assuring that there was no infant who showed the "difficult infant syndrome" on any one assessment day; and good modulation according to Als and Lewis (1975) (about 75% of the Bielefeld infants were well modulated on each assessment day).

The two factors, Orienting Ability and Irritability, that emerged from the factor analysis accounted for 33.5%, 36.2%, and 36.9% of the total variance on the three assessment days, respectively. The factor scores for orienting ability were negatively correlated with the factor scores for irritability ($r = -.37, p < .003$).

Orientation factor scores for infants classified as securely attached to their mothers at 12 months were higher for two of the three assessments. The item that showed the clearest differentiation between infants later classified as group B ($N = 16$) and group A ($N = 24$) was Orienting to Face ($p < .03$).

Neonatal differences between children later classified as securely versus insecurely attached are most obvious if the orientation and irritability factor scores are separated at the median. Twelve of the 16 children (75%) classified as securely attached to their mothers at 12 months had been good (above the median) orienters. This was true for only nine of the 24 children (37.5%) classified as insecure-avoidant ($p < .02$). Fourteen of the 24 group A children (58%) had been more irritable newborns, but so had seven (44%) of the group B children. A larger percentage of the more irritable group B children, however, had also been good orienters. As a group, the resistant (group C) infants did not receive unusual NBAS scale or factor scores. Half the infants classified as group C were good orienters as newborns, and only one scored above average on the irritability factor.

Thus only the orienting ability of the newborn was related to Strange Situation classification with the mother at 12 months, and this attentive response differentiated group B from group A infants but did not discriminate group C from the other two groups.

The newborns' orienting ability was also a significant predictor of the Strange Situation classifications with the father at 18 months, but the effect was not as strong: 68% of the infants classified as securely attached to the father ($N = 19$) had been good orienters as newborns, as compared to 32% of the infants classified as insecurely attached ($\chi^2[1] = 4,40, p < .05$). Considering the infants' responses to both parents, 60% or 29 of 48 infants had shown the secure attachment behavior pattern to at least one parent.[2] Twenty of these had been good orienters (69%). Of the 20 infants who were not classified as securely attached to either parent, only five (25%) had been good orienters. This difference is highly significant ($\chi^2[1] = 9, p < .01$).

Orienting ability, maternal sensitivity, and attachment classification.—Neonatal orientation factor scores were not related to maternal sensitivity at 2, 6, or 10 months ($r = .02, -.17, .15$, respectively). Thus in Bielefeld maternal sensitivity during the first year did not depend on the infants' attentiveness as newborns.

Figure 2 shows that newborns' orienting abilities and maternal sensitivity during the first half year both make independent contributions to the prediction of infant attachment classifications with mother at 12 months. The findings are presented as a Venn diagram.

Twelve of the 16 group B children had been good orienters (scored above the median), and 11 of them had sensitive mothers (sensitivity score > 5). Only eight group B infants were good orienters during the neonatal period and had sensitive mothers. On the other hand, 15 of the 16 group B children (94%) either were good orienters as newborns or had sensitive mothers. Only 52% of the group A infants and 67% of the group C infants either were good orienters or had sensitive mothers. The difference between groups A and B is significant (Fischer's Exact Probability Test, $p < .025$).

Figure 2 also shows, however, that 13 infants who scored above the median on newborn orientation ·and 13 infants whose mothers received

---

[2] We include in this number the two children who were classified as B to mother but whom we did not see with father. We exclude from the total the child who was classified as A with mother and whom we did not see with father.

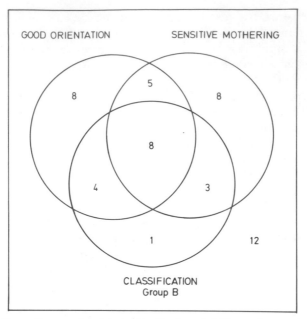

FIG. 2.—Venn diagram showing the distribution of children who were good orienters (above the median) as newborns, whose mothers were rated sensitive (rating of 5 and above) during the first half year, and who were classified as group B (secure) in the Strange Situation with their mothers at 12 months.

above average scores on maternal sensitivity were not classified as securely attached to their mothers at 12 months. Interestingly, there were even five infants with good newborn orientation and sensitive mothers who were classified as insecurely attached to their mothers in the Strange Situation.

DISCUSSION

In an attempt to replicate Ainsworth's careful quantitative and qualitative analyses of mother-infant interaction during the first year of life, we found some of the predicted associations between maternal sensitivity and infant behavior patterns at home (Ainsworth et al., 1978), but we also discovered that neonatal orienting ability made an independent contribution to the quality of the relationship as assessed by the Strange Situation. Cultural differences emerged not in the types of attachment patterns observed at home and in the Strange Situation but in the quantitative distribution of these patterns and in their relationship to maternal sensitivity assessed at 10 months.

General Findings

Both in the Bielefeld and in the Baltimore samples mothers of infants classified as securely attached in the Strange Situation at 1 year were more sensitive to their infants' signals during the first year of life. In the Bielefeld sample, maternal sensitivity assessed at 2 and 6 months (but not at 10 months) predicted the infant's attachment classification at 12 months. In addition, maternal and infant interactive behaviors were related to maternal sensitivity in both samples. Infants of sensitive mothers cried less, were held more, quieted more readily on being picked up, and protested less when they were put down again.

On the other hand, maternal sensitivity only partially accounted for the quality of attachment to mother in 12-month-olds. The infants' readiness as newborns to attend to incoming sensory stimuli was an independent second predictor of secure attachment to mother as assessed in the Strange Situation. Five infants showed the secure attachment pattern despite their mothers' lower sensitivity scores. Four of these infants had been good neonatal orienters. One might speculate that these infants were so ready and willing to interact that a good relationship was easily established even by a less sensitive mother or that they were able to tolerate less than optimal mothering. We are even more persuaded by the fact that 74% of the infants who did not show the secure attachment pattern to either parent had been lower than average in their orienting ability.

Cultural Differences

Although Baltimore and Bielefeld mothers had almost the same amount of close bodily contact with their 10-month-old infants, the quality of holding differed: the Bielefeld mothers were generally less tender and affectionate, their holding episodes were shorter, and their pickups were more frequently interfering as compared to the Baltimore mothers. The Bielefeld infants also seemed to communicate less with their mothers.

In the Strange Situation a much higher percentage of the Bielefeld sample was classified as group A (avoidant) than in the Baltimore sample (49% vs. 26%). We interpret this part of our findings with respect to the cultural values that we believe to be dominant in North Germany, where people tend to keep a larger interpersonal distance. As soon as infants become mobile, most mothers feel that they should now be weaned from close bodily contact. To carry a baby who can move on its own or to respond to its every cry by picking it up would be considered as spoiling. The ideal is an independent, nonclinging infant who does not make demands on the parents but rather unquestioningly obeys their commands. One is reminded of Lewin's observations about social-psychological differences between the United States and Germany:

> For someone who comes from Germany the degree of freedom and independence of children and adolescents in the United States is astounding. Especially impressive is the lack of a submissive attitude of the child toward adults or of students toward their professors. The adults too treat the child as their equal, whereas in Germany it appears to be the natural right of the adult to dominate and the duty of the child to obey. The natural relationship between the adult and the child in the United States is not considered as one between a master and a subordinate but as one between two individuals of basically equal rights. Parents seem to treat their children more respectfully. When they ask the child to bring something, they usually ask for it in a polite manner. In a situation in which a German father or a German mother would most probably utter brief commands, parents in the United States will let the child feel that they enjoy its compliance. It is often the case in the United States that one hears a father or a mother say "thank you" after such compliant behavior. [Lewin, 1936/1948, p. 27][3]

Despite the tremendous attitudinal and political changes that have occurred in the last 50 years or so, traditional attitudes of the kind described by Lewin still seem to be somewhat alive in many homes where they have never been the subject of parental reflection. It should be stressed, however, that Erikson's dark and grave picture of the utterly insensitive and authoritarian father of the German family belongs definitely to the past (Erikson, 1963).

We believe that, in our North German sample, a mother's lower sensitivity to infant signals during the first half year may reflect a desire to comply with cultural norms rather than indicating an underlying rejecting attitude toward the child. This interpretation is supported by two findings. First, the Bielefeld group A mothers were rated higher on maternal sensitivity than the Baltimore group A mothers (with a mean difference of two points). Indeed, their mean scores were the same as the sensitivity scores of the Baltimore group B_1/B_2 mothers. Second, maternal sensitivity and maternal rejection were not correlated in the Bielefeld sample even though they were highly correlated for the Baltimore sample (Ainsworth et al., 1978). Hence, the infant's avoidance of the mother during the reunion episodes of the Strange Situation may best be interpreted as a temporary disturbance of the relationship due to premature demands on self-reliance. Early weaning of close bodily contact puts most of the children under stress and seems to

[3] Translated by K. E. Grossmann.

make them ill at ease with their mothers at 12 months. As children grow and are able to carry out more independent activities, nonrejecting parents will become proud of their children's achievements and support the next developmental step appropriately. The outlook for such a relationship seems less grave than the withholding of physical contact based on rejection. Comparing the North German (Bielefeld) and South German (Regensburg) findings, we could speculate that in South Germany independence training is begun later. Our everyday, unsystematic observations would confirm this hypothesis, but we do not have data to substantiate it at present.

A further difference between the Bielefeld and the Baltimore mothers concerns the sensitivity of mothers whose infants were classified in subgroup B_3. Group B_3 mothers behaved less sensitively during the 10-month visit than during the 2- and 6-month observations. Although group B mothers picked up their crying babies more often than group A or group C mothers, the Bielefeld group B mothers offered a toy in response to their infants' distress signals about three times as often as Baltimore mothers (Bell & Ainsworth, 1972), thus diverting the infants from close bodily proximity. They often tried to relieve the infants' distress by other means than picking them up, which was quite successful in many instances. From the decline in B_3 mothers' sensitivity scores at 10 months, we can infer that they now also enforced independence (see Grossmann & Grossmann, 1981b, for a discussion of this issue). But in view of the fact that these babies did show secure attachment patterns at 12 months, we may conclude that insensitivity for the sake of complying with cultural norms is not equivalent to rejection.

More generally, we suspect that in U.S. samples the less frequent A and C classifications may provide a reliable indicator of insecure relationships, whereas the more common B classification may not be as reliably linked to optimal infant-parent attachment. Our suggestion is based on the surprising finding that some abused infants in U.S. samples showed the secure patterns of reunion behavior in the Strange Situation despite objectively assessed events indicating an impaired mother-infant relationship (Egeland & Farber, 1984; Gaensbauer & Harmon, 1982). In North Germany, by contrast, the B pattern may be a more reliable assessment of security than it is in the United States, but the more common A pattern may characterize a wider range of less optimal relationships.

With the aim of further clarifying the meaning of North German infants' avoidant reunion behavior, we reanalyzed episodes 2, 5, and 8 of the Strange Situation, during which parent and child are together. By focusing on the communicative outcome of the infant's behavior vis-à-vis the parent, especially on vocal, gestural, and facial expressions, we were able to assess infant signals in terms of their social consequences for dyadic functioning. Our preliminary results show that self-reliance in the manipulation of objects, object-centered initiations of interaction, and less communication and dampened facial/vocal expressiveness do indeed tend to characterize avoidant (group A) infants (Grossmann, Grossmann, & Schwan, in press).

We shall be able to answer further related questions in the near future. At present, we have begun to assess paternal caretaking and emotional involvement with the infant during the first year. This will allow us to examine whether paternal behavior and neonatal orienting ability predict Strange Situation classification with the father at 18 months.

With regard to the mother-child interactions, we are using the narrative reports and audiorecordings of the home visits to discover how early verbal communications are used to replace close bodily contact and at what age some infants are developmentally able to accept this substitute for bodily proximity and contact. We are paying close attention to the content of maternal demands and to maternal styles of establishing obedience. We are also testing the predictive validity of the mother-child interaction measures from the first year by analyzing play situations of the same mother-child pairs at 2 years of age (Grossmann, 1984) as well as at 3 years of age (Luetkenhaus, 1984). At these ages there is an emphasis on the parents' teaching styles as well as on their emotional supportiveness.

The main conclusion to be drawn from our findings is, however, that the development of attachment has to be given much more scrutiny of the kind provided by Ainsworth and her co-workers in Baltimore. In the Baltimore project, reunion patterns in the Strange Situation could be predicted from mother-infant interactions at home. On the basis of that validation, the Strange Situation as an observation-based measure has profitably been used by a number of researchers. It is nevertheless a shortcut method. By equating a wider attachment concept with a narrower operationalization based on a single standardized assessment procedure, we run the risk of losing much of the rich background and potential of the original attachment concept (Grossmann et al., in press). Although this appears to be the most likely fate of any simplification, such an approach may lead to highly misleading findings in intercultural research. For purposes of cross-cultural comparisons, the Strange Situation does not provide an easy way out. Thorough descriptions of the development of attachment patterns in the context of particular cultural values and practices are vital. Fortunately, more work toward gaining a better understanding of attachment relationships is already under way in a number of research teams in different parts of the world.

XI. SECURITY OF INFANT-MOTHER, -FATHER, AND -METAPELET ATTACHMENTS AMONG KIBBUTZ-REARED ISRAELI CHILDREN

ABRAHAM SAGI

University of Haifa

MICHAEL E. LAMB AND KATHLEEN S. LEWKOWICZ

University of Utah

RONIT SHOHAM AND RACHEL DVIR

University of Haifa

DAVID ESTES

University of Michigan

Although the Strange Situation procedure was developed two decades ago, it was until recently used exclusively in the United States. Only in the late 1970s did researchers begin using the procedure in other countries, notably, Sweden (Lamb, Hwang, Frodi, & Frodi, 1982), West Germany (Grossmann et al., 1981; Grossmann et al., in this vol.), and Japan (Miyake et al., in this vol.). What follows is a report of our attempt to use the Strange Situation procedure to explore the effects of kibbutz rearing practices on

This research was made possible by the School of Social Work and the Research Authority of the University of Haifa. The authors are grateful to Gaby Lanyi, Atalia Gidron, Abraham Landau, Michael Nathan, Zvi Lavi, the staff of Oranim, the Institute for Research on Kibbutz Education, and the staff of Na'Amat and Wizo (day-care centers) as well as to the child-care coordinators, metaplot, and parents who made this research possible by their gracious cooperation. We also wish to thank Yona Berkovitz, Ronit Bogler, Racheli Goldman, Tinika Polak, Rachel Roler, Adar Lavi, and Aaron Cohen for their assistance in the collection and reduction of the data and William P. Gardner and Daniel Cerro for assistance with the data analysis.

the development of infant-mother, infant-father, and infant-caretaker attachments in a sample of kibbutz-reared Israeli infants.

Our study had two interrelated goals. One was to see whether the proportion of insecure attachment relationships observed among infants on the kibbutzim differed from the proportion typically observed among infants in traditional American families. The question was important because, as indicated below, kibbutz child-rearing practices differ substantially from those that are considered desirable by attachment theorists (e.g., Ainsworth, 1973). Consequently, attachment theory led us to expect that there would be an increase in the number of insecure attachments among kibbutz-reared infants. Our second goal was to see whether the insecurity of specific relationships was lawfully related to the occurrence of events or circumstances that should, on theoretical grounds, be associated with attachment insecurity. Since most of the available evidence was derived from one hypothesis-generating study (Ainsworth et al., 1974), findings concerning the antecedents of attachment security and insecurity were also of great potential importance, regardless of whether the distribution of infants across attachment classifications was different from the norm.

When the first kibbutzim were founded by Zionist pioneers early in the twentieth century, the exigencies of survival made it necessary for as many adults as possible to be involved in economically productive work. This was one of the reasons why the few children were placed in the care of specially designated caretakers ("metapelet"; plural, "metaplot"). Over the years, this system of communal child care became institutionalized. In "traditional" kibbutzim today, mothers are granted brief maternity leaves to allow them to care for their infants at home. Between 6 and 12 weeks postpartum, mothers begin a phased return to work. At the same time that mothers begin returning to work, infants are usually assigned to beds in the communal *beit tinokot* ("infants' homes") to which they return each evening after periods of interaction with their parents. During the hours that mothers are working, their children are cared for by metaplot assigned to three or four children of the same age. Children typically stay with the same metapelet until 12–15 months of age, when they are reassigned. In most cases, two metaplot combine their groups into a single group of six to eight children each of whom is thus familiar with two regular caretakers. In keeping with the policy of many kibbutzim, the women appointed as metaplot may or may not be enthusiastic about serving in this role. There is thus considerable variation in the motivation, enthusiasm, and expertise of the individuals responsible for basic child care.

Once their mothers have returned to full-time work—usually by the children's first birthdays—children are with peers and metaplot throughout the daylight hours except between 4:00 and 7:00 P.M. every day, when they are with their parents rather than metaplot. However, parents are permitted to and often do visit their children at other times during the day. During the night, all the children in the kibbutz, distributed among several *beit tinokot* and *beit yeladim* ("children's homes"), are cared for by watchwomen. In some kibbutzim a single person in a central location monitors the children through intercoms placed in each *beit yeladim* or *beit tinokot*. In other cases, an adult may sleep in the building, while in others watchwomen monitor the children by walking from residence to residence. Because many women in the kibbutz take turns as watchwomen, the adult attending to a distressed infant at night is often quite unfamiliar and may be inexperienced. Further, in some kibbutzim there may be considerable delays at night between the onset of distress and the arrival of an adult.

Over the last decade, 91 of the 222 nonreligious kibbutzim in the country have shifted from communal to "familistic" sleeping arrangements for their young children, and a few others are planning to change. Under the familistic arrangement, children go home with their parents at 4:00 P.M. and do not return to the *beit yeladim* until early the next morning. However, our study was conducted exclusively in kibbutzim that still maintained the traditional arrangement.

Because the traditional kibbutz child-care practices are so unlike those traditionally considered by psychologists (e.g., Ainsworth, 1973; Bowlby, 1969/1982b, 1973) to be universally desirable and appropriate (i.e., primary care by the child's mother figure), many researchers have sought to determine what effects these practices have on child development, especially social, emotional, and personality development (e.g., Bettelheim, 1971; Fox, 1977; Maccoby & Feldman, 1972; Rabin, 1965; Spiro, 1958). Unfortunately, many of the earlier studies were conducted by investigators with predetermined views about the desirability or undesirability of kibbutz rearing practices, and few involved appropriate comparison groups or employed objective measures of known reliability. Most also focused on older children rather than infants. Consequently, such studies will not be discussed here.

The studies by Fox (1977) and Maccoby and Feldman (1972) are more pertinent, however, because they involved attempts to determine whether infants formed attachments to their mothers and metaplot. Maccoby and Feldman concluded that 2-, 3-, and 4-year-olds were attached to their mothers from evidence that the children protested separation from their mothers and used their mothers as secure bases from which to explore. Fox showed that 8–20-month-olds protested separation from both mothers and metaplot; this led him to conclude that the kibbutz child-rearing practices do not prevent infants from forming attachments to their mothers; they simply allow children to form other attachments as well.

Our study was designed to extend the findings of Fox and of Maccoby and Feldman. Assuming that the infants on kibbutzim indeed formed attachments to their mothers, fathers, and metaplot, we sought to assess the security or insecurity of these relationships using the Strange Situation procedure. These data would allow us to answer two questions. Are insecure attachments more common among kibbutz-reared children than in other samples of Israeli or American children? and, What factors are associated with attachment security and insecurity within the kibbutz sample? Ainsworth et al. (1974) have argued that the security of infant-adult attachments is determined by the quality of interaction—notably the sensitivity of the adult to the infant's signals and needs. Ainsworth (1973) and Blehar (1974) have also suggested that repeated separations (as in day care) increase the likelihood of insecure attachments, which implies that the kibbutz child-care practices should have this effect. Likewise, the common failure of familiar caretakers to respond to the child's needs at night, the frequently delayed responsiveness to distress at night, and the low motivation and commitment of some metaplot are all factors that seem likely to increase the number of insecure attachments among kibbutz-reared infants. Among kibbutzim, meanwhile, there is variation in the experience, training, stability, and motivation of metaplot, in the extent to which the parents have regular or irregular separations (of several days or longer) imposed on them, and in the extent to which the kibbutz child-rearing practices are consistent or inconsistent with those with which the parents and metaplot grew up and feel familiar. These factors seem likely to affect the security/insecurity of individual infant-adult attachments if our current beliefs about the antecedents of attachment security are correct (cf. Ainsworth et al., 1974; Lamb, Thompson, Gardner, Charnov, & Estes, 1984). The study was thus designed to yield data concerning the effects of kibbutz rearing practices on socioemotional development as well as theoretically important data concerning the antecedents and thus interpretation of individual differences in Strange Situation behavior.

The Strange Situation procedure was designed to allow researchers to observe changes in the organization of attachment behavior in the context of gradually increasing stress occasioned by taking the child to an unfamiliar room, introducing an unfamiliar female, and engineering brief separations from, followed by reunions with, the attachment figure (Ainsworth & Wittig, 1969). Under stress, securely attached infants should seek comfort and security from their attachment figures and should use the adults as secure bases from which to explore the environment (Ainsworth et al., 1978). Insecurely attached infants fail to use their attachment figures in this fashion. Instead, some avoid, rather than seek proximity to, their attachment figures, while others mingle angry, rejecting behavior and strong contact-seeking behavior, creating the impression of ambivalence.

As indicated earlier, it is widely believed that the way infants behave in the Strange Situation is determined by their prior experiences—most importantly by their interactions with the specific adult (Ainsworth et al.,

1978). Infants often behave differently in the Strange Situation with their mothers and fathers (Grossmann et al., 1981; Lamb, 1978; Lamb et al., 1982; Main & Weston, 1981), suggesting that characteristics of interaction with the particular person, rather than some general temperamental trait, determine behavior in the Strange Situation. Thus the mothers of securely attached infants are said to have been sensitively responsive to their infants' signals and needs, whereas the mothers of insecurely attached infants are insensitive. Unfortunately, although the association between maternal behavior and security of attachment (as assessed in the Strange Situation) is widely described, the only published data were gathered in one exploratory longitudinal study (Ainsworth et al., 1971, 1972, 1974). There is thus a need for further research on the antecedents or correlates of individual differences in the security of attachment. One goal of the present study, as mentioned earlier, was to see whether we could identify specific aspects of each infant's experiences that were systematically related to the security or insecurity of that infant's attachments to mother, father, and metapelet as assessed in the Strange Situation. Although these data would not affirm the importance of parental sensitivity, they would at least speak to the importance of the infant's social history in shaping the security of attachment. To address this issue, we used questionnaires to gather information about caretaking arrangements and change therein as well as about family circumstances. Meanwhile, by examining the distribution of infants across the major variations in attachment security, we hoped to determine whether the child-rearing practices of the kibbutzim in themselves had a general effect on the security of infant-adult attachments. Changes in the frequency of secure (group B), insecure-avoidant (A), insecure-resistant (C), and dependent (B_4) attachment classifications were determined by comparing the frequencies of each category observed in the kibbutz sample with distributions obtained in the United States and in a small Israeli city sample we recruited.

Our attempts to identify the correlates of secure and insecure attachments using the above strategies are important not only to broaden the data base on which assumptions about the meaning of Strange Situation behavior are based but also to determine whether the procedure is valid as an index of the quality of infant-adult relationships when employed in a cultural context very different from that in which it was developed and standardized. The developing literature involving the Strange Situation has led many researchers to employ it in studies outside the United States, such as West Germany (Grossmann et al., 1981; Grossmann et al., in this vol.), Japan (Miyake et al., in this vol.), and Sweden (Lamb et al., 1982). It is clearly essential to determine whether the procedure is indeed suitable for use in these contexts. In fact, some of our findings raise questions about the meaning of the Strange Situation classifications of kibbutz-reared infants.

METHOD

Subjects

Eighty-six infants, along with their mothers, fathers, and metaplot, served as subjects in this research. Thirty-seven of the infants were first-borns, and 49 were second- or thirdborns. Thirty-nine of the infants were girls. We aimed to include only infants who had been assigned to the same metapelet for at least 3 months prior to data collection. We later found that 20% of the infants had been with their metaplot for 1–3 months, 13% for 3–6 months, 30% for 6–9 months, and 38% for 9–12 months. As indicated below, however, there was no significant relationship between the security of attachment and the recency of assignment to the metaplot. The subjects were drawn from a total of 18 kibbutzim in Northern Israel, nine affiliated with each of the major kibbutz movements (Takam and Artzi). All the kibbutzim had maintained the traditional pattern of infant care, with infants housed in central living quarters rather than with their families. Such arrangements are maintained by 69 of the 70 kibbutzim in the Artzi movement but by only 67 of the 152 kibbutzim affiliated with Takam. Kibbutznikim typically have at least a high school education and a middle-class lifestyle even when, following the needs and dictates of the kibbutz, many are engaged in more menial forms of work.

For purposes of comparison, two additional, smaller samples were recruited. One consisted of 36 infants and their city-dwelling mothers. All came from middle-class backgrounds and were recruited through day-care centers where the infants were enrolled full-time while their mothers were employed. All came from intact middle-class families and were in other ways similar to the major kibbutz sample. Our original intention was to recruit a larger sample of city-reared children. However, when collection of data on this sample was terminated prematurely by the war in Lebanon, we had observed only 36 dyads. The second special sample consisted of eight infants and their metaplot working on the same kibbutzim from which the major sample was derived. These infants and metaplot were observed in the Strange Situation in the mornings so that we could assess the effects of time of day on the patterns of infant behavior observed in the Strange Situation. For the purposes of analysis, this small special sample was augmented by 19 of the metapelet-infant dyads in the major kibbutz sample who had to be assessed in the mornings.

Procedure

Infants in the main sample were observed in the Strange Situation three times, once each with their mothers, fathers, and metaplot. The assessments took place 6 weeks apart when the infants were 11, 12½, and 14 months old, and the order in which the three adults were involved was systematically counterbalanced to control for order effects. Immediately prior to each Strange Situation assessment, the infants' sociability toward an unfamiliar female and an unfamiliar male was assessed using a brief, nonintrusive procedure developed by Stevenson and Lamb (1979). The sociability data have not yet been analyzed and will be reported elsewhere.

Most of the sessions took place between 4:00 and 6:00 P.M., a time at which the infants were rested and would typically be at home with their parents. All observations took place in a room of a *beit yeladim* other than that in which the infant was housed. Camera operators filmed unobtrusively through a crack in the curtains from outside. After the three assessments had been completed, the child-care coordinator for the kibbutz completed a brief questionnaire concerning the care arrangements, significant separations from either parent, family life events, et cetera. In most cases, the coordinators completed the questionnaires with the assistance of both parents and metaplot.

The Strange Situation procedure employed was identical to that described by Ainsworth et al. (1978). The strangers were drawn from a pool of nine female students, 20–27 years of age, who took turns in the role and participated in roughly equivalent numbers of sessions. All were completely unfamiliar to the infants, and different strangers were involved in each Strange Situation. Assessments of the security of attachment were later conducted using the videotapes. Ainsworth et al.'s interactive rating scales were completed for each episode before an overall judgment about the security of attachment was made. All tapes were rated independently by two to five of the authors, trained by author Lamb, who personally participated in the rating of 90% of the tapes. When scoring any tape, the raters were unaware of the infant's behavior in other sessions—something that was easy to ensure with 296 sessions to rate. Raters always worked independently, comparing their ratings after each episode and discussing any disagreements of one point or more on any scale until consensus was reached. Similarly, each rater assigned the child to a group and subgroup independently. Agreement in the use of the interactive scales was extremely high (range = 93%–97%, $M = 95\%$), as was agreement in the assignment of group and subgroup labels (86%). Disagreements about classification were usually resolved by discussion, perhaps with a re-review of the tape. In extremely ambiguous or difficult cases, the tape was also set aside for recoding.

Contrary to our prior experience in the United States and Sweden, a considerable number (80) of the 251 sessions involving kibbutz-reared infants had to be terminated prematurely—either without any or after only one brief separation—because the child was inconsolably distressed. In some cases, the session ended after episodes 3 or 5. In other cases, the stranger was asked to leave after episode 3, and when the child had calmed, we proceeded to episode 6 (child alone). As indicated below, attempts were made to classify these attachments using the limited available information; most were classified as C_2 because of the infant's passivity and failure to gain comfort from the adult.

The questionnaires completed by the kibbutz child-care coordinators contained items concerning the age at which the infant first began sleeping in the infant house; its age when mother returned to some, half-time, three-quarter-time, or full-time work; how long the infant had been in the care of the metapelet with whom it was seen in the Strange Situation; whether it had previously been in the care of another metapelet; the occurrence and length of regular separations from mother and father; the occurrence, frequency, and length of any irregular separations from either parent; the frequency of maternal and paternal visits to the infant home during the day; the occurrence of hospitalizations; the origins (kibbutz born, Israeli born, or immigrant) of mother, father, and metapelet; and the metapelet's own parental status, experience, training, and desire for the job.

Comparable data (where relevant to the city context) were gathered by questionnaires from the mothers of the 36 infants in the day-care comparison group. Additional questions focused on the reasons for maternal employment, maternal satisfaction with employment, maternal perceptions of their ability to function as mothers, and the nature of the mothers' and fathers' jobs.

RESULTS

Effects of Infant Gender, Kibbutz Movement, and Order of Assessment

Chi-square tests were employed to determine whether there was any association between the security of attachment classification and whether the assessment was first, second, or third in sequence. Three analyses were performed: one concerned with relative numbers of A, B, B_4, and C group infants; one with relative numbers of insecure (A and C) and secure (B_1, B_2, and B_3) infants; and one with relative proportions of anxious (A, C, and B_4) and secure (B_1, B_2, and B_3) infants. Similar groupings were used for most of the analyses reported below unless otherwise noted. Tests revealed no order effects, so the data were combined for subsequent analyses.

There were also no sex differences, so the data for boys and girls were combined for later analyses.

There was, however, one significant effect for movement: more infants were classified as insecurely attached to their mothers on Takam kibbutzim than on Artzi kibbutzim, $\chi^2 = 7.06$, $df = 1$, $p < .01$, with B_4 considered insecure; $\chi^2 = 6.88$, $df = 1$, $p < .01$, with B_4 not included. This relationship was not evident when all four categories (A, B, B_4, and C) were distinguished. There were also no relationships between movement affiliation and the apparent security of infant-father and infant-metapelet attachment. Because the movement effects were not consistent across adults and were not readily explained and because the sample was too small to split in two, we decided to combine data from both movements in the analyses that follow. None of the major findings reported here is different for the two movements.

Distribution across Attachment Categories

Compared with samples studied previously in the United States, we found a somewhat greater number of infants assigned insecure classifications in the kibbutz sample. As illustrated in Table 1 (for the full kibbutz sample), 41% of the mother-infant and 47% of the metapelet-infant relationships were classified as either avoidant or resistant. If we also consider the dependent and clingy B_4 relationships to be nonsecure or anxious, then the total number of nonsecure relationships with both mothers and metaplot is around 50%, compared with 30%–35% in most samples. Also notable is the proportion of insecure attachments falling into the resistant category. Infants of this type have been rare in the United States (Ainsworth et al., 1978), Sweden (Lamb et al., 1982), and North Germany (Grossmann et al., 1981) but here constituted a third of the sample—three times more than is typical. The distribution of infant-mother attachments across the four categories (A, B, B_4, and C) differed significantly from the distribution reported by Ainsworth et al., $\chi^2 = 17.89$, $df = 3$, $p < .001$.[1] Likewise, the distribution of metapelet-infant relationships differed significantly from the distribution reported for mothers by Ainsworth et al., $\chi^2 = 12.99$, $df = 3$, $p < .005$. Interestingly, the distribution of avoidant, resistant, dependent, and secure father-infant attachments did not differ significantly from the proportions reported by Ainsworth et al.

---

[1] We compared our distributions with those of Ainsworth et al. (1978) because their's is the largest and best-known sample group. Previous studies in the United States and Sweden have reported no deviations from Ainsworth et al.'s distributions whether they studied mothers (Lamb, 1978; Lamb et al., 1982; Main & Weston, 1981; Thompson et al., 1979; Vaughn et al., 1979; Waters, 1978) or fathers (Lamb, 1978; Lamb et al., 1982; Main & Weston, 1981). Previous studies with fathers in the United States employed smaller samples than Ainsworth et al. and do not provide necessary information regarding subgroup assignment, so we chose instead to use Ainsworth's data concerning mothers. We are aware of no prior studies in which the Strange Situation has been used to explore attachments between infants and nonfamilial caretakers similar to metaplot.

TABLE 1

CLASSIFICATION OF INFANT-ADULT RELATIONSHIPS INTO ATTACHMENT CATEGORIES

	AVOIDANT (A)		SECURE (B)		DEPENDENT (B_4)		RESISTANT (C)	
	N	%	N	%	N	%	N	%
U.S. sample:								
Mother ($N = 105$)[a]	22	21	66	63	4	4	13	12
Full kibbutz sample:								
Mother ($N = 83$)[b]	7	8	40	48	7	8	28	33
Father ($N = 83$)[c]	9	11	45	54	9	11	18	22
Metapelet ($N = 84$)[d]	13	15	38	45	6	7	27	32
Nonabbreviated sessions for kibbutz sample:								
Mother ($N = 52$)	7	13	33	63	3	6	9	17
Father ($N = 56$)	8	14	43	77	1	2	4	7
Metapelet ($N = 59$)	13	22	35	59	3	5	8	14
Abbreviated sessions for kibbutz sample:								
Mother ($N = 30$)	0	0	7	23	4	13	19	63
Father ($N = 25$)	1	4	2	8	8	32	14	56
Metapelet ($N = 25$)	0	0	3	12	3	12	19	76

[a] Data from Ainsworth et al. (1978).
[b] One unclassified.
[c] Two unclassified.
[d] One unattached.

Complete versus incomplete assessments.—As mentioned earlier, a considerable number (35%) of Strange Situation sessions had to be terminated prematurely or modified by eliminating episodes 3 and 4 because the infants were inconsolably distressed. Most of these infants were later classified in the C_2 category. If we exclude from consideration those infants whose sessions were abbreviated, the resultant distributions of infants across attachment categories for mother-infant, father-infant, or metapelet-infant attachments do not deviate significantly from U.S. norms (see Table 1, for nonabbreviated sessions). By contrast, the distributions for abbreviated sessions differed dramatically from U.S. norms, χ^2 = 42.17, 50.86, and 50.71 for mothers, fathers, and metaplot, respectively, $df = 1$, $p < .001$. Thus the overall deviations reported above are accounted for by a group of infants who manifested unusual degrees of distress and were extremely difficult to soothe.

Comparison between the Kibbutz and Israeli City Samples

The fact that there were increases in the number of C and B_4 classifications, especially in relation to mothers and metaplot, raises the possibility that there is a cultural difference—perhaps in temperament or child-rearing style—that accounts for the differences between the distributions observed in Israel and those observed previously in the United States. For this reason, we recruited a sample of city-raised Israeli infants from comparable backgrounds who were enrolled in full-time day care. Because this comparison group was small, however, we were not able to perform statistical comparisons of the relative proportions of A, B, B_4, and C group classifications in the city, kibbutz, and U.S. samples.

The distribution of attachment classifications for the 36 Israeli city infants differed from the distribution obtained for the kibbutz infants. Only one city infant was classified as group A (3%), 27 infants (75%) fell in groups B_1, B_2, or B_3, two infants (6%) were classified as group B_4, and six infants (16%) as group C. Analyses showed that significantly fewer infants were securely attached to their mothers in the kibbutz sample than in the city sample, $\chi^2 = 7.00$, $df = 1$, $p < .01$, with B_4 considered insecure; $\chi^2 = 6.72$, $df = 1$, $p < .01$, with B_4 not included. The relative proportions of secure and insecure infants in the city sample did not differ from the typical U.S. distribution. On the other hand, the kibbutz and city samples did not differ significantly in the relative proportions of avoidant and resistant or avoidant and resistant/dependent categories with mothers, fathers, or metaplot. As in the kibbutz sample, however, the city sample differed from the U.S. distribution in the relative proportions of avoidant and resistant ($p = .02$, Fisher exact test) and of avoidant and resistant/dependent ($p = .01$, Fisher exact test) classifications. These data suggest that, while there may be some cultural difference between Israeli and American children in the frequency of certain attachment categories, the kibbutz child-rearing arrangements may have an additional independent effect.

Effects of Time of Day

An alternative possibility we needed to consider was that the unusual distribution we observed was an artifact of our assessment procedure—specifically, the fact that almost all assessments occurred in the afternoon at a time when infants were used to going home with their parents. Infants may thus have found our procedures discrepant from their everyday routine, especially when they stayed for assessments with the metaplot. To examine this, we compared the distribution across attachment categories in groups of infants assessed with their metaplot in the afternoon ($N = 66$) or morning ($N = 27$). There was no significant difference between the distributions observed in the morning and afternoon assessments, $\chi^2 = 1.67$, $df = 3$. Unfortunately, the organization of kibbutz life is such that we could not assess sufficient numbers of father-infant and mother-infant attachments in the morning to assess the effects of time of day on the security of these relationships, but there is reason to believe (as noted above) that time of assessment would affect infant-metapelet relationships most. Thus the distributions we observed seem related to implementation of the kibbutz system of child care and not to procedural artifacts.

Relationships between Attachment Classifications and Questionnaire Data

It seems that the kibbutz child-care arrangements are responsible for an increase in the number of insecure, especially insecure-resistant, classifications. Clearly, however, these effects are not inevitable, as nearly half the sample had relationships that were classified as secure (49%) and a further 12% were placed in the insecure-avoidant categories. Consequently, our next goal was to determine whether there were systematic relationships between the classifications and the events or characteristics explored using the questionnaires.

Ten items were related to the security of infant-mother attachment, six to infant-father attachments, and eight to infant-metapelet attachments. These items were related individually and in the context of composite risk scores combining the most important risk items, which were selected a priori (six for mother, five for father, and four for metaplot).[2] Only a chance number of these associations were statistically significant, however; so these will not be discussed. Some insight into the correlates of secure and insecure classifications was also sought by attempting comparable analyses using data from the small city sample. There were again no significant associations.

Another analysis revealed one important finding, however. Sixteen of the metaplot in the study were observed with more than one of the infants in their care (total of 39 infants). In seven cases, all the attachments with a given metapelet were of the same type (secure or insecure), and in an additional five cases, the majority of the three or four attachments with a given metapelet were of the same type. In only four cases did dissimilarity exceed or equal the degree of similarity. Although difficult to test statistically, this finding is important because it strongly suggests that the security of infant-

---

[2] The items for mother were (a) the age at which the infant moved to the *beit tinokot;* (b) the occurrence of regular separations (> 24 hours) from mother; (c) the occurrence of irregular separations from mother lasting 2 weeks or longer; (d) the occurrence of long irregular separations from father; (e) whether mother visited child regularly during the day; and (f) the occurrence of overnight hospitalizations. The items for father were a, d, and f above as well as (g) the occurrence of regular separations (> 24 hours) from father and (h) whether father visited the child during the day. The items for metaplot were a and f above as well as (i) whether metapelet wanted to engage in child care or was assigned to it and (j) whether the metapelet had been with the infant for more or less than 3 months prior to observation.

metapelet attachment as assessed in the Strange Situation is determined by the characteristics and quality of their prior interaction. Some metaplot apparently have characteristics that potentiate insecure attachments, whereas others have characteristics that potentiate secure attachments. These findings thus support Ainsworth's contention that adult characteristics are more influential than infant characteristics in shaping the security of attachment.

Intraindividual Consistency in Security of Attachment

Tables 2, 3, and 4 show, respectively, the relationships between mother-infant and metapelet-infant relationships, mother-infant and father-infant attachments, and metapelet-infant and father-infant relationships. For these analyses, we were able to consider only secure and insecure groups because the number was too small to permit a 16-cell chi-square analysis in which all four categories (A, B, B_4, and C) were distinguished. Note also that, because not all infants were seen with every adult, the number of subjects differs from table to table. Whether the B_4 infants were excluded or considered anxious/insecure, there was a significant similarity between the security of infant-father and infant-metapelet relationships, $\chi^2 = 10.77$, $df = 1$, $p < .005$, with B_4 not considered; $\chi^2 = 9.97$, $df = 1$, $p < .005$, with B_4 considered anxious/insecure. By contrast, there was no significant similarity between the mother-infant and father-infant or infant-mother and infant-metapelet relationships. Our findings concerning the lack of relationship between the security of infant-mother and infant-father attachments are consistent with those of other researchers (Grossmann et al., 1981; Lamb, 1978; Lamb et al., 1982; Main & Weston, 1981). Most researchers consider this as evidence that the Strange Situation taps the quality of specific relationships rather than temperament or personality traits.

Intraindividual Consistency in Termination
or Modification of the Procedures

Other data gathered in this study, however, suggest that some dimensions of emotionality, other than characteristics of the specific relationship, may be tapped by the Strange Situation. As indicated on Table 5, the need to terminate or modify any one assessment was significantly related to the need for termination or modification of other assessments.[3] Thus when the

[3] Note that the number of subjects in these tables differ from those in Table 1 because we include here cases where the relationship was not classified or the infant was deemed unattached. These were excluded from Table 1.

TABLE 2

CLASSIFICATIONS OF INFANTS OBSERVED WITH MOTHERS AND METAPLOT

	OBSERVED WITH MOTHER			
OBSERVED WITH METAPELET	Avoidant (A)	Secure (B)	Dependent (B$_4$)	Resistant (C)
Avoidant (A)	2	9	0	2
Secure (B)	4	20	3	10
Dependent (B$_4$)	1	3	0	2
Resistant (C)	0	8	4	13

TABLE 3

CLASSIFICATIONS OF INFANTS OBSERVED WITH MOTHERS AND FATHERS

	OBSERVED WITH MOTHER			
OBSERVED WITH FATHER	Avoidant (A)	Secure (B)	Dependent (B$_4$)	Resistant (C)
Avoidant (A)	1	6	1	1
Secure (B)	6	22	3	13
Dependent (B$_4$)	0	3	0	5
Resistant (C)	0	8	3	6

TABLE 4

CLASSIFICATIONS OF INFANTS OBSERVED WITH FATHERS AND METAPLOT

	OBSERVED WITH FATHER			
OBSERVED WITH METAPELET	Avoidant (A)	Secure (B)	Dependent (B$_4$)	Resistant (C)
Avoidant (A)	5	6	0	2
Secure (B)	2	27	4	3
Dependent (B$_4$)	1	2	1	2
Resistant (C)	1	9	4	10

Strange Situations with mothers were complete, the assessments with metaplot, $\chi^2 = 13.63$, $df = 1$, $p < .002$, and fathers, $\chi^2 = 7.99$, $df = 1$, $p < .01$, tended to be complete, and vice versa. Likewise, when the assessments with fathers were modified or terminated, the assessments with metaplot were likely to be terminated as well, $\chi^2 = 14.88$, $df = 1$, $p < .001$. This suggests that for either constitutional or experiential reasons some infants were unusually and consistently distressed by the procedures. Recall also that it was these infants who accounted for the unusually large proportion of resistant-insecure infants in the kibbutz sample.

TABLE 5

INTRAINDIVIDUAL CONSISTENCY IN MODIFICATION
OF PROCEDURES

A. MOTHERS/METAPLOT

OBSERVED WITH METAPELET	OBSERVED WITH MOTHER	
	Modified	Complete
Modified	16	8
Complete	14	45

B. MOTHERS/FATHERS

OBSERVED WITH FATHER	OBSERVED WITH MOTHER	
	Modified	Complete
Modified	15	11
Complete	14	41

C. FATHERS/METAPLOT

OBSERVED WITH METAPELET	OBSERVED WITH FATHER	
	Modified	Complete
Modified	15	9
Complete	11	47

Birth Order

When the classifications of relationships to all three adults were combined, significant birth order effects were evident (see Table 6). More of the firstborns than of the later borns were rated as secure whether the B_4 infants were excluded from, $\chi^2 = 3.79$, $df = 1$, $p < .10$, or included with the anxious/insecure groups, $\chi^2 = 4.98$, $df = 1$, $p < .05$. The association was not significant when the four groupings (A, B, B_4, and C) were distinguished, $\chi^2 = 5.38$, N.S. When relationships to mothers, fathers, and metaplot were considered separately, none of the chi-square tests was significant, although the same pattern was evident in each case (see Table 6).

DISCUSSION

The primary goal of this study was to investigate the antecedents of individual differences in Strange Situation behavior. This goal was ad-

TABLE 6

Adult and Birth Order	Avoidant (A)		Secure (B)		Depen- dent (B₄)		Resistant (C)	
	N	$\%$	N	$\%$	N	$\%$	N	$\%$
Mother:								
First ($N = 37$) 2		5	21	57	2	5	12	32
Later ($L = 46$)[a] 5		11	19	41	5	11	16	35
Father:								
First ($N = 36$)[a] 4		11	22	61	3	8	6	17
Later ($N = 47$)[a] 5		11	23	49	6	13	12	26
Metapelet:								
First ($N = 37$) 5		14	20	54	2	5	10	27
Later ($N = 48$)[b] 8		17	18	38	4	8	17	35

[a] Includes one unclassified infant.
[b] Includes one unattached infant.

dressed in two ways: by comparing the distribution of infants across attachment categories in the kibbutzim with that observed in samples of American and Israeli city-reared children and by relating the insecurity/security of specific attachment relationships to events or circumstances likely to affect the quality of dyadic interaction in the months preceding assessment in the Strange Situation. The results obtained appear important for at least three reasons. First, they confirm speculations that infant behavior in the Strange Situation is systematically related to aspects of the infant's history and experience. Second, they raise questions about the extent to which aspects of the infant's temperament or emotionality (whether of constitutional or experiential origin) affect the behavior of at least some infants in the Strange Situation. Third, they raise questions about the validity of the Strange Situation procedure for assessing security of attachment in at least one cultural context. Let us consider these issues in more detail.

Our results revealed an increase in the number of insecure-resistant attachments in the kibbutz sample relative to the number typically observed in the United States and an increase in the number of (avoidant and resistant) insecure attachments relative to that observed in a small sample of Israeli city children. However, the Israeli city and kibbutz samples did not differ with respect to the relative proportions of avoidant and resistant attachments. Consequently, we cannot say that the kibbutz rearing practices were associated with an increase in the number of insecure-resistant attachments; rather, some aspect of Israeli rearing practices, or a cultural difference in temperament or emotionality, appears to be responsible.

Nevertheless, one set of analyses indicated that, at least in the case of metaplot, there was an association between Strange Situation behavior and the prior interaction between the metapelet and a specific infant. In cases where the same metapelet was observed with two or more infants, all or the majority of the relationships were of the same type in 12 out of 16 cases. As infant temperament is unassociated with assignment to a specific metapelet, our findings suggest that certain metaplot have characteristics that potentiate secure or insecure attachments. Unfortunately, we were not able to determine what these characteristics were. Both in this subsample of 39 infants and in the entire sample there were no significant associations between the security of infant-mother, -father, or -metapelet attachments as assessed in the Strange Situation and a number of events or circumstances that should, on the basis of theory and prior research (Ainsworth et al., 1978; Bowlby, 1973; Thompson et al., 1982; Vaughn et al., 1979), be associated with individual differences in Strange Situation behavior. This does not necessarily mean that infant experiences had no effect on the security of attachment. There was substantial homogeneity with respect to the variables we examined, whereas there was unexplored variability in dimensions that we were not able to explore. For example, we do not have data on the promptness with which adults responded to infant distress at night, the parents' attitudes to the kibbutz child-rearing arrangements, the extent to which parents used visits during the day to interact with their infants rather than the metaplot, or the timing (relative to the time of the Strange Situation assessments) of the parent-child separations. All these are factors that seem likely to influence the development of C-type relationships in the view of Ainsworth and her colleagues (1978).

Whereas these data suggested that the Strange Situation assessments tapped characteristics of specific relationships rather than characteristics of specific infants, other findings suggested that the latter may be important as well. One third of the Strange Situation procedures had to be modified or terminated prematurely because the infants were intensely and inconsolably distressed. There was significant intraindividual consistency in the need for termination or modification of procedures, suggesting that some infants were consistently too distressed to complete the procedure. We cannot, of course, say whether these consistent individual differences were of experiential or constitutional origin, but we can that, for, say, these infants, behavior in the Strange Situation reflected—at least in part—a characteristic of the infant rather than of a specific infant-adult relationship. Similar characteristics may also be important—if only for some infants—in samples drawn from countries other than Israel.

Most of the infants whose assessments were terminated or modified were later rated resistantly attached (C_2 subgroup). In fact, it was this group of infants who accounted for the unusually large number of resistant infants in the kibbutz sample. In the absence of additional information about the validity of Strange Situation assessments in this cultural context, we cannot say whether these infants were clearly insecure or whether the procedures

were inappropriate. Evidently, the validity of the Strange Situation procedure as an instrument for assessing individual differences hinges on its
success in subjecting all infants to a qualitatively similar experience (Ainsworth et al., 1978; Lamb et al., 1984). Thus we have to entertain the possibility that the procedures created for this subgroup of infants a psychological
state of distress so intense that its effects were qualitatively different than
that typically observed. One may need to entertain similar questions concerning the validity of Grossmann et al.'s (1981) assessments in Germany.
We cannot assume that Strange Situation assessments in specific cultures are
valid indices of security of attachment unless there are data showing clear
and theoretically predictable relationships among Strange Situation behavior, prior characteristics of the infant-adult relationship, and/or subsequent
characteristics of the child's socioemotional performance. Compelling data
are not yet available for either Israel or West Germany.

In our kibbutz sample, the subgroup of infants whose sessions were
terminated were often rendered distraught by the entrance of the stranger
in episode 3. Thus the common characteristic appeared to be an unusual
degree of stranger anxiety. Once they were distressed, however, neither the
stranger's departure nor the attachment figure's ministrations were successful in calming the infants. Although sociability assessments before the
Strange Situation do not appear to have affected Strange Situation behavior
in the United States (Thompson et al., 1982) or Sweden (Lamb et al., 1982),
they may have helped escalate the degree of distress experienced by the
infants in this subgroup of kibbutz-reared infants.

Less important, although still interesting, were the birth-order effects
we observed. These findings are of interest in light of Fox's (1977) report
that firstborn kibbutz-reared infants were more distressed by separation and
reunion from mothers and metaplot and by the entrance of a stranger than
later born infants were. He speculated that the separations were more stressful to firstborns because they were less used to separations and being with
strangers in the evening hours than were secondborns, who had to share
their parents' attention with a sibling. Our results were not consistent with
Fox's findings. Instead, we found more secondborns falling in the C and B_4
categories, which comprise infants noted for high degrees of distress. There
is no obvious reason for the discrepancy between Fox's findings and our
own. Given the apparent inconsistency of the birth-order effects, speculations about their meaning appear premature.

In sum, our results raise interesting and important questions about the
validity of the Strange Situation procedure as a means of assessing the
security of infant-adult attachment. On the one hand, our findings concerning the striking intrametapelet consistency in the security/insecurity of their
charges confirms hypotheses linking Strange Situation behavior to aspects of
the infants' prior experience with the attachment figure. On the other hand,

we were unable to determine what events were associated with the security/ insecurity of relationships to mothers, fathers, or metaplot. Furthermore, our findings indicated that individual differences in temperament or emotionality (whether of constitutional or experiential origin) affect the behavior of at least some infants in the Strange Situation. Even if this occurs only in certain cultural contexts, the finding raises questions about the validity of the Strange Situation procedure for assessing security of attachment. If temperament affects Strange Situation behavior in cultures other than Israel, we would have to conclude that Strange Situation behavior is affected by factors other than the security of attachment. Like Grossmann et al. (in this vol.), therefore, we are uncertain about the appropriateness of assuming that Strange Situation behavior in different cultural contexts can be interpreted in the same way as Strange Situation behavior in the United States. Clearly, these are important issues for future research to address.

XII. INFANT TEMPERAMENT, MOTHER'S MODE OF INTERACTION, AND ATTACHMENT IN JAPAN: AN INTERIM REPORT

KAZUO MIYAKE AND SHING-JEN CHEN

Hokkaido University

JOSEPH J. CAMPOS

University of Denver

INTRODUCTION

The objective of our research is to investigate the possible relationships among several variables: the infant's temperamental disposition, the mother's mode of interaction, and the quality of the subsequent mother-infant attachment. Our ultimate objective is to understand how processes in early infancy lay the basis for important individual differences in both personality and cognitive style in later childhood (Azuma, Kashiwagi, & Hess, 1981; Miyake, Tajima, & Usui, 1980).

Specifically, our research concerns the relationship between the infant's temperamental characteristics and the attachment to his or her mother; the

This research was supported by grants 803173 and 813083 from the Toyota Foundation and a grant from the Japan Society for the Promotion of Science facilitating cross-national exchange between Japan and the United States. Further support was provided by the Ministry of Education, Science and Culture of the Government of Japan and by the John D. and Catherine T. MacArthur Research Network for the Study of the Transition from Infancy to Early Childhood. The authors would like to thank Jerome Kagan for his invaluable suggestions, Keiko Takahashi and Donna L. Bradshaw for their assistance and comments in various phases of this project and Drs. Seiichiro Fujimoto and Katsuya Uzuki for permitting access to their patients. We also thank Drs. Hiroshi Azuma, Keiko Kashiwagi, and Giyoo Hatano for their conceptual discussions and Nobumoto Tajima, Kimiharu Satoh, Akashi Ishikawa, Hiroshi Usui, Tatsuo Ujiie, Shigeru Nakano, Yuko Kanaya, Etsuko Minamide, Masako Maruyama, Aoi Noda, and Mayumi Aida for data collection and analysis.

relationship between mother-infant interaction and the infant's subsequent attachment to the mother; and the relationship between the infant's temperament and mother-infant interaction observed both in the home and in free-play laboratory assessments. In this report, we will discuss the first two objectives, and we will reserve for future publication the findings relevant to the third objective.

Temperament and the Assessment of Attachment Relationships

Special affective and behavioral dispositions that are called "the attachment relationship" are believed to be created by specific experiences taking place during interaction with the mother during the first year of life (Ainsworth et al., 1978; Bowlby, 1969/1982b, 1973, 1980). Ainsworth and her colleagues have consistently emphasized the role of the mother's sensitivity in shaping the quality of the infant's attachment, as assessed by the Strange Situation technique. However, we think it is more appropriate to consider maternal variables in relation to infant variables. In this study, we chose to investigate some aspects of the infant's behavioral characteristics that are related to temperament. By temperament we mean biologically based dispositions that are stable over reasonably long periods of time and that have the capacity to influence interactions with the caretaker and others in the environment (Goldsmith & Campos, 1982). Specific instances of temperament-related behaviors include dispositions to cry, smile, become irritable, or be motorically active or inactive.

Temperament may be related to the measurement of attachment in a number of ways. Kagan (1982), for instance, believes that temperamental differences in the proneness to distress in uncertain situations confound the assessment of attachment in paradigms like the Strange Situation. Rather than reflecting "quality of attachment," as Ainsworth et al. (1978) proposed, infants categorized as A, B, or C in the Strange Situation may, according to Kagan, simply differ in proneness to distress. An A baby may be a temperamentally calm infant who is less prone to becoming wary in the Strange Situation by separation from the mother and therefore show no special reaction to her on her return. Although A babies in the familiar home environment may become upset at separation (Ainsworth et al., 1978), they do so for reasons other than wariness in response to uncertainty. A C baby, on the other hand, may be highly susceptible to distress in response to uncertainty and may thus appear inconsolable, tense, angry, and ambivalent on reunion following a brief separation from the mother. The modal temperamental reaction to stress is that shown by the B babies. In Kagan's view, the temperamental contribution to individual differences in Strange Situation performance must be partialed out before one can infer the role of mother-infant interaction in Strange Situation performance, but no one has yet adequately done such partialing.

In addition to confounding the assessment of attachment, temperament may also influence directly or indirectly the mother-infant interaction, which in turn determines the quality of a baby's attachment relation with the caretaker. This view is similar to that of Thomas and Chess (1977), who proposed the notion of the "goodness of fit" between maternal characteristics and infant propensities in the determination of subsequent healthy cognitive and personality development. Waters and Deane (1982) also discussed this position as one among several possible mechanisms determining the quality of an infant's attachment to the mother.

Not many studies on attachment have considered the infant's temperamental dispositions and assessed how those dispositions are related to both the mother's mode of interaction and the quality of attachment an infant develops. An up-to-date review of the few studies on this issue has been recently published (Campos, Barrett, Lamb, Goldsmith, & Stenberg, 1983), and the reader is referred there for greater detail. One noteworthy study on this issue is that of Waters et al. (1980). They recently showed that infant characteristics assessed by the Brazelton Neonatal Behavioral Assessment Scale (NBAS) during the first week after birth were related to individual differences in attachment as assessed by the Strange Situation at 12 months, although NBAS assessments taken a few days later did not significantly predict patterns of attachment. Crockenberg (1981) also reported reliable relationships between irritability in the neonatal period and later Strange Situation assessments, although only in dyads in which mothers received low social support. A constitutional or biological correlate, and possible determinant, of individual differences in attachment behaviors of 1-year-olds was recently reported by Tennes (1982). In her study, cortisol levels assessed during a nonstressful day when infants were at home with their mothers predicted the degree of separation distress on a subsequent experimental day when the mother left the home. She reported that the highest postseparation levels of cortisol were excreted by infants who greeted the mother happily, moderate levels by infants who greeted her ambivalently, and lowest levels by infants who ignored her.

Potential Importance of Studying Temperament-Attachment Relations in Japan

Studies of Japanese infants should elucidate the role of infant temperament on social development because there is evidence that children of Oriental descent, especially when tested in their own cultures, may be temperamentally quite different from Caucasian infants (Hsu, Soong, Stigler,

Hong, & Liang, 1981). Although Freedman (1974) has reported that Chinese neonates are more placid than Caucasian neonates, more extensive research has shown that Oriental infants are more temperamentally inhibited and less reactive in unfamiliar situations and to unfamiliar incentives than Caucasian infants (Kagan et al., 1978). Japanese infants have also been reported to be significantly more negative in mood and less adaptive and rhythmic than American infants on the Carey-McDevitt scale (Ohyama, Murai, & Nihei, 1982). Japanese neonates also differ from American newborns on a number of Brazelton NBAS items (Kosawa, 1980). We caution that these temperamental differences need not imply racial differences: by 3 months of age, fourth-generation Japanese-American infants show significantly less distress vocalizations than either American infants or Japanese infants in Japan (who, in agreement with the other studies cited above, showed the greatest amount of distress vocalizations [Caudill & Frost, 1972]). By studying infants whose initial temperamental characteristics are quite different from those of Caucasians and by relating these initial characteristics both to the pattern of mother-infant interaction in the home and lab and to Strange Situation assessment, we hope to identify the precise role that temperament plays in both the development of attachment and its assessment in later infancy.

Mother-Infant Interaction and Attachment Relationships:
A Japanese Perspective

As to the second issue we have been investigating, we assume that the manner and quality of affective exchange in the mother-infant interaction are major determinants of the infant's subsequent attachment. Investigations of non-Western societies where maternal behaviors differ considerably from those in the United States can clarify this issue. Available data imply that Japanese mothers encourage considerable emotional dependence in their children, in contrast to the emphasis on independence normally found in America (Azuma et al., 1981). The Japanese psychoanalyst Doi (1973) has described a two-stage process of social development in Japanese infants Prior to 7 months of age, infants experience what Doi has called a sense of "perfect oneness" with their social environment, an experience similar to what in other cultures is called "symbiosis" (Mahler et al., 1975). Doi goes on to argue that the Japanese mother encourages in the infant the development of a unique characteristic he calls *amae*, by which he refers to the tendency of a person self-indulgently to expect and even to take advantage of the help and support of individuals and groups close to him or her. *Amae* does not begin until the age of 7–8 months, when the infant starts to become aware that his or her mother exists as an entity separate from himself or herself.

Not only does the Japanese infant long for a return to the state of "perfect oneness" with the mother, but he or she also longs to preserve the state of *amae*. Thus Doi's speculations suggest to us that for two reasons—one of which is unique to the Japanese culture—the Japanese child is strongly motivated to prevent any separation from the mother.

Observational studies comparing American and Japanese mother-infant interaction suggest major differences between the interactional styles of the two different cultures. Caudill and Weinstein (1969) presented data suggesting that, despite some similarities in basic care of their infants, Japanese mothers differed from American mothers in employing a more proximal mode of interaction (emphasizing physical contact, for instance). American mothers, on the other hand, seemed to employ a more distal mode of interaction (one emphasizing verbal communication to the baby). Caudill and Weinstein inferred that the Japanese mothers seemed intent on producing a quiet, contented baby who has a close and intense relationship with the mother, while the American mothers wanted an active, vocal baby who is more independent.

Two other studies are in close agreement with Caudill and Weinstein's analysis about the Japanese mother's emphasis on proximal contact. Vogel (1963) reported that Japanese children and their mothers are rarely apart, and the American custom of baby-sitting is practically nonexistent. This is true even in contemporary nuclear Japanese families. Lebra (1976) similarly reported that mother-child relationships in Japan are characterized by a good deal of close physical contact (e.g., breast-feeding, co-bathing, sleeping together, communicating tactually, transporting the child on the mother's back, toilet training the child by physically holding him or her above the toilet, etc.).

It is possible that an interactive relationship characterized primarily by close physical contact and infrequent separation may lead to the establishment of an attachment that is qualitatively different from one that involves less physical contact and a great deal of distal interaction. From the research cited above, it seems reasonable to expect Japanese infants to show a different pattern of attachment behaviors by 12 months of age than that shown by infants in other cultures.

The Measurement of Attachment in Cross-national Research

The precise way of measuring individual differences in attachment has always been controversial (Cohen, 1974; Lamb et al., 1984), and no consensus exists about which is the best outcome measure in studies of the development of attachment. However, of all the methods extant, the Ainsworth Strange Situation (Ainsworth et al., 1978) is at present not only the most thoroughly studied but also the one with the best construct validation. As

Ainsworth et al. (1978) note, individual differences in the Strange Situation have been reported to reflect differences in the mother-infant interaction assessed in the home in the first year of life and also to predict individual differences in the infant's problem-solving competence and social functioning in later childhood (Lamb et al., 1984; Sroufe, 1983). Moreover, individual differences in the Strange Situation have been reported to be stable over a period of several months (e.g., Waters, 1978). For these and other reasons to be discussed shortly, we chose the Ainsworth Strange Situation as our principal index of attachment.

There are at least two ways of using the Strange Situation in a study of attachment that is carried out with a cultural group other than the one in which it was developed. One way is to apply literally the scoring rules and procedures developed in the United States to the performance of infants in the other culture. The second approach uses the Strange Situation as a rich source of individual differences in emotional and attachment-related behavior but does not assume that morphologically-similar behavior patterns in the two cultures imply similar quality of attachment. Rather one searches for patterns of behavior more appropriate for the ultimate goal of predicting the infant's social, emotional, and cognitive adaptation in the other culture. For the purposes of this report, we are treating the Strange Situation in the first way, but on acquiring a sufficient body of longitudinal data, we will shift to treating the attachment assessment in the second way.

The literal application of Strange Situation scoring rules can sometimes be valid, but the investigator must be very careful not to confuse the contextual determinants of Strange Situation performance with "quality of attachment." Ainsworth and her colleagues (1978) themselves highlighted the contextual influence on Strange Situation performance when they noted that retest of babies on the paradigm a mere 2 weeks later resulted in the infants showing considerable distress and quite a different pattern of attachment behaviors, with no babies being classified as A on retest and more being classified as C.

There are a number of contextual factors in Strange Situation assessment that make it likely that the pattern of behaviors Japanese infants show in the Strange Situation will differ, sometimes markedly so, from that reported for middle-class American infants. First of all, the degree of "strangeness" of the Strange Situation will be a function of the frequency with which an infant is placed in novel situations. Second, the degree of stress produced by an unfamiliar adult will depend to a large extent on the experience the child has had interacting with other adults in the home and elsewhere. Third, the degree of disturbance experienced by a child on being left alone will in all likelihood reflect both the child's prior experiences with maternal separation and the mother's own unease at being temporarily separated from her child. Takahashi and Miyake (1984) have discussed these notions more extensively and describe why the Japanese infant is likely to be very different from American infants on these three factors.

The combined influence in Japanese infants of greater temperamental proneness to inhibition and crying, more proximal interaction, infrequent separation from the mother, and less experience with situations approximating the Strange Situation paradigm lead us to predict that the distribution of A, B, and C infants will differ radically between Japan and other countries. In this report, we present data relevant to this prediction. Specifically, we predict that Japanese infants will be overrepresented in the Ainsworth C classification and underrepresented in the Ainsworth A classification, a prediction that is based on the assumption that the greater the infant's proneness to distress (for constitutional, experiential, or contextual reasons) the greater the likelihood that an infant will be classified as C and the less the likelihood that the infant will be classified as A. We make this prediction not because Japanese infants are more prone to insecure attachment but because the testing context of the Strange Situation differs markedly among cultures.

The present report, then, deals with a preliminary analysis of data from a longitudinal study that extends from the prenatal period to preschool. We will present some of the data that we have gathered in the first year of life in a cohort of 29 middle-class Japanese infants in Sapporo. We will address three issues: how our sample of Japanese infants compares with infants in other countries on Ainsworth Strange Situation classifications; how early temperamental differences relate to Strange Situation attachment assessments; and how some maternal behaviors similarly are related to subsequent attachment.

METHOD

Subjects

Data were obtained from 31 mother-infant pairs selected for longitudinal study from a larger group of 36 pairs nominated to participate in our study by obstetricians. Three mothers refused to participate when contacted because they planned to return to work and could not make a long-term commitment to participate in the study. Two additional infants died in the first week of life. All families contacted were predominantly middle class, and each parent had at least a high school education. The fathers were engaged in white-collar or professional occupations, and the mothers at the time of recruitment planned not to be employed full-time. Infants were firstborn, and all but three were full-term (the others being 35–37 weeks conceptional age but normal in weight for gestational age) with no serious pre- or perinatal complications. Mothers were between 24 and 35 years old.

Data from only 20 pairs (with seven male infants and 13 female) were obtained during all assessments planned for the first year of life. Attrition was produced by the family moving from the city ($N = 1$), maternal resumption of employment ($N = 3$), and unwillingness to participate further ($N = 7$).

To increase the sample size for the Strange Situation analyses as well as for follow-ups planned for the second and subsequent years of life, we recruited an additional nine mother-infant pairs at 11 months from the same population of infants tested from birth.

Procedures

Assessments were taken at the Hokkaido University Hospital during the 32- and 38-week prenatal clinics as well as during the newborn period and at 7.5 months. They were taken in the home at 1 and 3 months and at the Research and Clinical Center for Child Development of Hokkaido University at 7½, 11, and 12 months.

The prenatal assessment taken at 32 weeks involved an interview and two questionnaires dealing with maternal anxiety in general and anxiety about pregnancy in particular, whereas those taken at 38 weeks involved an assessment of preparation for delivery, feeding plans, and child-care objectives. However, these and other maternal interview measures will not be discussed further in this report.

Newborn Assessments

The reaction of infants to the interruption of sucking produced by the removal of a nipple (Bell, Weller, & Waldrop's, 1971, RIS task) was selected to assess neonatal temperament. This task was chosen because it permits estimation of threshold to distress, a parameter linked closely to infant temperament (Goldsmith & Campos, 1982). Moreover, previous research with this task has shown promising continuity of individual differences between the neonatal period and early childhood (Bell et al., 1971; Yang & Halverson, 1976). RIS was administered twice, on the second and fifth or sixth day after birth. Five trials were administered on both test days in the morning while the infant was not crying or asleep, after an average of 40 minutes after the last feeding, and after the daily bath. The trials consisted of 20 seconds during which the infant was allowed to suck on a rubber nipple, after which the nipple was gently removed. Infant reactions were videotaped.

Two interviews of the mother were conducted during the 1-week lying-in period customary in Japan. One addressed maternal impressions about her baby, and the other addressed her impressions about the baby's feeding behavior.

Assessments at 1 and 3 Months in the Home

Two research assistants visited the subjects' home for 2 hours starting about 1:00 P.M. One assistant interviewed the mother, while the second assistant observed the behavior of the infant and recorded the presence of preselected behaviors every 30 seconds, using a checklist. The categories employed included activity, inactivity, sleep and wakefulness, crying, fussing, noncrying vocalizations, smiling, and mouthing. At 3 months, an additional category, thumb sucking, was included.

Assessments at 7.5 Months

Infants were tested for stranger and separation distress in a sparsely furnished room (4 m. by 3 m.) while the infant and mother awaited a routine well-baby examination. No one else was present in the room, and the mother had previously been instructed about the procedure to be used with the infant. Electrocardiograph telemetry leads were attached to the infant's chest just prior to testing. The procedure consisted of a series of six episodes: (a) baseline (3 min. with mother and infant alone); (b) stranger entry (2-min. period during which a male adult stranger approached to within .8 m. of the infant, talked to both the infant and the mother, then shook the infant's hand); (c) mother departure (2-min. period during which the infant remained alone in the room with the stranger); (d) stranger departure (2-min. period during which the infant and mother remained alone in the room); (e) stranger reentry (2-min. period during which the stranger behaved as in episode b but with no infant pickup); and (f) mother reentry.

The infant's reactions were recorded from a television camera located in an unobtrusive position in the testing room and a videorecorder located in an adjacent room. The heart-rate readout, representing the average of each three beats, was recorded onto the sound track of the videorecorder by a microphone mixer.

On the same day, two other procedures were administered: a mother-infant interaction session and testing of the infant's reactions to auditory and visual stimuli. These were conducted in a different location and were completed 30 minutes before the stranger and separation reactions were elicited. The mother-infant interaction was videotaped in an unstructured free-play situation lasting for 10 minutes. The data obtained during the auditory and visual stimulation assessments will not be discussed further here.

Eleven-Month Assessments

Free play and cognitive measurements were taken in the same playroom that had been used for the observation of mother-infant interaction at 7.5 months. The infant's play behavior was observed for 10 minutes in a room with many toys while the mother sat in one corner of the room conversing with a female experimenter. The mother was instructed not to interact with her baby unless necessary during the 10-minute session. Infant behaviors were videotaped. Cognitive assessments consisted of the Uzgiris-Hunt Object Permanence Scale (Uzgiris & Hunt, 1975).

Twelve-Month Assessments

At 12 months, the Ainsworth Strange Situation assessment was conducted following the procedures described in Ainsworth et al. (1978). Two female students alternated in the role of stranger. Episodes 4, 6, and 7 of the Strange Situation were curtailed if distress lasted a maximum of 2 minutes. (It was necessary to shorten the separation time for one child in episode 4, for 21 children in episode 6, and for 15 children in episode 7.) In addition, episode 6, the infant-alone situation, was skipped for one mother-infant pair whose mother was reluctant to leave the room after episode 5.

Prior to the Strange Situation procedure, the mother was given detailed written instructions about it. The Strange Situation assessment was recorded by using three cameras, and a narrative account was taped by one observer.

Coding of the Strange Situation classifications was done by three separate raters.[1] There was only one disagreement in classifying infants, which was resolved by independent review of the tape by a fourth scorer.

[1] All Strange Situation variables were scored by Keiko Takahashi of Soka University in Tokyo, who consulted with L. A. Sroufe and Mary Main on Strange Situation assessment, and by Yuko Kanaya and Tatsuo Ujiie of Hokkaido University, who were trained by Donna Bradshaw. Bradshaw was trained in the system used at the University of Virginia and the University of Utah. Additional details concerning Strange Situation scoring, including further analysis of discrete response variables, will be provided in Takahashi (in preparation) as well as in future reports by the current authors.

RESULTS

We will present our findings in the following way. First, we will describe the results of Strange Situation classifications performed at 12 months of age on our sample of Sapporo infants. Then we will discuss several anteced-ents of this classification: neonatal and early infant temperament assess-ments, differential behavioral responsiveness evident at 7.5 months of age to strangers on maternal separation, and, finally, mother-infant interactional differences observed at 1, 3, and 7.5 months of age.

Attachment Behaviors in the Strange Situation at 12 Months

On the basis of three factors—the role of temperament in Strange Situation classification, the likelihood of greater irritability in Japanese in-fants, and the infrequency of separation in Japanese mother-infant dyads— we predicted that more Japanese infants would be classified as C and fewer infants as A than in normative American samples. This prediction was strongly supported. No infants, out of 29 tested, were classified as A babies. Seven infants were unambiguously classified as C babies by all the judges. In addition, four infants were classified as "pseudo-C" infants (a designation conceived by Miyake et al., 1983). These babies showed the typical pattern of C babies (such as extreme crying, difficulty in soothing, and moderate levels of resistance on reunion) during the second separation and reunion but before then were B-like, especially in not showing much resistance in the first reunion. The combined C plus pseudo-C classification thus totaled 38% of our sample, and prototypical C infants constituted 28% of the 25 infants who were unambiguously classified. There were no apparent sex differences in Strange Situation classification. The proportion of infants in the supple-mental sample recruited at 11 months ($N = 9$) was 67% B and 33% un-equivocal C.

These findings corroborate the reports of other investigations of non-American groups, which reveal dramatically different distributions of A, B, and C babies as a function of country of rearing. Table 1 presents such data from studies by Grossmann et al. (1981; see also Grossmann et al., in this vol.) using West German infants, by Sagi et al. (in this vol.) using kibbutz babies in Israel, by Lamb et al. (1982) in Sweden, and by various inves-tigators in the United States as compiled in Campos et al. (1983). As can be seen, Grossmann et al. report many more A babies in Germany, Lamb et al. report fewer C infants in Sweden, and Sagi et al., in agreement with our findings, report many more C infants in Israel than are typically found in American middle-class samples.

Analyses of discrete response variables (including crying, touching the mother, looking to mother, and smiling) confirmed the assignment of sub-

TABLE 1

PERCENTAGE OF B, C, AND A CLASSIFICATIONS IN DIFFERENT COUNTRIES

Type	B	C	A	
Sapporo	72.0	28.0	.0	$N = 25$, clearly classified
United States ...	62.0	15.0	23.0	Compilation in Campos et al. (1983)
Germany	32.7	12.2	49.0	$N = 49$, by Grossmann et al. (1981)
Sweden	74.5	3.9	21.6	$N = 51$, by Lamb et al. (1982)
Israel	37.5	50.0	12.5	$N = 56$, by Sagi et al. (in this vol.)

jects by global judgment into B versus C categories. These discrete response variables (interscorer reliabilities of which averaged 96% for perfect agreement between two scorers, range 85%–100%) provided a picture of greater hedonic negativity in the combined group of C plus pseudo-C babies in the Strange Situation. In light of the great emphasis frequently given to reunion episodes in the Strange Situation, it is interesting to note that differences between B and non-B babies were evident in all variables even before maternal separation and reunion, that is, in episodes 2 and 3. The discrete response variables scored to date are presented in Figure 1.

Because of the close link noted in some previous studies between proneness to cry and C classification (e.g., Ainsworth et al., 1978; Campos et al., 1983), we were especially interested in whether B and C infants differed in crying during the Strange Situation episodes. In Figure 1 we present the number of 10-second epochs in which crying was observed in each episode of the Strange Situation. As can be seen, the incidence of crying in our combined C plus pseudo-C grouping was higher in every episode, and the differences reached significance by t test with 27 df in episodes 4, 7, and 8 ($t = 2.12, 2.16$, and 8.86, respectively) and approached significance ($p < .10$) in episodes 2, 3, and 5 ($t = 2.04, 1.78$, and 1.92, respectively).

Crying, however, was not the only discrete response variable differentiating the two Strange Situation groups: the incidence of touching the mother, quantified as the number of 10-second epochs in which touching was observed, was also higher for the C-type infants in every one of the Strange Situation episodes in which the behavior could be manifested and reached significance in episodes 3, 5, and 8 ($t = 3.37, 2.24$, and 2.95, respectively).

By contrast, the number of babies who smiled at the mother during each episode of the attachment test was greater for the B than for the C-type babies in every episode in which the mother was present, a tendency that approached significance in episode 3 (Fisher Exact Probability Test, $p = .13$ [Siegel, 1956]) and was marginally significant in episode 8 (Fisher test, $p = .07$).

The C-type infants also showed significantly greater looking to the

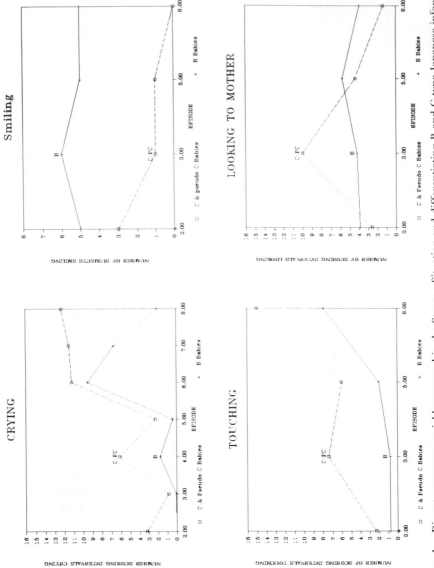

Fig. 1.—Discrete response variables assessed in the Strange Situation and differentiating B and C-type Japanese infants

mother in episode 3, when the stranger entered (t = 4.95, df = 27, $p <$ .001), but showed significantly less looking to the mother in episode 8 (t = 2.71, df = 27, $p < .05$), perhaps as a function of being held longer by the mother in that episode.

The Relationship between Neonatal Temperament Assessments and Strange Situation Classification

Although temperament involves much more than irritability, which we define here as proneness to cry, the major temperament variables we have analyzed thus far relate to individual differences in crying. We have focused on irritability since there is ample evidence that crying is stable over a period of time (Crockenberg, 1981; Korner, Hutchinson, Kopcrski, Kraemer, & Schneider, 1981), that it influences the mother-infant interaction in powerful ways (Thomas & Chess, 1977), and that, as we have seen, it may be a discrete variable related to subsequent Strange Situation classification (Ainsworth et al., 1978, Table 9).

The major assessment of neonatal temperament relevant to the goals of this report concerns individual differences in infants' reactions to interruption of sucking (Bell et al , 1971). The fundamental data used in this analysis included (a) the latency in seconds to the first observable response of any sort (e.g., grimace, vocalization, or head movement), (b) latency to full cry, defined as a rhythmic cry that lasted over a minimum of 5 seconds, and (c) the difference in seconds between the first observable response and full cry, which we term here "crying rise time." We also tabulated the number of subjects who cried at all or who did not cry on any of the 10 trials administered over the two neonatal tests.

Because of difficulties in videorecording, data from three subjects were lost in the neonatal period, and data from an additional seven subjects were lost through attrition over the first year of life. Accordingly, the data presented have come from a sample of 19 infants, 11 B and eight C plus pseudo-C. They show a significant difference between future-B- and -C-type infants in crying parameters taken during the neonatal period. Despite the small sample sizes, t tests comparing the 11 future-B babies with the eight future-C babies proved significant for the log-transformed rise time index (M = 9.97 vs. M = 16.07, t = 2.12, $p < .05$), and one was also marginally significant for the latency to full cry (M = 17.27 vs. M = 19.78, t = 1.54, $p < .10$, one-tailed). Furthermore, there was a statistically significant trend toward more babies who cried on the RIS task as neonates to be classified as C-type (seven of eight) rather than B-type (six of 11) infants when tested on the Strange Situation 12 months later (Fisher test, $p < .05$). By way of contrast, no meaningful difference was obtained on a noncry index, the latency to any observable response.

The Consistency of Infant Irritability

At 1 and 3 months of age, the home observation coding sheets were scored for several behaviors related to irritability, including fussing (negative vocalizations that are not crying), crying, and, at 3 months, thumb sucking (which was presumed to index self-soothing). Some of these behaviors were roughly analogous to those assessed in the RIS task administered in the neonatal period, and all were scored well before the infants were tested in the Strange Situation.

Although necessarily computed on small numbers, these data reveal substantial stability of infant irritability between the newborn period and the 3-month assessment: 10 infants were classified as irritable both as newborns and at 3 months (meaning that they met the criterion of "full cry," defined above, on four of the five RIS trials on either neonatal session and a criterion of any crying or fussing at 1 month or any crying/fussing and the emergent index of self-soothing, thumb sucking, at 3 months). Three of these consistently irritable infants were future-B babies (i.e., 27% of the future-B group), and seven were future-C infants (i.e., 87% of the future-C group). The difference between future-B and future-C infants in the proportion of consistency of irritability from the newborn period to 3 months of age reached significance by Fisher's test ($p < .05$).

There was also a trend for consistency of irritability to be more frequent in the future-C than the future-B infants between the newborn period and 1 month as well as between 1 and 3 months. However, possibly because of the small sample sizes, the differences in consistency between the two groups of infants did not reach statistical significance at these ages.

Although consistency of irritability was proportionally greater in future-C-like infants than in future-B infants, an appropriate tentative conclusion is that, while Strange Situation C-type infants may be prone to irritability in early infancy, not all infants who are prone to irritability in that age period necessarily become C babies.

Mother-Infant Interaction Variables at 1- and
3-Month Home Observations

A long-term goal of this research project is to describe the modal pattern of mother-infant interaction in Japanese mothers, to relate individual differences in mother-infant interaction to subsequent patterns of attachment, and to confirm the ways in which the Japanese mother's style of interaction with the baby differs from that used typically by mothers in Western cultures. As a first step in analyzing maternal variables believed related to differential attachment patterns, we focused at the 1- and 3-month home observations on the mother's behavior when the infant was in a quiet state and when the infant was fussy or irritated. The frequencies of the following maternal behaviors were scored from the behavior checklists: looks at infant, holds infant, rocks infant, affectionate contact, stimulates infant, and talks to infant.

At both 1 and 3 months of age, only one of the maternal response categories differentiated future-B and future-C infants. At 1 month, mothers of the future-B infants held their babies during twice as many scoring epochs as did the other mothers ($M = 75.72$ and 37.86, $t = 2.60$, $df = 12$, $p < .05$); and at 3 months of age, mothers of future-C infants responded to their infants' irritability by talking in a greater number of epochs ($M = 70.50$ and 47.42, $t = 1.86$, $df = 15$, $p < .10$).

Because further analyses are in progress, using more detailed and quantitative analyses and scoring schemes that better reflect the affective quality as well as the contingency of the mother's interaction with her baby, we caution that these data should be treated as preliminary only.

Antecedents of Strange Situation Classification at 7.5 months

The pattern of greater proneness to distress observed in future-C infants in the neonatal and first quarter-year observations was again evident in the assessment of infants' reactions to strangers and to maternal separation at 7.5 months of age.

Mean heart rate (HR) data for eight future-C and 12 future-B infants were computed during four episodes: the 20-second baseline that preceded the entry of a stranger, the first 20 seconds of stranger entry, the first 20 seconds after the mother exited the room, and the last 20 seconds prior to mother's reentry. Although these HR data did not reach statistical significance, there was a trend toward a more acceleratory baseline HR in future-C infants (HR = 150.25 bpm) than in future-B infants (HR = 146.45 bpm). There was also a nonsignificant tendency toward a more acceleratory HR level in the last 20 seconds of the mother exit procedure in the future-C infants (HR = 175.4 bpm) than in future-B infants (HR = 165.0 bpm).

Although there were no overt behavioral differences observed prior to stranger entry in the two groups, there were differences observed during the stranger entry episode. Four behavioral categories were scored: avoidance (defined as pulling away when the stranger extends his hands or approaches the baby), approach (defined as the infant extending his or her hands toward the stranger without being invited), and negative vocalization (any fret, fuss, or cry). A global judgment of fearfulness was also derived, computed as the presence of avoidance and negative vocalization, together with a decrease in play behavior relative to the baseline prior to the stranger

TABLE 2

INFANT BEHAVIOR AT 7.5 MONTHS BY ATTACHMENT CLASSIFICATION

Future Classification in Strange Situation	Avoid	Approach	Negative Vocal	Fearful
		Stranger Entry		
B	1/7	2/7	3/7	2/7
C type	4/8	2/8	3/8	7/8
		Mother Exit		
B	2/7	3/7	4/7	3/7
C type	5/8	2/8	4/8	7/8

approach. These data are presented in Table 2, for both the stranger-entry and the mother-exit periods.

Seven out of eight future-C infants were judged to be "fearful" in both the stranger-entry and the mother-exit episodes, whereas only two of seven future-B infants were similarly judged in the former episode and three of seven in the latter. The difference in incidence of "fearful" classification was significantly different ($p < .01$) by Fisher's Exact Probability Test for the stranger entry episode and nearly significant in the mother-exit episode. Six out of the seven fearful infants were the same as the seven who in the neonatal and 3-month assessment proved irritable. Moreover, on both the stranger-entry and the mother-exit episodes, future C-type infants showed significantly more avoidance (Fisher, $p < .05$). The differences between the two groups in the other two scoring categories were not significant.

Thus, by 7.5 months of age, future-C infants tended to be more wary, as evident in resting heart-rate levels, in cardiac responsiveness to maternal absence, and in behavioral reactivity to stranger entry and maternal departure.

Mother-infant interaction was also assessed at 7.5 months of age and was scored from videotapes for four dimensions of maternal responsiveness. The categories were as follows: stimulation (defined as any action on the part of the mother directed toward her baby), effectiveness of stimulation (defined as any maternal action that successfully elicits a response on the part of the baby), responsiveness (meaning any reaction on the part of the mother that both is in response to the baby's behavior and elicits a response of any sort from the baby), and intrusiveness (which was any maternal behavior that both interrupted the baby's ongoing activity without a bid by the baby and resulted in a change in the baby's behavior, such as crying, shift to playing with a new toy, etc.). The frequencies of each of these four categories were measured during the 10-minute interaction.

The results of the mother-infant interaction analysis clearly demonstrated that, like infant temperament, some mother-infant interactional variables predicted Strange Situation classification. Mothers of future-B infants were found to be significantly less intrusive ($M = 2.3$ and $5.8, t = 2.54$, $p < .005$) than mothers of future-C infants. Both groups of mothers showed equivalent rates of stimulation of their infants, and their stimulation was equivalently effective.

Thus, at 7.5 months of age, future-B and future-C infants differed significantly in terms of their reactivity to strangers and to maternal separation and in how their mothers behaved toward them in an unstructured laboratory observation session.

Antecedents of Strange Situation Classification at 11 Months

Future-B and future-C infants differed in task persistence at 11 months: future-C infants tended to spend less time in manipulation of toys than did future-B infants (12.95 sec. vs. 17.36 sec., $t = 2.04, p < .10$) and also tended to interrupt their play activities more frequently (4.71 vs. 2.55 times), though not significantly so. The latter activity was done in the service of proximity seeking since the infants left the toys to approach the mother. No other free-play assessments reached significance. It was not possible to assess maternal variables at this age.

In summary, our preliminary findings from the longitudinal study of Japanese infants and their mothers reveal that Japanese infants are far more likely to be classified as C infants than are infants in Western countries like Sweden, Germany, and the United States. Moreover, we have found a thread of continuity between the neonatal period and 12-month attachment assessment in proneness to irritability, a proneness evident in a variety of settings, including home observations and laboratory tests of stranger approach and maternal separation. We have also confirmed that maternal variables such as intrusiveness are antecedents of Strange Situation classification. We emphasize that these findings are preliminary only. Future analyses will permit us to determine the extent to which maternal variables interact with infant variables to determine attachment patterns and to verify which aspects of Strange Situation performance in Japan may successfully predict an infant's social and cognitive adaptation.

DISCUSSION

Our preliminary findings document the role of both constitutional factors and of mother-infant interaction in the determination of individual differences in patterns of attachment in the first year of life. We have also documented the existence of major differences in Strange Situation performance of Japanese infants relative to those in other countries, such as the United States and Germany. We now discuss the implications of these findings for attachment theory (Ainsworth et al., 1978) and for the formation of relationships in early life.

Implications of Cross-national Differences in Strange Situation Performance

The cross-national differences in Strange Situation classification now being consistently reported raise the issue of the difference between "index" and "construct" in the assessment of attachment. There has often been a subtle implication that the Ainsworth B pattern represents the one to which the human infant is phylogenetically adapted and that the A and C classifications reflect failures of adaptation (i.e., "insecure attachment"). We believe that this facile equation of index with construct is misleading within national groups and is especially problematic in cross-national comparisons. In cognitive development, it is well-known that inferences about level of cognitive competence in a cultural group often differ, depending on the appropriateness of the materials used for the cognitive assessment. Similar contextual factors constrain inferences about level of social competence from observations of specific levels of social behavior.

There is no doubt that cultural factors constrain performance on social assessments like the Strange Situation. The mothers of our 12-month-olds reported that the infant was left alone or with another adult (usually the father or grandmother) only 2.5 times a month. Separation from the mother is thus a very unusual occurrence in Japan and may create far greater stress in Japanese infants than it does in countries where brief mother-infant separations are more customary. This factor alone assures that contextual influences confound the inferences possible from the Strange Situation. Thus we do not consider the classification of Japanese infants as C to reflect a greater proneness to be "insecurely attached." It will be necessary for us to review for our Japanese mothers and babies which patterns of attachment behaviors in the Strange Situation reflect emotionally unstable or problematic mother-infant interactions in the first year of life and which patterns predict subsequent social and cognitive competence after 1 year of age.

The Role of Temperament in Strange Situation Classification

Although the findings reported here represent only a preliminary analysis of data collected in an extensive longitudinal investigation, one conclusion is already clear: infant characteristics in the first days of life play a role in the subsequent classification of babies into Ainsworth Strange Situation A, B, and C categories. The clearest relationship observed to date exists between early irritability and subsequent C classification. This finding has been reported now by Crockenberg (1981), Waters et al. (1980), Sagi et al. (in this vol.), and the present study. Moreover, the conclusion that early irritability predicts later Strange Situation classification is consistent with data presented by Ainsworth and her colleagues (1978) on home observations made in the Baltimore study. In the study included in this *Monograph*, Grossmann et al. provide further support for the conclusion that neonatal characteristics predict subsequent Strange Situation classification: in their study, future-B infants were significantly more prone to orient to the environment on the Brazelton NBAS. The link reported by Grossmann et al. (in this vol.) between neonatal temperament and later attachment assessment was observed over as long as 18 months. However, Grossmann et al. did not report a significant relationship between neonatal irritability and C classification, which suggests that not all ways of operationalizing "irritability" will reveal continuities in the first year of life.

It is not yet clear how temperamental factors like irritability influence Strange Situation classification. Possibly, constitutionally determined predispositions to become distressed in part account for the infant's reaction to the stresses imposed in the Strange Situation, as Connell and Goldsmith (1982) have maintained. Kagan (1982) has argued even more forcefully that the Strange Situation does not assess individual differences in quality of the mother's interaction as much as it does the infant's temperament.

The Role of Mother-Infant Interaction in Strange Situation Assessment

Because of the consistent finding that patterns of attachment to the father are often independent of those to the mother in the Strange Situation (Lamb et al., 1984), we feel that endogenous constitutional characteristics cannot fully account for the individual differences observed in the Strange Situation. More likely, temperamental and maternal factors interact to determine the patterns of observed attachment behavior. Accordingly, we are examining our data to see how maternal characteristics may interact with endogenous temperamental factors to produce the individual differences that are of interest in the Strange Situation. There is evidence from the present study that infant irritability alone does not inevitably result in C classification. Of the 10 infants whom we found to be consistently irritable in the first 3 months of life, seven became distress-prone C-type babies, and three became B. Were there some maternal factors that maintained the infant's proneness to distress? Were there some other maternal interventions that prevented the continued expression of irritability in some infants?

If so, what were these variables? Our data suggest that the mother's intrusiveness played a major role in the infant's distress. Other data suggest that the mother's sensitivity to the infant's goals, needs, and social signals are crucial determinants of individual differences (see Ainsworth et al., 1978; Grossmann et al., in this vol.; Lamb et al., 1984).

Our own data on the effects of the mother's intrusiveness at 7.5 months indicate that the effects of the mother's interaction are indeed different, according to the level of the infant's proneness to irritability. There was a suggestion that the mother's proneness to interrupt her baby was not a factor in classification of infants into B or C several months later if her infant was a temperamentally calm baby. However, if the infant was prone to distress, the mother's proneness to interrupt the baby was decisive in determining future-B versus future-C classification: the more the mother was prone to interrupt, the more the baby was likely to be classified later as a C infant. This suggestion of an infant temperament × maternal behavioral style interaction merits confirmation in future research.

Future Studies Planned or in Progress in Sapporo

Because the present study suffered from extensive sample attrition and other problems, we were not able to conduct as extensive and detailed analyses of individual differences in early mother-infant interaction as we had intended. Nor were we able to assess a promising psychophysiological index of temperamental disposition to wariness—Kagan et al.'s (1978) notion that high and stable heart rates to cognitive discrepancies characterize wary babies. Accordingly, we have begun the testing of a second cohort of mother-infant pairs in Sapporo—a cohort that will enable us to obtain data relevant to several issues: the assessment of the role of the mother's contingency and affective quality in interaction with her infant; the interaction between infant temperament and maternal interactional dispositions in accounting for attachment patterns at 1 year of age and later and the confirmation of the major findings obtained to date with the first cohort of subjects. In fact, as this chapter goes to press, we have already confirmed the findings reported here regarding the distribution of A, B, and C infants in Japan (Miyake, 1984; Takahashi & Miyake, 1984).

This second longitudinal cohort of 30 pairs of mothers and infants also starts from the late pregnancy period and continues to the preschool period. In this second cohort, there are several innovations: our mother-infant interaction assessments in the home are videotaped; they are longer in duration; and they will permit more objective scoring of both the affective quality of the mother's interaction with the baby and the contingency of the mother's response to her infant's signals. We are also devoting special attention to minimizing problems of subject attrition. Very significantly, cohort 2 will also permit us to move away from the classification of mother-infant relationships into A, B, or C (which we feel may be culture bound—see Takahashi, in preparation) and to address more directly individual differences in the quality of the emotional communication between the mother and her infant in the Strange Situation and in other contexts as well. Such individual differences in emotional communication may manifest themselves particularly clearly during the preseparation episodes (2 and 3). These episodes have been neglected in Strange Situation research but clearly permit assessment of the infant's use of mother as a secure base for exploration as well as the positive affective sharing between mother and child. We feel that such a shift would take Bowlby's attachment theory in exciting new directions.

REFERENCES

Adam, K. S. (1982). Loss, suicide and attachment. In C. M. Parkes & J. Stevenson-Hinde (Eds.), *The place of attachment in human behavior* (pp. 269–294). New York: Basic.

Ainsworth, M. D. S. (1967). *Infancy in Uganda: Infant care and the growth of love.* Baltimore: Johns Hopkins University Press.

✓Ainsworth, M. D. S. (1972). Attachment and dependency: A comparison. In J. L. Gewirtz (Ed.), *Attachment and dependency* (pp. 97–137). Washington, DC: Winston.

✓ Ainsworth, M. D. S. (1973). The development of infant-mother attachment. In B. M. Caldwell & H. N. Ricciuti (Eds.), *Review of child development research* (Vol. **3**, pp. 1–94). Chicago: University of Chicago Press.

Ainsworth, M. D. S. (1977). Attachment theory and its utility in cross-cultural research. In P. H. Leiderman, S. R. Tulkin, & R. Rosenfeld (Eds.), *Culture and infancy* (pp. 49–67). New York: Academic Press.

Ainsworth, M. D. S. (1980). Attachment and child abuse. In G. Gerbner, J. D. Ross, & E. Zigler (Eds.), *Child abuse: An agenda for action* (pp. 35–47). New York: Oxford University Press.

Ainsworth, M. D. S. (1982). Attachment: Retrospect and prospect. In C. M. Parkes & J. Stevenson-Hinde (Eds.), *The place of attachment in human behavior* (pp. 3–30). New York: Basic.

Ainsworth, M. D. S. (1983). Patterns of infant-mother attachment as related to maternal care. In D. Magnusson & V. Allen (Eds.), *Human development: An interactional perspective* (pp. 35–55). New York: Academic Press.

Ainsworth, M. D. S. (1984, April). *Adaptation and attachment.* Paper presented at the International Conference on Infant Studies, New York.

Ainsworth, M. D. S., & Bell, S. M. (1969). Some contemporary patterns in the feeding situation. In A. Ambrose (Ed.), *Stimulation in early infancy* (pp. 133–170). London: Academic Press.

Ainsworth, M. D. S., Bell, S. M., & Stayton, D. J. (1971). Individual differences in strange situation behavior of one-year-olds. In H. R. Schaffer (Ed.), *The origins of human social relations* (pp. 17–57). London: Academic Press.

Ainsworth, M. D. S., Bell, S. M., & Stayton, D. J. (1972). Individual differences in the development of some attachment behaviors. *Merrill-Palmer Quarterly*, **18**, 123–143.

Ainsworth, M. D. S., Bell, S. M., & Stayton, D. J. (1974). Infant-mother attachment and social development: "Socialization" as a product of reciprocal responsiveness to signals. In M. P. Richards (Ed.), *The integration of the child into a social world* (pp. 99–135). London: Cambridge University Press.

Ainsworth, M. D. S., Blehar, M. C., Waters, E., & Wall, S. (1978). *Patterns of attachment: A psychological study of the Strange Situation.* Hillsdale, NJ: Erlbaum.

298

Ainsworth, M. D. S., & Wittig, B. A. (1969). Attachment and the exploratory behavior of one-year-olds in a strange situation. In B. M. Foss (Ed.), *Determinants of infant behavior* (Vol. **4**, pp. 113–136). London: Methuen.

Aleksandrowicz, M. K., & Aleksandrowicz, D. R. (1975). The molding of personality: A newborn's innate characteristics in interaction with parents' personalities. *Child Psychiatry and Human Development,* **4,** 231–241.

Allen, M. G. (1967). Childhood experience and adult personality—a cross-cultural study using the concept of ego-strength. *Journal of Social Psychology,* **71,** 53–68.

Als, H., & Lewis, M. (1975, April). *The contribution of the infant to the interaction with his mother.* Paper presented at the biennial meeting of the Society for Research in Child Development, Denver.

Anderson, J. W. (1972). Attachment behaviour out of doors. In N. Blurton Jones (Ed.), *Ethological studies of child behaviour* (pp. 199–215). Cambridge: Cambridge University Press.

Arend, R., Gove, F., & Sroufe, L. A. (1979). Continuity of individual adaptation from infancy to kindergarten: A predictive study of ego-resiliency and curiosity in preschoolers. *Child Development,* **50,** 950–959.

Azuma, H., Kashiwagi, K., & Hess, R. (1981). *Hahaoya no taido koudou to kodomo no chiteki hattatsu* [The influence of maternal teaching style on the cognitive development of children] (Text in Japanese, English monograph forthcoming). Tokyo: University of Tokyo Press.

Baers, M. (1954). Women workers and home responsibilities. *International Labor Review,* **69,** 338–355.

Baldwin, J. M. (1911). *The individual and society.* Boston: Goreham.

Bandura, A. (1971). Analysis of modeling processes. In A. Bandura (Ed.), *Psychological modeling* (pp. 1–62). New York: Aldine-Atherton.

Barkow, J. H. (1977). Human ethology and intraindividual systems. *Science Information,* **16,** 133–145.

Bates, E., Bretherton, I., Beeghly, M., & McNew, S. (1982). Social bases of language development: A reassessment. In H. W. Reese & L. P. Lipsitt (Eds.), *Advances in child development and behavior* (Vol. **16,** pp. 7–75). New York: Academic Press.

Bates, E., Camaioni, L., & Volterra, V. (1975). The acquisition of performatives prior to speech. *Merrill-Palmer Quarterly,* **21,** 205–226.

Bates, J. E. (1983). Issues in the assessment of difficult temperament: A reply to Thomas, Chess and Korn. *Merrill-Palmer Quarterly,* **29,** 89–97.

Bates, J. E., & Bayles, K. (1984). Objective and subjective components in mothers' perception of their children from age 6 months to 3 years. *Merrill-Palmer Quarterly,* **30,** 111–130.

Bates, J. E., Freeland, C. A. B., & Lounsbury, M. L. (1979). Measurement of infant difficultness. *Child Development,* **50,** 794–803.

Bates, J. E., Olson, S. L., Pettit, G. S., & Bayles, K. (1982). Dimensions of individuality in the mother-infant relationship at six months of age. *Child Development,* **53,** 446–461.

Bates, J. E., Pettit, G. S., & Bayles, K. (1981, April). *Antecedents of behavior problems at age 3 years.* Paper presented at the biennial meeting of the Society for Research in Child Development, Boston.

Bateson, G., & Mead, M. (1942). *Balinese character: A photographic analysis.* New York: New York Academy of Sciences.

Baumrind, D. (1967). Child care practices anteceding three patterns of preschool behavior. *Genetic Psychology Monographs,* **76,** 43–88.

Baumrind, D. (1968). Authoritarian and authoritative parental control. *Adolescence,* **3,** 255–279.

Bayley, N. (1969). *The Bayley scales of infant development*. New York: Psychological Corp.

Behar, L. B. (1977). The preschool behavior questionnaire. *Journal of Abnormal Child Psychology*, **5**, 265–275.

Behar, L., & Stringfield, S. (1974). A behavior rating scale for the preschool child. *Developmental Psychology*, **10**, 601–610.

Bell, R. Q. (1979). Parent, child, and reciprocal influences. *American Psychologist*, **34**, 821–826.

Bell, R. Q., Weller, G., & Waldrop, M. (1971). Newborn and preschooler: Organization of behavior and relations between periods. *Monographs of the Society for Research in Child Development*, **36**(1–2, Serial No. 142).

Bell, S. M., & Ainsworth, M. D. S. (1972). Infant crying and maternal responsiveness. *Child Development*, **43**, 1171–1190.

Belsky, J. (1980). Child maltreatment: An ecological integration. *American Psychologist*, **35**, 320–335.

Belsky, J. (1984). The determinants of parenting: A process model. *Child Development*, **55**, 83–96.

Belsky, J., Rovine, M., & Taylor, D. G. (1984). The Pennsylvania Infant and Family Development Project, 3: The origins of individual differences in infant-mother attachment: Maternal and infant contributions. *Child Development*, **55**, 718–728.

Belsky, J., & Steinberg, L. D. (1978). The effects of day care: A critical review. *Child Development*, **49**, 929–949.

Belsky, J., Steinberg, L. D., & Walker, A. (1982). The ecology of daycare. In M. Lamb (Ed.), *Childrearing in nontraditional families* (pp. 71–116). Hillsdale, NJ: Erlbaum.

Bem, D., & Funder, D. (1978). Predicting more of the people more of the time: Assessing the personality of situations. *Psychological Review*, **85**, 485–501.

Bender, L., & Yarnell, H. (1941). An observation nursery: A study of 250 children on the Psychiatric Division of Bellevue Hospital. *American Journal of Psychiatry*, **97**, 1158–1172.

Benedek, P. (1949). The psychosomatic implications of the primary unit: Mother-child. *American Journal of Orthopsychiatry*, **19**, 642–654.

Berger, M., & Kennedy, H. (1975). Pseudobackwardness in children. *Psychoanalytic Study of the Child*, **30**, 279–306.

Bettelheim, B. (1967). *The empty fortress*. New York: Free Press.

Bettelheim, B. (1971). *Children of the dream*. London: Paladin.

Bischof, N. (1975). A systems approach toward the functional connections of attachment and fear. *Child Development*, **46**, 801–817.

Blehar, M. C. (1974). Anxious attachment and defensive reactions associated with day care. *Child Development*, **45**, 683–692.

Blehar, M. C., Lieberman, A. F., & Ainsworth, M. D. S. (1977). Early face-to-face interaction and its relation to later infant-mother attachment. *Child Development*, **48**, 182–194.

Block, J. (1971). *Lives through time*. Berkeley: Bancroft.

Block, J. (1978). *The Q-sort method in personality assessment and psychiatry research*. Palo Alto, CA: Consulting Psychologists Press. (Original work published 1961)

Block, J. H. (1969a). A comparative study of parents of schizophrenic, neurotic, asthmatic, and congenitally ill children. *Archives of General Psychiatry*, **20**, 659–674.

Block, J. H. (1969b). *Retrospective reports revisited: Evidence for validity*. Paper presented at the meeting of the Society for Research in Child Development, Santa Monica, CA.

Block, J. H., & Block, J. (1980). The role of ego-control and ego-resiliency in the organization of behavior. In A. Collins (Ed.), *Minnesota symposium of child psychology* (Vol. **13**, pp. 39–101). Hillsdale, NJ: Erlbaum.

Bower, G. (1981). Mood and memory. *American Psychologist*, **36**, 129–148.

Bowlby, J. (1958). The nature of the child's tie to his mother. *International Journal of Psycho-Analysis*, **39,** 350–373.

Bowlby, J. (1973). *Attachment and loss: Vol. 2. Separation*. New York: Basic.

Bowlby, J. (1979). The making and breaking of affectional bonds. *British Journal of Psychiatry*, **130,** 201–210, 421–431.

Bowlby, J. (1980). *Attachment and loss: Vol. 3. Loss, sadness and depression*. New York: Basic.

Bowlby, J. (1982a). Attachment and loss: Retrospect and prospect. *American Journal of Orthopsychiatry*, **52,** 664–678.

Bowlby, J. (1982b). *Attachment and loss: Vol. 1. Attachment* (2d). New York: Basic. (Original work published 1969)

Bradley, R. H., & Caldwell, B. M. (1980). The relation of home environment, cognitive competence, and IQ among males and females. *Child Development*, **51,** 1140–1148.

Brazelton, T. B. (1973). *Neonatal behavioral assessment scale* (Clinics in Developmental Medicine, no. 50). Philadelphia: Lippincott.

Brazelton, T. B. (1977). Implications of infant development among the Mayan Indians of Mexico. In P. H. Leiderman, S. R. Tulkin, & A. Rosenfeld (Eds.), *Culture and infancy* (pp. 151–187). New York: Academic Press.

Brazelton, T. B., Als, H., Tronick, E., & Lester, B. M. (1979). Specific neonatal measures: The Brazelton Neonatal Assessment Scale. In J. D. Osofsky (Ed.), *Handbook of infant development* (pp. 185–215). New York: Wiley.

Brazelton, T. B., Koslowski, B., & Main, M. (1974). The origins of mother-infant interaction. In M. Lewis & L. A. Rosenblum (Eds.), *The effect of the infant on its caregiver* (pp. 49–76). New York: Wiley.

Bretherton, I. (1980). Young children in stressful situations: The supporting role of attachment figures and unfamiliar caregivers. In G. V. Coelho & P. Ahmed (Eds.), *Uprooting and development* (pp. 179–210). New York: Plenum.

Bretherton, I. (1984). Representing the social world in symbolic play: Reality and fantasy. In I. Bretherton (Ed.), *Symbolic play: The development of social understanding* (pp. 3–11). New York: Academic Press.

Bretherton, I., & Ainsworth, M. D. S. (1974). Responses of one-year-olds to a stranger in a strange situation. In M. Lewis & L. A. Rosenblum (Eds.), *The origins of fear* (pp. 131–164). New York: Wiley.

Bretherton, I., & Bates, E. (1979). The emergence of intentional communication. In I. Uzgiris (Ed.), *New Directions for Child Development*, **4,** 81–100.

Bretherton, I., Bates, E., Benigni, L., Camaioni, L., & Volterra, V. (1979). Relationships between cognition, communication and quality of attachment. In E. Bates, L. Benigni, I. Bretherton, L. Camaioni, & V. Volterra, *The emergence of symbols: Cognition and communication in infancy* (pp. 223–269). New York: Academic Press.

Bretherton, I., McNew, S., & Beeghly-Smith, M. (1981). Early person knowledge as expressed in verbal and gestural communication. When do infants acquire a "theory of mind"? In M. E. Lamb & L. R. Sherrod (Eds.), *Infant social cognition* (pp. 333–373). Hillsdale, NJ: Erlbaum.

Bretherton, I., O'Connell, B., & Tracy, R. (1980, March). *Styles of mother-infant and stranger-infant interaction*. Paper presented at the International Conference on Infant Studies, New Haven, CT.

Bridges, K. M. B. (1932). Emotional development in early infancy. *Child Development*, **3,** 324–341.

Brim, O. G., Jr., & Kagan, J. (1980). Constancy and change: A view of the issues. In O. G. Brim, Jr., & J. Kagan (Eds.), *Constancy and change in human development* (pp. 1–25). Cambridge, MA: Harvard University Press.

Brim, O. G., Jr., & Ryff, C. D. (1980). On the properties of life events. In P. B. Baltes &

O. G. Brim, Jr. (Eds.), *Lifespan development and behavior* (Vol. **3,** pp. 368–388). New York: Academic Press.

Bronson, W., Katten, E., & Livson, N. (1959). Patterns of authority and affection in two generations. *Journal of Abnormal and Social Psychology,* **58,** 143–152.

Brookhart, J., & Hock, E. (1976). The effects of experimental context and experiential background on infants' behavior toward their mothers and a stranger. *Child Development,* **47,** 333–340.

Bruner, J. (1975). The ontogenesis of speech acts. *Journal of Child Language,* **2,** 1–19.

Burns, R. B. (1976). Attitudes to self and attitudes to others. *British Journal of Social and Clinical Psychology,* **15,** 319–321.

Buss, D. M., Block, J. H., & Block, J. (1980). Preschool activity level: Personality correlates and developmental implications. *Child Development,* **51,** 401–408.

Butterworth, G. (1979, September). *What minds have in common is space: A perceptual mechanism for joint reference in infancy.* Paper presented to the Developmental Section, British Psychological Society, Southampton.

Caldwell, B. M. (1969). A new "APPROACH" to behavioral ecology. In J. P. Hill (Ed.), *Minnesota symposium of child psychology* (Vol. **2,** pp. 74–109). Minneapolis: University of Minnesota Press.

Caldwell, B. M. (1979). *Home observation for measurement of the environment.* Little Rock: University of Arkansas, Center for Early Development and Education.

Campbell, S. B., Szumowski, E. K., Ewing, L. J., Gluck, D. S., & Breaux, A. M. (1982). A multidimensional assessment of parent-identified behavior problem toddlers. *Journal of Abnormal Child Psychology,* **10,** 569–592.

Campos, J. J., Barrett, K., Lamb, M. E., Goldsmith, H., & Stenberg, C. R. (1983). Socioemotional development. In M. M. Haith & J. J. Campos (Eds.), P. H. Mussen (Series Ed.), *Handbook of child psychology: Vol. 2. Infancy and developmental psychobiology* (pp. 783–915). New York: Wiley.

Campos, J. J., & Stenberg, C. R. (1981). Perception, appraisal and emotion: The onset of social referencing. In M. E. Lamb & L. R. Sherrod (Eds.), *Infant social cognition* (pp. 273–314). Hillsdale, NJ: Erlbaum.

Carey, W. B., & McDevitt, S. (1978). Revision of the infant temperament questionnaire. *Pediatrics,* **61,** 735–739.

Cassidy, J. (1985, April). *Attachment and the self at six.* Paper presented at the biennial meeting of the Society for Research in Child Development, Toronto.

Cassidy, J., & Main, M. (1984, April). *Quality of attachment from infancy to six years: Security is stable but behavior changes.* Paper presented at the International Conference on Infant Studies, New York.

Cattell, R. B., & Scheier, I. H. (1963). *Handbook for the IPAT Anxiety Scale* (2d ed.). Champaign, IL: Institute of Personality and Ability Testing.

Caudill, W., & Frost, L. (1972). A comparison of maternal care and infant behavior in Japanese-American, American and Japanese families. In U. Bronfenbrenner (Ed.), *Influences on human development* (pp. 329–342). Hinsdale, IL: Dryden.

Caudill, W., & Weinstein, S. (1969). Maternal care and infant behavior in Japan and America. *Psychiatry,* **32,** 12–43.

Charlesworth, W. R., & Fitzpatrick, L. (1979). *Tool using behavior in young children.* Unpublished manuscript, University of Minnesota at Minneapolis St. Paul, Institute of Child Development.

Chess, S., & Thomas, A. (1982). Reply to Sroufe and Waters. *American Journal of Orthopsychiatry,* **52,** 746–747.

Cicchetti, D., & Rizley, R. (1981). Developmental perspectives on the etiology, intergenerational transmission, and sequelae of child maltreatment. *New Directions in Child Development*, **11**, 31–55.

Cicchetti, D., & Schneider-Rosen, K. (1984). Theoretical and empirical considerations in the investigation of the relationship between affect and cognition. In C. Izard, J. Kagan, & R. Zajonc (Eds.), *Emotions, cognitions, and behavior* (pp. 366–406). New York: Cambridge University Press.

Cicchetti, D., & Serafica, F. C. (1981). The interplay among behavioral systems: Illustrations from the study of attachment, affiliation, and wariness in young Down Syndrome children. *Developmental Psychology*, **17**, 36–49.

Clarke-Stewart, K. A. (1973). Interactions between mothers and their young children: Characteristics and consequences. *Monographs of the Society for Research in Child Development*, **38**(5–6, Serial No. 153).

Clarke-Stewart, K. A. (1982). *The Chicago Study of child care and development.* Unpublished manuscript. University of California, Department of Social Ecology.

Clarke-Stewart, K. A., & Fein, G. (1983). Early childhood programs. In M. M. Haith & J. J. Campos (Eds.), P. H. Mussen (Series Ed.), *Handbook of child psychology: Vol. 2. Infancy and developmental psychobiology* (pp. 917–999). New York: Wiley.

Coates, B., Anderson, E., & Hartup, W. (1972). Interrelations in the attachment behavior of human infants. *Developmental Psychology*, **6**, 218–230.

Cochran, M. M. (1977). A comparison of group day and family child-rearing patterns in Sweden. *Child Development*, **48**, 702–707.

Cochrane, R., & Robertson, A. (1973). The life event inventory: A measure of the relative severity of psycho-social stressors. *Journal of Psychosocial Research*, **17**, 135–139.

Cohen, J. (1960). A coefficient of agreement for nominal scales. *Educational and Psychological Measurement*, **20**, 37–46.

Cohen, L. (1974). The operational definition of human attachment. *Psychological Bulletin*, **81**, 207–217.

Cohen, S. E., & Beckwith, L. (1979). Preterm infant interaction with the caregiver in the first year of life and competence at age two. *Child Development*, **50**, 767–776.

Cohler, B., & Grunebaum, H. (1981). *Mothers, grandmothers and daughters.* New York: Wiley.

Connell, D. B. (1976). *Individual differences in attachment: An investigation into stability, implications and relationships to structure of early language development.* Unpublished doctoral dissertation, University of Syracuse.

Connell, J. P., & Goldsmith, H. H. (1982). A structural modelling approach to the study of attachment and Strange Situation behaviors. In R. Emde & R. Harmon (Eds.), *The development of attachment and affiliative systems* (pp. 213–243). New York: Plenum.

Cooley, C. H. (1902). *Human nature and the social order.* New York: Scribner's.

Cottrell, L. (1969). Interpersonal interaction and the development of the self. In D. A. Goslin (Ed.), *Handbook of socialization theory and research* (pp. 543–570). Chicago: Rand-McNally.

Craik, K. (1943). *The nature of explanation.* Cambridge: Cambridge University Press.

Crittenden, P. M. (1981). Abusing, neglecting, problematic, and adequate dyads: Differentiating by patterns of interaction. *Merrill-Palmer Quarterly*, **27**, 201–208.

Crockenberg, S. B. (1981). Infant irritability, mother responsiveness, and social support influences on the security of mother-infant attachment. *Child Development*, **52**, 857–865.

Cummings, E. M. (1980). Caregiver stability and day care. *Developmental Psychology*, **16**, 31–37.

Deane, K., & Waters, E. (1984). *Security, dependency, and sociability: A Q-sort analysis of conceptual and empirical relationships among related constructs in infancy and early childhood.* Unpublished manuscript, State University of New York at Stony Brook.

Denenberg, V. H. (1979). Paradigms and paradoxes in the study of behavioral development. In E. Thoman (Ed.), *Origins of the infant's social responsiveness* (pp. 251–289). Hillsdale, NJ: Erlbaum.

Dennis, W., & Najarian, T. (1957). Infant development under environmental handicap. *Psychological Monographs, 71*(Whole No. 436).

Doi, T. (1973). *The anatomy of dependence.* Tokyo: Kodansha.

Dontas, C. (1977). *Application of convergent analyses in mother-infant interaction research: Implications for the study of individual differences in separation-induced protest.* Unpublished doctoral dissertation, University of Minnesota.

Doyle, A. (1975). Infant development in day care. *Developmental Psychology, 4,* 655–656.

Easterbrooks, M. A., & Goldberg, W. A. (1984). Toddler development in the family: Impact of father involvement and parenting characteristics. *Child Development, 55,* 740–752.

Eckblad, G. (1981). *Scheme theory: A conceptual framework for cognitive-motivational processes.* New York: Academic Press.

Eckerman, C. O., & Whatley, J. L. (1977). Toys and social interaction between infant peers. *Child Development, 48,* 1645–1656.

Egeland, B. (1983). Comments on Kopp, Krakow, and Vaughn's chapter. In M. Perlmutter (Ed.), *Minnesota symposium in child psychology* (Vol. **16,** pp. 129–135). Hillsdale, NJ: Erlbaum.

Egeland, B., Breitenbucher, M., & Rosenberg, D. (1980). Prospective study of the significance of life stress in the etiology of child abuse. *Journal of Consulting and Clinical Psychology, 48,* 195–205.

Egeland, B., & Brunnquell, D. (1979). An at-risk approach to the study of child abuse. *Journal of the American Academy of Child Psychiatry, 18,* 219–235.

Egeland, B., Deinard, A., & Sroufe, L. A. (1977). *Early maladaptation and competence: A prospective, transactional study.* Project proposal submitted to the Office of Maternal and Child Health.

Egeland, B., & Farber, E. A. (1984). Infant-mother attachment: Factors related to its development and changes over time. *Child Development, 55,* 753–771.

Egeland, B., & Sroufe, L. A. (1981a). Attachment and early maltreatment. *Child Development, 52,* 44–52.

Egeland, B., & Sroufe, L. A. (1981b). Developmental sequelae of maltreatment in infancy. In R. Rizley & D. Cicchetti (Eds.), *Developmental perspectives in child maltreatment* (pp. 77–92). San Francisco: Jossey-Bass.

Elmer, E. (1977). *Fragile families, troubled children.* Pittsburgh, PA: University of Pittsburgh Press.

Emde, R. N. (1980). Emotional availability: A reciprocal award system for infants and parents with implications for prevention of psychosocial disorders. In P. M. Taylor (Ed.), *Parent-infant relationships* (pp. 87–115). New York: Grune & Stratton.

Emde, R. N. (1983). The prerepresentational self and its affective core. *Psychoanalytic Study of the Child, 38,* 165–192.

Emery, R. E. (1982). Interparental conflict and the children of discord and divorce. *Psychological Bulletin, 2,* 310–333.

Epstein, S. (1973). The self-concept revisited or a theory of a theory. *American Psychologist, 28,* 404–416.

Epstein, S. (1976). Anxiety, arousal and the self-concept. In I. G. Saranson & C. D. Spielberger (Eds.), *Stress and anxiety* (pp. 185–229). Washington, DC: Hemisphere.

Epstein, S. (1979). Natural healing processes of the mind: 1. Acute schizophrenic disorganization. *Schizophrenia Bulletin*, **5**, 315–321.

Epstein, S. (1980). The self-concept: A review and the proposal of an integrated theory of personality. In E. Staub (Ed.), *Personality: Basic aspects and current research* (pp. 82–131). Englewood Cliffs, NJ: Prentice-Hall.

Epstein, S. (1983). *The mother-father-peer scale.* Unpublished manuscript, University of Massachusetts—Amherst.

Epstein, S. (in press). Implications of cognitive self-theory for psychopathology and psychotherapy. In N. Cheshire & H. Thoma (Eds.), *Self-esteem and psychotherapy.* New York: Wiley.

Epstein, E., & Erskine, N. (1983). The development of personal theories of reality from an interactional perspective. In M. Magnussen & V. Allen (Eds.), *Human development: An interactional perspective* (pp. 133–147). New York: Academic Press.

Erickson, M. F., & Crichton, L. (1981, April). *Antecedents of compliance in two-year-olds from a high risk sample.* Paper presented at the biennial meeting of the Society for Research in Child Development, Boston.

Erickson, M. F., & Egeland, B. (1981). *Behavior problem scale technical manual.* Unpublished manuscript, University of Minnesota at Minneapolis St. Paul.

Erickson, M. F., Farber, E. A., & Egeland, B. (1982, August). *Antecedents and concomitants of compliance in high-risk preschool children.* Paper presented at the annual meeting of the American Psychological Association, Washington, DC.

Erikson, E. H. (1963). *Childhood and society* (2d ed.). New York: Norton.

Escher-Graeub, D., & Grossmann, K. E. (1983). *Bindungssicherheit im zweiten Lebensjahr—die Regensburger Querschnittuntersuchung* [Attachment security in the second year of life—the Regensburg longitudinal study] (Research Report). University of Regensburg.

Eysenck, H. J., & Eysenck, S. B. G. (1978). Psychopathy, personality, and genetics. In R. D. Hare & D. Schalling (Eds.), *Psychopathic behavior: Approaches to research* (pp. 191–302). New York: Wiley.

Fairbairn, W. R. D. (1940). *Psychoanalytic studies of the personality.* London: Tavistock.

Fairbairn, W. R. D. (1946). Object-relationships and dynamic structure. *International Journal of Psychoanalysis*, **27**, 30–37.

Farber, E. A., & Egeland, B. (1982). Developmental consequences of out-of-home care for infants in a low income population. In E. Zigler & E. Gordon (Eds.), *Day care* (pp. 102–125). Boston: Auburn.

Farran, D. C., & Ramey, C. T. (1977). Infant day care and attachment behaviors toward mothers and teachers. *Child Development*, **48**, 1112–1116.

Faschingbauer, R. R. (1974). A 166-item short form of the group MMPI: The FAM. *Journal of Consulting and Clinical Psychology*, **42**, 645–655.

Feinman, S., & Lewis, M. (1983). Social referencing at ten months: A second-order effect on infants' responses to strangers. *Child Development*, **54**, 878–887.

Feldman, S. S., & Ingham, M. E. (1975). Attachment behavior: A validation study in two age groups. *Child Development*, **46**, 319–330.

Field, D. (1981). Retrospective reports by healthy, intelligent elderly people of personal events of their adult lives. *International Journal of Behavioral Development*, **4**, 77–97.

Firth, R. (1936). *We, the Tikopia.* London: Allen & Unwin.

Fleiss, J., Cohen, J., & Everitt, B. (1969). Large sample standard errors of Kappa and weighted Kappa. *Psychological Bulletin*, **72**, 323–327.

Fox, N. (1977). Attachment of kibbutz infants to mother and metapelet. *Child Development*, **48**, 1228–1239.

Fraiberg, S. (1969). Libidinal object constancy and mental representation. *Psychoanalytic Study of the Child*, **24**, 9–47.

Fraiberg, S., Adelson, E., & Shapiro, V. (1975). Ghosts in the nursery: A psychoanalytic approach to the problems of impaired infant-mother relationships. *Journal of the American Academy of Child Psychiatry*, **14**, 387–421.

Frankel, K. F., & Bates, J. E. (1984). *Mother-toddler interactions while solving problems: Correlations with attachment security and interaction at home.* Unpublished manuscript, Indiana University, Department of Psychology.

Freedman, D. G. (1974). *Human infancy: An evolutionary perspective.* Hillsdale, NJ: Erlbaum.

Freud, A. (1952). The mutual influences in the development of ego and id. *Psychoanalytic Study of the Child*, **7,** 42–50.

Freud, A., & Dann, S. (1951). An experiment in group upbringing. *Psychoanalytic Study of the Child*, **6,** 127–168.

Freud, S. (1940). An outline of psychoanalysis. In J. Strachey (Ed. and Trans.), *The standard edition of the complete psychological works of Sigmund Freud* (Vol. **23**, pp. 137–207). London: Hogarth.

Frommer, E., & O'Shea, G. (1973a). Antenatal identification of women liable to have problems in managing their infants. *British Journal of Psychiatry*, **123,** 149–156.

Frommer, E., & O'Shea, G. (1973b). The importance of childhood experience in relation to problems of marriage and family building. *British Journal of Psychiatry*, **123,** 161–167.

Fu, V. R., Hinkle, D. E., & Hanna, M. K. (1983, April). *A three-generation study of the development of individual dependence and family interdependence.* Paper presented at the meeting of the Society for Research in Child Development, Detroit.

Gaensbauer, T. J., & Harmon, R. J. (1982). Attachment behavior in abused/neglected and premature infants: Implications for the concept of attachment. In R. N. Emde & R. J. Harmon (Eds.), *Attachment and affiliative systems* (pp. 245–279). New York: Plenum.

Garbarino, J., & Gilliam, G. (1980). *Understanding abusive families.* Lexington, MA: Lexington Books.

Garcia Coll, C., Kagan, J., & Reznick, J. S. (1984). Behavioral inhibition in young children. *Child Development*, **55,** 1005–1019.

George, C., Kaplan, N., & Main, M. (1984). *Attachment interview for adults.* Unpublished manuscript, University of California, Berkeley.

George, C., & Main, M. (1979). Social interactions of young abused children: Approach, avoidance, and aggression. *Child Development*, **50,** 306–318.

Gersten, M., Coster, W., Schneider-Rosen, K., Carlson, V., & Cicchetti, D. (in press). The socio-emotional bases of communicative functioning: Quality of attachment, language development, and early maltreatment. In M. Lamb, A. L. Brown, & B. Rogoff (Eds.), *Advances in developmental psychology* (Vol. **4**). Hillsdale, NJ: Erlbaum.

Ghiselli, E., Campbell, J., & Zedeck, S. (1981). *Measurement theory for the behavioral sciences.* San Francisco: Freeman.

Giovacchini, P. (1970). Effects of adaptive and disruptive aspects of early object relations upon later parental functioning. In E. Anthony & R. Benedek (Eds.), *Parenting: Its psychology and psychopathology* (pp. 525–537). Boston: Little Brown.

Giovannoni, J. M., & Becerra, R. M. (1979). *Defining child abuse.* New York: Free Press.

Goldfarb, W. (1943). Infant rearing and problem behavior. *American Journal of Orthopsychiatry*, **13,** 249–256.

Goldsmith, H. H., & Campos, J. J. (1982). Toward a theory of infant temperament. In R. N. Emde & R. Harmon (Eds.), *The development of attachment and affiliative systems* (pp. 161–185). New York: Plenum.

Gove, F. (1982). *Continuity of adaptation from 12 to 24 months in an economically disadvantaged population.* Unpublished doctoral dissertation, University of Minnesota at Minneapolis St. Paul.

Greenberg, J. R., & Mitchell, S. A. (1983). *Object relations in psychoanalytic theory.* Cambridge, MA: Harvard University Press.

Greenfield, P. M., & Smith, J. H. (1976). *The structure of communication in early development.* New York: Academic Press.

Grossmann, K. (1984, April). *Development of infants' relationships during the first two years.* Paper presented at the International Conference on Infant Studies, New York.

Grossmann, K., & Grossmann, K. E. (in press). Newborn behavior, early parenting quality, and later toddler-parent relationships in a group of North German infants. In J. K. Nugent, B. M. Lester, & T. B. Brazelton (Eds.), *The cultural context of infancy* (Vol. 2). Norwood, NJ: Ablex.

Grossmann, K. E. (1977). *Die Entwicklung der Lernfähigkeit in der sozialen Umwelt* [The development of learning competence in the social environment]. Munich: Kindler.

Grossmann, K. E., & Grossmann, K. (1981a). Parent-infant attachment relationships in Bielefeld. In K. Immelmann, G. Barlow, L. Petrovich, & M. Main (Eds.), *Behavioral development: The Bielefeld interdisciplinary project* (pp. 694–699). New York: Cambridge University Press.

Grossmann, K. E., & Grossmann, K. (1981b). The mother-child relationship. *German Journal of Psychology,* **5,** 237–252.

Grossmann, K. E., Grossmann, K., Huber, F., & Wartner, U. (1981). German children's behavior toward their mothers at 12 months and their fathers at 18 months in Ainsworth's Strange Situation. *International Journal of Behavioral Development,* **4,** 157–181.

Grossmann, K. E., Grossmann, K., & Schwan, A. (in press). Capturing the wider view of attachment: A reanalysis of Ainsworth's Strange Situation. In C. E. Izard & P. B. Read (Eds.), *Measuring emotions in infants and children* (Vol. 2). New York: Cambridge University Press.

Gunnarson, L. (1978). *Children in day care and family care in Sweden: A follow-up* (Bulletin No. 21). University of Gothenburg, Department of Educational Research.

Hall, F., & Pawlby, S. (1981). Continuity and discontinuity in the behavior of British working-class mothers and their first-born children. *International Journal of Behavioral Development,* **4,** 13–36.

Hall, F., Pawlby, S., & Wolkind, S. (1979). Early life experiences and later mothering behaviors: A study of mothers and their 20-week-old babies. In D. Shaffer & J. Dunn (Eds.), *The first year of life* (pp. 153–174). New York: Wiley.

Hansburg, H. G. (1972). *Adolescent separation anxiety: A method for the study of adolescent separation problems.* Springfield, IL: Thomas.

Harter, S. (1982). The perceived competence scale for children. *Child Development,* **53,** 81–86.

Harter, S. (1983). Developmental perspectives on the self-system. In E. M. Hetherington (Ed)., P. H. Mussen (Series Ed.), *Handbook of child psychology: Vol. 4. Socialization, personality, and social development* (pp. 275–385). New York: Wiley.

Hartup, W. W. (1970). Peer interaction and social organization. In P. H. Mussen (Ed.), *Carmichael's manual of child psychology* (Vol. **2,** pp. 361–456). New York: Wiley.

Hay, D. F. (1980). Multiple functions of proximity seeking in infancy. *Child Development,* **51,** 636–645.

Hays, W. L. (1963). *Statistics for psychologists.* New York: Holt, Rinehart, & Winston.

Heinicke, C., & Westheimer, I. (1966). *Brief separations.* New York: International Universities Press.

Hetherington, E. M., & Martin, B. (1979). Family interaction. In H. C. Quay & J. S. Werry (Eds.), *Psychopathological disorders of childhood* (2d ed., pp. 247–302). New York: Wiley.

Hinde, R. A. (1976). On describing relationships. *Journal of Child Psychology and Psychiatry,* **17,** 1–19.

Hinde, R. A. (1979). *Towards understanding relationships.* London: Academic Press.

Hinde, R. A. (1982a). Attachment: Some conceptual and biological issues. In C. Parkes & J. Stevenson-Hinde (Eds.), *The place of attachment in human behavior* (pp. 60–76). New York: Basic.

Hinde, R. A. (1982b). *Ethology.* New York: Oxford University Press.

Hock, E. (1980). Working and nonworking mothers and their infants: A comparative study of maternal caregiving characteristics and infant social behavior. *Merrill-Palmer Quarterly,* **26,** 79–101.

Hoffman, L. W. (1979). Maternal employment. *American Psychologist,* **34,** 859–865.

Hsu, C., Soong, W., Stigler, J. W., Hong, C., & Liang, C. (1981). The temperamental characteristics of Chinese babies. *Child Development,* **52,** 1337–1340.

Jackson, D. N. (1974). *Personality research form manual.* Goshen, NY: Research Psychological Press.

Joffe, L. S., & Vaughn, B. E. (1982). Infant-mother attachment: Theory, assessment and implications for development. In B. Wolman (Ed.), *Handbook of developmental psychology* (pp. 190–206). Englewood Cliffs, NJ: Prentice-Hall.

Kagan, J. (1982). *Psychological research on the human infant: An evaluative summary.* New York: W. T. Grant.

Kagan, J., Kearsley, R., & Zelazo, P. (1978). *Infancy: Its place in human development.* Cambridge, MA: Harvard University Press.

Kaplan, N. (1984). *Internal representations of separation experiences in six year olds: Related to actual experiences of separation.* Unpublished masters' thesis, University of California, Berkeley.

Karangelis, A. (1959). *Psychomotor development of infants residing in a model institution.* Unpublished doctoral dissertation, University of Athens.

Kell, L., & Aldous, J. (1960). Trends in childcare over three generations. *Marriage and Family Living,* **22,** 176–177.

Kerlinger, F. M., & Pedhazur, E. J. (1973). *Multiple regression in behavioral research.* New York: Holt.

Kiser, L. J., Bates, J. E., Maslin, C. A., & Bayles, K. (1983). *Mother-infant play at 6 months as a predictor of attachment security at thirteen months.* Unpublished manuscript, Indiana University, Department of Psychology.

Klagsbrun, M., & Bowlby, J. (1976). Responses to separation from parents: A clinical test for young children. *British Journal of Projective Psychology,* **21,** 7–21.

Klinnert, M. D., Campos, J. J., Sorce, J. F., Emde, R. N., & Svejda, M. (1983). Emotions as behavior regulators: Social referencing in infancy. In R. Plutchik & H. Kellerman (Eds.), *The emotions: Vol. 2. Emotions in early development* (pp. 57–86). New York: Academic Press.

Kobak, R. (1985). *Attitudes towards attachment relations and social competence among first year college students.* Unpublished doctoral dissertation, University of Virginia.

Korner, A. F., Hutchinson, C. A., Koperski, J. A., Kraemer, H. C., & Schneider, P. A. (1981). Stability of individual differences of neonatal motor and crying patterns. *Child Development,* **52,** 83–90.

Kosawa, Y. (1980). *The influence of the infant upon the early development of mother-child relationships.* Unpublished doctoral dissertation, University of Tokyo.

Krentz, M. S. (1983, March). *Qualitative differences between mother-child and caregiver-child attachments and infants in family daycare.* Paper presented at the biennial meeting of the Society for Research in Child Development, Detroit.

LaBarre, M., Jessner, L., & Ussery, L. (1960). The significance of grandmothers in the psychopathology of children. *American Journal of Orthopsychiatry,* **30,** 175–185.

LaFreniere, P., & Sroufe, L. A. (1985). Profiles of peer competence in the preschool: Interrelations between measures, influence of social ecology, and relation to attachment history. *Developmental Psychology*, **21**, 56–68.

Lamb, M. E. (1976). The role of the father: An overview. In M. E. Lamb (Ed.), *The role of the father in child development* (pp. 1–63). New York: Wiley.

Lamb, M. E. (1977). Father-infant and mother-infant interaction in the first year of life. *Child Development*, **48**, 167–181.

Lamb, M. E. (1978). Qualitative aspects of mother-infant and father-infant attachments. *Infant Behavior and Development*, **1**, 265–275.

Lamb, M. E., Hwang, C. P., Frodi, A., & Frodi, M. (1982). Security of mother- and father-infant attachment and its relation to sociability with strangers in traditional and nontraditional Swedish families. *Infant Behavior and Development*, **5**, 355–367.

Lamb, M. E., Thompson, R. A., Gardner, W., Charnov, E. L., & Estes, C. (1984). Security of attachment as assessed in the Strange Situation: Its study and biological interpretation. *Behavioral and Brain Sciences*, **7**, 127–147.

Lambert, W. W., Triandis, L. M., & Wolf, M. (1959). Some correlates of beliefs in the malevolence and benevolence of supernatural beings—a cross-cultural study. *Journal of Abnormal and Social Psychology*, **58**, 162–169.

Laudenslager, M. L., Reite, M., & Harbeck, R. J. (1982). Suppressed immune response in infant monkeys associated with maternal separation. *Behavioral and Neural Biology*, **36**, 40–48.

Lebra, T. S. (1976). *Japanese patterns of behavior*. Honolulu: University of Hawaii Press.

Lee, C., & Bates, J. (1984). *Mother-child interaction at age two years and perceived difficult temperament*. Unpublished manuscript, Indiana University, Department of Psychology.

Lenssen, B. G. (1975, April). *Infants' reactions to peer strangers*. Paper presented at the biennial meeting of the Society for Research in Child Development, Denver.

Lewin, K. (1948). *Resolving social conflicts*. New York: Harper. (Original work published 1936)

Lewis, M., & Brooks, J. (1974). Self, other and fear: Infants' reactions to people. In M. Lewis & L. A. Rosenblum (Eds.), *The origins of fear* (pp. 195–227). New York: Wiley.

Li-Repac, D. (1982). *The impact of acculturation on the child-rearing attitudes and practices of Chinese-American families*. Unpublished doctoral dissertation, University of California, Berkeley.

Littenberg, R., Tulkin, S., & Kagan, J. (1971). Cognitive components of separation anxiety. *Developmental Psychology*, **4**, 387–388.

Lobitz, G. K., & Johnson, S. M. (1975). Normal versus deviant children: A multimethod comparison. *Journal of Abnormal Child Psychology*, **3**, 353–374.

Loevinger, J. (1957). Objective tests as instruments of psychological theory. *Psychological Reports*, **3**(Monograph No. 9), 635–694.

Loftus, E. F. (1979). *Eyewitness testimony*. Cambridge, MA. Harvard University Press.

Londerville, S., & Main, M. (1981). Security of attachment, compliance and maternal training methods in the second year of life. *Developmental Psychology*, **17**, 289–299.

Lorenz, K. Z. (1935). Der Kumpan in der Umwelt des Vogels [Companionship in bird life]. *Journal of Ornithology*, **83**, 137–213. (English trans. in C. H. Schiller [Ed.], *Instinctive behavior* [pp. 83–128]. New York: International Universities Press, 1957)

Lorenz, K. (1965). *The evolution and modification of behavior*. Chicago: University of Chicago Press.

Lounsbury, M. L., & Bates, J. E. (1982). The cries of infants of differing levels of perceived temperamental difficultness: Acoustic properties and effects on listeners. *Child Development*, **53**, 677–686.

Luetkenhaus, P. (1984). Pleasure derived from mastery in 3-year-olds: Its function for persistence and the influence of maternal behavior. *International Journal of Behavioral Development, 7,* 343–359.

Lytton, H. (1980). *Parent-child interaction.* New York: Plenum.

Lytton, H., & Zwirner, W. (1975). Compliance and its controlling stimuli observed in a natural setting. *Developmental Psychology, 11,* 769–779.

Maccoby, E. E., & Feldman, S. S. (1972). Mother-attachment and stranger-reactions in the third year of life. *Monographs of the Society for Research in Child Development, 37*(1, Serial No. 146).

Maccoby, E. E., & Masters, J. C. (1970). Attachment and dependency. In P. H. Mussen (Ed.), *Carmichael's manual of child psychology* (3d ed., Vol. **2,** pp. 73–157). New York: Wiley.

Mahler, M., Pine, F., & Bergman, A. (1975). *The psychological birth of the human infant.* New York: Basic.

Main, M. (1973). *Play, exploration and competence as related to child-adult attachment.* Unpublished doctoral dissertation, Johns Hopkins University.

Main, M. (1981). Avoidance in the service of attachment: A working paper. In K. Immelmann, G. Barlow, L. Petrinovich, & M. Main (Eds.), *Behavioral development: The Bielefeld interdisciplinary project* (pp. 651–693). New York: Cambridge University Press.

Main, M. (1985, April). *An adult attachment classification system.* Paper presented at the biennial meeting of the Society for Research in Child Development, Toronto.

Main, M. (in press). Parental observed aversion to physical contact with the infant: Stability, consequences and reasons. In T. B. Brazelton & K. Barnard (Eds.), *Touch.* New York: International Universities Press.

Main, M., & Goldwyn, R. (in press). Predicting rejection of her infant from mother's representation of her own experiences: A preliminary report. *International Journal of Child Abuse and Neglect.*

Main, M., & Solomon, J. (in press). Discovery of an insecure disorganized/disoriented attachment pattern: Procedures, findings and implications for the classification of behavior. In M. Yogman & T. B. Brazelton (Eds.), *Affective development in infancy.* Norwood, NJ: Ablex.

Main, M., & Stadtman, J. (1981). Infant response to rejection of physical contact by the mother: Aggression, avoidance and conflict. *Journal of the American Academy of Child Psychiatry, 20,* 292–307.

Main, M., Tomasini, L., & Tolan, W. (1979). Differences among mothers of infants judged to differ in security. *Developmental Psychology, 15,* 472–473.

Main, M., & Weston, D. R. (1981). The quality of the toddler's relationship to mother and to father: Related to conflict behavior and the readiness to establish new relationships. *Child Development, 52,* 932–940.

Main, M., & Weston, D. R. (1982). Avoidance of the attachment figure in infancy: Descriptions and interpretations. In C. M. Parkes & J. Stevenson-Hinde (Eds.), *The place of attachment in human behavior* (pp. 31–59). New York: Basic.

Mandler, J. H. (1979). Categorical and schematic organization in memory. In C. R. Puff (Ed.), *Memory organization and structure* (pp. 259–299). New York: Academic Press.

Mandler, J. H. (1983). Representation. In J. H. Flavell & E. M. Markman (Eds.), P. H. Mussen (Series Ed.), *Handbook of child psychology: Vol. 3. Cognitive development* (pp. 420–494). New York: Wiley.

Maratos, O., Tsitsikas, H., Solman, M., Staikou, A., Mitsotakis, P., & Karangelis, A. (1982). Effects of age and rearing condition on Brazelton Neonatal Assessment Scale performance. In L. P. Lipsitt & T. M. Field (Eds.), *Infant behavior and development: Perinatal risk and newborn behavior* (pp. 9–20). Norwood, NJ: Ablex.

Marvin, R. S. (1972). *Attachment and cooperative behavior in two-, three-, and four-year-olds.* Unpublished doctoral dissertation, University of Chicago.

Marvin, R. S. (1977). An ethological-cognitive model for the attenuation of mother-child attachment behavior. In T. M. Alloway, L. Krames, & P. Pliner (Eds.), *Advances in the study of communication and affect: Vol. 3. The development of social attachments* (pp. 25–60). New York: Plenum.

Marvin, R. S., Greenberg, M. T., & Mosler, D. G. (1976). The early development of conceptual perspective taking: Distinguishing among multiple perspectives. *Child Development, 17,* 511–514.

Maslin, C. A. (1983). *Anxious and secure attachments: Antecedents and consequences in the mother-infant system.* Unpublished doctoral dissertation, Indiana University.

Masters, J., & Wellman, H. (1974). Human infant attachment: A procedural critique. *Psychological Bulletin, 81,* 218–237.

Matas, L., Arend, R. A., & Sroufe, L. A. (1978). Continuity of adaptation in the second year: The relationship between quality of attachment and later competence. *Child Development, 49,* 547–556.

Maudry, M., & Nekula, M. (1939). Social relations between children of the same age during the first two years of life. *Journal of Genetic Psychology, 54,* 193–215.

McGlaughlin, A. (1981). Generational continuities in child-rearing practices. In R. Chester, P. Diggory, & M. B. Sutherland (Eds.), *Changing patterns of child bearing and child rearing* (pp. 97–112). New York: Academic Press.

McNair, D. M., Lorr, M., & Droppleman, L. L. (1971). *Profile of mood states manual.* San Diego: Educational & Industrial Testing Service.

Mead, G. H. (1934). *Mind, self and society.* Chicago: University of Chicago Press.

Medinnus, G., & Curtis, F. (1963). The relations between maternal self-acceptance and children's acceptance. *Journal of Consulting Psychology, 27,* 542–544.

Meehl, P. E. (1973). *Psychodiagnosis: Selected papers.* New York: Norton.

Miller, A. (1981). *Prisoners of childhood: The drama of the gifted child.* New York: Basic.

Minturn, L., & Lambert, W. W. (1964). *Mothers of six cultures: Antecedents of child rearing.* New York: Wiley.

Mitera Babies' Center (1975). *Twenty year report: 1955–1975.*

Miyake, K. (1984, April). *The study of attachment in Japanese infants.* Paper presented at the meeting of the International Conference on Infant Studies, New York.

Miyake, K., Chen, S., Ujiie, T., Tajima, N., Satoh, K., & Takahashi, K. (1983). Infants' temperamental disposition, mother's mode of interaction, quality of attachment, and infants' receptivity to socialization—interim report (RCCCD Annual Report, 1981–1982). Hokkaido University, Faculty of Education.

Miyake, K., Tajima, N., & Usui, H. (1980). *Jiyuasobi bamen ni okeru boshi sougoukosho to youji no chiteki hattatsu: Nichibei hikaku kenkyu* [A cross-national study of mother child interactions in an unstructured situation and child's cognitive development]. *Bulletin of the Faculty of Education, Hokkaido University, 37,* 1–76.

Morris, D. (1980). *Infant attachment and problem solving in the toddler: Relations to mother's family history.* Unpublished doctoral dissertation, University of Minnesota.

Morris, D. (1981). Attachment and intimacy. In G. Stricker (Ed.), *Intimacy* (pp. 305–323). New York: Plenum.

Moskowitz, D. S., & Schwarz, J. C. (in press). Toward better personality measures. *Journal of Personality and Social Psychology.*

Moskowitz, D. S., Schwarz, J. C., & Corsini, D. A. (1977). Initiating day care at three years of age: Effects on attachment. *Child Development, 48,* 1271–1276.

Mueller, C. W., & Parcel, T. L. (1981). Measures of socioeconomic status: Alternatives and recommendations. *Child Development, 52,* 13–30.

Mueller, E., & Brenner, J. (1977). The origins of social skills and interaction among playgroup toddlers. *Child Development*, **48,** 854–861.

Mueller, E., & Vandell, D. L. (1978). Infant-infant interaction. In J. D. Osofsky (Ed.), *Handbook of infant development* (pp. 599–622). New York: Wiley.

Nelson, K. (1981). Social cognition in a script framework. In J. H. Flavell & L. Ross (Eds.), *Social cognitive development* (pp. 97–118). Cambridge, MA: Cambridge University Press.

Nelson, K., & Gruendel, J. (1981). Generalized event representations: Basic building blocks of cognitive development. In M. E. Lamb & A. Brown (Eds.), *Advances in developmental psychology* (Vol. **1,** pp. 131–158). Hillsdale, NJ: Erlbaum.

Nelson, K., & Ross, G. (1982). The generalities and specifics of long-term memory in infants and young children. In M. Perlmutter (Ed.), *Naturalistic approaches to memory* (pp. 87–101). San Franscisco: Jossey-Bass.

Nock, S. L., & Rossi, P. H. (1979). Household types and social standing. *Social Forces*, **57,** 1325–1345.

Norman, D. A., & Rumelhart, D. E. (1975). Memory and knowledge. In D. A. Norman & D. E. Rumelhart (Eds.), *Explorations in cognition* (pp. 3–32). San Francisco: W. H. Freeman.

O'Brien, E. (1981). *The self-report inventory: Construction and validation of a multidimensional measure of the self-concept and sources of self-esteem.* Unpublished doctoral dissertation, University of Massachusetts—Amherst.

Ohyama, M., Murai, N., & Nihei, Y. A. (1982). *Kishitsu to hattatsu ni tsuite no tsuisekiteki kenkyu (I): 2. Kokusai hikaku to seisa* [A follow-up study of temperament and development—cross-national comparison and sex differences] (Manuscript in Japanese). Paper presented at the meeting of the Japanese Psychological Association.

Olson, S. L., Bates, J. E., & Bayles, K. (1982). Maternal perceptions of infant and toddler behavior: A longitudinal construct validation study. *Infant Behavior and Development*, **5,** 397–410.

Olson, S. L., Bates, J. E., & Bayles, K. (1984). Mother-infant interaction and the development of individual differences in children's cognitive competence. *Developmental Psychology*, **20,** 166–179.

Osofsky, J. D. (1982, August). *The concept of attachment and psychoanalysis.* Paper presented at the meeting of the American Psychological Association, Washington, DC.

Osofsky, J. D., & Osofsky, H. J. (1984). Psychological and developmental perspectives on expectant and new parenthood. In R. D. Parke, R. N. Emde, H. P. MacAdoo, & G. P. Sackett (Eds.), *Review of child development research* (Vol. **7,** pp. 372–397). Chicago: University of Chicago Press.

Parke, R. D., & Asher, S. R. (1983). Social and personality development. *Annual Review of Psychology*, **34,** 465–509.

Parkes, C. M. (1971). Psychosocial transitions: A field of study. *Social Science and Medicine*, **5,** 101–115.

Parkes, C. M. (1982). Attachment and the prevention of mental disorders. In C. M. Parkes & J. Stevenson-Hinde (Eds.), *The place of attachment in human behavior* (pp. 295–309). New York: Basic.

Pastor, D. L. (1981). The quality of mother-infant attachment and its relationship to toddler's initial sociability with peers. *Developmental Psychology*, **17,** 323–335.

Pawlby, S., & Hall, F. (1980). Early and later language development of children who come from disrupted families of origin. In T. Field, S. Goldberg, D. Stern, & A. Sostek (Eds.), *High-risk infants and children: Adult and peer interaction* (pp. 61–75). New York: Academic Press.

Pettit, G. S., & Bates, J. E. (1983, April). *Description and prediction of adaptation in the family system.* Paper presented at the biennial meeting of the Society for Research in Child Development, Detroit.

Pettit, G. S., & Bates, J. E. (1984). Continuity of individual differences in the mother-infant relationship from six to thirteen months. *Child Development,* **55,** 729–739.

Piaget, J. (1954). *The construction of reality in the child.* New York: Basic.

Piaget, J. (1960). Comments in discussion. In J. M. Tanner & B. Inhelder (Eds.), *Discussions on child development* (Vol. **4,** pp. 87–91). London: Tavistock.

Piaget, J. (1967). *Six psychological studies.* New York: Random House.

Piaget, J. (1981). *Intelligence and affectivity.* New York: Annual Reviews.

Piaget, J., & Inhelder, B. (1973). *Memory and intelligence.* New York: Basic.

Plomin, R. (1981). Ethological behavioral genetics and development. In K. Immelmann, G. W. Barlow, L. Petrinovich, & M. Main (Eds.), *Behavioral development: The Bielefeld interdisciplinary project* (pp. 252–276). New York: Cambridge University Press.

Plomin, R. (1983). Childhood temperament. In B. Lahey & A. Kazdin (Eds.), *Advances in clinical child psychology* (Vol. **6,** pp. 45–92). New York: Plenum.

Portnoy, F. C., & Simmons, C. H. (1978). Day care and attachment. *Child Development,* **49,** 239–242.

Quinton, D., & Rutter, M. (in press). Parenting behavior of mothers raised "in care." In R. Nichol (Ed.), *Practical lessons from longitudinal studies.* Chichester: Wiley.

Rabin, A. I. (1965). *Growing up in the kibbutz.* New York: Springer.

Radloff, L. (1977). The CES-D scale: A self-report depression scale for research in the general population. *Applied Psychological Measurement,* **1,** 385–401.

Ragozin, A. S. (1980). Attachment behavior of day-care children: Naturalistic and laboratory observations. *Child Development,* **51,** 409–415.

Reite, M., Short, R., Seiler, C., & Pauley, J. D. (1981). Attachment, loss and depression. *Journal of Child Psychology and Psychiatry,* **22,** 141–169.

Ricciuti, H. N. (1974). Fear and the development of social attachments in the first year of life. In M. Lewis & L. A. Rosenblum (Eds.), *The origins of fear* (pp. 73–106). New York: Wiley.

Richman, M., Stevenson, J., & Graham, P. J. (1982). *Preschool to school: A behavioral study.* London: Academic Press.

Ricks, M. H. (1982, April). *Origins of individual differences in attachment: Maternal, familial and infant variables.* Paper presented at the International Conference on Infant Studies, Austin, TX.

Ricks, M. H. (1983). *Individual differences in the preschoolers' competence: Contributions of attachment history and concurrent environmental support.* Unpublished doctoral dissertation, University of Massachusetts—Amherst.

Ricks, M. H., & Noyes, D. (1984). Secure babies have secure mothers. Unpublished manuscript, University of Massachusetts—Amherst.

Roberts, G. C., Block, J. H., & Block, J. (1984). Continuity and change in parents' child-rearing practices. *Child Development,* **55,** 586–597.

Robertson, J (1953). Some responses of young children to loss of maternal care. *Nursing Care,* **49,** 382–386.

Robertson, J., & Bowlby, J. (1952). Responses of young children to separation from their mothers. *Courrier du Centre International de l'Enfance,* **2,** 131–142.

Robertson, J., & Robertson, J. (1967–1972). *Young children in brief separations* [Film series]. London: Tavistock Institute of Human Relations.

Robertson, J., & Robertson, J. (1971). Young children in brief separation: A fresh look. *Psychoanalytic Study of the Child,* **26,** 264–315.

Rohner, R. P. (1975). *They love me, they love me not.* New Haven, CT: HRAF.

Roopnarine, J., & Lamb, M. E. (1978). The effects of day care on attachment and exploratory behavior in a strange situation. *Merrill-Palmer Quarterly,* **24,** 85–95.

Roper, R., & Hinde, R. A. (1978). Social behavior in a play group: Consistency and complexity. *Child Development*, **49**, 570–579.

Ross, H. S., & Kay, D. A. (1980). The origins of social games. In K. H. Rubin (Ed.), *Children's play* (pp. 17–48). San Francisco: Jossey-Bass.

Rothbart, M. K., & Derryberry, D. (1981). Development of individual differences in temperament. In M. E. Lamb (Ed.), *Advances in developmental psychology* (Vol. **1**, pp. 17–86). Hillsdale, NJ: Erlbaum.

Rushton, J., Brainerd, C., & Pressley, M. (1983). Behavioral development and construct validity: The principle of aggregation. *Psychological Bulletin*, **94**, 18–38.

Rutter, M. (1972). Relationships between child and adult psychiatric disorders. *Acta Psychiatrica Scandinavia*, **48**, 3–21.

Rutter, M. (1979). Maternal deprivation, 1972–1978: New findings, new concepts, new approaches. *Child Development*, **50**, 283–305.

Rutter, M. (1981). Social-emotional consequences of day care for preschool children. *American Journal of Orthopsychiatry*, **51**, 4–28.

Rutter, M., & Madge, N. (1976). *Cycles of disadvantage: A review of research.* London: Heinemann.

Rutter, M., Quinton, D., & Liddle, C. (1983). Parenting in two generations: Looking backwards and looking forwards. In N. Madge (Ed.), *Families at risk* (pp. 60–98). London: Heinemann.

Sameroff, A. J. (1982). Development and dialectic: The need for a systems approach. In W. A. Collins (Ed.), *Minnesota symposium on child psychology* (Vol. **15**, pp. 187–244). Hillsdale, NJ: Erlbaum.

Sameroff, A. J., & Chandler, M. J. (1975). Reproductive risk and the continuum of caretaking casualty. In F. D. Horowitz (Ed.), *Review of child development research* (Vol. **4**, pp. 187–244). Chicago: University of Chicago Press.

Sander, L. (1975). Infant and caretaking environment. In E. J. Anthony (Ed.), *Explorations in child psychiatry* (pp. 129–166). New York: Plenum.

Sander, L. (1977). The regulation of exchange in the infant-caregiver system and some aspects of the context-content relationship. In M. Lewis & L. A. Rosenblum (Eds.), *Interaction, conversation and the development of language* (pp. 133–156). New York: Wiley.

Scaife, M., & Bruner, J. S. (1975). The capacity for joint visual attention in the infant. *Nature*, **253**, 265–266.

Schaefer, E., & Bayley, N. (1967). *Validity and consistency of mother-infant observations, adolescent maternal interviews and adult retrospective accounts of maternal behavior* (Proceedings of the 75th Annual Convention of the American Psychological Association). Washington, DC: American Psychological Association.

Schaffer, H. R. (1963). Some issues for research in the study of attachment behaviour. In B. M. Foss (Ed.), *Determinants of infant behaviour* (Vol. **2**, 179–199). New York: Wiley.

Schaffer, H. R., & Crook, C. K. (1979). Maternal control techniques in a directed play situation. *Child Development*, **50**, 989–996.

Schaffer, H. R., & Emerson, P. E. (1964). The development of social attachments in infancy. *Monographs of the Society for Research in Child Development*, **29**(3, Serial No. 94).

Schank, R. C., & Abelson, R. P. (1977). *Scripts, plans, goals and understanding.* Hillsdale, NJ: Erlbaum.

Schneider-Rosen, K., & Cicchetti, D. (1984). The relationship between affect and cognition in maltreated infants: Quality of attachment and the development of visual self-recognition. *Child Development*, **55**, 648–658.

Schwartz, P. (1983). Length of day-care attendance and attachment behavior in eighteen-month-old infants. *Child Development*, **54**, 1073–1078.

Schwarz, J. C. (1979). Childhood origins of psychopathology. *American Psychologist,* **34,** 879–885.

Schwarz, J. C., Strickland, R. G., & Krolick, G. (1974). Infant day care: Behavioral effects at preschool age. *Developmental Psychology,* **10,** 502–506.

Serafica, F. C., & Cicchetti, D. (1976). Down's syndrome children in a strange situation: Attachment and exploratory behaviors. *Merrill-Palmer Quarterly,* **21,** 137–150.

Shantz, C. U. (1983). Social cognition. In J. H. Flavell & E. M. Markman (Eds.), P. H. Mussen (Series Ed.), *Handbook of child psychology: Vol. 3. Cognitive development* (pp. 495–555). New York: Wiley.

Shepher, J. (1971). Mate selection among second generation kibbutz adolescents and adults. *Archives of Sexual Behavior,* **1,** 293–307.

Sherefsky, P. M., & Yarrow, L. J. (1976). *Psychological aspects of a first pregnancy and early postpartum adaptation.* New York: Raven.

Siegel, S. (1956). *Nonparametric statistics.* New York: McGraw-Hill.

Skodak, M., & Skeels, H. M. (1949). A final follow-up study of one hundred adopted children. *Journal of Genetic Psychology,* **75,** 85–125.

Sorce, J. F., & Emde, R. N. (1981). Mother's presence is not enough: Effect of emotional availability on infant explorations. *Developmental Psychology,* **17,** 737–745.

Spangler, G. (1981). *Entwicklung einer Methode und quantitative Analyse der Interaktion zwischen Müttern und ihren 10 Monate alten Kindern: Reaktion auf Weinen und Anlass für und Reaktion auf das Aufnehmen und Absetzen des Kindes* [Development of a method for quantitative analysis of mother-child interactions related to crying and close bodily contact]. Diplom thesis, University of Regensburg.

Spangler, G. (1982). *Beschreibung und Handanweisung für das Programmsystem PSABeP: Programmsystem zur Analyse von Beobachtungsprotokollen* [Description and instructions for the PAOP program package: Program for analyzing observation protocols]. Unpublished manuscript, University of Regensburg.

Spanier, G. B. (1976). Measuring dyadic adjustment: New scales for assessing the quality of marriage and similar dyads. *Journal of Marriage and the Family,* **38,** 15–20.

Spiro, M. E. (1958). *Children of the kibbutz.* Cambridge, MA: Harvard University Press.

Spiro, M. E., & D'Andrade, R. G. (1958). A cross-cultural study of some supernatural beliefs. *American Anthropologist,* **60,** 456–466.

Spitz, R. (1946). Anaclitic depression. *Psychoanalytic Study of the Child,* **2,** 313–342.

Spitz, R. (1966). Metapsychology and direct infant observation. In R. M. Loewenstein, L. M. Newman, M. Shure, & A. J. Solnit (Eds.), *Psychoanalysis: A general psychology* (pp. 123–151). New York: International Universities Press.

Sroufe, L. A. (1979). The coherence of individual development. *American Psychologist,* **34,** 834–841.

Sroufe, L. A. (1983). Infant-caregiver attachment and patterns of adaptation in preschool: The roots of maladaptation and competence. In M. Perlmutter (Ed.), *Minnesota symposium in child psychology* (Vol. **16,** pp 41–81). Hillsdale, NJ: Erlbaum.

Sroufe, L. A., & Fleeson, J. (in press). Attachment and the construction of relationships. In W. Hartup & Z. Rubin (Eds.), *The nature and development of relationships.* Hillsdale, NJ: Erlbaum.

Sroufe, L. A., Fox, N. E., & Pancake,V. R. (1983). Attachment and dependency in developmental perspective. *Child Development,* **54,** 1615–1627.

Sroufe, L. A., Schork, E., Motti, E., Lawroski, N., & LaFreniere, P. (1984). The role of affect in emerging social competence. In C. Izard, J. Kagan, & R. Zajonc (Eds.), *Emotion, cognition and behavior* (pp. 289–319). New York: Cambridge University Press.

Sroufe, L. A., & Waters, E. (1977). Attachment as an organizational construct. *Child Development,* **48,** 1184–1199.

Sroufe, L. A., & Waters, E. (1982). Issues of temperament and attachment. *American Journal of Orthopsychiatry,* **52,** 743–746.

Stayton, D. J., & Ainsworth, M. D. S. (1973). Individual differences in infant responses to brief everyday separations as related to other infant and maternal behaviors. *Developmental Psychology,* **9,** 226–235.

Stayton, D. J., Ainsworth, M. D. S., & Main, M. (1973). Development of separation behavior in the first year of life. *Developmental Psychology,* **9,** 213–225.

Stayton, D. J., Hogan, R., & Ainsworth, M. D. S. (1971). Infant obedience and maternal behavior: The origins of socialization reconsidered. *Child Development,* **42,** 1057–1070.

Stephenson, W. (1953). *The study of behavior: Q-technique and its methodology.* Chicago: University of Chicago Press.

Stern, D. (1977). *The first relationship: Infant and mother.* Cambridge, MA: Harvard University Press.

Stevens, A. G. (1968). "One of the greatest institooshuns," notes on a psychiatrist's love affair with Babies Centre Metera. *Clinical Pediatrics,* **7**(No. 12), 8A–28A.

Stevenson, M. B., & Lamb, M. E. (1979). Effects of sociability and the caretaking environment on infant cognitive performance. *Child Development,* **50,** 340–349.

Strage, A., & Main, M. (1984). *Attachment and parent-child discourse patterns.* Unpublished manuscript, University of California, Berkeley.

Suess, G. (1981). *Die Analyse von Beobachtungsprotokollen über Interaktionen zwischen 10 Monate alten Kindern und ihren Müttern in einer häuslichen Situation: Zusammenspiel gegenüber Beeinträchtigung, mütterliches Verhalten gegenüber dem kindlichen Weinen sowie kindliches Verhalten gegenüber Kommen und Gehen der Mütter* [Analysis of interactions between 10-month-olds and their mothers in the home: Cooperation versus interference, maternal responsiveness to crying, and infant responses to mother's coming and going]. Diplom thesis, University of Regensburg.

Sullivan, H. S. (1953). *The interpersonal theory of psychiatry.* New York: Norton.

Takahashi, K. (in preparation). *What do we mean by A-, B-, C-type infants? Culture-boundedness of the Strange Situation procedure.* Soka University.

Takahashi, K., & Miyake, K. (1984, April). *Culture-boundedness of the A, B, or C classification by the Strange Situation procedure: A study of Japanese infants and mothers.* Paper presented at the International Conference on Infant Studies, New York.

Tennes, K. (1982). The role of hormones in mother-infant transactions. In R. N. Emde & R. Harmon (Eds.), *The development of attachment and affiliative systems* (pp. 75–79). New York: Plenum.

Thomas, A. (1981). Current trends in developmental theory. *American Journal of Orthopsychiatry,* **51,** 580–609.

Thomas, A., & Chess, S. (1977). *Temperament and development.* New York: Brunner/Mazel.

Thomas, A., Chess, S., & Birch, H. G. (1968). *Temperament and behavior disorders in children.* New York: New York University Press.

Thompson, R. A., Lamb, M. E., & Estes, D. (1982). Stability of infant-mother attachment and its relationship to changing life circumstances in an unselected middle-class sample. *Child Development,* **53,** 144–148.

Thompson, R. A., Lamb, M. E., & Estes, D. (1983). Harmonizing discordant notes: A reply to Waters. *Child Development,* **54,** 521–524.

Tracy, R. L., & Ainsworth, M. D. S. (1981). Maternal affectionate behavior and infant-mother attachment patterns. *Child Development,* **52,** 1341–1343.

Tracy, R. L., Lamb, M. E., & Ainsworth, M. D. S. (1976). Infant approach behavior as related to attachment. *Child Development,* **47,** 571–578.

Trevarthen, C., & Hubley, P. (1979). Secondary intersubjectivity: Confidence, confiding, and acts of meaning in the first year. In A. Lock (Ed.), *Action, gesture and symbol* (pp. 183–229). New York: Academic Press.

Tronick, E., Ricks, M., & Cohn, J. (1982). Maternal and infant affective exchange: Patterns of adaptation. In T. Field & A. Fogel (Eds.), *Emotion and interaction: Normal and high-risk infants* (pp. 83–100). Hillsdale, NJ: Erlbaum.

Tulving, E. (1972). Episodic and semantic memory. In E. Tulving & W. Donaldson (Eds.), *Organization of memory* (pp. 382–403). New York: Academic Press.

Unzner, L. (1981). *Die Analyse von Beobachtungsprotokollen über Interaktionenzwischen 10 Monate alten Kindern und ihren Müttern in einer häuslichen Situation: Feinfühligkeit versus Unempfindlichkeit gegenüber den Signalen des Babys, sowie Reaktion auf Körperlichen Kontakt* [Analysis of interactions between 10-month-olds and their mothers in the home: Maternal sensitivity to infant signals and infant responses to close bodily contact]. Diplom thesis, University of Regensburg.

Urban Institute. (1980). *The subtle revolution: Women at work.* Washington, DC: Urban Institute.

Uzgiris, I., & Hunt, J. (1975). *Assessment in infancy.* Champaign-Urbana: University of Illinois Press.

Vandell, D. L. (1980). Sociability with peer and mother during the first year. *Developmental Psychology, 16,* 355–361.

Vaughn, B., Egeland, B., Sroufe, L. A., & Waters, E. (1979). Individual differences in infant-mother attachment at twelve and eighteen months: Stability and change in families under stress. *Child Development, 50,* 971–975.

Vaughn, B., Gove, F. L., & Egeland, B. (1980). The relationship between out-of-home care and the quality of infant-mother attachment in an economically disadvantaged population. *Child Development, 51,* 971–975.

Vogel, E. (1963). *Japan's new middle class.* Berkeley: University of California Press.

Waters, E. (1978). The reliability and stability of individual differences in infant-mother attachment. *Child Development, 49,* 483–494.

Waters, E. (1983). The stability of individual differences in infant attachment: Comments on the Thompson, Lamb, and Estes contributions. *Child Development, 54,* 516–520.

Waters, E., & Deane, K. E. (1982). Infant-mother attachment: Theories, models, recent data and some tasks for comparative developmental analysis. In L. W. Hoffman & R. J. Gandelman (Eds.), *Parenting: Its causes and consequences* (pp. 19–54). Hillsdale, NJ: Erlbaum.

Waters, E., Garber, J., Gornal, M., & Vaughn, B. (1983). Q-sort correlations of visual regard among preschool peers: Validation of a behavioral index of social competence. *Developmental Psychology, 19,* 550–560.

Waters, E., Matas, L., & Sroufe, L. (1975). Infant reactions to an approaching stranger: Description, validation, and functional significance of wariness. *Child Development, 46,* 348–356.

Waters, E., Noyes, D. M., Vaughn, B., & Ricks, M. H. (in press). Q-sort definitions of social competence and self-esteem: Discriminant validity of related constructs in theory and data. *Developmental Psychology.*

Waters, E., & Sroufe, L. A. (1983). Social competence as a developmental construct. *Developmental Review, 3,* 79–97.

Waters, E., Vaughn, B. E., & Egeland, B. R. (1980). Individual differences in infant-mother attachment relationships at age one: Antecedents in neonatal behavior in an urban, economically disadvantaged sample. *Child Development, 51,* 208–216.

Waters, E., Wippman, J., & Sroufe, L. A. (1979). Attachment, positive affect, and competence in the peer group: Two studies in construct validation. *Child Development, 50,* 821–829.

317

Wechsler, D. (1981). *Wechsler Adult Intelligence Scales—revised.* New York: Psychological Corp.

Weinraub, M., Brooks, J., & Lewis, M. (1977). The social network: A reconsideration of the concept of attachment. *Human Development, 20,* 31–47.

Werner, H. (1957). *Comparative psychology of mental development.* New York: International Universities Press.

Whiting, J. W. M. (1959). Sorcery, sin and superego: A crosscultural study of some mechanisms of social control. In M. R. Jones (Ed.), *Nebraska symposium on motivation, 1959* (pp. 174–197). Lincoln: University of Nebraska Press.

Whiting, J. W. M., & Child, I. (1953). *Child training and personality: A cross-cultural study.* New Haven, CT: Yale University Press.

Wilson, R. S., & Matheny, A. P. (1983). Assessment of temperament in infant twins. *Developmental Psychology, 19,* 172–183.

Winnicott, D. (1965). *The family and individual development.* London: Tavistock.

Wolkind, S., Hall, F., & Pawlby, S. (1977). Individual differences in mothering behavior: A combined epidemiological and observational approach. In P. J. Graham (Ed.), *Epidemiological approaches in child psychiatry* (pp. 107–124). London: Academic Press.

Yang, R. K., & Halverson, C. F., Jr. (1976). A study of the "inversion of intensity" between newborn and preschool-age behavior. *Child Development, 47,* 350–359.

Yarrow, L. J. (1967). The development of focused relationships during infancy. In J. Hellmuth (Ed.), *Exceptional infant* (Vol. 1, pp. 227–242). Seattle: Special Child.

Zimmerman, I., Steiner, V., & Pond, R. (1979). *Preschool Language Scale, revised edition.* Columbus, OH: Charles E. Merrill.

STATEMENT OF EDITORIAL POLICY

At the beginning of each year, we plan to provide a Statement of Editorial Policy to inform authors who may be considering a submission to *Monographs*.

The *Monographs* series is one of the longest continuing publications in the field of child development. It is intended to provide for publication of significant research reports that require longer presentations than that permitted in journal-length articles. Because of its circulation (over 5,000 copies are automatically distributed) and because single copies are available through the University of Chicago Press, this archival series may offer unique publication opportunities for investigators who are completing major programmatic projects.

Longitudinal studies are a special priority for the *Monographs*. Studies that utilize successive measurements on the same subjects are of particular importance to the field of child development and for understanding developmental processes. Longitudinal studies are apt to require considerable space, not only to describe the context of the study, but also to discuss methods, data, and theoretical implications. Special consideration is also given to studies of relevance to more than one discipline. Interdisciplinary collaborative research is often particularly enlightening for understanding developmental processes. Reports of multiple experiments on a single problem are also a priority for *Monographs*, when a unified report is more suitable than a series of articles. This category of priority may involve a diversity of methods focused around a central theme or a single method for studying several variables. Still, a series of experiments that does not have a necessary unity, even though it has a programmatic thrust, would be more appropriately published as a series of articles.

Among the important priorities for *Monographs* are reports of new directions in developmental research. We hope that *Monographs* can help catalyze the initiation and development of new research areas. Several formats may be suitable, and innovation is encouraged. *Monographs* can publish the proceedings of a particularly exciting and generative conference or symposium. It is anticipated that such a collection would involve a group of scientists who link more than one discipline with one or more problem areas and a symposium discussant who would provide introductory and concluding sections. The subject matter should be of interest to a substantial number of people, and the problems discussed should be developmental and remarkably innovative for submission in this category.

Other traditional categories for publication in *Monographs* include studies of physical growth and cross-cultural studies, and this practice will continue.

A few caveats. Perhaps the most important is that Ph.D. dissertations are rarely considered appropriate submissions for *Monographs;* usually the editor returns such submissions without review. There are many reasons for this policy. Most dissertations are written to demonstrate to a faculty that a student is competent. For this purpose, dissertations contain extensive reviews of the literature, tabular material, rationales for planning and execution, and lengthy discussions concerning errors, unanticipated results, and speculative applications. Most dissertations should be reduced and published as single articles.

Another caveat concerns the substantive nature of the work. Authors should ask themselves the following questions. Is the work truly developmental? Does it clearly represent the state of the art and science for reliable and valid observations, relevant controls, and data analytic procedures? Finally, as Robert Sears said of a prospective submission to *Monographs* in an editorial policy statement written in 1971, "It should be meat for a full section of a textbook chapter, not for a footnote. It should start a new field or put an end to an old one. It should be one that a *lot* of developmentalists care about and want to see some data on. A monograph should add a building block on which other researchers can step, not just an *i*-dotting or *t*-crossing of the latest fad" (Robert R. Sears, *Child Development*, 1971, **42**, 341).

Every attempt will be made to obtain at least two expert reviewers who are experienced and competent in the areas of submitted manuscripts accepted for review. Reviewers will be asked to bear the above priorities in mind as they look at a manuscript for scientific excellence and for results that will provide archival data to which other investigators will repeatedly return.

Monographs, like *Child Development*, accepts manuscripts from nonmembers of the Society for Research in Child Development as well as from members. A manuscript should be no briefer than 70 pages, including references, tables, and figures; the upper limit of 150–175 pages is somewhat more flexible because of the possibility of publishing a "double issue" *Monographs*. The style and format required by *Monographs* adheres to that of the current publication manual of the American Psychological Association (3d Ed.). *All* material should be typed double-spaced.

Potential authors may wish to consult the editor directly about matters of appropriate length, topic, and style. A more detailed "Guidelines to Authors and Typists" is available on request from the editor and should be obtained before the final typing of the manuscript.

Send all manuscripts and editorial correspondence to the editor: Robert N. Emde, Department of Psychiatry, University of Colorado School of Medicine, 4200 East Ninth Avenue, Box C268, Denver, Colorado 80262.

Children should be seen – and heard, and studied

Review of Child Development Research, Volume 7

Interest in the family has undergone a resurgence in recent years, and **RCDR 7** emphasizes the all-important role the family plays in a child's development. The volume investigates the vital role of mothers, fathers, and siblings and examines the family unit itself and its connection with its class, community, and ethnic heritage. As all families face a variety of life experiences and events which call for adaptation and coordination, **RCDR 7** illustrates how the ways in which families deal with these changes can facilitate our understanding of the intricacies of family functioning.

F. F. Strayer, Biological Approaches to the Study of the Family

G. Mitchell and **C. Shively,** Naturalistic and Experimental Studies of Nonhuman Primate and Other Animal Families

Irving E. Sigel, Albert S. Dreyer, and **Ann V. McGillicuddy-DeLisi,** Psychological Perspectives of the Family

Glen H. Elder, Jr., Families, Kin, and the Life Course: A Sociological Perspective

Tamara Hareven, Themes in the Historical Development of the Family

Robert D. Hess and **Susan D. Holloway,** Family and School as Educational Institutions

Lois Wladis Hoffman, Work, Family, and the Socialization of the Child

Urie Bronfenbrenner, Phyllis Moen, and **James Garbarino,** Child, Family, and Community

Algea Harrison, Felicisima Serafica, and **Harriette McAdoo,** Ethnic Families of Color

Joy D. Osofsky and **Howard J. Osofsky,** Psychological and Developmental Perspectives on Expectant and New Parenthood

E. Mavis Hetherington and **Kathleen A. Camara,** Families in Transition: The Processes of Dissolution and Reconstitution

---

Review of Child Development Research, Volume 7. Edited by **Ross D. Parke.** (Cloth, est. 450p. ISBN: 0-226-64666-1. LC: 64-20472.) $30.00. For more information write The University of Chicago Press, 11030 S. Langley Ave., Chicago, IL 60628.

6/84

THE UNIVERSITY OF CHICAGO PRESS